RUSSIA

On the Eve

O F

War and Revolution

RUSSIA

On the Eve

OF

War and Revolution

BY

Sir Donald Mackenzie Wallace

EDITED AND INTRODUCED BY

Cyril E. Black

PRINCETON UNIVERSITY PRESS
PRINCETON, NEW JERSEY

Published by Princeton University Press, 41 William Street,
Princeton, New Jersey 08540
Copyright © 1961 by Random House, Inc.
First Princeton Paperback printing, 1984

LIBRARY OF CONGRESS CATALOGING IN PUBLICATION
DATA
Wallace, Donald Mackenzie, Sir, 1841-1919.
  Russia: on the eve of war and revolution.

  Reprint. Originally published: New York: Vintage
Books, c1961. (Vintage Russian library)
  Includes bibliographical references.
    1. Soviet Union—Politics and government—19th century.
  2. Peasantry—Soviet Union. 3. Soviet Union—Nobility.
  4. Soviet Union—Industries—History—19th century.
  5. Soviet Union—Religious life and customs. I. Black,
Cyril Edwin, 1915-   II. Title.
  DK262.W29   1984   947.08   83-43100

  ISBN 0-691-05405-3 (alk. paper)
  ISBN 0-691-00774-8 (pbk.)

Reprinted by arrangement with Random House, Inc.
Printed in the United States of America by
Princeton University Press, Princeton, New Jersey

Introduction

CYRIL E. BLACK

ON THE OCCASION of the death of Sir Donald Mackenzie Wallace in 1919 at the age of seventy-seven, the *Times* of London noted that his *Russia* had been regarded since the publication of the first edition in 1877 as "the standard description of the life and institutions of Russia as it was before the cataclysm of the last couple of years." [1] It must be acknowledged that the *Times* prefaced this encomium with a qualification—it was "for Englishmen the standard description"—but it added that the work had been translated into "most European and some Asiatic languages, including several of the Indian vernaculars," and that it had been "crowned" by the French Academy. The *Dictionary of National Biography* was even more emphatic, stating without qualifications that Wallace's work "remains the standard authority on Russia before the revolution of 1917." [2] But let the reader be the judge. Wallace was widely traveled and his book was widely read in his lifetime. For us it is a valuable eyewitness account of a world we will never see.

It was appropriate that the *Times* should devote three columns to Wallace's obituary, for he had spent some of the most fruitful years of his life as a correspondent for that paper. He went to St. Petersburg briefly for the *Times* in 1878, attended the Congress of Berlin in June and July of that year, and was then assigned to Constantinople, where he spent the next six years. There he gained a reputation as

[1] The *Times*, January 11, 1919, page 6.
[2] *Dictionary of National Biography, 1912-1921* (London, 1927), page 549.

a specialist on the Balkans and Egypt, and was an eyewitness of many of the dramatic events of the 1880's. He then became private secretary to Lord Dufferin, during his five years as Viceroy of India from 1884 to 1889. In 1891 he returned to the *Times* as the first Director of the Foreign Department, and for eight years he supervised the activities of the world-wide organization of correspondents which gave that paper its reputation for authority and reliability in its reporting on foreign affairs. In 1900, Wallace became the editor of the *Encyclopaedia Britannica*, which had just been taken over by the *Times*, and in this capacity he supervised the preparation of the Tenth Edition. He returned to the *Times* briefly in 1905 to serve as its correspondent at the Peace Conference between Russia and Japan at Portsmouth, New Hampshire, and then retired to travel and study. He revisited Russia on a number of occasions, and revised his account of that country in 1905 and again in 1912. He also assisted in the preparation of the *Russian Supplement* of the *Times*, which was published on December 15, 1911.

In the course of his busy life, Wallace's interests extended well beyond the country with which his name is principally associated. His years in India brought him close to the governing circles of Great Britain, and he was a friend and adviser of the royalty and statesmen of many countries. In 1890-91 he accompanied the then crown prince of Russia, who was to ascend the throne in 1894 as Nicholas II, on a tour of India and Ceylon. Ten years later he accompanied the Duke of Cornwall and York, soon to be crowned as George V, on a tour of the Dominions. He also found time to write two books which reflected the understanding gained from his experiences in the British overseas possessions: *Egypt and the Egyptian Question* (1883), and *The Web of Empire* (1902).

Wallace was a scholar-publicist of a type which was not uncommon in his urbane generation, but is now much rarer in this age of jet travel and rapidly trained area specialists. He was born in Scotland in 1841 to a family of means, and although orphaned at the age of ten he had the determination to achieve the sort of education reserved in those days for young men destined for public life. After several years at the universities of Glasgow and Edinburgh, he went abroad to study law and jurisprudence in Paris, Berlin, and Heidelberg, receiving a degree of Doctor of Laws from the latter institution at the age of twenty-six.

Until this time he had not been to Russia, and his special knowledge of that country came to him almost by chance. He had acquired from his reading of Baron Haxthausen's account of Russia[3] a particular interest in the Ossetes in the Caucasus, and an invitation from a friend in St. Petersburg seemed to offer him an opportunity to pursue his study of this remote tribe. "In accepting this invitation of my Petersburg friend," he wrote later, "my intention was to spend about a year in studying the Russian language and certain Russian institutions which specially interested me, and then to devote one, two, or three years to a thorough study of the Ossetes. Gradually I saw reason to change my plans. On closer inspection the Russians turned out to be a much more, and the Ossetes a much less, interesting subject of study than I expected, and instead of one I devoted six years to Russia proper." [4]

The result was his *Russia,* the unique qualities of which have received such wide recognition. To his own generation Wallace brought an intimate view of a country which was almost daily in the headlines as a cold-war enemy during the last decades of the nineteenth century and as a somewhat uncongenial associate after the Anglo-Russian agreement of 1907. While Russia was certainly much more accessible in Wallace's day than it is now, and on the whole better understood, his account reflects a knowledge of the country which few could match. Indeed, his principal contribution lay in the painstaking care with which he read through masses of documents and prowled around the countryside in search of source materials and personal impressions. His study of the Zemstvo institutions is a good example of his method. He went to Novgorod, persuaded the president of the local Zemstvo to let him see their documents and statistics, accompanied Zemstvo officials on

[3] August Freiherr von Haxthausen, *Studien uber die innern Zustände, das Volksleben und insbesondere die ländlichen Einrichtungen Russlands* (3 vols.; Hanover, 1847-52).

[4] Quoted in *The Times,* January 11, 1919, page 6.

their visits to schools and hospitals, attended meetings of Zemstvo assemblies at both district and provincial levels, talked with the members, and throughout took copious notes. When he wished to learn about the beliefs of religious sects, he sought out their elders and talked with them into the early hours of the morning until his curiosity was satisfied. He came to know Russians of all walks of life, and many of them took him into their confidence. In the last years of Stalin's rule, when Russia was very largely closed to foreign travel, Western social scientists wrote extensively about studying a society at a distance. This is a problem that Wallace did not face.

In the Preface to the first edition of his work, Wallace mentions the difficulty which he had in selecting from his notes the topics of the greatest importance so as "to convey a general idea of the country and the people." In abridging his somewhat larger third edition for publication in an inexpensive format, an editor is faced with a similar problem. Wallace's material was already greatly condensed, and the problem of selection is not easy. The general principle followed here has been to select those chapters bearing on the main social groups and institutions. Although Wallace had a narrative style of considerable Victorian charm, and includes many colorful thumbnail sketches of people and places, his primary interest was in the comparative study of institutions. His own academic training was in this field, and the most prominent issues of public debate in Russia during the more than four decades of his association with that country were concerned with the extent and nature of its assimilation of European values and institutions. Almost two-thirds of the material in the edition of 1912 has been retained in the present abridged version, and these chapters have been rearranged topically for the convenience of the contemporary reader. Within these chapters occasional paragraphs have been omitted, but on the whole Wallace's views are so cogently expressed that editorial tampering of this sort in the interest of condensation did not seem justified.

Wallace was a warm friend of Russia, and followed with great sympathy the rapid changes which were in progress during his lifetime, but his pragmatic British outlook prevented him from adopting the widely prevalent view that Russia was going to resemble an England or a France within the foreseeable future. He recognized that the historical experience of Russia had been very different from that of the Western countries, and that a strongly centralized governmental structure had been essential to the establishment of Russia as a great power. He also recognized the heavy burden of problems which accompanied this well-entrenched statism, and especially the extent to which the state had become an end in itself, abstracted from the interests of the population at large. He therefore became impatient with the Russian reformers who expected their country to change overnight as a result of legislative action, and he was particularly aroused when liberals talked glibly about the application of modern scientific principles to society without being willing themselves to go to the trouble of rolling up their sleeves and getting to work.

The latter part of the nineteenth century was a great time for high-flown theorizing in Russia, and Wallace was not taken in by it. What impressed him was the profound difference between the historically rooted institutions of Russia and those which he knew in the West, and his ability to convey an understanding of this difference is one of the principal qualities of his work. His attitude often got him into sharp arguments with his Russian friends, however. After 1905 the Constitutional Democrats were particularly incensed by his view that they should not expect to achieve a smoothly working system of parliamentary government immediately and that it might take eight or ten years. "Eight or ten years?" one of them remarked in dismay. "We cannot wait so long as that." They are still waiting.

To say that Wallace was skeptical as to the possibilities of a rapid Europeanization of Russian society is not to say that he did not think it could be done. Rather he believed that it would take several generations, and would be accomplished in a manner somewhat different from the way it had come about in the West. Since "the modern scientific spirit," as he called it, was not native to Russia, it had to be adopted in an advanced form and imposed on the country by the government. Indeed, it was at first only imposed on the nobles and the urban population, and the great mass of Russians had at the turn of the century still been left almost untouched. There were thus two Russias, and during the eighteenth and most of the nineteenth centuries the gap between them became wider rather than narrower. Wallace studied both Russias, and his depiction of rural life is in many respects more vivid than that of the official world.

In reading Wallace's comments one cannot fail to see the reflection of his own philosophy, which was rooted in the belief that "Western civilization," to use his term, was the goal toward which Russia was slowly moving. Yet it must be recognized that in certain fundamental respects Wallace himself was not particularly attuned to the modern world. He had been raised as a member of the privileged order, and the hungry curiosity and sharp analysis which he lavished on so many aspects of Russian life did not extend to the newer forms of industrialism. He ridiculed the fear expressed by many Russians that the peasants might become a proletariat and "swallow up society," noting that those in the West "who habitually live in the midst of it" did not fear the proletariat. "Of course it is quite possible that their view of the subject is truer than ours," he nevertheless remarks, "and that we may some day, like the people who live tranquilly on the slopes of a volcano, be rudely awakened from our fancied security." This rather apprehensive approach to the emerging mass society is also reflected in his attitude toward the radical movements. The nihilists and populists he can handle well enough, but by the turn of the century the radicals were becoming somewhat less picturesque and Wallace did not feel at home with their programs and attitudes. Indeed it did not seem worthwhile to reproduce his chapter on "The Japanese War and its Consequences," because his account of the revolution of 1905 lacks his customary color and conviction. One also regrets that his Victorian reserve, or perhaps it was his professional reticence as a prominent publicist, prevented him from sharing his familiarity with some of the major actors on the Russian stage. He knew Nicholas II personally, and had long talks with Witte, Stolypin, and many others, but with few exceptions their personalities do not emerge very clearly and we are given only a few generalizations as to their views. Despite the reservations that one may entertain about certain of his judgments, his profound understanding of post-emancipation Russia is most impressive.

Some representative examples of the lighter vein of Wallace's writing have unfortunately been sacrificed to the requirements of abridgment. He has many anecdotes about the tribulations of the traveler in Russia, his experiences with provincial medical care, and descriptions of the outlying provinces to the north, east, and south, which foreigners did not penetrate very frequently. The omission of these chapters is regrettable not only because of their intrinsic interest, but also because it deprives the reader of the sense of diversity of Russian society. As it is, Russia is too often thought of as the land of the Great Russians alone, and the many minority peoples with their varying institutions and customs tend to be lost sight of. Other casualties of abridgment represent less of a loss. Although Wallace was present at the Portsmouth conference which concluded the Russian-Japanese war, he has little of interest to say about it. On similar grounds it also seemed fitting to omit his account of the revolution of 1905, as already noted, although a more adequate treatment would have made a suitable concluding chapter for the section on industrialization and revolution.

At the start of the First World War Wallace was called upon to write a pamphlet explaining Russia's position as an ally of Britain.[5] This assignment gave him an opportunity to set forth in general terms his interpretation of Russian developments. He recognized Russia's backwardness, which he explained on geopolitical grounds—"she did not get a fair start"—and he focused his readers' attention on the gains that had been made since the Crimean War. The reforms of the 1860's had enjoyed a wide success, he noted, but many Russians had been disappointed that progress was not more rapid and a revolutionary movement arose which culminated in the assassination of Alexander II. A new period of reform had been inaugurated after 1905, and he felt that by this time all classes were imbued with the desire to reproduce a European level of civilization on

[5] *Our Russian Ally*, London, 1914.

Russian soil. Wallace was particularly hopeful of the political education of the Russians. Although the form in which his views were expressed in this pamphlet may have been influenced by wartime loyalty to an ally, they no doubt accurately reflected enlightened Western opinion in 1914. The difference between Russia's traditions and those of the West were never lost sight of, but the rapid change of recent decades gave reason to expect that Russia would develop along European lines.

The war was to change all this, sapping the strength of a country still underdeveloped and undermining the authority of its government. But it is too much to ask that Wallace should have foreseen the violent explosion that was to come, and as a Western observer of Russia as it was under the last three Tsars, he has few peers.

Contents

5 : *Religion*

6 : *Industrialization and Revolution*

1 : *State and Society*

CHAPTER I

The Imperial Administration and the Officials

My administrative studies were begun in Novgorod. One of my reasons for spending a winter in that provincial capital was that I might study the provincial administration, and as soon as I had made the acquaintance of the leading officials I explained to them the object I had in view. With the kindly *bonhomie* which distinguishes the Russian educated classes, they all volunteered to give me every assistance in their power, but some of them, on mature reflection, evidently saw reason to check their first generous impulse. Among these was the Vice-Governor, a gentleman of German origin, and therefore more inclined to be pedantic than a genuine Russian. When I called on him one evening and reminded him of his friendly offer, I found to my surprise that he had in the meantime changed his mind. Instead of answering my first simple inquiry, he stared at me fixedly, as if for the purpose of detecting some covert, malicious design, and then, putting on an air of official dignity, informed me that as I had not been authorized by the Minister to make these investigations, he could not assist me, and would certainly not allow me to examine the archives.

This was not encouraging, but it did not prevent me from applying to the Governor, and I found him a man of a very different stamp. Delighted to meet a foreigner who seemed anxious to study seriously in an unbiased frame of mind the institutions of his much-maligned native country, he willingly explained to me the mechanism of the administration which he directed and controlled, and kindly placed at my disposal the books and documents in which I could find the historical and practical information which I required. This friendly attitude of his Excellency towards me soon became generally known in the town, and from that moment my difficulties were at an end. The minor officials no longer hesitated to initiate me into the mysteries of their respective departments, and at last even the Vice-Governor threw off his reserve and followed the example of his colleagues. The elementary information thus acquired I had afterwards abundant opportunities of completing by observation and study in other parts of the Empire, and I now propose to communicate to the reader a few of the more general results.

The gigantic administrative machine which holds together all the various parts of the vast Empire has been gradually created by successive generations, but we may say roughly that it was first designed and constructed by Peter the Great. Before his time the country was governed in a rude, primitive fashion. The Grand Princes of Moscow, in subduing their rivals and annexing the surrounding principalities, merely cleared the ground for a great homogeneous State. Wily, practical politicians, rather than statesmen of the doctrinaire type, they never dreamed of introducing uniformity and symmetry into the administration as a whole. They developed the ancient institutions so far as these were useful and consistent with the exercise of autocratic power, and made only such alterations as practical necessity demanded. And these necessary alterations were more frequently local than general. Special decisions, instructions to particular officials, and charters for particular communes or proprietors, were much more common than general legislative measures.

In short, the old Muscovite Tsars practiced a hand-to-mouth policy, destroying whatever caused temporary inconvenience, and giving little heed to what did not force itself upon their attention. Hence, under their rule the administration presented not only territorial peculiarities, but also an ill-assorted combination of different systems in the same district—a conglomeration of institutions belonging to different epochs, like a fleet composed of triremes, three-deckers, and ironclads.

This irregular system, or rather want of system, seemed highly unsatisfactory to the logical mind of Peter the Great, and he conceived the grand design of sweeping it away, and putting in its place a symmetrical bureaucratic machine. It is scarcely necessary to say that this magnificent project, so foreign to the traditional ideas and customs of the people, was not easily realized. Imagine a man, without technical knowledge, without skilled workmen, without good tools, and with no better material than soft, crumbling sandstone, endeavoring to build a palace on a marsh! The undertaking would seem to reasonable minds utterly absurd, and yet it must be admitted that Peter's project was scarcely more feasible. He had neither technical knowledge, nor the requisite materials, nor a firm foundation to build on. With his usual titanic energy he demolished the old structure, but his attempts to construct were little more than a series of failures. In his numerous ukases he has left us a graphic description of his efforts, and it is at once instructive and pathetic to watch the great worker toiling indefatigably at his self-imposed task. His instruments are constantly breaking in his hands. The foundations of the building are continually giving way, and the lower tiers crumbling under the superincumbent weight. Now and then a whole section is found to be unsuitable, and is ruthlessly pulled down, or falls of its own accord. And yet the builder toils on, with a perseverance and an energy of purpose that compel admiration, frankly confessing his mistakes and failures, and patiently seeking the means of remedying them, never allowing a word of despondency to escape him, and never despairing of ultimate success. And at length death comes, and the mighty builder is snatched away suddenly in the midst of his unfinished labors, bequeathing to his successors the task of carrying on the great work.

None of these successors possessed Peter's genius and energy—with the exception perhaps of Catherine II—but they were all compelled by the force of circumstances to adopt his plans. A return to the old rough-and-ready rule of the local *Voyevods* was impossible. As the autocratic power became more and more imbued with Western ideas, it felt more and more the need of new means for carrying them out, and accordingly it strove to systematize and centralize the administration.

In this change we may perceive a certain analogy with the history of the French administration from the reign of Philippe le Bel to that of Louis XIV. In both countries we see the central power bringing the local administrative organs more and more under its control, till at last it succeeds in creating a thoroughly centralized bureaucratic organization. But under this superficial resemblance lie profound differences. The French kings had to struggle with provincial sovereignties and feudal rights, and when they had annihilated this opposition, they easily found materials with which to build up the bureaucratic structure. The Russian sovereigns, on the contrary, met with no such opposition, but they had great difficulty in finding bureaucratic material amongst their uneducated, undisciplined subjects, notwithstanding the numerous schools and colleges which were founded and maintained simply for the purpose of preparing men for the public service.

The administration was thus brought much nearer to the West European ideal, but some people have grave doubts as to whether it became thereby better adapted to the practical wants of the people for whom it was created. On this point, a well-known Slavophil once made to me some remarks which are worthy of being recorded. "You have observed," he said, "that till very recently there was in Russia an enormous amount of official peculation, extortion, and misgovernment of every kind, that the courts of law were dens of iniquity, that the people often committed perjury, and much more of the same sort, and it must be admitted that all this has not yet entirely disappeared. But what does it prove? That the Russian people are morally inferior to the German? Not at all. It simply proves that the German system of administration, which was forced upon the Russians without their consent, was utterly unsuited to their nature. If a young growing boy be compelled to wear very tight boots, he will probably burst them, and the ugly rents will doubtless produce an unfavorable impression on the passers-by; but surely it is better that the boots should burst than that the feet should be deformed. Now, the Russian people was compelled to put on not only tight boots, but also a tight jacket, and, being young and vigorous, it burst them. Narrow-minded, pedantic Germans can neither understand nor provide for the wants of the broad Slavonic nature."

From the time of Peter the Great down to the beginning of the present century the Russian administration was a magnificent specimen of paternal, would-be beneficent despotism, working through a complicated system of highly centralized bureaucracy. Let me briefly describe the structure as depicted in the Imperial Code of Laws, previous to the creation of the Duma.

At the top of the pyramid stands the Emperor, "the autocratic monarch," as Peter the Great described him, "who has to give an account of his acts to no one on earth, but has power and authority to rule his States and lands as a Christian sovereign according to his own will and judgment." Immediately below his Majesty we see the Council of State, the Committee of Ministers, and the Senate, which represent respectively the legislative, the administrative, and the judicial power. At the first glance an Englishman might imagine that the Council of State is a kind of Parliament, and the Committee of Ministers a cabinet in our sense of the term, but in reality both institutions are simply incarnations of the autocratic power. Though the Council is entrusted with many important functions—such as discussing bills, criticizing the annual budget, declaring war and concluding peace—it has merely a consultative character, and the Emperor is not bound by its decisions. The Committee is not at all a cabinet as we understand the word. The Ministers are directly and individually responsible to the Emperor, and therefore the Committee has no common responsibility or other cohesive force. As to the Senate, it has descended from its high estate. It was originally entrusted with the supreme power during the absence or minority of the monarch, and was intended to exercise a controlling in-

fluence in all sections of the administration, but now its
activity is restricted to judicial matters, and it is little
more than a supreme court of appeal.

Immediately below these three institutions stand the
Ministries, ten in number. They are the central points, in
which converge the various kinds of territorial administration, and from which radiates the Imperial will all over the
Empire.

For the purpose of territorial administration Russia
proper—that is to say, European Russia, exclusive of Poland, the Baltic Provinces, Finland and the Caucasus—
is divided into forty-nine provinces or "governments"
(*gubernii*), and each government is subdivided into districts (*uyezdy*). The average area of a province is about
the size of Portugal, but some provinces are as small as
Belgium, whilst one has nearly thirty times the area of that
little kingdom. The population, however, does not corre-
spond to the amount of territory. In the largest province,
that of Archangel, there are only about 438,000 inhabitants, whilst more than a dozen of the smaller ones have
each over three million. The districts likewise vary greatly
in size. Some are smaller than Oxfordshire or Buckingham,
and others are bigger than the whole of the United
Kingdom.

Over each province is placed a Governor, who is assisted in his duties by a Vice-Governor and a small
council. According to the legislation of Catherine II, which
still appears in the Code and has only been partially repealed, the Governor is termed "the steward of the province," and is entrusted with so many and such delicate
duties, that in order to obtain qualified men for the post,
it would be necessary to realize the great Empress's
design of creating, by education, "a new race of people."
Down to the time of the Crimean War the Governors understood the term "stewards" in a very literal sense, and
ruled in a most arbitrary, high-handed style, often exercising an important influence on the civil and criminal tribunals. These extensive and vaguely defined powers have
now been very much curtailed, partly by positive legislation, and partly by increased publicity and improved
means of communication. All judicial matters have been

placed theoretically beyond the Governor's control, and many of his former functions are now fulfilled by the Zemstvo—the organ of local self-government created by Alexander II in 1864. Besides this, all ordinary current affairs are regulated by an already big and ever-growing body of instructions, in the form of Imperial orders and ministerial circulars, and as soon as anything not provided for by the instructions happens to occur, the Minister is consulted through the post office or by telegraph.

Even within the sphere of their lawful authority the Governors have now a certain respect for public opinion, and occasionally a very wholesome dread of casual newspaper correspondents. Thus the men who were formerly described by the satirists as "little satraps" have sunk to the level of subordinate officials. I can confidently say that many (I believe the great majority) of them are honest, upright men, who are perhaps not endowed with any unusual administrative capacities, but who perform their duties faithfully according to their lights. If any representatives of the old "satraps" still exist, they must be sought for in the outlying Asiatic provinces.

Independent of the Governor, who is the local representative of the Ministry of the Interior, are a number of resident officials, who represent the other ministries, and each of them has a bureau, with the requisite number of assistants, secretaries, and scribes.

To keep this vast and complex bureaucratic machine in motion it is necessary to have a large and well-drilled army of officials. These are drawn chiefly from the ranks of the Noblesse and the Clergy, and form a peculiar social class called *chinóvniks,* or men with *chins.* As the *chin* plays an important part in Russia, not only in the official world, but also to some extent in social life, it may be well to explain its significance.

All offices, civil and military, are, according to a scheme invented by Peter the Great, arranged in fourteen classes or ranks, and to each class or rank a particular name is attached. As promotion is supposed to be given according to personal merit, a man who enters the public service for the first time must, whatever be his social position, begin in the lower ranks, and work his way upwards. Educational certificates may exempt him from the necessity of passing through the lowest classes, and the Imperial will may disregard the restrictions laid down by law, but as a general rule a man must begin at or near the bottom of the official ladder, and he must remain on each step a certain specified time. The step on which he is for the moment standing, or, in other words, the official rank or *chin* which he possesses, determines what offices he is competent to hold. Thus rank or *chin* is a necessary condition for receiving an appointment, but it does not designate any actual office, and the names of the different ranks are extremely apt to mislead a foreigner.

We must always bear this in mind when we meet with those imposing titles which Russian tourists sometimes put on their visiting cards, such as "Conseiller de Cour," "Conseiller d'État," "Conseiller privé de S.M. l'Empéreur de toutes les Russies." It would be uncharitable to suppose that these titles are used with the intention of misleading, but that they do sometimes mislead there cannot be the least doubt. I shall never forget the look of intense disgust which I once saw on the face of an American who had invited to dinner a "Conseiller de Cour," on the assumption that he would have a Court dignitary as his guest, and who casually discovered that the personage in .question was simply an insignificant official in one of the public offices. No doubt other people have had similar experiences. The unwary foreigner who has heard that there is in Russia a very important institution called the "Conseil d'État," naturally supposes that a "Conseiller d'État" is a member of that venerable body; and if he meets "Son Excellence le Conseiller privé," he is pretty sure to assume— especially if the word "actuel" has been affixed—that he sees before him a real living member of the Russian Privy Council. When to the title is added, "de S.M. l'Empéreur de toutes les Russies," a boundless field is opened up to the non-Russian imagination. In reality these titles are not nearly so important as they seem. The *soi-disant* "Conseiller de Cour" has probably nothing to do with the Court. The Conseiller d'État is so far from being a member of the Conseil d'État that he cannot possibly become a member till he receives a higher *chin*.[1] As to the Privy Councillor, it is sufficient to say that the Privy Council, which had a very odious reputation in its lifetime, died more than a century ago, and has not since been resuscitated. The explanation of these anomalies is to be found in the fact that the Russian *chins*, like the German honorary titles—*Hofrath, Staatsrath, Geheimrath*—of which they are a literal translation, indicate not actual office, but simply honorary official rank. Formerly the appointment to an office generally depended on the *chin;* now there is a tendency to reverse the old order of things and make the *chin* depend upon the office actually held.

The reader of practical mind who is in the habit of considering results rather than forms and formalities desires probably no further description of the Russian bureaucracy, but wishes to know simply how it works in practice. What has it done for Russia in the past, and what is it doing in the present?

At the present day, when faith in despotic civilizers and paternal government has been rudely shaken, and the advantages of a free, spontaneous national development are fully recognized, centralized bureaucracies have everywhere fallen into bad odor. In Russia the dislike for them is particularly strong, because it has there something more than a purely theoretical basis. The recollection of the reign of Nicholas I, with its stern military regime, and minute, pedantic formalism, makes many Russians condemn in no measured terms the administration under which they live, and most Englishmen will feel inclined to endorse this condemnation. Before passing sentence, however, we ought to know that the system has at least an historical justification, and we must not allow our love of constitutional liberty and local self-government to blind us to the distinction between theoretical and historical possibility. What seems to political philosophers abstractly the best possible government may be utterly inapplicable in certain concrete cases. We need not attempt to decide whether it is better for humanity that Russia should ex-

[1] In Russian the two words are quite different; the Council is called *Gosudarstvenny Sovêt,* and the title *Státski Sovêtnik.*

ist as a nation, but we may boldly assert that without a
strongly centralized administration Russia would never
have become one of the great European powers. Until
comparatively recent times the part of the world which is
known as the Russian Empire was a conglomeration of
independent or semi-independent political units, animated
with centrifugal as well as centripetal forces; and even at
the present day it is far from being a compact homogeneous State. It was the autocratic power, with the centralized
administration as its necessary complement, that first
created Russia, then saved her from dismemberment and
political annihilation, and ultimately secured for her a
place among European nations by introducing Western
civilization.

Whilst thus recognizing clearly that autocracy and a
strongly centralized administration were necessary first for
the creation and afterwards for the preservation of national independence, we must not shut our eyes to the evil
consequences which resulted from this unfortunate necessity. It was in the nature of things that the Government,
aiming at the realization of designs which its subjects
neither sympathized with nor clearly understood, should
have become separated from the nation; and the reckless
haste and violence with which it attempted to carry out
its schemes aroused a spirit of positive opposition among
the masses. A considerable section of the people long
looked on the reforming Tsars as incarnations of the spirit
of evil, and the Tsars in their turn looked upon the people
as raw material for the realization of their political designs. This peculiar relation between the nation and the
Government has given the keynote to the whole system of
administration. The Government has always treated the
people as minors, incapable of understanding its political
aims, and not fully competent to look after their own local
affairs. The officials have naturally acted in the same spirit.
Looking for direction and approbation merely to their
superiors, they have systematically treated those over
whom they were placed as a conquered or inferior race.
The State has thus come to be regarded as an abstract
entity, with interests entirely different from those of the
human beings composing it; and in all matters in which

State interests are supposed to be involved, the rights of individuals are ruthlessly sacrificed.

If we remember that the difficulties of centralized administration must be in direct proportion to the extent and territorial variety of the country to be governed, we may readily understand how slowly and imperfectly the administrative machine necessarily works in Russia. The whole of the vast region stretching from the Polar Ocean to the Caspian, and from the shores of the Baltic to the confines of the Celestial Empire, is administered from St. Petersburg. The genuine bureaucrat has a wholesome dread of formal responsibility, and generally tries to avoid it by taking all matters out of the hands of his subordinates, and passing them on to the higher authorities. As soon, therefore, as affairs are caught up by the administrative machine they begin to ascend, and probably arrive some day at the cabinet of the Minister. Thus the Ministries are flooded with papers—many of the most trivial import—from all parts of the Empire; and the higher officials, even if they had the eyes of an Argus and the hands of a Briareus, could not possibly fulfill conscientiously the duties imposed on them. In reality the Russian administrators of the higher ranks recall neither Argus nor Briareus. They commonly show neither an extensive nor a profound knowledge of the country which they are supposed to govern, and seem always to have a fair amount of leisure time at their disposal.

Besides the unavoidable evils of excessive centralization, Russia has had to suffer much from the jobbery, venality, and extortion of the officials. When Peter the Great one day proposed to hang every man who should steal as much as would buy a rope, his Procurator-General frankly replied that if his Majesty put his project into execution there would be no officials left. "We all steal," added the worthy official; "the only difference is that some of us steal larger amounts and more openly than others." Since these words were spoken nearly two centuries have passed, and during all that time Russia has been steadily making progress, but until the accession of Alexander II in 1855 little change took place in the moral character of the administration. Some people still living can remember the time when they could have repeated, without much exaggeration, the confession of Peter's Procurator-General.

To appreciate aright this ugly phenomenon we must distinguish two kinds of venality. On the one hand there was the habit of exacting what are vulgarly termed "tips" for services performed, and on the other there were the various kinds of positive dishonesty. Though it might not be always easy to draw a clear line between the two categories, the distinction was fully recognized in the moral consciousness of the time, and many an official who regularly received "sinless revenues" (*bezgréshniye dokhódi*), as the tips were sometimes called, would have been very indignant had he been stigmatized as a dishonest man. The practice was, in fact, universal, and could be, to a certain extent, justified by the smallness of the official salaries. In some departments there was a recognized tariff. The "brandy farmers," for example, who worked the State Monopoly for the manufacture and sale of alcoholic liquors, paid regularly a fixed sum to every official, from the Governor to the policeman, according to his rank. I knew of one case where the official, on receiving a larger sum than was customary, conscientiously handed back the change! The other and more heinous offenses were by no means so common, but were still fearfully frequent. Many high officials and important dignitaries were known to receive large revenues, to which the term "sinless" could not by any means be applied, and yet they retained their position, and were received in society with respectful deference.

The Sovereigns were well aware of the abuses, and strove more or less to root them out, but the success which attended their efforts does not give us a very exalted idea of the practical omnipotence of autocracy. In a centralized bureaucratic administration, in which each official is to a certain extent responsible for the sins of his subordinates, it is always extremely difficult to bring an official culprit to justice, for he is sure to be protected by his superiors; and when the superiors are themselves habitually guilty of malpractices, the culprit is quite safe from exposure and punishment. An energetic Tsar might do much towards exposing and punishing offenders if he could venture to call in public opinion to his assistance, but in reality the Head of the State is very apt to become a party to the system of hushing up official delinquencies. He is himself the first official in the realm, and he knows that the abuse of power by a subordinate has a tendency to produce hostility towards the fountain of all official power. Frequent punishment of officials might, it is thought, diminish public respect for the Government, and undermine that social discipline which is necessary for the public tranquillity. It is therefore considered expedient to give to official delinquencies as little publicity as possible.

Besides this, strange as it may seem, a Government which rests on the arbitrary will of a single individual is, notwithstanding occasional outbursts of severity, much less systematically severe than authority founded on free public opinion. When delinquencies occur in very high places the Tsar is almost sure to display a leniency approaching to tenderness. If it be necessary to make a sacrifice to justice, the sacrificial operation is made as painless as may be, and illustrious scapegoats are not allowed to die of starvation in the wilderness—the wilderness being generally Paris or the Riviera. This fact may seem strange to those who are in the habit of associating autocracy with Neapolitan dungeons and the mines of Siberia, but it is not difficult to explain. No individual, even though he be the Autocrat of all the Russias, can so case himself in the armor of official dignity as to be completely proof against personal influences. The severity of autocrats is reserved for political offenders, against whom they naturally harbor a feeling of personal resentment. It is so much easier for us to be lenient and charitable towards a man who sins against public morality, than towards one who sins against ourselves!

In justice to the bureaucratic reformers in Russia, it must be said that they have preferred prevention to cure. Refraining from all Draconian legislation, they have put their faith in a system of ingenious checks and a complicated formal procedure. When we examine the complicated formalities and labyrinthine procedure by which the administration is controlled, our first impression is that administrative abuses must be almost impossible. Every possible act of every official seems to have been foreseen, and every possible outlet from the narrow path of honesty seems to have been carefully walled up. As the English reader has probably no conception of formal procedure in a highly centralized bureaucracy, let me give, by way of illustration, an instance which accidentally came to my knowledge.

In the residence of a Governor-General one of the stoves is in need of repairs. An ordinary mortal may assume that a man with the rank of Governor-General may be trusted to expend a few shillings conscientiously, and that consequently his Excellency will at once order the repairs to be made and the payment to be put down among the petty expenses. To the bureaucratic mind the case appears in a very different light. All possible contingencies must be carefully provided for. As a Governor-General may possibly be possessed with a mania for making useless alterations, the necessity for the repairs ought to be verified; and as wisdom and honesty are more likely to reside in an assembly than in an individual, it is well to entrust the verification to a council. A council of three or four members accordingly certifies that the repairs are necessary. This is pretty strong authority, but it is not enough. Councils are composed of mere human beings, liable to error and subject to be intimidated by a Governor-General. It is prudent, therefore, to demand that the decision of the council be confirmed by the Procureur, who is directly subordinated to the Minister of Justice. When this double confirmation has been obtained, an architect examines the stove, and makes an estimate. But it would be dangerous to give *carte blanche* to an architect, and therefore the estimate has to be confirmed, first by the aforesaid council and afterwards by the Procureur.

When all these formalities—which require sixteen days and ten sheets of paper—have been duly observed, his Excellency is informed that the contemplated repairs will cost two rubles and forty kopeks, or about five shillings of our money. Even here the formalities do not stop, for the Government must have the assurance that the architect who made the estimate and superintended the repairs has not been guilty of negligence. A second architect is therefore sent to examine the work, and his report, like the estimate, requires to be confirmed by the council and the Procureur. The whole correspondence lasts thirty days, and requires no less than thirty sheets of paper! Had the person who desired the repairs been not a Governor-General but an ordinary mortal, it is impossible to say how long the procedure might have lasted.[2]

It might naturally be supposed that this circuitous and complicated method, with its registers, ledgers, and minutes of proceedings, must at least prevent pilfering; but this *à priori* conclusion has been emphatically belied by experience. Every new ingenious device had merely the effect of producing a still more ingenious means of evading it. The system did not restrain those who wished to pilfer, and it had a deleterious effect on honest officials, by making them feel that the Government reposed no confidence in them. Besides this, it produced among all officials, honest and dishonest alike, the habit of systematic falsification. As it was impossible for even the most pedantic of men—and pedantry, be it remarked, is a rare quality among Russians—to fulfill conscientiously all the prescribed formalities, it became customary to observe the forms merely on paper. Officials certified facts which they never dreamed of examining, and secretaries gravely wrote the minutes of meetings that had never been held! Thus, in the case above cited, the repairs were in reality begun and ended long before the architect was officially authorized to begin the work. The comedy was nevertheless gravely played out to the end, so that anyone afterwards revising the documents would have found that everything had been done in perfect order.

Perhaps the most ingenious means for preventing administrative abuses was devised by the Emperor Nicholas

[2] In fairness, I feel constrained to add that incidents of this kind occasionally occur—or at least occurred as late as 1886—in our Indian Administration. I remember an instance of a pane of glass being broken in the Viceroy's bedroom in the Viceregal Lodge at Simla, and it would have required nearly a week, if the official procedure had been scrupulously observed, to have it replaced by the Public Works Department.

I. Fully aware that he was regularly and systematically deceived by the ordinary officials, he formed a body of well-paid officers, called the "Gendarmerie," who were scattered over the country, and ordered to report directly to his Majesty whatever seemed to them worthy of attention. Bureaucratic minds considered this an admirable expedient; and the Tsar confidently expected that he would, by means of these official observers, who had no interest in concealing the truth, be able to know everything, and to correct all official abuses. In reality the institution produced few good results, and in some respects had a very pernicious influence. Though picked men and provided with good salaries, these officers were all more or less permeated with the prevailing spirit. They could not but feel that they were regarded as spies and informers—a humiliating conviction, little calculated to develop that feeling of self-respect which is the main foundation of uprightness—and that all their efforts could do but little good. They were, in fact, in pretty much the same position as Peter's Procurator-General, and, with true Russian *bonhomie,* they disliked ruining individuals who were no worse than the majority of their fellows. Besides this, according to the received code of official morality, insubordination was a more heinous sin than dishonesty, and political offenses were regarded as the blackest of all. The gendarmerie officers shut their eyes, therefore, to the prevailing abuses, which were believed to be incurable, and directed their attention to real or imaginary political delinquencies. Oppression and extortion remained unnoticed, whilst an incautious word or a foolish joke at the expense of the Government was too often magnified into an act of high treason.

This force still exists under a modified form. Towards the close of the reign of Alexander II (1880), when Count Loris Méliko, with the sanction and approval of his august master, was preparing to introduce a system of liberal political reforms, it was intended to abolish the gendarmerie as an organ of political espionage, and accordingly the direction of it was transferred from the so-called Third Section of his Imperial Majesty's Chancery to the Ministry of the Interior; but when the benevolent monarch was, a few months afterwards, assassinated by revolutionists, the project was naturally abandoned, and the Corps of Gendarmes, while remaining under the Minister of the Interior, recovered a good deal of its previous authority. It serves now as a kind of supplement to the ordinary police, and is generally employed for matters in which secrecy is required. Unfortunately, it is not bound by those legal restrictions which protect the public against the arbitrary will of the ordinary authorities. In addition to its regular duties it has a vaguely defined roving commission to watch and arrest all persons who seem to it in any way dangerous or *suspectes*, and such persons may be kept in confinement for an indefinite time, or be exiled to some distant and inhospitable part of the Empire, without undergoing a regular trial. It is, in short, the ordinary instrument for punishing political dreamers, suppressing secret societies, counteracting political agitations, and in general executing the extralegal orders of the Government.

My relations with this anomalous branch of the administration were somewhat peculiar. After my experience with the Vice-Governor of Novgorod I determined to place myself above suspicion, and accordingly applied to the "Chef des Gendarmes" for some kind of official document which would prove to all officials with whom I might come in contact that I had no illicit designs. My request was granted, and I was furnished with the necessary documents; but I soon found that in seeking to avoid Scylla I had fallen into Charybdis. In calming official suspicions, I inadvertently aroused suspicions of another kind. The documents proving that I enjoyed the protection of the Government made many people suspect that I was an emissary of the gendarmerie, and greatly impeded me in my efforts to collect information from private sources. As the private were for me more important than the official sources of information, I refrained from asking for a renewal of the protection, and wandered about the country as an ordinary unprotected traveler. For some time I had no cause to regret this decision. I knew that I was pretty closely watched, and that my letters were occasionally opened in the post office, but I was subjected to

no further inconvenience. At last, when I had nearly
forgotten all about Scylla and Charybdis, I one night unexpectedly ran upon the former, and, to my astonishment,
found myself formally arrested! The incident happened in
this wise.

I had been visiting Austria and Serbia, and after a
short absence, returned to Russia through Moldavia. On
arriving at the Pruth, which there formed the frontier, I
found an officer of the gendarmerie, whose duty it was to
examine the passports of all passers-by. Though my passport was completely *en règle,* having been duly *visé* by
the British and Russian consuls at Galatz, this gentleman
subjected me to a searching examination regarding my
past life, actual occupation, and intentions for the future.
On learning that I had been for more than two years
traveling in Russia at my own expense, for the simple purpose of collecting miscellaneous information, he looked in-
credulous, and seemed to have some doubts as to my being
a genuine British subject; but when my statements were
confirmed by my traveling companion, a Russian friend
who carried awe-inspiring credentials, he countersigned
my passport, and allowed us to depart. The inspection of
our luggage by the custom-house officers was soon got
over; and as we drove off to the neighboring village, where
we were to spend the night, we congratulated ourselves
on having escaped for some time from all contact with the
official world. In this we were "reckoning without the
host." As the clock struck twelve that night I was roused
by a loud knocking at my door, and after a good deal of
parley, during which someone proposed to effect an en-
trance by force, I drew the bolt. The officer who had
signed my passport entered, and said, in a stiff, official
tone, "I must request you to remain here for twenty-four
hours."

Not a little astonished by this announcement, I ventured to inquire the reason for this strange request.

"That is my business," was the laconic reply.

"Perhaps it is; still you must, on mature consideration,
admit that I too have some interest in the matter. To my
extreme regret I cannot comply with your request, and
must leave at sunrise."

"You shall not leave. Give me your passport."

"Unless detained by force, I shall start at four o'clock; and as I wish to get some sleep before that time, I must request you instantly to retire. You had the right to stop me at the frontier, but you have no right to come and disturb me in this fashion, and I shall certainly report you. My passport I shall give to none but a regular officer of police."

Here followed a long discussion on the rights, privileges, and general character of the gendarmerie, during which my opponent gradually laid aside his dictatorial tone, and endeavored to convince me that the honorable body to which he belonged was merely an ordinary branch of the administration. Though evidently irritated, he never, I must say, overstepped the bounds of politeness, and seemed only half convinced that he was justified in interfering with my movements. When he found that he could not induce me to give up my passport he withdrew, and I again lay down to rest; but in about half an hour I was again disturbed. This time an officer of regular police entered, and demanded my "papers." To my inquiries as to the reason of all this disturbance, he replied, in a very polite, apologetic way, that he knew nothing about the reason, but he had received orders to arrest me, and must obey. To him I delivered my passport, on condition that I should receive a written receipt, and should be allowed to telegraph to the British ambassador in St. Petersburg.

Early next morning I telegraphed to the ambassador, and waited impatiently all day for a reply. I was allowed to walk about the village and the immediate vicinity, but of this permission I did not make much use. The village population was entirely Jewish, and Jews in that part of the world have a wonderful capacity for obtaining and spreading intelligence. By the early morning there was probably not a man, woman, or child in the place who had not heard of my arrest, and many of them felt a not unnatural curiosity to see the malefactor who had been caught by the police. To be stared at as a malefactor is not very agreeable, so I preferred to remain in my room, where, in the company of my friend, who kindly remained with me and made small jokes about the boasted liberty of British subjects, I spent the time pleasantly enough. The most disagreeable part of the affair was the uncertainty as to how many days, weeks, or months I might be detained, and on this point the police officer would not even hazard a conjecture.

The detention came to an end sooner than I expected. On the following day—that is to say, about thirty-six hours after the nocturnal visit—the police officer brought me my passport, and at the same time a telegram from the British Embassy informed me that the central authorities had ordered my release. On my afterwards pertinaciously requesting an explanation of the unceremonious treatment to which I had been subjected, the Minister for Foreign Affairs declared that the authorities expected a person of my name to cross the frontier about that time with a quantity of false banknotes, and that I had been arrested by mistake. I must confess that this explanation, though official, seemed to me more ingenious than satisfactory, but I was obliged to accept it for what it was worth. At a later period I had again the misfortune to attract the attention of the secret police, but I reserve that incident till I come to speak of my relations with the revolutionists.

From all I have seen and heard of the gendarmerie I am disposed to believe that the officers are for the most part polite, well-educated men, who seek to fulfill their disagreeable duties in as inoffensive a way as possible. It must, however, be admitted that they are generally regarded with suspicion and dislike, even by those people who fear the attempts at revolutionary propaganda which it is the special duty of the gendarmerie to discover and suppress. Nor need this surprise us. Though very many people believe in the necessity of capital punishment, there are few who do not feel a decided aversion to the public executioner.

The only effectual remedy for administrative abuses lies in placing the administration under public control. This has been abundantly proved in Russia. All the efforts of the Tsars during many generations to check the evil by means of ingenious bureaucratic devices proved utterly fruitless. Even the iron will and gigantic energy of Nicholas I were insufficient for the task. But when, after the Crimean War, there was a great moral awakening, and the Tsar called the people to his assistance, the stubborn, deep-rooted evils immediately disappeared. For a time venality and extortion were unknown, and since that period they have never been able to regain their old force.

At the present moment it cannot be said that the administration is immaculate, but it is incomparably purer than it was in old times. Though public opinion is no longer so powerful as it was in the early sixties, it is still strong enough to repress many malpractices which in the time of Nicholas I and his predecessors were too frequent to attract attention. On this subject I shall have more to say hereafter.

If administrative abuses are rife in the Empire of the Tsars, it is not from any want of carefully prepared laws. In no country in the world, perhaps, is the legislation more voluminous, and in theory, not only the officials, but even the Tsar himself, must obey the laws he has sanctioned, like the meanest of his subjects. This is one of those cases, not infrequent in Russia, in which theory differs somewhat from practice. In real life the Emperor may at any moment override the law by means of what is called a Supreme Command (*vysocháishiye poveléniyé*), and a minister may "interpret" a law in any way he pleases by means of a circular. This is a frequent cause of complaint even among those who wish to uphold the autocratic power. In their opinion law-respecting autocracy wielded by a strong Tsar is an excellent institution for Russia; it is arbitrary autocracy wielded by irresponsible ministers that they object to.

As Englishmen may have some difficulty in imagining how laws can come into being without a Parliament or legislative chamber of some sort, I shall explain briefly how they were manufactured by the Russian bureaucratic machine before the creation of the Duma in 1906.

When a minister considered that some institution in his branch of the service required to be reformed, he began by submitting to the Emperor a formal report on the matter. If the Emperor agreed with his minister as to the necessity for reform, he ordered a Commission to be appointed for the purpose of considering the subject and pre-

paring a definitive legislative project. The Commission
set to work in what seemed a very thorough way. It first
studied the history of the institution in Russia from the
earliest times downwards—or rather, it listened to an es-
say on the subject, especially prepared for the occasion by
some official who had a taste for historical studies and
possessed an agreeable literary style. The next step—to
use a phrase which often occurs in the minutes of such
Commissions—consisted in "shedding the light of science
on the question" (*prolít' na dyélo svêt naúki*). This important operation was performed by preparing a memorial
containing the history of similar institutions in foreign
countries, and an elaborate exposition of numerous theories
held by French and German philosophical jurists. In these
memorials it was often considered necessary to include
every European country except Turkey; and sometimes
the small German states and principal Swiss cantons were
treated separately.

To illustrate the character of these wonderful productions, let me give an example. From a pile of such papers lying before me I take one almost at random. It is a
memorial relating to a proposed reform of benevolent institutions. First I find a philosophical disquisition on
benevolence in general; next, some remarks on the Talmud
and the Koran; then a reference to the treatment of pau-
pers in Athens after the Peloponnesian War, and in Rome
under the emperors; then some vague observations on the
Middle Ages, with a quotation that was evidently intended to be Latin; lastly comes an account of the poor-
laws of modern times, in which I meet with "the Anglo-
Saxon domination," King Egbert, King Ethelred; "a
remarkable book of Icelandic laws, called Hragas"; Sweden
and Norway, France, Holland, Belgium, Prussia, and
nearly all the minor German States. The most wonderful thing is that all this mass of historical information, extending from the Talmud to the most recent legislation of
Hesse-Darmstadt, is compressed into twenty-one octavo
pages! The doctrinal part of the memorandum is not less
rich. Many respected names from the literature of Germany, France, and England are forcibly dragged in; and
the general conclusion drawn from this mass of raw, un-

digested materials is believed to be "the latest results of science."

Does the reader suspect that I have here chosen an extremely exceptional case? If so, let us take the next paper in the file. It refers to a project of law regarding imprisonment for debt. On the first page I find references to "the Salic laws of the fifth century," and the "Assises de Jerusalem, A.D. 1099." That, I think, will suffice. Let us pass, then, to the next step.

When the quintessence of human wisdom and experience had thus been extracted, the Commission considered how the valuable product might be applied to Russia, so as to harmonize with the existing general conditions and local peculiarities. For a man of practical mind this was, of course, the most interesting and most important part of the operation, but from Russian legislators it received comparatively little attention. Very often have I turned to this section of official papers in order to obtain information regarding the actual state of the country, and in every case I was grievously disappointed. Vague general phrases, founded on *à priori* reasoning rather than on observation, together with a few statistical tables—which the cautious investigator should avoid as he would an ambuscade —were too often all that was to be found. Through the thin veil of pseudo-erudition the real facts were clear enough. These philosophical legislators, who spent their lives in the official atmosphere of St. Petersburg, knew as much about Russia as the genuine cockney knows about Great Britain, and in this part of their work they derived no assistance from the learned German treatises which supplied an unlimited amount of historical facts and philosophical speculation.

From the Commission the project passed to the Council of State, where it was certainly examined and criticized, and perhaps modified, but was not likely to be improved from the practical point of view, because the members of the Council were merely *ci-devant* members of similar Commissions, hardened by a few additional years of official routine. The Council was, in fact, an assembly of *chinóvniks* who knew little of the practical, everyday wants of the unofficial classes. No merchant, manufacturer, or farmer ever entered its sacred precincts, so that its bureaucratic serenity was rarely disturbed by practical objections. It is not surprising, therefore, that it occasionally passed laws which were found at once to be absolutely unworkable.

From the Council of State the bill was taken to the Emperor, and he generally began by examining the signatures. The "Ayes" were in one column and the "Noes" in another. If his Majesty was not specially acquainted with the matter—and he could not possibly be acquainted with all the matters submitted to him—he usually signed with the majority, or on the side where he saw the names of officials in whose judgment he had special confidence; but if he had strong views of his own, he placed his signature in whichever column he thought fit, and it outweighed the signatures of any number of Councillors. In this way a small minority might be transformed into a majority. When the important question, for example, as to how far Latin and Greek should be taught in the higher schools was considered by the Council, only two members signed in favor of classical education, which was excessively unpopular at the moment; but the Emperor Alexander III, disregarding public opinion and the advice of his Councillors, threw his signature into the lighter scale, and the classicists were victorious.

CHAPTER · II

The Zemstvo and Local Self-Government

AFTER the emancipation of the serfs, the reform most urgently required was the improvement of the provincial
administration. In the time of serfage the Emperor Nicholas, referring to the landed proprietors, used to say in a
jocular tone that he had in his Empire 50,000 most zealous
and efficient hereditary police masters. By the Emancipation Law the authority of these hereditary police masters
was forever abolished, and it became urgently necessary
to put something else in its place. Peasant self-government was accordingly organized on the basis of the rural
Commune; but it fell far short of meeting the requirements of the situation. Its largest unit was the *Vólost*,
which comprised merely a few contiguous Communes, and
its action was confined exclusively to the peasantry. Evidently it was necessary to create a larger administrative
unit, in which the interests of all classes of the population
could be attended to, and for this purpose Alexander II, in
November, 1859, more than a year before the Emancipation Edict, instructed a special Commission to prepare a
project for giving to the inefficient, dislocated provincial
administration greater unity and independence. The project was duly prepared, and after being discussed in the
Council of State it received the Imperial sanction in January, 1864. It was supposed to give, in the words of an
explanatory memorandum, "as far as possible a complete
and logical development to the principle of local self-

government." Thus was created the Zemstvo,[1] which has attracted considerable attention in Western Europe.

My personal acquaintance with this interesting institution dates from 1870. Very soon after my arrival at Novgorod in that year, I made the acquaintance of a gentleman who was described to me as "the president of the provincial Zemstvo bureau," and finding him amiable and communicative, I suggested that he might give me some information regarding the institution of which he was the chief local representative. With the utmost readiness he proposed to be my mentor, introduced me to his colleagues, and invited me to come and see him at his office as often as I felt inclined. Of this invitation I made abundant use. At first my visits were discreetly few and short, but when I found that my new friend and his colleagues really wished to instruct me in all the details of Zemstvo administration, and had arranged a special table in the president's room for my convenience, I became a regular attendant, and spent daily several hours in the bureau, studying the current affairs, and noting down the interesting bits of statistical and other information which came before the members, as if I had been one of their number. When they went to inspect the hospital, the lunatic asylum, the seminary for the preparation of village schoolmasters, or any other Zemstvo institution, they invariably invited me to accompany them, and made no attempt to conceal from me any defects which they happened to discover.

I mention all this because it illustrates the readiness of most Russians to afford every possible facility to a foreigner who wishes seriously to study their country. They believe that they have long been misunderstood and systematically calumniated by foreigners, and they are extremely desirous that the prevalent misconceptions regarding their country should be removed. It must be said to their honor that they have little or none of that false patriotism which seeks to conceal national defects; and in judging themselves and their institutions they

[1] The term Zemstvo is derived from the word *Zemlyá*, meaning land, and might be translated, if a barbarism were permissible, by Land-dom, on the analogy of Kingdom, Dukedom, etc.

are inclined to be oversevere rather than unduly lenient. In the time of Nicholas I those who desired to stand well with the Government proclaimed loudly that they lived in the happiest and best-governed country of the world, but this shallow official optimism has long since gone out of fashion. During all the years which I spent in Russia I found everywhere the utmost readiness to assist me in my investigations, and very rarely noticed that habit of "throwing dust in the eyes of foreigners" of which some writers have spoken so much.

The Zemstvo is a kind of local administration which supplements the action of the rural Communes, and takes cognizance of those higher public wants which individual Communes cannot possibly satisfy. Its principal duties are to keep the roads and bridges in proper repair, to provide means of conveyance for the rural police and other officials, to look after primary education and sanitary affairs, to watch the state of the crops and take measures against approaching famine, and, in short, to undertake, within certain clearly defined limits, whatever seems likely to increase the material and moral well-being of the population. In form the institution is parliamentary—that is to say, it consists of an assembly of deputies which meets regularly once a year, and of a permanent executive bureau elected by the Assembly from among its members. If the Assembly be regarded as a local Parliament, the bureau corresponds to the Cabinet. In accordance with this analogy my friend the president was sometimes jocularly termed the Prime Minister. Once every three years the deputies are elected in certain fixed proportions by the landed proprietors, the rural Communes, and the municipal corporations. Every province (*gubérniya*) and each of the districts (*uyézdy*) into which the province is subdivided has such an assembly and such a bureau.

Not long after my arrival in Novgorod I had the opportunity of being present at a District Assembly. In the ballroom of the "Club de la Noblesse" I found thirty or forty men seated round a long table covered with green cloth. Before each member lay sheets of paper for the purpose of taking notes, and before the president—the Marshal of Noblesse for the district—stood a small hand bell, which

he rang vigorously at the commencement of the proceedings and on all occasions when he wished to obtain silence.
To the right and left of the president sat the members of
the executive (*upráva*), armed with piles of written and
printed documents, from which they read long and tedious extracts, till the majority of the audience took to
yawning and one or two of the members positively went
to sleep. At the close of each of these reports the president
rang his bell—presumably for the purpose of awakening
the sleepers—and inquired whether anyone had remarks
to make on what had just been read. Generally someone
had remarks to make, and not infrequently a discussion
ensued. When any decided difference of opinion appeared,
a vote was taken by handing round a sheet of paper, or by
the simpler method of requesting the Ayes to stand up and
the Noes to sit still.

What surprised me most in this assembly was that it
was composed partly of nobles and partly of peasants—
the latter being decidedly in the majority—and that no
trace of antagonism seemed to exist between the two
classes. Landed proprietors and their *ci-devant* serfs,
emancipated only ten years before, evidently met for the
moment on a footing of equality. The discussions were carried on chiefly by the nobles, but on more than one occasion peasant members rose to speak, and their remarks,
always clear, practical, and to the point, were invariably
listened to with respectful attention. Instead of that violent antagonism which might have been expected, considering the constitution of the Assembly, there was too
much unanimity—a fact indicating plainly that the majority of the members did not take a very deep interest in
the matters presented to them.

This assembly for the district was held in the month
of September. At the beginning of December the Assembly
for the Province met, and during nearly three weeks I was
daily present at its deliberations. In general character and
mode of procedure it resembled closely the District Assembly. Its chief peculiarities were that its members were
chosen, not by the primary electors, but by the assemblies
of the ten districts which compose the province, and that it
took cognizance merely of those matters which concerned

more than one district. Besides this, the peasant **deputies** were very few in number—a fact which somewhat surprised me, because I was aware that, according to the law, the peasant members of the District Assemblies were eligible, like those of the other classes. The explanation is that the District Assemblies choose their most active members to represent them in the Provincial Assemblies, and consequently the choice generally falls on landed proprietors. To this arrangement the peasants make no objection, for attendance at the Provincial Assemblies demands a considerable pecuniary outlay, and payment of the deputies is expressly prohibited by law.

To give the reader an idea of the elements composing this assembly, let me introduce him to a few of the members. A considerable section of them may be described in a single sentence. They are commonplace men, who have spent part of their youth in the public service as officers in the army, or officials in the civil administration, and have since retired to their estates, where they gain a modest competence by farming. Some of them add to their agricultural revenues by acting as justices of the peace.[2] A few may be described more particularly.

You see there, for instance, that fine-looking old general in uniform, with the St. George's Cross at his buttonhole— an order given only for bravery in the field. That is Prince Suvórov, a grandson of the famous field marshal who won victories for the Empress Catherine. He has filled high posts in the Administration without ever tarnishing his name by a dishonest or dishonorable action, and has spent a great part of his life at Court without ceasing to be frank, generous, and truthful. Though he has no intimate knowledge of current affairs, and sometimes gives way a little to drowsiness, his sympathies in disputed points are always on the right side, and when he gets to his feet he always speaks in a clear, soldier-like fashion.

The tall gaunt man, somewhat over middle age, who sits a little to the left is Prince Vassílchikov. He, too, has an historical name, but he cherishes above all things personal independence, and has consequently always kept

[2] That is no longer possible. The institution of justices elected and paid by the Zemstvo was abolished in 1889.

aloof from the Imperial Administration and the Court. The leisure thus acquired he has devoted to study, and he has produced several valuable works on political and social science. An enthusiastic but at the same time cool-headed abolitionist at the time of the Emancipation, he has since constantly striven to ameliorate the condition of the peasantry by advocating the spread of primary education, the establishment of rural credit associations in the villages, the preservation of the Communal institutions, and numerous important reforms in the financial system. Both of these gentlemen, it is said, generously gave to their peasants more land than they were obliged to give by the Emancipation Law. In the Assembly Prince Vassílchikov speaks frequently, and always commands attention; and of all important committees he is a leading member. Though a warm defender of the Zemstvo institutions, he thinks that their activity ought to be confined to a comparatively narrow field, and he thereby differs from some of his colleagues, who are ready to embark in hazardous, not to say fanciful, schemes for developing the natural resources of the province. His neighbor, Mr. P——, is one of the ablest and most energetic members of the Assembly. He is president of the executive bureau in one of the districts, where he has founded many primary schools and created several rural credit associations on the model of those which bear the name of Schultze Delitsch in Germany. Mr. S——, who sits beside him, was for some years an arbiter between the proprietors and emancipated serfs, then a member of the Provincial Executive Bureau, and is now director of a bank in St. Petersburg.

To the right and left of the president—who is Marshal of Noblesse for the province—sit the members of the bureau. The gentleman who reads the long reports is my friend "the Prime Minister," who began life as a cavalry officer, and after a few years of military service retired to his estate; he is an intelligent, able administrator, and a man of considerable literary culture. His colleague, who assists him in reading the reports, is a merchant, and director of the municipal bank. The next member is also a merchant, and in some respects the most remarkable man in the room. Though born a serf, he is already, at middle age, an important personage in the Russian commercial world. Rumor says that he laid the foundation of his fortune by one day purchasing a copper caldron in a village through which he was passing on his way to St. Petersburg, where he hoped to gain a little money by the sale of some calves. In the course of a few years he amassed an enormous fortune; but cautious people think that he is too fond of hazardous speculations, and prophesy that he will end life as poor as he began it.

All these men belong to what may be called the party of progress, which anxiously supports all proposals recognized as "liberal," and especially all measures likely to improve the condition of the peasantry. Their chief opponent is that little man with close-cropped, bullet-shaped head and small piercing eyes, who may be called the Leader of the Opposition. He condemns many of the proposed schemes, on the ground that the province is already overtaxed, and that the expenditure ought to be reduced to the smallest possible figure. In the District Assembly he preaches this doctrine with considerable success, for there the peasantry form the majority, and he knows how to use that terse, homely language, interspersed with proverbs, which has far more influence on the rustic mind than scientific principles and logical reasoning; but here, in the Provincial Assembly, his following composes only a respectable minority, and he confines himself to a policy of obstruction.

The Zemstvo of Novgorod had at that time the reputation of being one of the most enlightened and energetic, and I must say that the proceedings were conducted in a businesslike, satisfactory way. The reports were carefully considered, and each article of the annual budget was submitted to minute scrutiny and criticism. In several of the provinces which I afterwards visited I found that affairs were conducted in a very different fashion: quorums were formed with extreme difficulty, and the proceedings, when they at last commenced, were treated as mere formalities and despatched as speedily as possible. The character of the Assembly depends, of course, on the amount of interest taken in local public affairs. In some districts this interest is considerable; in others it is very near zero.

The birth of this new institution in 1864 was hailed with enthusiasm, and produced great expectations. At that time a large section of the Russian educated classes had a simple, convenient criterion for institutions of all kinds. They assumed as a self-evident axiom that the excellence of an institution must always be in proportion to its "liberal" and democratic character. The question as to how far it might be appropriate to the existing conditions and to the character of the people, and as to whether it might not, though admirable in itself, be too expensive for the work to be performed, was little thought of. Any organization which rested on "the elective principle," and provided an arena for free public discussion, was sure to be well received, and these conditions were fulfilled by the Zemstvo.

The expectations excited were of various kinds. People who thought more of a political than economic progress saw in the Zemstvo the basis of boundless popular liberty. Prince Vassílchikov, for example, though naturally of a phlegmatic temperament, became for a moment enthusiastic, and penned the following words: "With a daring unparalleled in the chronicles of the world, we have entered on the career of public life." If local self-government in England had, in spite of its aristocratic character, created and preserved political liberty, as had been proved by several learned Germans, what might be expected from institutions so much more liberal and democratic? In England there had never been county parliaments, and the local administration had always been in the hands of the great landowners; whilst in Russia every district would have its elective assembly, in which the peasant would be on a level with the richest landed proprietors. People who were accustomed to think of social rather than political progress expected that they would soon see the country provided with good roads, safe bridges, numerous village schools, well-appointed hospitals, and all the other requisites of civilization. Agriculture would become more scientific, trade and industry would be rapidly developed, and the material, intellectual, and moral condition of the peasantry would be enormously improved. The listless apathy of provincial life and the hereditary indifference to local public affairs were now, it was thought, about to be dispelled; and in view of this change, patriotic mothers took their children to the annual assemblies in order to accustom them from their early years to take an interest in the public welfare.

It is hardly necessary to say that these inordinate expectations were not realized. From the very beginning there had been a misunderstanding regarding the character and functions of the new institutions. During the short period of universal enthusiasm for reform, the great officials had used incautiously some of the vague liberal phrases then in fashion, but they never seriously intended to confer on the child which they were bringing into the world a share in the general government of the country; and the rapid evaporation of their sentimental liberalism, which began as soon as they undertook practical reforms, made them less and less conciliatory. When the vigorous young child, therefore, showed a natural desire to go beyond the humble functions accorded to it, the stern parents proceeded to snub it and put it into its proper place. The first reprimand was administered publicly in the capital. The St. Petersburg Provincial Assembly, having shown a desire to play a political part, was promptly closed by the Minister of the Interior, and some of the members were exiled for a time to their homes in the country.

This warning produced merely a momentary effect. As the functions of the Imperial Administration and of the Zemstvo had never been clearly defined, and as each was inclined to extend the sphere of its activity, friction became frequent. The Zemstvo had the right, for example, to co-operate in the development of education, but as soon as it organized primary schools and seminaries it came into contact with the Ministry of Public Instruction. In other departments similar conflicts occurred, and the *chinóvniks* came to suspect that the Zemstvo had the ambition to play the part of a parliamentary Opposition. This suspicion found formal expression in at least one secret official document, in which the writer declares that "the Opposition has built itself firmly a nest in the Zemstvo." Now, if we mean to be just to both parties in this little family quarrel, we must admit that the Zemstvo, as I shall explain in a future chapter, had ambitions of that kind, and it would have been better perhaps for the country at the present moment if it had been able to realize them. But this is a West European idea. In Russia there is, and can be, no such thing as "His Majesty's Opposition." To the Russian official mind the three words seem to contain a logical contradiction. Opposition to officials, even within the limits of the law, is equivalent to opposition to the autocratic power, of which they are the incarnate emanations; and opposition to what they consider the interests of autocracy comes within measurable distance of high treason. It was considered necessary, therefore, to curb and suppress the ambitious tendencies of the wayward child, and accordingly it was placed more and more under the tutelage of the provincial Governors.

To show how the change was effected, let me give an illustration. In the older arrangements the Governor could suspend the action of the Zemstvo only on the ground of its being illegal or *ultra vires,* and when there was an irreconcilable difference of opinion between the two parties, the question was decided judicially by the Senate; under the more recent arrangements his Excellency can interpose his veto whenever he considers that a decision, though it may be perfectly legal, is not conducive to the public good, and differences of opinion are referred, not to the Senate, but to the Minister of the Interior, who is always naturally disposed to support the views of his subordinate.

In order to put an end to all this insubordination Count Tolstoy, the reactionary Minister of the Interior in the reign of Alexander III, prepared a scheme of reorganization in accordance with his antiliberal views, but he died before he could carry it out, and a much milder reorganization was adopted in the law of June 24th, 1890. The principal changes introduced by that law were that the number of delegates in the Assemblies was reduced by about a fourth, and the relative strength of the different social classes was altered. Under the old law the Noblesse had about 42 per cent and the peasantry about 38 per cent of the seats; by the new electoral arrangements the former have 57 per cent and the latter about 30. It does not necessarily follow, however, that the Assemblies are more conservative or more subservient on that account. Liberalism and insubordination are much more likely to be found among the nobles than among the peasants.

In addition to all this, as there was an apprehension in the higher official spheres of St. Petersburg that the opposition spirit of the Zemstvo might find public expression in a printed form, the provincial Governors received extensive rights of preventive censure with regard to the publication of the minutes of Zemstvo Assemblies and similar documents.

What the bureaucracy, in its zeal to defend the integrity of the autocratic power, feared most of all was combination for a common purpose on the part of the Zemstvos of different provinces. It vetoed, therefore, all such combinations, even for statistical purposes; and when it discovered, on one occasion, that leading members of the Zemstvos from all parts of the country were holding private meetings in Moscow for the ostensible purpose of discussing economic questions, it ordered them to return to their homes.

Even within its proper sphere, as defined by law, the Zemstvo has not accomplished what was expected of it. The country has not been covered with a network of macadamized roads, and the bridges are by no means as safe as could be desired. Village schools and infirmaries are still far below the requirements of the population. Little or nothing has been done for the development of trade or manufactures; and the villages remain very much what they were under the old Administration. Meanwhile the local rates have been rising with alarming rapidity; and many people draw from all this the conclusion that the Zemstvo is a worthless institution which has increased the taxation without conferring any corresponding benefit on the country.

If we take as our criterion in judging the institution the exaggerated expectations at first entertained, we may feel inclined to agree with this conclusion, but this is merely tantamount to saying that the Zemstvo has performed no miracles. Russia is much poorer and much less densely populated than the more advanced nations which she takes as her model. To suppose that she could at once

create for herself by means of an administrative reform all
the conveniences which those more advanced nations enjoy, was as absurd as it would be to imagine that a poor
man can at once construct a magnificent palace because
he has received from a wealthy neighbor the necessary
architectural plans. Not only years, but generations, must
pass before Russia can assume the appearance of Germany, France, or England. The metamorphosis may be accelerated or retarded by good government, but it could not
be effected at once, even if the combined wisdom of all
the philosophers and statesmen in Europe were employed
in legislating for the purpose.

The Zemstvo has, however, done much more than the
majority of its critics admit. It fulfills tolerably well, without scandalous peculation and jobbery, its commonplace,
everyday duties, and it has created a new and more equitable system of rating by which landed proprietors and
house owners are made to bear their share of the public
burdens. It has done a very great deal to provide medical
aid and primary education for the common people, and it
has improved wonderfully the condition of the hospitals,
lunatic asylums, and other benevolent institutions committed to its charge. In its efforts to aid the peasantry it
has helped to improve the native breeds of horses and cattle, and it has created a system of obligatory fire insurance,
together with means for preventing and extinguishing fires
in the villages—a most important matter in a country
where the peasants live in wooden houses and big fires are
fearfully frequent. After neglecting for a good many years
the essential question as to how the peasants' means
of subsistence can be increased, it has latterly . . .
helped them to obtain improved agricultural implements
and better seed, encouraged the formation of small credit
associations and savings banks, and appointed agricultural
inspectors to teach them how they may introduce modest
improvements within their limited means.[3] At the same
time, in many districts it has endeavored to assist the home

[3] The amount expended on these objects in 1897, the latest
year for which I have statistical data, was about a million and a
half rubles, or, roughly speaking, £150,000, distributed under
the following heads:

industries which are threatened with annihilation by the
big factories, and whenever measures have been proposed
for the benefit of the rural population, such as the lower-
ing of the land-redemption payments and the creation of
the Peasant Land Bank, it has invariably given them its
cordial support.

If you ask a zealous member of the Zemstvo why it
has not done more he will probably tell you that it is because its activity has been constantly restricted and counteracted by the Government. The Assemblies were obliged
to accept as presidents the Marshals of Noblesse, many of
whom were men of antiquated ideas and retrograde principles. At every turn the more enlightened, more active
members found themselves opposed, thwarted, and finally
checkmated by the Imperial officials. When a laudable
attempt was made to tax trade and industry more equi-
tably the scheme was vetoed, and consequently the mercantile class, sure of being always taxed at a ridiculously
low maximum, have lost all interest in the proceedings.
Even with regard to the rating of landed and house
property a low limit is imposed by the Government, because it is afraid that if the rates were raised much it
would not be able to collect the heavy Imperial taxation.
The uncontrolled publicity which was at first enjoyed by
the Assemblies was afterwards curtailed by the bureaucracy. Under such restrictions all free, vigorous action, it
was said, became impossible, and the institutions failed to
effect what was reasonably anticipated. All this is true
in a certain sense, but it is not the whole truth. If we examine some of the definite charges brought against the institution we shall understand better its real character.

The most common complaint made against it is that it
has enormously increased the rates. On that point there
is no possibility of dispute. At first its expenditure in the

1. Agricultural tuition	£ 41,100
2. Experimental stations, museums, etc.	19,800
3. Scientific agriculturists	17,400
4. Agricultural industries	26,700
5. Improving breeds of horses and cattle	45,300
	£ 150,300

thirty-four provinces in which it existed was under six millions of rubles; in two years (1868) it had jumped up to
fifteen millions; in 1875 it was nearly twenty-eight millions; in 1885 over forty-three millions, and at the end of
the century it had attained the respectable figure of 95,-
800,000 rubles. As each province had the right of taxing
itself, the increase varied greatly in different provinces.
In Smolensk, for example, it was only about 30 per cent,
whilst in Samara it was 436, and in Viatka, where the
peasant element predominates, no less than 1,262 per cent!
In order to meet this increase, the rates on land rose from
under ten millions in 1868 to over forty-seven millions in
1900. No wonder that the landowners who find it difficult
to work their estates at a profit should complain!

Though this increase is disagreeable to the ratepayers,
it does not follow that it is excessive. In all countries rates
and local taxation are on the increase, and it is in the backward countries that they increase most rapidly. In France,
for example, the average yearly increase has been 2.7 per
cent, while in Austria it has been 5.59. In Russia it ought
to have been more than in Austria, whereas it has been, in
the provinces with Zemstvo institutions, only about four
per cent. In comparison with the Imperial taxation the
local does not seem excessive when compared with other
countries. In England and Prussia, for instance, the State
taxation as compared with the local is as a hundred to
fifty-four and fifty-one, whilst in Russia it is as a hundred
to sixteen.[4] A reduction in the taxation as a whole would
certainly contribute to the material welfare of the rural
population, but it is desirable that it should be made in the
Imperial taxes rather than in the rates, because the latter
may be regarded as something akin to productive investments, whilst the proceeds of the former are expended
largely on objects which have little or nothing to do with
the wants of the common people. In speaking thus I am
assuming that the local expenditure is made judiciously,
and this is a matter on which, I am bound to confess, there
is by no means unanimity of opinion.

[4] These figures are taken from the best available authorities,
chiefly Schwanebach and Scalon, but I am not prepared to
guarantee their accuracy.

Hostile critics can point to facts which are, to say the least, strange and anomalous. Out of the total of its revenue the Zemstvo spends about twenty-eight per cent under the heading of public health and benevolent institutions; and about fifteen per cent for popular education, whilst it devotes only about six per cent to roads and bridges, and until lately it neglected, as I have said above, the means for improving agriculture and directly increasing the income of the peasantry.

Before passing sentence with regard to these charges we must remember the circumstances in which the Zemstvo was founded and has grown up. In the early times its members were well-meaning men who had had very little experience in administration or in practical life of any sort except the old routine in which they had previously vegetated. Most of them had lived enough in the country to know how much the peasants were in need of medical assistance of the most elementary kind, and to this matter they at once turned attention. They tried to organize a system of doctors, hospital assistants, and dispensaries by which the peasant would not have to go more than fifteen or twenty miles to get a wound dressed or to have a consultation or to obtain a simple remedy for an ordinary ailment. They felt the necessity, too, of thoroughly reorganizing the hospitals and the lunatic asylums, which were in a very unsatisfactory condition. Plainly enough, there was here good work to be done. Then there were the higher aims. In the absence of practical experience there were enthusiasms and theories. Amongst these was the enthusiasm for education, and the theory that the want of it was the chief reason why Russia had remained so far behind the nations of Western Europe. "Give us education," it was said, "and all other good things will be added thereto. Liberate the Russian people from the bonds of ignorance as you have liberated it from the bonds of serfage, and its wonderful natural capacities will then be able to create everything that is required for its material, intellectual, and moral welfare."

If there was anyone among the leaders who took a more sober, prosaic view of things he was denounced as an ignoramus and a reactionary. Willingly or unwillingly, everybody had to swim with the current. Roads and bridges were not entirely neglected, but the efforts in that direction were confined to the absolutely indispensable. For such prosaic concerns there was no enthusiasm, and it was universally recognized that in Russia the construction of good roads, as the term is understood in Western Europe, was far beyond the resources of any Administration. Of the necessity for such roads few were conscious. All that was required was to make it *possible* to get from one place to another in ordinary weather and ordinary circumstances. If a stream was too deep to be forded, a bridge had to be built or a ferry had to be established; and if the approach to a bridge was so marshy or muddy that vehicles often sank *quite* up to the axles and had to be dragged out by ropes, with the assistance of the neighboring villagers, repairs had to be made. Beyond this the efforts of the Zemstvo rarely went. Its road-building ambition remained within very modest bounds.

As for the impoverishment of the peasantry and the necessity for improving their system of agriculture, that question had hardly appeared above the horizon. It might have to be dealt with in the future, but there was no need for hurry. Once the rural population were educated, the question would solve itself. It was not till about the year 1885 that it was recognized to be more urgent than had been supposed, and some Zemstvos perceived that the people might starve before its preparatory education was completed. Repeated famines pushed the lesson home, and the landed proprietors found their revenues diminished by the fall in the price of grain on the European markets. Thus was raised the cry: "Agriculture in Russia is on the decline! The country has entered on an acute economic crisis! If energetic measures be not taken promptly the people will soon find themselves confronted by starvation!"

To this cry of alarm the Zemstvo was neither deaf nor indifferent. Recognizing that the danger could be averted only by inducing the peasantry to adopt a more intensive system of agriculture, it directed more and more of its attention to agricultural improvements, and tried to get them adopted.[5] It did, in short, all it could, according to its

[5] *Vide,* pp. 38 and 366.

lights and within the limits of its moderate resources. Unfortunately, its available resources were small, for it was forbidden by the Government to increase the rates, and it could not well dismiss doctors and close dispensaries and schools when the people were clamoring for more. So at least the defenders of the Zemstvo maintain, and they go so far as to contend that it did well not to grapple with the impoverishment of the peasantry at an earlier period, when the real conditions of the problem and the means of solving it were only very imperfectly known: if it had begun at that time it would have made great blunders and spent much money to little purpose.

However this may be, it would certainly be unfair to condemn the Zemstvo for not being greatly in advance of public opinion. If it endeavors strenuously to supply all clearly recognized wants, that is all that can reasonably be expected of it. What it may be more justly reproached with is, in my opinion, that it is, to a certain extent, imbued with that unpractical, pedantic spirit which is commonly supposed to reside exclusively in the Imperial Administration. But here again it simply reflects public opinion and certain intellectual peculiarities of the educated classes. When a Russian begins to write on a simple everyday subject, he likes to connect it with general principles, philosophy, or history, and begins, perhaps, by expounding his views on the intellectual and social developments of humanity in general and of Russia in particular. If he has sufficient space at his disposal he may even tell you something about the early period of Russian history previous to the Mongol invasion before he gets to the simple matter in hand. In the previous chapter I have described the process of "shedding on a subject the light of science" in Imperial legislation.[6] In Zemstvo activity we often meet with pedantry of a similar kind.

If this pedantry were confined to the writing of reports it might not do much harm. Unfortunately, it often appears in the sphere of action. To illustrate this I take an instance from the province of Nizhni-Novgorod. The Zemstvo of that province received from the central Government in 1895 a certain amount of capital for road im-

[6] *Vide supra,* pp. 24 and 26.

provement, with instructions from the Ministry of Interior that it should classify the roads according to their relative importance and improve them accordingly. Any intelligent person well acquainted with the region might have made, in the course of a week or two, the required classification accurately enough for all practical purposes. Instead of adopting this simple procedure, what does the Zemstvo do? It chooses one of the eleven districts of which the province is composed, and instructs its statistical department to describe all the villages with a view to determining the amount of traffic which each will probably contribute to the general movement, and then it verifies its *à priori* conclusions by means of a detachment of specially selected "registrars," posted at all the crossways during six days of each month. These registrars doubtless inscribed every peasant cart as it passed and made a rough estimate of the weight of its load. When this complicated and expensive procedure was completed for one district it was applied to another; but at the end of three years, before all the villages of this second district had been described and the traffic estimated, the energy of the statistical department seems to have flagged, and, like a young author impatient to see himself in print, it published a volume at the public expense which no one will ever read.

The cost entailed by this procedure is not known, but we may form some idea of the amount of time required for the whole operation. It is a simple rule-of-three sum. If it took three years for the preparatory investigation of a district and a half, how many years will be required for eleven districts? More than twenty years! During that period it would seem that the roads are to remain as they are, and when the moment comes for improving them it will be found that, unless the province is condemned to economic stagnation, the "valuable statistical material" collected at such an expenditure of time and money is in great part antiquated and useless. The statistical department will be compelled, therefore, like another unfortunate Sisyphus, to begin the work anew, and it is difficult to see how the Zemstvo, unless it becomes a little more practical, is ever to get out of the vicious circle.

In this case the evil result of pedantry was simply unnecessary delay, and in the meantime the capital was accumulating, unless the interest was entirely swallowed up by the statistical researches; but there are cases in which the consequences are more serious. Let me take an illustration from the enlightened province of Moscow. It was observed that certain villages were particularly unhealthy, and it was pointed out by a local doctor that the inhabitants were in the habit of using for domestic purposes the water of ponds which were in a filthy condition. What was evidently wanted was good wells, and a practical man would at once have taken measures to have them dug. Not so the District Zemstvo. It at once transformed the simple fact into a "question" requiring scientific investigation. A commission was appointed to study the problem, and after much deliberation it was decided to make a geological survey in order to ascertain the depth of good water throughout the district as a preparatory step towards preparing a project which will some day be discussed in the District Assembly, and perhaps in the Assembly of the province. Whilst all this is being done according to the strict principles of bureaucratic procedure the unfortunate peasants, for whose benefit the investigation was undertaken, continue to drink the muddy water of the dirty ponds.

Incidents of that kind, which I might multiply almost to any extent, remind one of the proverbial formalism of the Chinese; but between Chinese and Russian pedantry there is an essential difference. In the Middle Kingdom the sacrifice of practical considerations proceeds from an exaggerated veneration of the wisdom of ancestors; in the Empire of the Tsars it is due to an exaggerated adoration of the goddess *Naúka* (Science), and a habit of appealing to abstract principles and scientific methods when only a little plain common sense is required.

The absence of this plain common sense sometimes becomes painfully evident during the debates of the Assemblies, and gives an air of unreality to the proceedings. On one occasion, I remember, in a District Assembly of the province of Riazán, when the subject of primary schools was being discussed, an influential member stood up and proposed that an obligatory system of education should at

once be introduced throughout the whole district. Strange
to say, the motion was very nearly carried, though all the
members present knew—or at least might have known if
they had taken the trouble to inquire—that the actual
number of schools would have to be multiplied twenty-
fold, and all were agreed that the local rates must not be
increased. To preserve his reputation for liberalism, the
honorable member further proposed that, though the system should be obligatory, no fines, punishments, or other
means of compulsion should be employed. How a system
could be obligatory without using some means of compulsion, he did not condescend to explain. To get out of the
difficulty, one of his supporters suggested that the peasants who did not send their children to school should be
excluded from serving as office bearers in the Communes;
but this proposition merely created a laugh, for many
deputies knew that the peasants would regard this supposed punishment as a valuable privilege. And whilst this
discussion about the necessity for introducing an ideal system of obligatory education was being carried on, the
street before the windows of the room was covered with a
stratum of mud nearly two feet in depth! The other streets
were in a similar condition; and a large number of the
members always arrived late, because it was almost impossible to come on foot, and there was only one public
conveyance in the town. Many members had, fortunately,
their private conveyances, but even in these locomotion
was by no means easy. One day, in the principal thor-
oughfare, a member had his *tarantass* overturned, and he
himself was thrown into the mud!

It is hardly fair to compare the Zemstvo with the older
institutions of a similar kind in Western Europe, and especially with our own local self-government. Our institutions have all grown out of real, practical wants, keenly
felt by a large section of the population. Cautious and conservative in all that concerns the public welfare, we regard change as a necessary evil, and put off the evil day
as long as possible, even when convinced that it must inevitably come. Thus our administrative wants are always
in advance of our means for satisfying them, and we use
vigorously those means as soon as they are supplied. Our

method of supplying the means, too, is peculiar. Instead of making a *tabula rasa,* and beginning from the foundations, we utilize to the utmost what we happen to possess, and add merely what is absolutely indispensable. Metaphorically speaking, we repair and extend our political edifice according to the changing necessities of our mode of life, without paying much attention to abstract principles or the contingencies of the distant future. The building may be an aesthetic monstrosity, belonging to no recognized style of architecture, and built in defiance of the principles laid down by philosophical art critics, but it is well adapted to our requirements, and every hole and corner of it is sure to be utilized.

Very different has been the political history of Russia during the last two centuries. It may be briefly described as a series of revolutions effected peaceably by the autocratic power. Each young energetic sovereign has attempted to inaugurate a new epoch by thoroughly remodeling the Administration according to the most approved foreign political philosophy of the time. Institutions have not been allowed to grow spontaneously out of popular wants, but have been invented by bureaucratic theorists to satisfy wants of which the people were often still unconscious. The administrative machine has therefore derived little or no motive force from the people, and has always been kept in motion by the unaided energy of the central Government. Under these circumstances it is not surprising that the repeated attempts of the Government to lighten the burdens of centralized administration by creating organs of local self-government should not have been very successful.

The Zemstvo, it is true, offered better chances of success than any of its predecessors. A large portion of the nobles had become alive to the necessity for improving the Administration, and the popular interest in public affairs was much greater than at any former period. Hence there was at first a period of enthusiasm, during which great preparations were made for future activity, and not a little was actually effected. The institution had all the charm of novelty, and the members felt that the eyes of the public were upon them. For a time all went well, and the Zemstvo was so well pleased with its own activity that the satirical journals compared it to Narcissus admiring his image reflected in the pool. But when the charm of novelty had passed and the public turned its attention to other matters, the spasmodic energy evaporated, and many of the most active members looked about for more lucrative employment. Such employment was easily found, for at that time there was an unusual demand for able, energetic, educated men. Several branches of the civil service were being reorganized, and railways, banks, and joint-stock companies were being rapidly multiplied. With these the Zemstvo had great difficulty in competing. It could not, like the Imperial service, offer pensions, decorations, and prospects of promotion, nor could it pay such large salaries as the commercial and industrial enterprises. In consequence of all this, the quality of the executive bureaus deteriorated at the same time as the public interest in the institution diminished.

To be just to the Zemstvo I must add that, with all its defects and errors, it is infinitely better than the institutions which it replaced. If we compare it with previous attempts to create local self-government, we must admit that the Russians have made great progress in their political education. What its future may be I do not venture to predict. From its infancy it has had, as we have seen, the ambition to play a great political part, and in 1904-5, when the disasters in the Far East were raising a storm of popular indignation against the Government, its leading representatives in conclave assembled took upon themselves to express what they considered the national demand for liberal representative institutions. The desire, which had previously from time to time been expressed timidly and vaguely in loyal addresses to the Tsar, that a central Zemstvo Assembly, bearing the ancient title of Zemski Sobór, should be convoked in the capital and endowed with political functions, was now put forward by the representatives in plain unvarnished form. This desire, as we shall see in the sequel, was not realized, but the impetus given to the reform movement at that time by the Zemstvo Liberals contributed largely to the creation of the Duma.

CHAPTER · III

❦ ❧

The Imperial Duma

THE first Duma, containing over four hundred members, reflected in some respects the contemporary state of Russia. Like the Empire, it was composed of many nationalities clustering round the dominant race. The chief ethnographical groups were the Great Russians (265), the Little Russians (62), the White Russians (12), the Poles (51), the Lithuanians (10), the Letts (6), the Estonians (4), the Germans (4), the Jews (13), the Tatars (8), and the Bashkirs (4); whilst the less important nationalities, each represented by one or two deputies, included the Mordvá, the Votiaks, the Tchuvash, the Circassians, and the Kalmyks. In respect of social status the diversity was equally remarkable. A spectator had only to glance at the costumes to perceive that the Assembly included the tamed nomad from the Steppe, the free Cossack, the unlettered peasant, the parish priest, the village schoolmaster, the unsophisticated landed proprietor, and some gentlemen who represented the latest products of West European culture. With regard to political tendencies and aims, the Duma was likewise a fair reflection of the state of things in the Empire. In the old times, when a National Assembly was still a dream of the future, my Russian friends used to assure me that if they were ever fortunate enough to possess a parliament, it would contain no rival parties, because all the members would devote themselves exclusively to securing and advancing the national welfare; but this prediction, as I warned my friends at the time, was not destined to be realized. In the first Duma there were as many parties, or at least rival groups, as there are usually in the parliaments of other countries. First in numbers and importance came the 153 Constitutional Democrats, or Cadets as they are usually called,[1] drawn from various sections of the educated classes— landed gentry, barristers, doctors, officials, professors, and literary men. Next came the Labor group of 107 members, drawn from lower social strata—the peasants, workmen, minor officials, schoolteachers, and the like. Apart from both of these were the Autonomists, 63 in number, representing the minor nationalities who objected to complete absorption in the great heterogeneous Empire, and the Independents, numbering 165, who hesitated to attach themselves to any party and were unable to form a party for themselves. As for the Conservatives and Reactionaries, they were so few that they hardly constituted a group, and they were so little in sympathy with the overwhelming majority of their colleagues that they rarely ventured to put forward their views.

If there was any truth in the current accusation that the authorities had exercised undue pressure on the electors, the pressure must have been singularly ineffectual, for the Chamber could not be called governmental in any sense of the term. On the contrary, it was not at all amenable to official influence, and its short, stormy life of seventy-two days was devoted almost entirely to a struggle with the Cabinet. Nearly all the groups of which it was composed were resolved to extort from the autocratic power a great deal more than had been granted by the manifestoes, the rescripts, the ukases, and the fundamental laws; and when they encountered stubborn resistance from the Executive, they directed their energies to discrediting the Government, to advertising their own benevolent intentions towards the people, and to increasing the popular discontent.

[1] This curious term *Cadet* deserves a word of explanation. Most of the parties and groups gave themselves such long names that it became customary to designate them by their initials. Thus the Constitutional Democrats (*Konstitutsionniye Demokraty*) were designated by the letters K. D., which are pronounced in Russian *Ka Deh*, exactly like the French word *Cadet*.

Of the groups above enumerated, and others which might be mentioned, the only one which had the characteristics of an organized political party was that of the Cadets. Though it included only about one-third of the House, it had so many allies in other groups that it could generally count on a majority in a division, and it directed the proceedings to such an extent that this first Assembly is often called the Cadet Duma to distinguish it from its successors.

In theory the Cadets were a moderate constitutional party, and if they had possessed a little more prudence and patience they might have led the country gradually into the paths of genuine constitutional government; but, like everyone in Russia at that time, they were in a hurry, and they greatly overestimated their own strength. Their impatience was curiously illustrated during a friendly conversation which I had one evening with a leader of the party. With all due deference, I ventured to suggest that, instead of maintaining an attitude of systematic and uncompromising hostility to the Ministry, the party might co-operate with the Government and thereby gradually create something like the English parliamentary system, for which they professed such admiration; possibly in eight or ten years this desirable result might be obtained. On hearing these last words my friend suddenly interrupted me and exclaimed:

"Eight or ten years? We cannot wait so long as that!"

"Well," I replied, "you must know your own affairs best; but in England, which constitutionalists of other countries often take as their model, we had to wait for several centuries."

Suggestions of this kind were most unwelcome to the Cadets, for they were resolved to obtain at once a full-fledged Constitution. In granting a kind of parliament, the Emperor had defined and limited its functions by fundamental laws which could be modified only on the initiative of the Crown, and he had reserved to the Sovereign the appointment of Ministers and the control of the Executive. Thus the new Russian Constitution, if Constitution it could be called, was of the German rather than of the English type. Now, what the Cadets wanted—and with them the

great majority of the educated classes—was a Constitution
in which the Cabinet and the Administration should be
responsible, not to the Emperor, but to the majority in the
Duma; and they began at once their campaign for the attainment of this object, which was inconsistent with the
fundamental laws just issued. Foreseeing clearly the probable consequences of this course, they resolved, at a party
conference, that they should seek to attain their ends, "un-
deterred by the possibility of an open rupture with the
Government," and that the Government should be made
to appear responsible for the conflict. That was the basis
of their strategy, and they acted accordingly. In their reply to the speech from the Throne they carefully abstained
from any expression of gratitude for rights and privileges
conferred, and they enumerated clearly their demands:
That no special laws should limit the Duma's legislative
competence; that the Council of the Empire should be
abolished; that the Ministry should be responsible to the
Duma; and that the Administration should be thoroughly
reorganized.

As soon as they were given to understand that these demands, being inconsistent with the fundamental laws,
could not be complied with, efforts were made to induce
the Ministers to resign in order that they might be replaced by a Cabinet formed from the majority of the
Chamber, and these efforts were continued almost daily
till the end of the session. Again and again the cry was
raised: "Resign! Resign! It is time for you to retire!" Want
of confidence, dissatisfaction, and even contempt were frequently and loudly expressed, and the Ministers were told,
sometimes in insulting terms, that in their retirement alone
was to be found the salvation of the Fatherland. Some of
the more impatient deputies of the Labor group proposed
to create at once an administrative organization independent of the Government by means of local committees
elected on the basis of manhood suffrage; and when their
demands were disregarded, their declamations assumed a
tone of menace: "We regard the Ministers as criminals; we
hope that their disgraceful rule may be put an end to, and
if that cannot be done by us, the people will settle accounts with them!" "Is it not time for all these rulers, great

and small, to understand that the moment is perhaps not
far distant when the Duma will find it impossible to protect them against the punishing hand of the enraged People?" "Surely the Government must perceive that a frightful wave of national indignation is rising, and that it may
reach heights hitherto unknown!"

When violent language of this kind was used by the
parties of the Left, the Cadets usually remained silent and
they never once protested. They could wax eloquent over
the atrocities instigated by the Reactionaries, but for revolutionary agitation and acts of terrorism they had no
word of condemnation; they regarded, in fact, the parties
of the Left as their allies, and hoped to use them as instruments for bringing pressure on the Government with a
view to raising themselves to the Ministerial benches.
Gradually this strategy came to be understood by the
members of the Labor group, and their relations with the
Cadets ceased to be cordial.

This struggle for power between the Government and
the Cadets went on for two months without any tangible
results, and at last the Cadets imprudently resolved to
bring about a general, decisive engagement. The battlefield chosen was the Agrarian question, in which revolutionary proposals were sure to evoke the sympathy and
support of the peasants. In the hope of counteracting
the Agrarian movement for the forcible expulsion of the
landed proprietors from their estates, the Government had
issued on July 2nd an official communication to the effect
that it regarded as inadmissible the compulsory alienation
of landed property in favor of the peasants. This seemed
to ordinary minds a natural and laudatory proceeding on
the part of the Government, but the Cadets, who did not
desire Agrarian tranquillity at that moment, denounced it
as "not only imprudent, but as a criminal attempt on the
part of the Executive to produce confusion in the minds
of the population." In order to prevent this evil effect, they
proposed to issue to the people a counterblast in the form
of a communication of the Duma, "the highest legislative
authority." The proposal was warmly supported by the
orators of the Left, who spoke very plainly: "If the Duma,"
they said, "does not wish to be a dead institution like the

bureaucracy, it must listen every day and every hour to the voice of the national will, and execute immediately the commands of the People. The demand for direct relations between the Duma and the People comes from all classes. . . . The slow, indirect method is no longer possible, now that at the head of the Administration remain authorities who have been declared by the voice of the People to be criminals, murderers, and executioners. From today onwards the People sees before it two contending powers: the power of the bureaucracy, and the power of the national representatives."

Not a few deputies, even in the ranks of the Cadets, had scruples about thus appealing to the People against the Government, but they refrained from offering strenuous opposition, and on July 19th, in a small House, the revolutionary proposal was carried by a majority of 124 to 53. At once the Government took up the challenge, and three days afterwards the Duma was dissolved.

This was a surprise for the Cadets. They believed that the Government would not dare to proceed to a dissolution, and that if it took such a step the whole population would rise in support of their representatives. In accordance with this belief, they went immediately to Finland and drew up at Vyborg a seditious proclamation in which they called upon the people to assume an attitude of passive resistance to the authorities by refusing recruits and declining to pay taxes.

If the Cadets really hoped to produce a serious popular movement against the Government, they must have been greatly surprised and disappointed, for their proclamation, in publishers' phrase, "fell still-born from the press." It was not obeyed even by its authors, for among those who had drawn up and signed it some went abroad a few days afterwards and showed no hesitation about paying the passport tax! Thus ended, not very heroically, what has been called "the Duma of the national indignation." It certainly expressed the anger of the nation against the Government in no measured terms, but it did little else. Having fulfilled this part of its mission, it might have settled down quietly to useful legislative work and co-operated with the Government in a series of practical reforms.

but it had no taste for such prosaic occupation. No one was satisfied with the concessions made by the Emperor, and all were clamoring for more. The moderate groups were demanding a Cabinet chosen from, and responsible to, themselves; while the groups of the Left were aiming at the substitution of a democratic republic for the autocratic regime.

In dissolving the first Duma the Emperor decided that another experiment should be made without any change in the electoral law, and a new Duma was accordingly convoked for March 5th, 1907.

There was some reason to suppose that the new Duma would be better than its predecessor: the public excitement had abated, and many illusions had been destroyed by experience. No one any longer imagined that autocracy, bureaucracy, and all the other evils from which Russia was suffering could be swept away by torrents of in-dignant rhetoric, and the ground be cleared for a beautiful new edifice, constructed according to the most modern and advanced principles of political architecture. Even the most doctrinaire of the Liberals or Socialists could hardly flatter themselves that the walls of the Imperial Jericho would fall spontaneously before the blast of democratic or revolutionary trumpets. The Government had shown that it possessed means of resistance, and now it had on its side a volunteer force drawn from the Conservative elements of the population, which had not been able to organize themselves for the first general election. Moreover, there was now a much stronger hand at the helm; for, at the moment of the dissolution, M. Stolýpin, the only member of the Cabinet who had succeeded in obtaining generally a respectful hearing in the Chamber, had replaced M. Goremýkin as Prime Minister; and he had now provided abundant occupation for such deputies as wished to undertake practical legislative work. Differing in this respect from his predecessor,[2] he had taken the precaution of preparing a big pile of bills, sufficient in

[2] In justice to M. Goremýkin I may mention that he was not to blame for appearing before the first Duma with empty hands, because he had been appointed Premier only about ten days before the opening of the Assembly.

quantity and quality to occupy fully for several years the energies of the most hard-working Parliament. There would be less excuse, therefore, for honorable members to waste time and create unnecessary friction by raising and discussing abstract constitutional questions.

All this gave reason to hope that the second Duma, which was about to assemble, would be less revolutionary and more capable of practical work than its predecessor; but these hopes were not destined to be realized. Though the political excitement had subsided in certain sections of the population, it was still so general that the fact of a candidate having been imprisoned or exiled was commonly regarded by the constituencies as a recommendation in his favor. Out of a total of 213 deputies elected in the twenty-five provinces for which I happen to possess statistics, no less than 55 had been in prison, in exile, or under police supervision, and 13 had been dismissed from the public service. Existing revolutionary groups were thereby strengthened, and they were reinforced by a new and powerful group—that of the Social Democrats, who had boycotted the first general election and had now gained more than sixty seats. The total of Socialist deputies was thus raised from 26 to 83—that is to say, from 5 to 17 per cent of the whole House.

Another undesirable change had been produced by the general election: the intellectual level of the deputies as a body had been lowered. Among the Cadets who had signed the Vyborg manifesto, not a few were men of exceptional ability and culture, and as they were being prosecuted on a charge of sedition they could not legally present themselves as candidates. Of the deputies who replaced them, the great majority were very far from being men of the same intellectual caliber, while the contingent of the totally uneducated was greatly reinforced. In contradistinction to "the Duma of the national indignation," the new Assembly could be described by a leading Conservative, without much exaggeration, as "the Duma of the national ignorance."

As soon as the formal business had been disposed of, the House began to show its real character. When M. Stolýpin had sketched in outline his legislative program, and expressed his readiness to place at the disposal of the Duma his loyal intentions and accumulated experience, he was answered by the Extreme Left in anything but a conciliatory tone. The leader of the Social Democrats, a young Georgian from the Caucasus, speaking in a calm, deliberate style, declared that the Prime Minister's speech had been received in silence because no cries or stormy demonstrations could adequately express the feelings of the People towards a Government which had dispersed the first Duma, created courts-martial, fettered the country by a state of siege, imprisoned its best sons, ruined the population, and squandered the money intended for famine relief. As the Executive would never voluntarily submit to the legislative power, the orator considered that the organized strength of the Government must be opposed by the organized strength of the People. For this purpose the accusing voice of the People's representatives must resound through the country and rouse to the struggle all who were not yet awake; and the Duma must, by means of legislative measures, organize and combine the awakened masses. This revolutionary plan of campaign, recommended with the calm assurance of conscientious conviction as if it had been an ordinary legislative proposal, was supported with great warmth by less phlegmatic members of the party, and gave rise to a very lively discussion, in which the Extreme Right protested in violent language. M. Stolýpin, on the Ministerial bench, listened attentively in silence to the various orators, and finally closed the debate by a short speech, delivered with calm dignity, but not without occasional indications of suppressed emotion. After referring to the thinly disguised threats of the Social Democrats, he turned to the leader of the party, drew himself up to his full height, and concluded with a short declaration, in a firm, defiant tone:

"These attacks are doubtless intended to paralyze the will and intellect of the Government; they are all tantamount to two words addressed to the constituted authority: 'Hands up!' To these two words the Government, completely self-possessed and conscious of its uprightness, can only reply: 'You do not frighten us!' "

During this significant discussion which foreshadowed

the whole history of the second Duma (March 5th to
June 16th) the Cadets remained silent, playing the part
of *tertius gaudens*. They clung as firmly as ever to their
aim of compelling the Government to grant parliamentary
institutions in the English sense of the term, and they had
still the ambition to form the first Cabinet in a parliament
of that kind; but they recognized the necessity of changing their tactics, and one of them expressed this in a picturesque way: "As the fortress cannot be taken by storm,
it must be forced to capitulate by a prolonged siege." In
one respect, however, their tactics remained the same:
they encouraged the activity of the Extreme Left, in the
hope that sooner or later the Government would be frightened by the revolutionary agitation and would accept as
the lesser of two evils a Cadet Ministry. For this reason
they could never be induced to support even an academic
resolution condemning acts of terrorism, and persistently
regarded all such proposals as traps laid by their rivals
for the purpose of sowing discord between them and their
revolutionary allies. The said allies, however, understood
the game perfectly; whilst refraining from unnecessary
conflicts with the Cadets, they regarded them as half-
hearted politicians who, in the event of an armed rising,
would view the proceedings at a safe distance and intervene merely to carry off the lion's share of the spoil.
M. Stolýpin likewise understood the Cadets' game, and
systematically rejected their advances; he had not forgotten the Vyborg manifesto and all that it implied. Nor
was he less cautious with regard to the avowed revolutionaries. He obstinately refused to swell the ranks of the
agitators and terrorists by recommending a general am-
nesty for political offenders, and he declined to relax in
any way his military precautions against an insurrection.

In such circumstances, with no moderate party strong
enough to command a majority when important legislative
questions were put to the vote, the Duma was incapable
of any useful work; but nearly all the sections of which it
was composed desired, for different reasons, to prolong its
existence. By all parties it was regarded as a convenient
instrument for ventilating their political opinions and aspirations, and as a means of keeping a door open for future

possibilities; but there was one group which was too impatient to continue indefinitely a waiting policy. That was the group of the Social Democrats, who were convinced that their aims could be attained only by an armed rising, in which the army should pass over to the side of the masses, or at least remain neutral. To attain this object they had created a secret organization with ramifications in the garrison towns all over the country and a central bureau in St. Petersburg, where the conspirators assembled in the apartment of one of the deputies.

This revolutionary activity was carried on so openly that it very soon became known to the Government, and M. Stolýpin determined to put a stop to it. On June 14th he accordingly came down to the House, announced formally that fifty-five members of the Social Democratic group had been conspiring to seduce the army from its allegiance and bring about an insurrection, and demanded that the Duma should consent to judicial proceedings being taken against them. In explanation and support of his demand, he caused a lengthy indictment to be read by a high official of the Judicial Department, and he gave it clearly to be understood that the matter must be treated as urgent. This placed the Cadets in an extremely awkward position: if they consented to the demand of the Prime Minister, they practically abandoned their allies of the Extreme Left; and if they refused, they ran a very serious risk of provoking a dissolution, which they were most anxious, for many reasons, to avoid. In this difficulty they took refuge in procrastination, and caused the matter to be referred to a Committee, which was instructed to report within twenty-four hours; but at the end of that time no decision was forthcoming, and an attempt was made to secure further delay. To these Fabian tactics the Government replied next morning by a decree of dissolution.

Thus ended, one might almost say by suicide, the second Duma, after an inglorious existence of a little more than three months, during which it showed its incapacity for practical legislative work. As insinuations have been made in various quarters that the conspiracy which produced the crisis was an invention of the police, it may be well to mention an incident which effectually refutes that theory. When the Cadets proposed to refer the matter to a Commission, Tsereteli, leader of the Social Democrats, courageously declared that such a procedure was unnecessary, because the indictment was true from beginning to end (*ot slova do slova*), and the accused were proud of what they had done: "We who are accused of having undertaken the political education of the masses, declare that this accusation fills our hearts with pride, and serves as a proof that we fulfilled honorably the obligations imposed on us."

As the Duma had thus twice shown its unfitness to fulfill the functions for which it had been created, the question was raised whether it should not be abolished, or at least radically transformed. Several members of the Cabinet answered this question in the affirmative. M. Stolýpin, on the contrary, urged that at least one more attempt should be made to lead the country gradually into the paths of constitutional life, and as a means of removing some of the worst evils he proposed certain modifications of the election law. In this course of action he was supported by the Emperor, who was likewise reluctant to return to the old system of Government; and the experiment was made with considerable success.

The change in the composition and spirit of the Assembly was evident at a glance. On returning home from one of the first sittings, I made the following entry in my diary, which indicates briefly the changes which had taken place and the prospects for the future:

"*November 23rd*, 1907.—This third Duma, in which I have just spent three hours listening attentively to the debates, and conversing, during the intervals, with some of the more influential members, is evidently very different from its predecessors. What struck me immediately was that most of the members are better dressed and have altogether a more civilized appearance; I saw no unkempt Bohemians and only a few peasants, none of whom were in peasant costume. If first impressions are to be trusted, this Assembly will not be known as 'the Duma of the national indignation,' nor as 'the Duma of the national ignorance.' Many of the peasants and village schoolmasters have been replaced by landed proprietors, and there are now, I am told, a few representatives of the big manufacturers, who were formerly conspicuous by their absence. The reactionary group has been greatly increased, whereas the avowedly revolutionary contingent has almost completely disappeared. Stolýpin seems to be, on the whole, satisfied with the result of the elections, but he prudently refrains from sanguine predictions.

"The change for the better may be attributed in some measure to the new electoral law and the progress made by the Government in the art of electioneering, but it is mainly due, I believe, to a great change which has taken place in public opinion. Under the influence of time and experience, the revolutionary excitement is evaporating, and those who have something to lose have become alarmed by the activity and defiant attitude of the aggressive Socialists. Cosmopolitanism, too, which favored the extravagant claim of the minor nationalities, has received a check, and there are significant symptoms that Russian nationalist feeling is being aroused. This is not surprising when we remember how, in the last Duma, deputies from the Caucasus, speaking Russian with a strong foreign accent, threatened the Government with an armed rising of the Russian people; how the Poles, while respecting scrupulously the rules of the House, held the balance for a time between the contending Russian parties; and how on one occasion an Armenian deputy allowed himself to cast an insult at the Russian army! The weak point in the present Assembly is that the Octobrists —the moderate party which accepts the famous October manifesto in its natural sense, and wishes to co-operate with the Government in legislative work—do not possess an absolute majority, and consequently they must ally themselves, permanently or intermittently, either with the Right or with the Cadets. Doubtless they would prefer the former as allies, but, unfortunately, the Right contains a large element of violent Reactionaries, who are more than suspected of a desire to wreck the parliamentary institutions and re-establish some sort of autocracy under their own control. On the other hand, an alliance with the Cadets, who still cling to their old tactics of trying to extort further concessions from the Crown, would inevitably lead to a conflict with the Government and probably to another dissolution."

The general character and the conflicting currents of this Duma were reflected in the debates on the address (November 26th, 1907). The text recommended by the Octobrists was as follows:

> "Your Imperial Majesty was graciously pleased to welcome us, members of the third State Duma, and to invoke the blessing of the Almighty on the legislative work which awaits us. We consider it our duty to express to your Imperial Majesty our feelings of devotion to the Supreme Leader of the Russian State, and our gratitude for the rights of national representation granted to Russia and confirmed by the fundamental laws of the Empire. Believe us, Sire, we shall apply all our strength, all our knowledge, all our experience, to strengthening the State organism, renewed in the manifesto of October 30 by your sovereign will; to tranquillizing the Fatherland, maintaining order, developing public instruction, increasing the general welfare, confirming the greatness of indivisible Russia, and justifying thereby the confidence shown us by the Sovereign and the country."

This address, which the Octobrist leader recommended as containing nothing of a party character, gave rise to a very curious and characteristic debate. Objections were raised both by the Right and by the Cadets. The former insisted on the insertion of the word *Autocrat,* which still appears among the Emperor's titles; whilst the latter insisted on the insertion of the word "Constitution," which has never received official sanction. These apparently futile amendments had a certain practical significance. On the one hand the insertion of the word Autocrat would be a public recognition of the fact that the Emperor was still, as his official title proclaimed, the Autocrat of All the Russias. On the other hand, if the word Constitution found a place in the document, and was allowed to pass without protest, the Cadets could in future maintain that what they called "the Constitution" had been officially recognized by the Emperor, and they could stigmatize as "unconstitutional" much that was really permissible according to the fundamental laws. In order to avoid these controversies, the Octobrists had adopted a neutral expression—"the State organism renewed in the manifesto of October 30th by your Sovereign will"—and this was finally carried, but not unanimously, for the Extreme Right and the Extreme Left abstained from voting.

When we contrast that address of November 26th, 1907, couched in respectful language and expressing gratitude to the Emperor, with the address presented by the "Duma of the national indignation," on May 17th, 1906, we realize the great progress which had been made towards pacification in the short space of a year and a half. For that remarkable change the merit belongs largely to M. Stolýpin. At the beginning of his Ministry he formed two resolves, and he clung to them with marvelous tenacity: To suppress disorders relentlessly by every means at his disposal, and to preserve the Duma as long as hopes could be entertained of its doing useful work, while keeping it strictly within the functions assigned to it by the Emperor. Until the assembling of the third Duma he found no cordial support in any of the parties or groups; all were leagued against him. For the Conservative and Reactionary Right, he was too liberal; for the Revolutionary Left, he was a pillar of autocracy, an advocate of police repression and drumhead courts-martial; for the Cadets, who were the predominant guiding power in the first two Dumas, he was an irreconcilable enemy, who systematically and watchfully prevented them from encroaching on the prerogatives of the Crown as defined by the fundamental laws. In spite of all this, like a courageous pilot, he steered the ship dexterously through successive storms, and at last brought her into comparatively calm water.

Thanks to his exertions, loyally supported by the Octobrists and the moderate Right, the third Duma did much useful legislative work. Favored by the gradual subsidence of the revolutionary excitement, it fulfilled successfully the functions of a Chamber of Deputies endowed with limited powers. Of the old bureaucratic Council of the Empire, which the October manifesto and subsequent edicts transformed into an Upper Chamber composed of Crown nom-

inees and elective members in equal numbers, it is too
soon to speak confidently; but there is good reason to hope
that it will likewise fulfill its functions successfully and
exercise eventually a restraining and regulating influence
on the parliamentary machine. No doubt there will be occasional friction between the two Houses, and between
them and the Government, but this is the necessary condition of parliamentary life in all countries, and there is
no reason why Russia should be an exception to the general rule.

In order to appreciate fully the difficulties of M. Stolýpin's task, we must remember that he had to struggle not
only with political opposition in the Duma and among the
Court officials, but also with the revolutionary agitation,
conspiracies, terrorism, and all manner of disorders
throughout the country. During the first five weeks of his
premiership he had to deal with five local mutinies in the
army and navy, and with a long series of murderous attacks with bombs and revolvers on provincial governors,
vice-governors, generals, minor officials, and policemen of
all grades. He himself had a very narrow escape. His villa
in St. Petersburg was blown up with bombs while he was
sitting in it at work; he remained unhurt, but a number of
his officials and servants were killed or wounded, and one
of his daughters, when extricated from the wreckage,
was found to be dangerously injured. As an instance of
the attacks on the police, an incident in Warsaw may
be quoted: According to a preconcerted arrangement,
twenty-six policemen and sentries were shot simultaneously by revolutionary agents in different quarters of the
town. In other parts of the country burglaries and acts of
brigandage were perpetrated with unprecedented audacity in wholesale fashion; banks were attacked by
armed youths in broad daylight, and postal trains were
held up and robbed. At first these attacks were directed
against Government property, and were technically called
"expropriations," but the "political expropriators" were
soon followed by ordinary robbers and thieves, who could
not be controlled by the revolutionary committees. For
more than a year this state of things continued, with considerable loss of life. In the month of May, 1907, for ex-

ample, the list of casualties resulting from the revolutionary disorders amounted to 291 killed and 326 wounded. All this time the agrarian disturbances were still going on in the rural districts, and the means of repression at the disposal of the local authorities was often very inadequate.

By ceaseless, persistent effort, attended necessarily with great severity, public order was gradually restored. For the severity M. Stolýpin was much criticized, especially by those who, like the Cadets, did not wish to see tranquillity restored until their political aims had been attained; but the unfavorable judgments passed on him in this respect were not confirmed by those who knew him personally, and who realized the situation in which he was placed. Naturally of a humane temperament and a singularly affectionate disposition, he would gladly have refrained from all severe measures, but he had to sacrifice his personal feelings to a sense of public duty. Firmly convinced that the vital interests of his country were at stake, he acted as a true patriot. His motives were indicated by a remark he made one day in the Duma. Defending his Government against an attack by a group of revolutionary deputies, he turned to them and said in a voice quivering with emotion: "*You* desire great commotions; *we* desire a great Russia!" As a boy he had been distinguished by his strong patriotic feelings, and in the last years of his life they were the keynote of his policy.

M. Stolýpin did not live to carry out his program, which aimed at consolidating representative institutions without destroying the Imperial authority. On September 18th, 1911, at a gala performance in the theater of Kiev, he was shot by a young Jew who was at one and the same time a Terrorist and an agent of the secret police; and four days afterwards he died from the effects of the wound. The post-mortem examination showed that he could not in any case have lived much longer; his health, never very robust, had been thoroughly undermined by overwork and anxieties. For a considerable time he knew that his end was near, but this merely increased his feverish energy, which was concealed under a grave yet cheerful manner. Of the many distinguished Russians whom I have known, he was certainly one of the most sympathetic, and even his enemies, while denying to him the qualities of a great statesman, were constrained to admit that he was an honest, courageous, truthful, and in all respects honorable man.[3]

[3] With regard to the dissolution of the second Duma, it has recently been asserted that there was no Social Democrat conspiracy, and that Tsereteli's confession was simply a piece of bravado. I may be permitted, therefore, to mention that I had an opportunity of examining the original documents on which the indictment was founded, and they convinced me that it was amply justified. On the other hand, it must be admitted that the modification of the Electoral Law was technically illegal.

CHAPTER · IV

The Reform of the Law Courts

AFTER serf-emancipation and local self-government, the subject which demanded most urgently the attention of reformers was the judicial organization, which had sunk to a depth of inefficiency and corruption difficult to describe.

In early times the dispensation of justice in Russia, as in other states of a primitive type, had a thoroughly popular character. The State was still in its infancy, and the duty of defending the person, the property, and the rights of individuals lay, of necessity, chiefly on the individuals themselves. Self-help formed the basis of the judicial procedure, and the State merely assisted the individual to protect his rights and to avenge himself on those who voluntarily infringed them.

By the rapid development of the autocratic power all this was changed. Autocracy endeavored to drive and regulate the social machine by its own unaided force, and regarded with suspicion and jealousy all spontaneous action in the people. The dispensation of justice was accordingly appropriated by the central authority, absorbed into the Administration, and withdrawn from public control. Themis retired from the marketplace, shut herself up in a dark room from which the contending parties and the public gaze were rigorously excluded, surrounded herself with secretaries and scribes who put the rights and claims of the litigants into whatever form they thought proper, weighed according to her own judgment the arguments presented to her by her own servants, and came forth from her seclusion merely to present a ready-made decision or to punish the accused whom she considered guilty.

This change, though perhaps to some extent necessary, was attended with very bad consequences. Freed from the control of the contending parties and of the public, the courts acted as uncontrolled human nature generally does. Injustice, extortion, bribery and corruption assumed gigantic proportions, and against these evils the Government found no better remedy than a system of complicated formalities and ingenious checks. The judicial functionaries were hedged in by a multitude of regulations, so numerous and complicated that it seemed impossible for even the most unjust judge to swerve from the path of uprightness. Explicit, minute rules were laid down for investigating facts and weighing evidence; every scrap of evidence and every legal ground on which the decision was based were committed to writing; every act in the complicated process of coming to a decision was made the subject of a formal document, and duly entered in various registers; every document and register had to be signed and countersigned by various officials who were supposed to control each other; every decision might be carried to a higher court and made to pass a second time through the bureaucratic machine. In a word, the legislature introduced a system of formal written procedure of the most complicated kind, in the belief that by this means mistakes and dishonesty would be rendered impossible.

It may be reasonably doubted whether this system of judicial administration can anywhere give satisfactory results. It is everywhere found by experience that in tribunals from which the healthy atmosphere of publicity is excluded justice languishes, and a great many ugly plants shoot up with wonderful vitality. Languid indifference, an indiscriminating spirit of routine, and unblushing dishonesty too often creep in through the little chinks and crevices of the barrier raised against them, and no method of hermetically sealing these chinks and crevices has yet been invented. The attempt to close them up by increasing the formalities and multiplying the courts of appeal and revision merely adds to the tediousness of the procedure, and withdraws the whole process still more completely from public control. At the same time the absence of free discussion between the contending parties renders the task of the judge enormously difficult. If the system is to succeed at all, it must provide a body of able, intelligent, thoroughly trained jurists, and must place them beyond the reach of bribery and other forms of corruption.

In Russia neither of these conditions was fulfilled. Instead of endeavoring to create a body of well-trained jurists, the Government went farther and farther in the direction of letting the judges be chosen for a short period by popular election from among men who had never received a juridical education, or a fair education of any kind; whilst the place of judge was so poorly paid, and stood so low in public estimation, that the temptations to dishonesty were difficult to resist.

The practice of choosing the judges by popular election was an attempt to restore to the courts something of their old popular character; but it did not succeed, for very obvious reasons. Popular election in a judicial organization is useful only when the courts are public and the procedure simple; on the contrary, it is positively prejudicial when the procedure is in writing and extremely complicated. And so it proved in Russia. The elected judges, unprepared for their work, and liable to be changed at short intervals, rarely acquired a knowledge of law or procedure. They were for the most part poor, indolent landed proprietors, who did little more than sign the decisions prepared for them by the permanent officials. Even when a judge happened to have some legal knowledge he found small scope for its application, for he rarely, if ever, examined personally the materials out of which a decision was to be elaborated. The whole of the preliminary work, which was in reality the most important, was performed by minor officials under the direction of the secretary of the court. In criminal cases, for instance, the secretary examined the written evidence—all evidence was taken down in writing—extracted what he considered the essential points, arranged them as he thought proper, quoted the laws which ought in his opinion to be applied, put all this into a report, and read the report to the judges. Of course the judges, if they had no personal interest in the decision, accepted the secretary's view of the case. If they did not, all the preliminary work had to be done anew by themselves—a task that few judges were able, and still fewer willing, to perform. Thus the decision lay virtually in the hands of the secretary and the minor officials, and in general neither the secretary nor the minor officials were fit persons to have such power.

There is no need to detail here the ingenious expedients by which they increased their meager salaries, and how they generally contrived to extract money from both parties.[1] Suffice it to say that in general the chancelleries of the courts were dens of pettifogging rascality, and the habitual, unblushing bribery had a negative as well as a positive effect. If a person accused of some crime had no money wherewith to grease the palm of the secretary he might remain in prison for years without being brought to trial. A well-known Russian writer once related to me that when visiting a prison in the province of Nizhni-Novgorod he found among the inmates undergoing preliminary arrest two peasant women, who were accused of setting fire to a hayrick to revenge themselves on a landed proprietor, a crime for which the legal punishment was from four to eight months' imprisonment. One of them had a son of seven years of age, and the other a son of twelve, both of whom had been born in the prison, and had lived there ever since among the criminals. Such a long preliminary arrest caused no surprise or indignation among those who heard of it, because it was quite a common occurrence. Everyone knew that bribes were taken not only by the secretary and his scribes, but also by the judges, who were elected by the local Noblesse from its own ranks.

With regard to the scale of punishments, notwithstanding some humanitarian principles in the legislation, they were very severe, and corporal punishment played amongst them a disagreeably prominent part. Capital sen-

[1] Old book catalogues sometimes mention a play bearing the significant title, *The Unheard-of Wonder; or, The Honest Secretary* (*Neslýkhannoe Chudo ili Chestny Sekretár*). I have never seen this curious production, but I have no doubt that it referred to the peculiarities of the old judicial procedure.

tences were abolished as early as 1753-54, but castigation
with the knout, which often ended fatally, continued until
1845, when it was replaced by flogging in the civil administration, though retained for the military and for insubordinate convicts. For the nonprivileged classes the
knout or the lash supplemented nearly all punishments for
criminal offenses. When a man was condemned, for example, to penal servitude, he received publicly from thirty to
one hundred lashes, and was then branded on the forehead
and cheeks with the letters K.A.T.—the first three letters
of *kátorzhnik* (convict). If he appealed he received his
lashes all the same, and if his appeal was rejected by the
Senate he received some more castigation for having troubled unnecessarily the higher judicial authorities. For the
military and for insubordinate convicts there was a barbarous punishment called *Spitsruten,* to the extent of 5,000
or 6,000 blows, which often ended in the death of the unfortunate.

The use of torture in criminal investigations was formally abolished in 1801, but if we may believe the testimony of a public prosecutor, it was occasionally used in
Moscow as late as 1850.

The defects and abuses of the old system were so
flagrant that they became known even to the Emperor
Nicholas I, and caused him momentary indignation, but
he never attempted seriously to root them out. In 1844,
for example, he heard of some gross abuses in a tribunal
not far from the Winter Palace, and ordered an investigation. Baron Korff, to whom the investigation was entrusted, brought to light what he called "a yawning abyss
of all possible horrors, which have been accumulating for
years," and his Majesty, after reading the report, wrote
upon it with his own hand: "Unheard-of disgrace! The
carelessness of the authority immediately concerned is incredible and unpardonable. I feel ashamed and sad that
such disorder could exist almost under my eyes and remain unknown to me." Unfortunately the outburst of Imperial indignation did not last long enough to produce any
remedial consequences. The only result was that one member of the tribunal was dismissed from the service, and the
Governor-General of St. Petersburg had to resign, but

the latter subsequently received an honorary reward, and
the Emperor remarked that he was himself to blame for
having kept the Governor-General so long at his post.

When His Majesty's habitual optimism happened to be
troubled by incidents of this sort he probably consoled
himself with remembering that he had ordered some
preparatory work, by which the administration of justice
might be improved, and this work was being diligently
carried out in the legislative section of his own chancery
by Count Bludov, one of the ablest Russian lawyers of his
time. Unfortunately, the existing state of things was not
thereby improved, because the preparatory work was not
of the kind that was wanted. On the assumption that any
evil which might exist could be removed by improving
the laws, Count Bludov devoted his efforts almost entirely
to codification. In reality, what was required was to
change radically the organization of the courts and the
procedure, and above all to let in on their proceedings the
cleansing atmosphere of publicity. This the Emperor Nicholas could not understand, and if he had understood it he
could not have brought himself to adopt the appropriate
remedies, because radical reform and control of officials
by public opinion were his two pet bugbears.

Very different was his son and successor, Alexander II,
in the first years of his reign. In his accession manifesto a
prominent place was given to his desire that justice and
mercy should reign in the courts of law. Referring to these
words in a later manifesto, he explained his wishes more
fully as "the desire to establish in Russia expeditious, just,
merciful, impartial courts of justice for all our subjects; to
elevate the judicial authority; to give it the proper independence, and in general to implant in the people that
respect for the law which ought to be the constant guide of
all and everyone from the highest to the lowest." These
were not mere vain words. Peremptory orders had been
given that the great work should be undertaken without
delay, and when the Emancipation question was being
discussed in the Provincial Committees, the Council of
State examined the question of judicial reform "from the
historical, the theoretical, and the practical point of
view," and came to the conclusion that the existing organization must be completely transformed.

The commission appointed to consider this important matter filed a lengthy indictment against the existing system, and pointed out no less than twenty-five radical defects. To remove these it proposed that the judicial organization should be completely separated from all other branches of the Administration; that the most ample publicity, with trial by jury in criminal cases, should be introduced into the tribunals; that Justice of Peace Courts should be created for petty affairs; and that the procedure in the ordinary courts should be greatly simplified.

These fundamental principles were published by Imperial command on September 29th, 1862—a year and a half after the publication of the Emancipation Manifesto —and on November 20th, 1864, the new legislation founded on these principles received the Imperial sanction.

Like most institutions erected on a *tabula rasa*, the new system is at once simple and symmetrical. As a whole, the architecture of the edifice is decidedly French, but here and there we may detect unmistakable symptoms of English influence. It is not, however, a servile copy of any older edifice; and it may be fairly said that, though every individual part was fashioned according to a foreign model, the whole has a certain originality.

The lower part of the building in its original form was composed of two great sections, distinct from, and independent of, each other—on the one hand the Justice of Peace Courts, and on the other the Regular Tribunals. Both sections contained an Ordinary Court and a Court of Appeal. The upper part of the building, covering equally both sections, was the Senate as Supreme Court of Revision (*Cour de Cassation*).

The distinctive character of the two independent sections may be detected at a glance. The function of the Justice of Peace Courts is to decide petty cases that involve no abstruse legal principles, and to settle, if possible by conciliation, those petty conflicts and disputes which arise naturally in the relations of everyday life; the function of the Regular Tribunals is to take cognizance of those graver affairs in which the fortune or honor of individuals or families is more or less implicated, or in which the public tranquillity is seriously endangered. The two kinds of courts were organized in accordance with these intended

functions. In the former the procedure is simple and conciliatory, the jurisdiction is confined to cases of little importance, and the judges were at first chosen by popular
election, generally from among the local inhabitants. In
the latter there is more of "the pomp and majesty of the
law." The procedure is more strict and formal, the jurisdiction is unlimited with regard to the importance of the
cases, and the judges are trained jurists nominated by
the Emperor.

The Justice of Peace Courts received jurisdiction over all
obligations and civil injuries in which the sum at stake was
not more than 500 rubles—about £ 50—and all criminal
affairs in which the legal punishment did not exceed
300 rubles—about £ 30—or one year of imprisonment.
When anyone had a complaint to make, he might go to
the Justice of the Peace (*Mirovói Sudyá*) and explain the
affair orally, or in writing, without observing any formalities; and if the complaint seemed well founded, the Justice
at once fixed a day for hearing the case, and gave the
other party notice to appear at the appointed time. When
the time appointed arrived, the affair was discussed publicly and orally, either by the parties themselves, or by
any representatives whom they might appoint. If it was a
civil suit, the Justice began by proposing to the parties to
terminate it at once by a compromise, and indicated what
he considered a fair arrangement. Many affairs were terminated in this simple way. If, however, either of the parties
refused to consent to a compromise, the matter was fully
discussed, and the Justice gave a formal written decision,
containing the grounds on which it was based. In criminal
cases the amount of punishment was always determined
by reference to a special Criminal Code.

If the sum at issue exceeded thirty rubles—about £ 3
—or if the punishment exceeded a fine of fifteen rubles—
about 30s.—or three days of arrest, an appeal might be
made to the Assembly of Justices (*Mirovói Syezd*). This
is a point in which English rather than French institutions
were taken as a model. According to the French system,
all appeals from a Juge de Paix are made to the "Tribunal
d'Arrondissement," and the Justice of Peace Courts are
thereby subordinated to the Regular Tribunals. Accord-

ing to the English system, certain cases may be carried on appeal from the Justice of the Peace to the Quarter Sessions. This latter principle was adopted and greatly developed by the Russian legislation. The Monthly Sessions, composed of all the Justices of the District (*uyézd*), considered appeals against the decisions of the individual Justices. The procedure was simple and informal, as in the lower court, but an assistant of the Procureur was always present. This functionary gave his opinion in some civil and in all criminal cases immediately after the debate, and the Court took his opinion into consideration in framing its judgment.

In the other great section of the judicial organization—the Regular Tribunals—there are likewise Ordinary Courts and Courts of Appeal, called respectively "Tribunaux d'Arrondissement" (*Okruzhniye Sūdý*) and "Palais de Justice" (*Sudêbniya Paláty*). Each Ordinary Court has jurisdiction over several Districts (*uyézdy*), and the jurisdiction of each Court of Appeal comprehends several Provinces. All civil cases are subject to appeal, however small the sum at stake may be, but criminal cases are decided *finally* by the lower court with the aid of a jury. Thus in criminal affairs the "Palais de Justice" is not at all a court of appeal, but as no regular criminal prosecution can be raised without its formal consent, it controls in some measure the action of the lower courts.

As the general reader cannot be supposed to take an interest in the details of civil procedure, I shall merely say on this subject that in both sections of the Regular Tribunals the cases are always tried by at least three judges, the sittings are public, and oral debates by officially recognized advocates form an important part of the proceedings. I venture, however, to speak a little more at length regarding the change which has been made in the criminal procedure—a subject that is less technical and more interesting for the uninitiated.

Down to the time of the recent judicial reforms the procedure in criminal cases was, as I have said above, secret and inquisitorial. The accused had little opportunity for defending himself, but, on the other hand, the State took endless formal precautions against condemning the innocent. The practical consequence of this system was that an innocent man might remain for years in prison until the authorities convinced themselves of his innocence, whilst a clever criminal might indefinitely postpone his condemnation.

In studying the history of criminal procedure in foreign countries, those who were entrusted with the task of preparing projects of reform found that nearly every country of Europe had experienced the evils from which Russia was suffering, and that one country after another had come to the conviction that the most efficient means of removing these evils was to replace the inquisitorial by litigious procedure, to give a fair field and no favor to the prosecutor and the accused, and allow them to fight out their battle with whatever legal weapons they might think fit. Further, it was discovered that, according to the most competent foreign authorities, it was well in this modern form of judicial combat to leave the decision to a jury of respectable citizens. The steps which Russia had to take were thus clearly marked out by the experience of other nations, and it was decided that they should be taken at once. The organs for the prosecution of supposed criminals were carefully separated from the judges on the one hand, and from the police on the other; oral discussions between the Public Prosecutor and the prisoner's counsel, together with oral examination and cross-questioning of witnesses, were introduced into the procedure; and the jury was made an essential factor in criminal trials.

When a case, whether civil or criminal, has been decided in the Regular Tribunals, there is no possibility of appeal in the strict sense of the term, but an application may be made for a revision of the case on the ground of technical informality. To use the French terms, there cannot be *appel*, but there may be *cassation*. According to the new Russian system, the sole Court of Revision is the Senate.

The Senate thus forms the regulator of the whole judicial system, but its action is merely regulative. It takes cognizance only of what is presented to it, and supplies to the machine no motive power. If any of the lower courts should work slowly or cease to work altogether, the

Senate might remain ignorant of the fact, and certainly could take no official notice of it. It was considered necessary, therefore, to supplement the spontaneous vitality of the lower courts, and for this purpose was created a special centralized judicial administration, at the head of which was placed the Minister of Justice. The Minister is "Procureur-Général," and has subordinates in all the courts. The primary function of this administration is to preserve the force of the law, to detect and repair all infractions of judicial order, to defend the interests of the State and of those persons who are officially recognized as incapable of taking charge of their own affairs, and to act in criminal matters as Public Prosecutor.

Viewed as a whole, and from a little distance, this grand judicial edifice seems perfectly symmetrical, but a closer and more minute inspection brings to light unmistakable indications of a change of plan during the process of construction. Though the work lasted only about half-a-dozen years, the style of the upper differs from the style of the lower parts, precisely as in those Gothic cathedrals which grew up slowly during the course of centuries. And there is nothing here that need surprise us, for a considerable change took place in the opinions of the official world during that short period. The reform was conceived at a time of uncritical enthusiasm for advanced liberal ideas, of boundless faith in the dictates of science, of unquestioning reliance on public spirit, public control, and public honesty —a time in which it was believed that the public would spontaneously do everything necessary for the common weal, if it were only freed from the administrative swaddling clothes in which it had been hitherto bound. Still smarting from the severe régime of Nicholas, men thought more about protecting the rights of the individual than about preserving public order, and under the influence of the socialistic ideas in vogue, malefactors were regarded as the unfortunate, involuntary victims of social inequality and injustice.

Towards the end of the period in question all this had begun to change. Many were beginning to perceive that liberty might easily turn to license, that the spontaneous public energy was largely expended in empty words, and that a certain amount of hierarchical discipline was necessary in order to keep the public administration in motion. It was found, therefore, in 1864, that it was impossible to carry out to their ultimate consequences the general principles laid down and published in 1862. Even in those parts of the legislation which were actually put in force, it was found necessary to make modifications in an indirect, covert way. Of these, one may be cited by way of illustration. In 1860 criminal inquiries were taken out of the hands of the police, and transferred to "Juges d'Instruction" (*Sudébniye Slédovateli*), who were almost entirely independent of the Public Prosecutor, and could not be removed unless condemned for some legal transgression by a Regular Tribunal. This reform created at first much rejoicing and great expectations, because it raised a barrier against the tyranny of the police and against the arbitrary power of the higher officials. But very soon the defects of the system became apparent. Many *juges d'instruction*, feeling themselves independent and knowing that they would not be prosecuted except for some flagrantly illegal act, gave way to indolence, and spent their time in inactivity.[2] In such cases it was always difficult, and sometimes impossible, to procure a condemnation—for indolence must assume gigantic proportions in order to become a crime—and the Minister had to adopt the practice of appointing, without Imperial confirmation, temporary *juges d'instruction* whom he could remove at pleasure.

It is unnecessary, however, to enter into these theoretical defects. The important question for the general public is: How do the institutions work in the local conditions in which they are placed?

This is a question which has an interest not only for Russians, but for all students of social science, for it tends to throw light on the difficult subject as to how far institutions may be successfully transplanted to a foreign soil. Many thinkers hold, and not without reason, that no institution can work well unless it is the natural product of previous historical development. Now we have here an opportunity of testing this theory by experience; we have even what Bacon terms an *experimentum crucis*. This new

[2] A flagrant case of this kind came under my own observation.

judicial system is an artificial creation constructed in accordance with principles laid down by foreign jurists. All that the elaborators of the project said about developing old institutions was mere talk. In reality, they made a *tabula rasa* of the existing organization. If the introduction of public oral procedure and trial by jury was a return to ancient customs, it was a return to what had been long since forgotten by all except antiquarian specialists, and no serious attempt was made to develop what actually existed. One form, indeed, of oral procedure had been preserved in the Code, but it had fallen completely into disuse, and seems to have been overlooked by the elaborators of the new system.[3]

Having in general little confidence in institutions which spring ready-made from the brains of autocratic legislators, I expected to find that this new judicial organization, which looks so well on paper, was well-nigh worthless in reality. Observation, however, has not confirmed my pessimistic expectations. On the contrary, I have found that these new institutions, though they are very far from being perfect, even in the human sense of the term, work on the whole remarkably well, and have already conferred immense benefit on the country.

In the course of a few years the Justice of Peace Courts, which may perhaps be called the newest part of the new institutions, became thoroughly acclimatized as if they had existed for generations. As soon as they were opened they became extremely popular. In Moscow the authorities had calculated that under the new system the number of cases would be more than doubled, and that on an average each justice would have nearly a thousand cases brought before him in the course of the year. The reality far exceeded their expectations: each justice had on an average 2,800 cases. In St. Petersburg and the other large towns the amount of work which the justices had to get through was equally great.

To understand the popularity of the Justice of Peace Courts, we must know something of the old police courts

[3] I refer to the so-called *Sûd po formê*, established by an ukase of Peter the Great, in 1723. I was much astonished when I accidentally stumbled upon it in the Code.

which they supplanted. The nobles, the military, and the small officials had always looked on the police with contempt, because their position secured them against interference, and the merchants acquired a similar immunity by submitting to blackmail, which often took the form of a fixed subsidy; but the lower classes in town and country stood in fear of the humblest policeman, and did not dare to complain of him to his superiors. If two workmen brought their differences before a police court, instead of getting their case decided on grounds of equity they were pretty sure to get scolded in language unfit for ears polite, or to receive still worse treatment. Even among the higher officers of the force many became famous for their brutality. A *Gorodnichi* of the town of Tcherkassy, for example, made for himself in this respect a considerable reputation. If any humble individual ventured to offer an objection to him, he had at once recourse to his fists, and any reference to the law put him into a state of frenzy. "The town," he was wont to say on such occasions, "has been entrusted to me by his Majesty, and you dare to talk to me of the law? There is the law for you!"—the remark being accompanied with a blow. Another officer of the same type, long resident in Kiev, had a somewhat different method of maintaining order. He habitually drove about the town with a Cossack escort, and when anyone of the lower classes had the misfortune to displease him, he ordered one of his Cossacks to apply a little corporal punishment on the spot without any legal formalities.

In the Justice of Peace Courts things were conducted in a very different style. The justice, always scrupulously polite without distinction of persons, listened patiently to the complaint, tried to arrange the affair amicably, and when his efforts failed, gave his decision at once according to law and common sense. No attention was paid to rank or social position. A general who would not conform to the police regulations was fined like an ordinary workman, and in a dispute between a great dignitary and a man of the people the two were treated in precisely the same way. No wonder such courts became popular among the masses; and their popularity was increased when it became known that the affairs were disposed of expeditiously,

without unnecessary formalities and without any bribes or
blackmail. Many peasants regarded the justice as they had
been wont to regard kindly proprietors of the old patriarchal type, and brought their griefs and sorrows to him
in the hope that he would somehow alleviate them. Often
they submitted most intimate domestic and matrimonial
concerns, of which no court could possibly take cognizance, and sometimes they demanded the fulfillment of
contracts which were in flagrant contradiction not only to
the written law, but also to ordinary morality.[4]

Of course, the courts were not entirely without blemishes. In the matter, for example, of making no distinction
of persons, some of the early justices, in seeking to avoid
Scylla, came dangerously near to Charybdis. Imagining
that their mission was to eradicate the conceptions and
habits which had been created and fostered by serfage,
they sometimes used their authority for giving lessons in
philanthropic liberalism, and took a malicious delight in
wounding the susceptibilities, and occasionally even the
material interests, of those whom they regarded as enemies to the good cause. In disputes between master and
servant, or between employer and workmen, the justice of
this type considered it his duty to resist the tyranny of
capital, and was apt to forget his official character of judge
in his assumed character of social reformer. Happily,
these aberrations on the part of the justices are already
things of the past, but they helped to bring about a reaction, as we shall see presently.

The extreme popularity of the Justice of Peace Courts
did not last very long. Their history resembled that of the
Zemstvo and many other new institutions in Russia: at
first, enthusiasm and inordinate expectations; then consciousness of defects and practical inconveniences; and,
lastly, in an influential section of the public, the pessimism
of shattered illusions, accompanied by the adoption of a
reactionary policy on the part of the Government. The
discontent appeared first among the so-called privileged
classes. To people who had all their lives enjoyed great

---

[4] Many curious instances of this have come to my knowledge,
but they are of such a kind that they cannot be quoted in a work
intended for the general public.

social consideration it seemed monstrous that they should be treated exactly on the same footing as the muzhik. When a general, for example, who was accustomed to be addressed as "Your Excellency," was accused of using abusive language to his cook, and found himself seated on the same bench with the menial, he naturally supposed that the end of all things was at hand. Similarly, a great civil official, who was accustomed to regard the police as created merely for the lower classes, was greatly scandalized when he suddenly found himself, to his inexpressible astonishment, fined for a contravention of police regulations! Naturally the justices were accused of dangerous revolutionary tendencies, and when they happened to bring to light some injustices on the part of the *chinóvniks* they were severely condemned for undermining the prestige of the Imperial authority!

For a time the accusations provoked merely a smile or a caustic remark among the Liberals, but about the middle of the eighties criticisms began to appear even in the Liberal press. No very grave allegations were made, but defects in the system and miscarriages of justice were put forward and severely commented upon. Occasionally it happened that a justice was indolent, or that at the Sessions in a small country town it was impossible to form a quorum on the appointed day. Overlooking the good features of the institution and the good services rendered by it, the critics, especially those in the reactionary camp, began to propose partial reorganization in the sense of greater control by the central authorities. It was suggested, for example, that the President of Sessions should be appointed by the Government, that the justices should be subordinated to the Regular Tribunals, and that the principle of election by the Zemstvo should be abolished.

These complaints were not at all unwelcome to the Government, because it had embarked on a reactionary policy, and in 1889 it suddenly granted to the critics a great deal more than they desired. In the rural districts of Central Russia the justices were replaced by the rural supervisors, of whom I have spoken in a previous chapter, and the part of their functions which could not well be entrusted to those new officials was transferred to judges of the

Regular Courts. In some of the larger towns and in the rural districts of outlying provinces the justices were preserved, but instead of being elected by the Zemstvo they were nominated by the Government.

The Regular Tribunals likewise became acclimatized in an incredibly short space of time. The first judges were not by any means profound jurists, and were too often deficient in that dispassionate calmness which we are accustomed to associate with the Bench; but they were at least honest, educated men, and generally possessed a fair knowledge of the law. Their defects were due to the fact that the demand for trained jurists far exceeded the supply, and the Government was forced to nominate men who, under ordinary circumstances, would never have thought of presenting themselves as candidates. At the beginning of 1870, in the 32 "Tribunaux d'Arrondissement" which then existed, there were 227 judges, of whom 44 had never received a judicial education. Even the presidents had not all passed through a school of law. Of course the courts could not become thoroughly effective until all the judges were men who had received a good special education, and had a practical acquaintance with judicial matters. This has now been effected, and the present generation of judges are better prepared and more capable than their predecessors. On the score of probity I have never heard any complaints.

Of all the judicial innovations, perhaps the most interesting is the jury.

At the time of the reforms the introduction of the jury into the judicial organization awakened among the educated classes a great amount of sentimental enthusiasm. The institution had the reputation of being "liberal," and was known to be approved of by the latest authorities in criminal jurisprudence. This was sufficient to insure it a favorable reception, and to excite most exaggerated expectations as to its beneficent influence. Ten years of experience somewhat cooled this enthusiasm, and voices might be heard declaring that the introduction of the jury was a mistake. The Russian people, it was held, was not yet ripe for such an institution, and numerous anecdotes were related in support of this opinion. One jury, for instance, was said to have returned a verdict of "*not* guilty with extenuating circumstances"; and another, being unable to come to a decision, was reported to have cast lots before an Icon, and to have given a verdict in accordance with the result! Besides this, juries often gave a verdict of "not guilty" when the accused made a full and formal confession to the court.

How far the comic anecdotes are true I do not undertake to decide, but I venture to assert that such incidents, if they really occur, are too few to form the basis of a serious indictment. The fact, however, that juries often acquit prisoners who openly confess their crime is beyond all possibility of doubt.

To most Englishmen this fact will probably seem sufficient to prove that the introduction of the institution was at least premature, but before adopting this sweeping conclusion, it will be well to examine the phenomenon a little more closely in connection with Russian criminal procedure as a whole.

In England the Bench is allowed very great latitude in fixing the amount of punishment. The jury can therefore confine themselves to the question of fact and leave to the judge the appreciation of extenuating circumstances. In Russia the position of the jury is different. The Russian criminal law fixes minutely the punishment for each category of crimes, and leaves very little latitude to the judges. The jury know that if they give a verdict of guilty, the prisoner will inevitably be punished according to the Code. Now the Code, borrowed in great part from foreign legislation, is founded on conceptions very different from those of the Russian people, and in many cases it attaches heavy penalties to acts which the ordinary Russian is wont to regard as mere peccadilloes, or positively justifiable. Even in those matters in which the Code is in harmony with the popular morality, there are many exceptional cases in which *summum jus* is really *summa injuria*. Suppose, for instance—as actually happened in a case which came under my notice—that a fire breaks out in a village, and that the Village Elder, driven out of patience by the apathy and laziness of some of his young fellow villagers, oversteps the limits of his authority as defined by

law, and accompanies his reproaches and exhortations
with a few lusty blows. Surely such a man is not guilty of
a very heinous crime—certainly he is not in the opinion of
the peasantry—and yet if he be prosecuted and convicted
he inevitably falls into the jaws of an article of the Code
which condemns to transportation for a long term of years.

In such cases what are the jury to do? In England they
might safely give a verdict of guilty, and leave the judge
to take into consideration all the extenuating circumstances; but in Russia they cannot act in this way, for
they know that the judge must condemn the prisoner according to the Criminal Code. There remains, therefore,
but one issue out of the difficulty—a verdict of acquittal;
and Russian juries—to their honor be it said—generally
adopt this alternative. Thus the jury, in those very cases in
which it is most severely condemned, provides a corrective
for the injustice of the criminal legislation. Occasionally, it
is true, they go a little too far in this direction and arrogate
to themselves a right of pardon, but cases of that kind
are, I believe, very rare. I know of only one well-authenticated instance. The prisoner had been proved guilty of a
serious crime, but it happened to be the eve of a great
religious festival, and the jury thought that in pardoning
the prisoner and giving a verdict of acquittal, they would
be acting as good Christians!

The legislation, of course, regards this practice as an
abuse, and has tried to prevent it by concealing as far
as possible from the jury the punishment that awaits the
accused if he be condemned. For this purpose it forbids
the counsel for the prisoner to inform the jury what punishment is prescribed by the Code for the crime in question. This ingenious device not only fails in its object, but
has sometimes a directly opposite effect. Not knowing
what the punishment will be, and fearing that it may be
out of all proportion to the crime, the jury sometimes acquit a criminal whom they would condemn if they knew
what punishment would be inflicted. And when a jury is,
as it were, entrapped, and finds that the punishment is
more severe than it supposed, it can take its revenge in the
succeeding cases. I know at least of one instance of this
kind. A jury convicted a prisoner of an offense which it

regarded as very trivial, but which in reality entailed, according to the Code, seven years of penal servitude! So surprised and frightened were the jurymen by this unexpected consequence of their verdict, that they obstinately acquitted, in the face of the most convincing evidence, all the other prisoners brought before them.

The most famous case of acquittal when there was no conceivable doubt as to the guilt of the accused was that of Vera Zasulich, who shot General Trepov, Prefect of St. Petersburg; but the circumstances were so peculiar that they will hardly support any general conclusion. I happened to be present, and watched the proceedings closely. Vera Zasulich, a young woman who had for some time taken part in the revolutionary movement, heard that a young revolutionist called Bogoliubov, imprisoned in St. Petersburg, had been flogged by orders of General Trepov,[5] and though she did not know the victim personally she determined to avenge the indignity to which he had been subjected. With this intention she appeared at the Prefecture, ostensibly for the purpose of presenting a petition, and when she found herself in the presence of the Prefect she fired a revolver at him, wounding him seriously, but not mortally. At the trial the main facts were not disputed, and yet the jury brought in a verdict of not guilty. This unexpected result was due, I believe, partly to a desire to make a little political demonstration, and partly to a strong suspicion that the prison authorities, in carrying out the Prefect's orders, had acted in summary fashion without observing the tedious formalities prescribed by the law. Certainly one of the prison officials, when under cross-examination, made on me, and on the public generally, the impression that he was prevaricating in order to shield his superiors.

At the close of the proceedings, which were dexterously conducted by counsel in such a way that, as the Emperor is reported to have said, it was not Vera Zasulich, but

[5] The reason alleged by General Trepov for giving these orders was that, during a visit of inspection, Bogoliubov had behaved disrespectfully towards him, and had thereby committed an infraction of prison discipline, for which the law prescribes the use of corporal punishment.

General Trepov, who was being tried, an eminent Russian journalist rushed up to me in a state of intense excitement and said: "Is not this a great day for the cause of political freedom in Russia?" I could not agree with him, and I ventured to predict that neither of us would ever again see a political case tried publicly by jury in an ordinary court. The prediction has proved true. Since that time political offenders have been tried by special tribunals without a jury, or dealt with "by administrative procedure" —that is to say, inquisitorially, without any regular trial.

The defects, real and supposed, of the present system are commonly attributed to the predominance of the peasant element in the juries; and this opinion, founded on *à priori* reasoning, seems to many too evident to require verification. The peasantry are in many respects the most ignorant class, and therefore, it is assumed, they are least capable of weighing conflicting evidence. Plain and conclusive as this reasoning seems, it is in my opinion erroneous. The peasants have, indeed, little education, but they have a large fund of plain common sense; and experience proves—so at least I have been informed by many judges and Public Prosecutors—that, as a general rule, a peasant jury is more to be relied on than a jury drawn from the educated classes. It must be admitted, however, that a peasant jury has certain peculiarities, and it is not a little interesting to observe what those peculiarities are.

In the first place, a jury composed of peasants generally acts in a somewhat patriarchal fashion, and does not always confine its attention to the evidence and the arguments adduced at the trial. The members form their judgment as men do in the affairs of ordinary life, and are sure to be greatly influenced by any jurors who happen to be personally acquainted with the prisoner. If several of the jurors know him to be a bad character, he has little chance of being acquitted, even though the chain of evidence against him should not be quite perfect. Peasants cannot understand why a notorious scoundrel should be allowed to escape because a little link in the evidence is wanting, or because some little judicial formality has not been duly observed. Indeed, their ideas of criminal procedure in general are extremely primitive. The Communal method of dealing with malefactors is best in accordance with their conceptions of well-regulated society. Until recently the *Mir* could, by a Communal decree and without a formal trial, have any of its unruly members transported to Siberia. This summary, informal mode of procedure seems to the peasants very satisfactory. They are at a loss to understand how a notorious culprit is allowed to "buy" an advocate to defend him, and are very insensible to the bought advocate's eloquence. To many of them, if I may trust to conversations which I have casually overheard in and around the courts, "buying an advocate" seems to be very much the same kind of operation as bribing a judge.

In the second place, the peasants, when acting as jurors, are very severe with regard to crimes against property. In this they are instigated by the simple instinct of self-defense. They are, in fact, continually at the mercy of thieves and malefactors. They live in wooden houses easily set on fire; their stables might be broken into by a child; at night the village is guarded merely by an old man, who cannot be in more than one place at a time, and in the one place he is apt to go to sleep; a police officer is rarely seen, except when a crime has actually been committed. A few clever horse stealers may ruin many families, and a fire raiser, in his desire to avenge himself on an enemy, may reduce a whole village to destitution. These and similar considerations tend to make the peasants very severe against theft, robbery, and arson; and a Public Prosecutor who desires to obtain a conviction against a man charged with one of these crimes endeavors to have a jury in which the peasant class is largely represented.

With regard to fraud in its various forms, the peasants are much more lenient, probably because the line of demarcation between honest and dishonest dealing in commercial affairs is not very clearly drawn in their minds. Many, for instance, are convinced that trade cannot be successfully carried on without a little clever cheating; and hence cheating is regarded as a venial offense. If the money fraudulently acquired be restored to the owner, the crime is supposed to be completely condoned. Thus when a *Vólost* Elder appropriates the public money, and succeeds in repaying it before the case comes on for trial, he is invariably acquitted—and sometimes even re-elected!

An equal leniency is generally shown by peasants to-wards crimes against the person, such as assaults, cruelty, and the like. This fact is easily explained. Refined sensi-tiveness and a keen sympathy with physical suffering are the result of a certain amount of material well-being, together with a certain degree of intellectual and moral culture, and neither of these is yet possessed by the Rus-sian peasantry. Anyone who has had opportunities of fre-quently observing the peasants must have been often as-tonished by their indifference to suffering, both in their own persons and in the persons of others. In a drunken brawl heads may be broken and wounds inflicted without any interference on the part of the spectators. If no fatal consequences ensue, the peasant does not think it neces-sary that official notice should be taken of the incident, and certainly does not consider that any of the combatants should be transported to Siberia. Slight wounds heal of their own accord without any serious loss to the sufferer, and therefore the man who inflicts them is not to be put on the same level as the criminal who reduces a family to beg-gary. This reasoning may, perhaps, shock people of sensi-tive nerves, but it undeniably contains a certain amount of plain, homely wisdom.

Of all kinds of cruelty, that which is perhaps most re-volting to civilized mankind is the cruelty of the husband towards his wife; but to this crime the Russian peasant shows especial leniency. He is still influenced by the old conceptions of the husband's rights, and by that low esti-mate of the weaker sex which finds expression in many popular proverbs.

The peculiar moral conceptions reflected in these facts are evidently the result of external conditions, and not of any recondite ethnographical peculiarities, for they are not found among the merchants, who are nearly all of peasant origin. On the contrary, the merchants are more severe with regard to crimes against the person than with regard to crimes against property. The explanation of this is simple. The merchant has means of protecting his prop-erty, and if he should happen to suffer by theft, his fortune is not likely to be seriously affected by it. On the other hand, he has a certain sensitiveness with regard to such crimes as assault; for though he has commonly not much more intellectual and moral culture than the peasant, he is accustomed to comfort and material well-being, which naturally develop sensitiveness regarding physical pain.

Towards fraud the merchants are quite as lenient as the peasantry. This may, perhaps, seem strange, for fraudulent practices are sure in the long run to undermine trade. The Russian merchants, however, have not yet arrived at this conception, and can point to many of the richest members of their class as a proof that fraudulent practices often create enormous fortunes. Long ago Samuel Butler justly remarked that we damn the sins we have no mind to.

As the external conditions have little or no influence on the religious conceptions of the merchants and the peasantry, two classes are equally severe with regard to those acts which are regarded as crimes against the Deity. Hence acquittals in cases of sacrilege, blasphemy, and the like, never occur unless the jury is in part composed of educated men.

In their decisions, as in their ordinary modes of thought, the jurors drawn from the educated classes are little, if at all, affected by theological conceptions, but they are sometimes influenced in a not less unfortunate way by conceptions of a different order. It may happen, for instance, that a juror who has passed through one of the higher educational establishments has his own peculiar theory about the value of evidence, or he is profoundly impressed with the idea that it is better that a thousand guilty men should escape than that one innocent man should be punished, or he is imbued with sentimental pseudo-philanthropy, or he is convinced that punishments are useless because they neither cure the delinquent nor deter others from crime; in a word, he may have in some way or other lost his mental balance in that moral chaos through which Russia has lately passed. In England, France, or Germany such an individual would have little influence on his fellow jurymen, for in these countries

there are very few people who allow new paradoxical ideas
to overturn their traditional notions and obscure their common sense; but in Russia, where even the elementary moral
conceptions are singularly unstable and pliable, a man of
this type may succeed in leading a jury. More than once I
have heard men boast of having induced their fellow jurymen to acquit every prisoner brought before them, not because they believed the prisoners to be innocent or the evidence to be insufficient, but because all punishments are
useless and barbarous.

One word in conclusion regarding the independence
and political significance of the new courts. When the
question of judicial reform was first publicly raised many
people hoped that the new courts would receive complete autonomy and real independence, and would thus
form a foundation for political liberty. These hopes, like
so many illusions of that strange time, have not been realized. A large measure of autonomy and independence was
indeed granted in theory. The law laid down the principle
that no judge could be removed unless convicted of a
definite crime, and that the courts should present candidates for all the vacant places on the Bench; but these and
similar rights have little practical significance. If the Minister cannot depose a judge, he can deprive him of all possibility of receiving promotion, and he can easily force him
in an indirect way to send in his resignation; and if the
courts have still the right to present candidates for vacant
places, the Minister has also the right, and can, of course,
always secure the nomination of his own candidate. By
the influence of that centripetal force which exists in all
centralized bureaucracies, the Procureurs have become
more important personages than the Presidents of the
courts.

From the political point of view the question of the independence of the courts has not yet acquired much practical importance, because the Government can always
have political offenders tried by a special tribunal, or can
send them to Siberia for an indefinite term of years without regular trial by the "administrative procedure" to
which I have above referred.

CHAPTER V

Social Classes

In these pages I repeatedly use the expression "social classes," and probably more than once the reader may feel inclined to ask, What are social classes in the Russian sense of the term? It may be well, therefore, before going farther, to answer this question.

If the question were put to a Russian it is not at all unlikely that he would reply somewhat in this fashion: "In Russia there are no social classes, and there never have been any. That fact constitutes one of the most striking peculiarities of her historical development, and one of the surest foundations of her future greatness. We know nothing, and have never known anything, of those class distinctions and class enmities which in Western Europe have often rudely shaken society in past times, and imperil its existence in the future."

This statement will not be readily accepted by the traveler who visits Russia with no preconceived ideas and forms his opinions from his own observations. To him it seems that class distinctions form one of the most prominent characteristics of Russian society. In a few days he learns to distinguish the various classes by their outward appearance. He notices perhaps nothing peculiar in the nobles, because they dress in the ordinary European fashion, but he easily recognizes the burly, bearded merchant in black cloth cap and long, shiny, double-breasted coat; the priest with his uncut hair and flowing robes; the peasant with his full, fair beard and unsavory, greasy sheepskin. Meeting everywhere those well-marked types, he naturally assumes that Russian society is composed of ex-

clusive castes; and this first impression will be fully confirmed by a glance at the Code. On examining that monu-
mental work, he finds that an entire volume—and by no
means the smallest—is devoted to the rights and obligations of the various classes. From this he concludes that
the classes have a legal as well as an actual existence. To
make assurance doubly sure he turns to the latest statistics,
and there he finds the following table:

Nobles and officials	...	...	1.5 per cent	
Clergy	...	...	.5	"
Merchants	...	...	.5	"
Burghers	...	...	10.7	"
Peasants	...	...	77.1	"
Cossacks	...	...	2.3	"
Miscellaneous	...	...	7.4	"
			100.0	"

Armed with these materials, the traveler goes to his
Russian friends who have assured him that their country
knows nothing of class distinctions. He is confident of being able to convince them that they have been laboring under a strange delusion, but he will be disappointed. They
will tell him that these laws and statistics prove nothing,
and that the categories therein mentioned are mere administrative fictions.

This apparent contradiction is to be explained by the
equivocal meaning of the Russian terms *Sosloviya* and
Sostoyaniya, which are commonly translated "social
classes." If by these terms are meant "castes" in the Oriental sense, then it may be confidently asserted that such
do not exist in Russia. Between the nobles, the clergy, the
burghers, and the peasants there are no distinctions of
race and no impassable barriers. The peasant often becomes a merchant, and there are many cases on record of
peasants and sons of parish priests becoming nobles. Until
very recently the parish clergy composed a peculiar and
exclusive class, with many of the characteristics of a caste;
but this has been changed, and it may now be said that
in Russia there are no castes in the Oriental sense.

If the word *Sosloviya* be taken to mean an organized

political unit with an esprit de corps and a clearly conceived political aim, it may likewise be admitted that there
are none in Russia. Among the subjects of the Tsar political life is still in its infancy, and political parties are
only beginning to be formed.

On the other hand, to say that social classes have never
existed in Russia, and that the categories which appear in
the legislation and in the official statistics are mere administrative fictions, is a piece of gross exaggeration.

From the very beginning of Russian history we can detect unmistakably the existence of social classes, such as
the princes, the *Boyárs*, or armed followers of the princes,
the peasantry, the slaves, and various others; and one
of the oldest documents which we possess—the "Russian
Right" (*Rússkaya Pravda*) of the Grand Prince Yaroslav
(1019-1054)—contains irrefragable proof, in the penalties
attached to various crimes, that these classes were formally recognized by the legislation. Since that time they
have frequently changed their character, but they have
never at any period ceased to exist.

In ancient times, when there was very little administrative regulation, the classes had perhaps no clearly defined
boundaries, and the peculiarities which distinguished them
from each other were actual rather than legal—lying in
the mode of life and social position rather than in peculiar
obligations and privileges. But as the autocratic power developed and strove to transform the nation into a State
with a highly centralized administration, the legal element
in the social distinctions became more and more prominent. For financial and other purposes the people had to
be divided into various categories. The actual distinctions
were of course taken as the basis of the legal classification,
but the classifying had more than a merely formal significance. The necessity of clearly defining the different
groups entailed the necessity of elevating and strengthening the barriers which already existed between them, and
the difficulty of passing from one group to another was
thereby increased.

In this work of classification Peter the Great especially
distinguished himself. With his insatiable passion for regulation, he raised formidable barriers between the different

categories, and defined the obligations of each with mi-
croscopic minuteness. After his death the work was carried on in the same spirit, and the tendency reached its
climax in the reign of Nicholas I, when the number of
students to be received in the universities was determined
by Imperial ukase!

In the reign of Catherine a new element was introduced
into the official conception of social classes. Down to her
time the Government had thought merely of class obligations; under the influence of Western ideas she introduced
the conception of class rights. She wished, as we have
seen, to have in her Empire a noblesse and a *tiers-état* like
those which existed in France, and for this purpose she
granted, first to the *Dvoryánstvo* and afterwards to the
towns, an Imperial Charter, or Bill of Rights. Succeeding
sovereigns have acted in the same spirit, and the Code
now confers on each class numerous privileges as well as
numerous obligations.

Thus, we see, the oft-repeated assertion that the Russian
social classes are simply artificial categories created by the
legislature is to a certain extent true, but is by no means
accurate. The social groups, such as peasants, landed proprietors, and the like, came into existence in Russia, as
in other countries, by the simple force of circumstances.
The legislature merely recognized and developed the social distinctions which already existed. The legal status,
obligations, and rights of each group were minutely defined and regulated, and legal barriers were added to the
actual barriers which separated the groups from each
other.

What is peculiar in the historical development of Russia is this: until lately she remained an almost exclusively agricultural Empire with abundance of unoccupied
land. Her history presents, therefore, few of those conflicts
which result from the variety of social conditions and the
intensified struggle for existence. Certain social groups
were, indeed, formed in the course of time, but they were
never allowed to fight out their own battles. The irresistible autocratic power kept them always in check and
fashioned them into whatever form it thought proper, defining minutely and carefully their obligations, their rights,

their mutual relations, and their respective positions in the political organization. Hence we find in the history of Russia almost no trace of those class hatreds which appear so conspicuously in the history of Western Europe.

The practical consequence of all this is that in Russia at the present day there is very little caste spirit or caste prejudice. Within half a dozen years after the emancipation of the serfs, proprietors and peasants, forgetting apparently their old relationship of master and serf, were working amicably together in the new local administration, and not a few similar curious facts might be cited. The confident anticipation of many Russians that their country will one day enjoy political life without political parties is, if not a contradiction in terms, at least a Utopian absurdity; but we may be sure that the Russian political parties of the future will be very different from those which exist in Germany, France, and England. . . .

2 : *The Noblesse*

CHAPTER · VI

The Noblesse

In the old times, when Russia was merely a collection of some seventy independent principalities, each reigning prince was surrounded by a group of armed men, composed partly of *Boyárs*, or large landed proprietors, and partly of knights, or soldiers of fortune. These men, who formed the Noblesse[1] of the time, were to a certain extent under the authority of the Prince, but they were by no means mere obedient, silent executors of his will. The *Boyárs* might refuse to take part in his military expeditions, and the "free lances" might leave his service and seek employment elsewhere. If he wished to go to war without their consent, they could say to him, as they did on one occasion, "You have planned this yourself, Prince, so we will not go with you, for we knew nothing of it." Nor was this resistance to the princely will always merely passive. Once, in the principality of Galich, the armed men seized their prince, killed his favorites, burned his mistress, and made him swear that he would in future live with his lawful wife. To his successor, who had married the wife of a priest, they spoke thus: "We have not risen against *you*, Prince, but we will not do reverence to a priest's wife: we will put her to death, and then you may marry whom you please." Even the energetic Bogolubski, one of the

[1] I use here a foreign, in preference to an English, term, because the word "Nobility" would convey a false impression. Etymologically the Russian word *Dvoryanín* means a Courtier (from *Dvor* = court); but this term is equally objectionable, because the great majority of the *Dvoryánstvo* have nothing to do with the Court.

most remarkable of the old princes, did not succeed in
having his own way. When he attempted to force the
Boyárs he met with stubborn opposition, and was finally
assassinated. From these incidents, which might be indefinitely multiplied from the old chronicles, we see that
in the early period of Russian history the *Boyárs* and
knights were a body of free men, possessing a considerable
amount of political power.

Under the Mongol domination this political equilibrium
was destroyed. When the country had been conquered,
the princes became servile vassals of the Khan, and arbitrary rulers towards their own subjects. The political significance of the nobles was thereby greatly diminished. It
was not, however, by any means annihilated. Though the
prince no longer depended entirely on their support, he
had an interest in retaining their services, to protect his
territory in case of sudden attack, or to increase his possessions at the expense of his neighbors when a convenient opportunity presented itself. Theoretically, such conquests were impossible, for all removing of the ancient
landmarks depended on the decision of the Khan; but in
reality the Khan gave little attention to the affairs of his
vassals, so long as the tribute was regularly paid; and
much took place in Russia without his permission. We find,
therefore, in some of the principalities the old relations
still subsisting under Mongol rule. The famous Dmitri of
the Don, for instance, when on his deathbed, speaks thus
to his *Boyárs:* "You know my habits and my character; I
was born among you, grew up among you, governed with
you—fighting by your side, showing you honor and love,
and placing you over towns and districts. I loved your children, and did evil to no one. I rejoiced with you in your
joy, mourned with you in your grief, and called you the
princes of my land." Then, turning to his children, he adds,
as a parting advice: "Love your *Boyárs,* my children;
show them the honor which their services merit, and
undertake nothing without their consent."

When the Grand Princes of Moscow brought the other
principalities under their power, and formed them into the
Tsardom of Muscovy, the nobles descended another step
in the political scale. So long as there were many princi-

palities they could quit the service of a prince as soon as
he gave them reason to be discontented, knowing that
they would be well received by one of his rivals; but now
they had no longer any choice. The only rival of Moscow
was Lithuania, and precautions were taken to prevent the
discontented from crossing the Lithuanian frontier. The
nobles were no longer voluntary adherents of a prince, but
had become subjects of a Tsar; and the Tsars were not as
the old princes had been. By a violent legal fiction they
conceived themselves to be the successors of the Byzantine Emperors, and created a new court ceremonial, borrowed partly from Constantinople and partly from the
Mongol Horde. They no longer associated familiarly with
the *Boyárs*, and no longer asked their advice, but treated
them rather as menials. When the nobles entered their
august master's presence they prostrated themselves in
Oriental fashion—occasionally as many as thirty times—
and when they incurred his displeasure they were liable to
be summarily flogged or executed, according to the Tsar's
good pleasure. In succeeding to the power of the Khans,
the Tsars had adopted, we see, a good deal of the Mongol
system of government.

It may seem strange that a class of men, which had formerly shown a proud spirit of independence, should have
submitted quietly to such humiliation and oppression
without making a serious effort to curb the new power,
which had no longer a Mongol Horde at its back to quell
opposition. But we must remember that the nobles, as
well as the princes, had passed in the meantime through
the school of the Mongol domination. In the course of two
centuries they had gradually become accustomed to despotic rule in the Oriental sense. If they felt their position
humiliating and irksome, they must have felt, too, how
difficult it was to better it. Their only resource lay in combining against the common oppressor; and we have only to
glance at the motley, disorganized group, as they cluster
round the Tsar, to perceive that combination was extremely difficult. We can distinguish there the mediatized
princes, still harboring designs for the recovery of their independence; the Moscow *Boyárs*, jealous of their family
honor and proud of Muscovite supremacy; Tatar *Murzi*,

who have submitted to be baptized and have received
land like the other nobles; the Novgorodian magnate, who
cannot forget the ancient glory of his native city; Lithuanian nobles, who find it more profitable to serve the Tsar
than their own sovereign; petty chiefs who have fled from
the oppression of the Teutonic order; and soldiers of fortune from every part of Russia. Strong, permanent political
factors are not easily formed out of such heterogeneous
material.

At the end of the sixteenth century the old dynasty became extinct, and after a short period of political anarchy,
commonly called "the troublous times" (*smútnoe vrémya*),
the Románov family were raised to the throne by the will
of the people, or at least by those who were assumed to be
its representatives. By this change the Noblesse acquired
a somewhat better position. They were no longer exposed to capricious tyranny and barbarous cruelty, such
as they had experienced at the hands of Ivan the Terrible,
but they did not, as a class, gain any political influence.
There were still rival families and rival factions, but there
were no political parties in the proper sense of the term,
and the highest aim of families and factions was to gain
the favor of the Tsar.

The frequent quarrels about precedence which took
place among the rival families at this period form one of
the most curious episodes of Russian history. The old patriarchal conception of the family as a unit one and indivisible was still so strong among these men that the elevation
or degradation of one member of a family was considered
to affect deeply the honor of all the other members. Each
noble family had its rank in a recognized scale of dignity,
according to the rank which it held, or had previously
held, in the Tsar's service; and a whole family would have
considered itself dishonored if one of its members accepted a post lower than that to which he was entitled.
Whenever a vacant place in the service was filled up, the
subordinates of the successful candidate examined the
official records and the genealogical trees of their families,
in order to discover whether some ancestor of their new
superior had not served under one of their own ancestors.
If the subordinate found such a case, he complained to

the Tsar that it was not becoming for him to serve under a man who had less family honor than himself.

Unfounded complaints of this kind often entailed imprisonment or corporal punishment, but in spite of this the quarrels for precedence were very frequent. At the commencement of a campaign many such disputes were sure to arise, and the Tsar's decision was not always accepted by the party who considered himself aggrieved. I have met at least with one example of a great dignitary voluntarily mutilating his hand in order to escape the necessity of serving under a man whom he considered his inferior in family dignity. Even at the Tsar's table these rivalries sometimes produced unseemly incidents, for it was almost impossible to arrange the places so as to satisfy all the guests. In one recorded instance a noble who received a place lower than that to which he considered himself entitled openly declared to the Tsar that he would rather be condemned to death than submit to such an indignity. In another instance of a similar kind the refractory guest was put on his chair by force, but saved his family honor by slipping under the table!

The next transformation of the Noblesse was effected by Peter the Great. Peter was by nature and position an autocrat, and could brook no opposition. Having set before himself a great aim, he sought everywhere obedient, intelligent, energetic instruments to carry out his designs. He himself served the State zealously—as a common artisan, when he considered it necessary—and he insisted on all his subjects doing likewise, under pain of merciless punishment. To noble birth and long pedigrees he habitually showed a most democratic, or rather autocratic, indifference. Intent on obtaining the service of living men, he paid no attention to the claims of dead ancestors, and gave to his servants the pay and honor which their services merited, irrespective of birth or social position. Hence many of his chief coadjutors had no connection with the old Russian families. Count Yaguzhinski, who long held one of the most important posts in the State, was the son of a poor sacristan; Count Devier was a Portuguese by birth, and had been a cabin boy; Baron Shafirov was a Jew; Hannibal, who died with the rank of Commander-in-Chief, was a Negro who had been bought in Constantinople; and his Serene Highness Prince Ménshikov had begun life, it was said, as a baker's apprentice! For the future, noble birth was to count for nothing. The service of the State was thrown open to men of all ranks, and personal merit was to be the only claim to promotion.

This must have seemed to the conservatives of the time a most revolutionary and reprehensible proceeding, but it did not satisfy the reforming tendencies of the great autocrat. He went a step farther, and entirely changed the legal status of the Noblesse. Down to his time the nobles were free to serve or not as they chose, and those who chose to serve enjoyed land on what we should call a feudal tenure. Some served permanently in the military or civil administration, but by far the greater number lived on their estates, and entered the active service merely when the militia was called out in view of war. This system was completely changed when Peter created a large standing army and a great centralized bureaucracy. By one of those "fell swoops" which periodically occur in Russian history, he changed the feudal into freehold tenures, and laid down the principle that all nobles, whatever their landed possessions might be, should serve the State in the army, the fleet, or the civil administration, from boyhood to old age. In accordance with this principle, any noble who refused to serve was not only deprived of his estate, as in the old times, but was declared to be a traitor and might be condemned to capital punishment.

The nobles were thus transformed into servants of the State, and the State in the time of Peter was a hard taskmaster. They complained bitterly, and with reason, that they had been deprived of their ancient rights, and were compelled to accept quietly and uncomplainingly whatever burdens their master chose to place upon them. "Though our country," they said, "is in no danger of invasion, no sooner is peace concluded than plans are laid for a new war, which has generally no other foundation than the ambition of the Sovereign, or perhaps merely the ambition of one of his Ministers. To please him our peasants are utterly exhausted, and we ourselves are forced to leave our homes and families, not as formerly for a

single campaign, but for long years. We are compelled to
contract debts and to entrust our estates to thieving over-
seers, who commonly reduce them to such a condition
that when we are allowed to retire from the service, in
consequence of old age or illness, we cannot to the end of
our lives retrieve our prosperity. In a word, we are so exhausted and ruined by the keeping up of a standing army,
and by the consequences flowing therefrom, that the most
cruel enemy, though he should devastate the whole Empire, could not cause us one-half of the injury." [2]

This Spartan regime, which ruthlessly sacrificed private
interests to considerations of State policy, could not long
be maintained in its pristine severity. It undermined its
own foundations by demanding too much. Draconian laws
threatening confiscation and capital punishment were of
little avail. Nobles became monks, inscribed themselves as
merchants, or engaged themselves as domestic servants, in
order to escape their obligations. "Some," says a contemporary, "grow old in disobedience and have never once
appeared in active service. . . . There is, for instance,
Theodore Mokeyev. . . . In spite of the strict orders sent
regarding him no one could ever catch him. Some of those
sent to take him he belabored with blows, and when he
could not beat the messengers, he pretended to be dangerously ill, or feigned idiocy, and, running into the pond,
stood in the water up to his neck; but as soon as the messengers were out of sight he returned home and roared
like a lion." [3]

After Peter's death the system was gradually relaxed,
but the Noblesse could not be satisfied by partial concessions. Russia had in the meantime moved, as it were, out of
Asia into Europe, and had become one of the great European powers. The upper classes had been gradually learning something of the fashions, the literature, the institutions, and the moral conceptions of Western Europe, and
the nobles naturally compared the class to which they
belonged with the aristocracies of Germany and France.
For those who were influenced by the new foreign ideas

[2] These complaints have been preserved by Vockerodt, a
Prussian diplomatic agent of the time.

[3] Posóshkov, "O skúdosti i bogátstvê."

the comparison was humiliating. In the West the Noblesse was a free and privileged class, proud of its liberty, its rights, and its culture; whereas in Russia the nobles were servants of the State, without privileges, without dignity, subject to corporal punishment, and burdened with onerous duties from which there was no escape. Thus arose in that section of the Noblesse which had some acquaintance with Western civilization a feeling of discontent, and a desire to gain a social position similar to that of the nobles in France and Germany. These aspirations were in part realized by Peter III, who, in 1762, abolished the principle of obligatory service. His consort, Catherine II, went much farther in the same direction, and inaugurated a new epoch in the history of the *Dvoryánstvo,* a period in which its duties and obligations fell into the background, and its rights and privileges came to the front.

Catherine had good reason to favor the Noblesse. As a foreigner and a usurper, raised to the throne by a Court conspiracy, she could not awaken in the masses that semi-religious veneration which the legitimate Tsars have always enjoyed, and consequently she had to seek support in the upper classes, who were less rigid and uncompromising in their conceptions of legitimacy. She confirmed, therefore, the ukase which abolished obligatory service of the nobles, and sought to gain their voluntary service by honors and rewards. In her manifestoes she always spoke of them in the most flattering terms, and tried to convince them that the welfare of the country depended on their loyalty and devotion. Though she had no intention of ceding any of her political power, she formed the nobles of each province into a corporation, with periodical assemblies, which were supposed to resemble the French Provincial Parliaments, and entrusted to each of these corporations a large part of the local administration. By these and similar means, aided by her masculine energy and feminine tact, she made herself very popular, and completely changed the old conceptions about the public service. Formerly service had been looked on as a burden; now it came to be looked on as a privilege. Thousands who had retired to their estates after the publication of the liberation edict now flocked back and sought appointments, and this tendency was greatly increased by the brilliant campaigns against the Turks, which excited the patriotic feelings and gave plentiful opportunities of promotion. "Not only landed proprietors," it is said in a comedy of the time,[4] "but all men, even shopkeepers and cobblers, aim at becoming officers, and the man who has passed his whole life without official rank seems to be not a human being."

And Catherine did more than this. She shared the idea —generally accepted throughout Europe since the brilliant reign of Louis XIV—that a refined, pomp-loving, pleasure-seeking Court Noblesse was not only the best bulwark of Monarchy, but also a necessary ornament of every highly civilized State; and as she ardently desired that her country should have the reputation of being highly civilized, she strove to create this national ornament. The love of French civilization, which already existed among the upper classes of her subjects, here came to her aid, and her efforts in this direction were singularly successful. The Court of St. Petersburg became almost as brilliant, as *galant*, and as frivolous as the Court of Versailles. All who aimed at high honors adopted French fashions, spoke the French language, and affected an unqualified admiration for French classical literature. The courtiers talked of the *point d'honneur*, discussed the question as to what was consistent with the dignity of a noble, sought to display "that chivalrous spirit which constitutes the pride and ornament of France," and looked back with horror on the humiliating position of their fathers and grandfathers. "Peter the Great," writes one of them, "beat all who surrounded him, without distinction of family or rank; but now, many of us would certainly prefer capital punishment to being beaten or flogged, even though the castigation were applied by the sacred hands of the Lord's Anointed."

The tone which reigned in the Court circle of St. Petersburg spread gradually towards the lower ranks of the *Dvoryánstvo*, and it seemed to superficial observers that a very fair imitation of the French Noblesse had been pro-

---

[4] *Khvastún*, by Knyazhnin.

duced; but in reality the copy was very unlike the model. The Russian *Dvoryanín* easily learned the language and assumed the manners of the French *gentilhomme,* and succeeded in changing his physical and intellectual exterior; but all those deeper and more delicate parts of human nature which are formed by the accumulated experience of past generations could not be so easily and rapidly changed. The French *gentilhomme* of the eighteenth century was the direct descendant of the feudal baron, with the fundamental conceptions of his ancestors deeply embedded in his nature. He had not, indeed, the old haughty bearing towards the Sovereign, and his language was tinged with the fashionable democratic philosophy of the time; but he possessed a large intellectual and moral inheritance that had come down to him directly from the palmy days of feudalism—an inheritance which even the Great Revolution, which was then preparing, could not annihilate. The Russian noble, on the contrary, had received from his ancestors entirely different traditions. His father and grandfather had been conscious of the burdens rather than the privileges of the class to which they belonged. They had considered it no disgrace to receive corporal punishment, and had been jealous of their honor, not as gentlemen or descendants of *Boyárs,* but as Brigadiers, College Assessors, or Privy Councillors. Their dignity had rested not on the grace of God, but on the will of the Tsar. Under these circumstances even the proudest magnate of Catherine's Court, though he might speak French as fluently as his mother tongue, could not be very deeply penetrated with the conception of noble blood, the sacred character of nobility, and the numerous feudal ideas interwoven with these conceptions. And in adopting the outward forms of a foreign culture the nobles did not, it seems, gain much in true dignity. "The old pride of the nobles has fallen!" exclaims one who had more genuine aristocratic feeling than his fellows.[5] "There are no longer any honorable families, but merely official rank and personal merits. All seek official rank, and as all cannot render direct services, distinctions are sought by every possible

[5] Prince Shcherbátov.

means—by flattering the Monarch and toadying the important personages." There was considerable truth in this complaint, but the voice of this solitary aristocrat was as of one crying in the wilderness. The whole of the educated classes—men of old family and *parvenus* alike—were, with few exceptions, too much engrossed with place-hunting to attend to such sentimental wailing.

If the Russian Noblesse was thus in its new form but a very imperfect imitation of its French model, it was still more unlike the English aristocracy. Notwithstanding the liberal phrases in which Catherine habitually indulged, she never had the least intention of ceding one jot or tittle of her autocratic power, and the Noblesse as a class never obtained even a shadow of political influence. There was no real independence under the new airs of dignity and hauteur. In all their acts and openly expressed opinions the courtiers were guided by the real or supposed wishes of the Sovereign, and much of their political sagacity was employed in endeavoring to discover what would please her. "People never talk politics in the salons," says a contemporary witness,[6] "not even to praise the Government. Fear has produced habits of prudence, and the Frondeurs of the Capital express their opinions only in the confidence of intimate friendship or in a relationship still more confidential. Those who cannot bear this constraint retire to Moscow, which cannot be called the center of opposition, for there is no such thing as opposition in a country with an autocratic Government, but which is the capital of the discontented." And even there the discontent did not venture to show itself in the Imperial presence. "In Moscow," says another witness, accustomed to the obsequiousness of Versailles, "you might believe yourself to be among republicans who have just thrown off the yoke of a tyrant, but as soon as the Court arrives you see nothing but abject slaves." [7]

Though thus excluded from direct influence in political affairs, the Noblesse might still have acquired a certain political significance in the State, by means of the Provin-

[6] Ségur, long Ambassador of France at the Court of Catherine.
[7] Sabathier de Cabres, *Catherine II et la Cour de Russie en 1772.*

cial Assemblies, and by the part they took in local administration; but in reality they had neither the requisite political experience nor the requisite patience, nor even the
desire to pursue such a policy. The majority of the proprietors preferred the chances of promotion in the Imperial
service to the tranquil life of a country gentleman; and
those who resided permanently on their estates showed
indifference or positive antipathy to everything connected
with the local administration. What was officially described
as "a privilege conferred on the nobles for their fidelity,
and for the generous sacrifice of their lives in their country's cause," was regarded by those who enjoyed it as a
new kind of obligatory service—an obligation to supply
judges and officers of rural police.

If we require any additional proof that the nobles
amidst all these changes were still as dependent as ever on
the arbitrary will or caprice of the Monarch, we have only
to glance at their position in the time of Paul I, the capricious, eccentric, violent son and successor of Catherine.
The autobiographical memoirs of the time depict in vivid
colors the humiliating position of even the leading men in
the State, in constant fear of exciting by act, word, or look
the wrath of the Sovereign. As we read these contemporary records we seem to have before us a picture of ancient Rome under the most despotic and capricious of her
Emperors. Irritated and embittered before his accession to
the throne by the haughty demeanor of his mother's favorites, Paul lost no opportunity of showing his contempt
for aristocratic pretensions, and of humiliating those who
were supposed to harbor them. "Apprenez, monsieur," he
said angrily on one occasion to Dumouriez, who had accidentally referred to one of the "considerable" personages of the Court, "Apprenez qu'il n'y a de considérable ici
que la personne à laquelle je parle et pendant le temps
que je lui parle!" [8]

From the time of Catherine down to the succession of
Alexander II in 1855 no important change was made in
the legal status of the Noblesse, but a gradual change
took place in its social character by the continual influx

[8] This saying is often falsely attributed to Nicholas I. The
anecdote is related by Ségur.

of Western ideas and Western culture. The exclusively
French culture in vogue at the Court of Catherine assumed a more cosmopolitan coloring, and permeated
downwards till all who had any pretensions to being
civilisés spoke French with tolerable fluency and possessed at least a superficial acquaintance with the literature of Western Europe. What chiefly distinguished them
in the eye of the law from the other classes was the privilege of possessing "inhabited estates"—that is to say, estates with serfs. By the emancipation of the serfs in 1861
this valuable privilege was abolished, and about one-half
of their landed property passed into the hands of the
peasantry. By the administrative reforms which have since
taken place, any little significance which the provincial
corporations may have possessed has been annihilated.
Thus at the present day the nobles are on a level with the
other classes with regard to the right of possessing landed
property and the administration of local affairs.

From this rapid sketch the reader will easily perceive
that the Russian Noblesse has had a peculiar historical
development. In Germany, France, and England the nobles were early formed into a homogeneous organized
body by the political conditions in which they were placed.
They had to repel the encroaching tendencies of the Monarchy on the one hand, and of the *bourgeoisie* on the
other; and in this long struggle with powerful rivals they
instinctively held together and developed a vigorous esprit
de corps. New members penetrated into their ranks, but
these intruders were so few in number that they were
rapidly assimilated without modifying the general character or recognized ideals of the class, and without rudely
disturbing the fiction of purity of blood. The class thus assumed more and more the nature of a caste with a peculiar intellectual and moral culture, and stoutly defended
its position and privileges till the ever increasing power of
the middle classes undermined its influence. Its fate in
various countries has been different. In Germany it clung
to its feudal traditions, and still preserves its social exclusiveness. In France it was deprived of its political influence by the Monarchy and crushed by the Revolution. In
England it moderated its pretensions, allied itself with the

middle classes, created under the disguise of constitutional
monarchy an aristocratic republic, and conceded inch by
inch, as necessity demanded, a share of its political influence to the ally that had helped it to curb the Royal
power. Thus the German baron, the French *gentilhomme,*
and the English nobleman represent three distinct, well-
marked types; but amidst all their diversities they have
much in common. They have all preserved to a greater or
less extent a haughty consciousness of innate inextinguish-
able superiority over the lower orders, together with a more
or less carefully disguised dislike for the class which has
been, and still is, an aggressive rival.

The Russian Noblesse has not these characteristics. It
was formed out of more heterogeneous materials, and
these materials did not spontaneously combine to form an
organic whole but were crushed into a conglomerate mass
by the weight of the autocratic power. It never became a
semi-independent factor in the State. What rights and
privileges it possesses it received from the Monarchy, and
consequently it has no deep-rooted jealousy or hatred of
the Imperial prerogative. On the other hand, it has never
had to struggle with the other social classes, and therefore
it harbors towards them no feelings of rivalry or hostility. If
we hear a Russian noble speak with indignation of autocracy or with acrimony of the *bourgeoisie,* we may be sure
that these feelings have their source, not in traditional
conceptions, but in principles learned from the modern
schools of social and political philosophy. The class to
which he belongs has undergone so many transformations
that it has no hoary traditions or deep-rooted prejudices,
and always willingly adapts itself to existing conditions. Indeed, it may be said in general that it looks more to the
future than the past, and is ever ready to accept any new
ideas that wear the badge of progress. Its freedom from
traditions and prejudices makes it singularly susceptible of
generous enthusiasm and capable of vigorous spasmodic
action, but calm moral courage and tenacity of purpose
are not among its prominent attributes. In a word, we find
in it neither the peculiar virtues nor the peculiar vices
which are engendered and fostered by an atmosphere of
political liberty.

However we may explain the fact, there is no doubt that the Russian Noblesse has little or nothing of what we call aristocratic feeling—little or nothing of that haughty, domineering, exclusive spirit which we are accustomed to associate with the word Aristocracy. We find plenty of Russians who are proud of their wealth, of their culture, or of their official position, but we rarely find a Russian who is proud of his birth or imagines that the fact of his having a long pedigree gives him any right to political privileges or social consideration. Hence there is a certain amount of truth in the oft-repeated saying that there is in reality no aristocracy in Russia.

Certainly the Noblesse as a whole cannot be called an aristocracy. If the term is to be used at all, it must be applied to a group of families which cluster around the Court and form the highest ranks of the Noblesse. This social aristocracy contains many old families, but its real basis is official rank and general culture rather than pedigree or blood. The feudal conceptions of noble birth, good family, and the like have been adopted by some of its members, but do not form one of its conspicuous features. Though habitually practicing a certain exclusiveness, it has none of those characteristics of a caste which we find in the German *Adel*, and is utterly unable to understand such institutions as *Tafelfähigkeit*, by which a man who has not a pedigree of a certain length is considered unworthy to sit down at a royal table. It takes rather the English aristocracy as its model, and harbors the secret hope of one day obtaining a social and political position similar to that of the nobility and gentry of England. Though it has no peculiar legal privileges, its actual position in the Administration and at Court gives its members great facilities for advancement in the public service. On the other hand, its semibureaucratic character, together with the law and custom of dividing landed property among the children at the death of their parents, deprives it of stability. New men force their way into it by official distinction, whilst many of the old families are compelled by poverty to retire from its ranks. The son of a small proprietor, or even of a parish priest, may rise to the highest offices of State, whilst the descendants of the half-mythical Rurik may descend to the position of peasants. It is said that not very long ago a certain Prince Krapotkin gained his living as a cabman in St. Petersburg!

It is evident, then, that this social aristocracy must not be confounded with the titled families. Titles do not possess the same value in Russia as in Western Europe. They are very common—because the titled families are numerous, and all the children bear their father's title, even while he is still alive—and they are by no means always associated with official rank, wealth, social position, or distinction of any kind. There are hundreds of princes and princesses who have not the right to appear at Court, and who would not be admitted into what is called in St. Petersburg *"la société"*—or, indeed, into refined society in any country.

The only genuine Russian title is *Knyaz,* commonly translated "Prince." It is borne by the descendants of Rurik, of the Lithuanian Prince Ghedimin, and of the Tatar Khans and Murzi officially recognized by the Tsars. Besides these, there are fourteen families who have adopted it by Imperial command during the last two centuries. The titles of count and baron are modern importations, beginning with the time of Peter the Great. From Peter and his successors about seventy families have received the title of count and ten that of baron. The latter are all, with two exceptions, of foreign extraction, and are mostly descended from Court bankers.[9]

There is a very common idea that Russian nobles are as a rule enormously rich. This is a mistake. The majority of them are poor. At the time of the Emancipation, in 1861, there were 100,247 landed proprietors, and of these more than 41,000 were possessors of fewer than twenty-one male serfs—that is to say, were in a condition of poverty. A proprietor who was owner of 500 serfs was not considered as by any means very rich, and yet there were only 3,803 proprietors belonging to that category. There were a few, indeed, whose possessions were enormous. Count Sheremetiev, for instance, possessed more than 150,000 male serfs, or in other words more than 300,000

[9] Besides these, there are of course the German counts and barons of the Baltic Provinces, who are Russian subjects.

souls; and forty years ago Count Orlov-Davydov owned considerably more than half a million of acres. The Demídov family derived colossal revenues from their mines, and the Strógonovs possessed estates which, if put together, would be sufficient in extent to form a small independent State in Western Europe. The very rich families, however, are not numerous, and a large proportion of them have become impoverished during the last half-century. The lavish expenditure in which Russian nobles used to indulge indicated too frequently not large fortune, but simply foolish ostentation and reckless improvidence.

Perhaps, after having spoken so much about the past history of the Noblesse, I ought to endeavor to cast its horoscope, or at least to say something of its probable future. Though predictions are always hazardous, it is sometimes possible, by tracing the great lines of history in the past, to follow them for a little distance into the future. If it be allowable to apply this method of prediction in the present matter, I should say that the Russian *Dvoryánstvo* will assimilate with the other classes, rather than form itself into an exclusive corporation. Hereditary aristocracies may be preserved—or at least their decomposition may be retarded—where they happen to exist, but it seems that they can no longer be created. In Western Europe there is a large amount of aristocratic sentiment, both in the nobles and in the people; but it exists in spite of, rather than in consequence of, actual social conditions. It is not a product of modern society, but an heirloom that has come down to us from feudal times, when power, wealth, and culture were in the hands of a privileged few. If there ever was in Russia a period corresponding to the feudal times in Western Europe, it has long since been forgotten. There is very little aristocratic sentiment either in the people or in the nobles, and it is difficult to imagine any source from which it could now be derived. More than this, the nobles do not desire to make such an acquisition. In so far as they have any political aspirations, they aim, with very few exceptions, at securing the political liberty of the people as a whole, and not at acquiring exclusive rights and privileges for their own class.

In that section which I have called a social aristocracy

there are a few individuals who desire to gain exclusive
political influence for the class to which they belong, but
there is very little chance of their succeeding. If their
desires were ever by chance realized, we should probably
have a repetition of the scene which occurred in 1730.
When in that year some of the great families raised the
Duchess of Courland to the throne on condition of her
ceding part of her power to a Supreme Council, the lower
ranks of the Noblesse compelled her to tear up the Constitution which she had signed! Those who dislike the
autocratic power dislike the idea of an aristocratic
oligarchy infinitely more. Nobles and people alike seem to
hold instinctively the creed of the French philosopher,
who thought it better to be governed by a lion of good
family than by a hundred rats of his own species.

Of the present condition of the Noblesse I shall again
have occasion to speak when I come to consider the consequences of the Emancipation.

CHAPTER · VII

❧ ❧

Landed Proprietors
of the Old School

OF all the foreign countries in which I have traveled, Russia certainly bears off the palm in the matter of hospitality. Every spring I found myself in possession of a large number of invitations from landed proprietors in different parts of the country—far more than I could possibly accept—and a great part of the summer was generally spent in wandering about from one country house to another. I have no intention of asking the reader to accompany me in all these expeditions—for, though pleasant in reality, they might be tedious in description—but I wish to introduce him to some typical examples of the landed proprietors. Among them are to be found nearly all ranks and conditions of men, from the rich magnate, surrounded with the refined luxury of West European civilization, to the poor, ill-clad, ignorant owner of a few acres which barely supply him with the necessaries of life. Let us take, first of all, a few specimens from the middle ranks.

In one of the central provinces, near the bank of a sluggish, meandering stream, stands an irregular group of wooden constructions—old, unpainted, blackened by time, and surmounted by high, sloping roofs of moss-covered planks. The principal building is a long, one-storied dwelling house, constructed at right angles to the road. At the front of the house is a spacious, ill-kept yard, and at the back an equally spacious shady garden, in which Art carries on a feeble conflict with encroaching Nature. At

the other side of the yard, and facing the front door—
or, rather, the front doors, for there are two—stand the
stables, hay shed, and granary, and near to that end of the
house which is farthest from the road are two smaller
houses, one of which is the kitchen and the other the
Lyudskáya, or servants' apartments. Beyond these we can
perceive, through a single row of lime trees, another group
of time-blackened wooden constructions in a still more dilapidated condition. That is the farmyard.

There is certainly not much symmetry in the disposition of these buildings, but there is nevertheless a certain
order and meaning in the apparent chaos. All the buildings which do not require stoves are built at a considerable distance from the dwelling house and kitchen, which
are more liable to take fire; and the kitchen stands by itself, because the odor of cookery, in which oil is copi-
ously used, is by no means agreeable, even for those whose
olfactory nerves are not very sensitive. The plan of the
house is likewise not without a certain meaning. The rigorous separation of the sexes, which formed a characteristic trait of old Russian society, has long since disappeared, but its influence may still be traced in houses
built on the old model. The house in question is one of
these, and consequently it is composed of three sections—
at the one end the male apartments, at the other the female apartments, and in the middle the neutral territory,
comprising the dining room and the *salon*. This arrangement has its conveniences, and explains the fact that
the house has two front doors. At the back is a third door,
which opens from the neutral territory into a spacious
veranda overlooking the garden.

Here lives, and has lived for many years, Ivan Ivanovich
K——, a gentleman of the old school, and a very worthy
man of his kind. If we look at him as he sits in his comfortable armchair, with his capacious dressing gown hanging loosely about him, we shall be able to read at a glance
something of his character. Nature endowed him with
large bones and broad shoulders, and evidently intended
him to be a man of great muscular power, but he has contrived to frustrate this benevolent intention, and has now
more fat than muscle. His close-cropped head is round as

a bullet, and his features are massive and heavy, but the heaviness is relieved by an expression of calm content-ment and imperturbable good nature, which occasionally blossoms into a broad grin. His face is one of those on which no amount of histrionic talent could produce a look of care and anxiety; and for this it is not to blame, for such an expression has never been demanded of it. Like other mortals he sometimes experiences little annoyances, and on such occasions his small gray eyes sparkle and his face becomes suffused with a crimson glow that sug-gests apoplexy; but ill fortune has never been able to get sufficiently firm hold of him to make him understand what such words as care and anxiety mean. Of struggle, disappointment, hope, and all the other feelings which give to human life a dramatic interest, he knows little by hearsay and nothing by experience. He has, in fact, always lived outside of that struggle for existence which modern philosophers declare to be the law of Nature.

Somewhere about seventy years ago Ivan Ivan'ich was born in the house where he still lives. His first lessons he received from the parish priest, and afterwards he was taught by a deacon's son who had studied in the ec-clesiastical seminary to so little purpose that he was un-able to pass the final examination. By both of these teach-ers he was treated with extreme leniency, and was al-lowed to learn as little as he chose. His father wished him to study hard, but his mother was afraid that study might injure his health, and accordingly gave him several holi-days every week. Under these circumstances his progress was naturally not very rapid, and he was still very slightly acquainted with the elementary rules of arithmetic when his father one day declared that he was already eighteen years of age, and must at once enter the service. But what kind of service? Ivan had no natural inclination for any kind of activity. The project of entering him as a *Junker* in a cavalry regiment, the colonel of which was an old friend of the family, did not at all please him. He had no love for military service, and positively disliked the prospect of an examination. Whilst seeming, therefore, to bow implicitly to the paternal authority, he induced his mother to oppose the scheme.

The dilemma in which Ivan found himself was this: in deference to his father he wished to be in the service and to gain that official rank which every Russian noble desires to possess, and at the same time, in deference to his mother and his own tastes, he wished to remain at home and continue his indolent mode of life. The Marshal of Noblesse, who happened to call one day, helped him out of the difficulty by offering to inscribe him as secretary in the *Dvoryánskaya Opéka*, a bureau which acts as curator for the estates of minors. All the duties of this office could be fulfilled by a paid secretary, and the nominal occupant would be periodically promoted as if he were an active official. This was precisely what Ivan required. He accepted eagerly the proposal, and obtained, in the course of seven years, without any effort on his part, the rank of "collegiate secretary," corresponding to the "capitaine-en-second" of the military hierarchy. To mount higher he would have had to seek some place where he could not have fulfilled his duty by proxy, so he determined to rest on his laurels, and sent in his resignation.

Immediately after the termination of his official life his married life began. Before his resignation had been accepted he suddenly found himself one morning on the high road to matrimony. Here again there was no effort on his part. The course of true love, which is said never to run smooth for ordinary mortals, ran smooth for him. He never had even the trouble of proposing. The whole affair was arranged by his parents, who chose as bride for their son the only daughter of their nearest neighbor. The young lady was only about sixteen years of age, and was not remarkable for beauty, talent, or any other peculiarity, but she had one very important qualification—she was the daughter of a man who had an estate contiguous to their own, and who might give as a dowry a certain bit of land which they had long desired to add to their own property. The negotiations, being of a delicate nature, were entrusted to an old lady who had a great reputation for diplomatic skill in such matters, and she accomplished her mission with such success that in the course of a few weeks the preliminaries were arranged and the day fixed for the wedding. Thus Ivan Ivan'ich won his bride as easily as he had won his *chin* of "collegiate secretary."

Though the bridegroom had received rather than taken to himself a wife, and did not imagine for a moment that he was in love, he had no reason to regret the choice that was made for him. Maria Petrovna was exactly suited by character and education to be the wife of a man like Ivan Ivan'ich. She had grown up at home in the society of nurses and maidservants, and had never learned anything more than could be obtained from the parish priest and from "Ma'mselle," a personage occupying a position midway between a maidservant and a governess. The first events of her life were the announcement that she was to be married and the preparations for the wedding. She still remembers the delight which the purchase of her trousseau afforded her, and keeps in her memory a full catalogue of the articles bought. The first years of her married life were not very happy, for she was treated by her mother-in-law as a naughty child who required to be frequently snubbed and lectured; but she bore the discipline with exemplary patience, and in due time became her own mistress and autocratic ruler in all domestic affairs. From that time she has lived an active, uneventful life. Between her and her husband there is as much mutual attachment as can reasonably be expected in phlegmatic natures after nearly half a century of matrimony. She has always devoted her energies to satisfying his simple material wants—of intellectual wants he has none—and securing his comfort in every possible way. Under this fostering care he "effeminated himself" (*obábilsya*), as he is wont to say. His love of shooting died out, he cared less and less to visit his neighbors, and each successive year he spent more and more time in his armchair.

The daily life of this worthy couple is singularly regular and monotonous, varying only with the changing seasons. In summer Ivan Ivan'ich gets up about seven o'clock, and puts on, with the assistance of his *valet de chambre*, a simple costume, consisting chiefly of a faded, plentifully stained dressing gown. Having nothing particular to do, he sits down at the open window and looks into the yard. As the servants pass he stops and questions them, and then gives them orders, or scolds them, as circumstances demand. Towards nine o'clock tea is announced, and he goes into the dining room—a long, narrow apartment with bare wooden floor and no furniture but a table and chairs, all in a more or less rickety condition. Here he finds his wife with the tea urn before her. In a few minutes the grandchildren come in, kiss their grandpapa's hand, and take their places round the table. As this morning meal consists merely of bread and tea, it does not last long; and all disperse to their several occupations. The head of the house begins the labors of the day by resuming his seat at the open window. When he has smoked some cigarettes and indulged in a proportionate amount of silent contemplation, he goes out with the intention of visiting the stables and farmyard, but generally before he has crossed the court he finds the heat unbearable, and returns to his former position by the open window. Here he sits tranquilly till the sun has so far moved round that the veranda at the back of the house is completely in the shade, when he has his armchair removed thither, and sits there till dinnertime.

Maria Petrovna spends her morning in a more active way. As soon as the breakfast table has been cleared, she goes to the larder, takes stock of the provisions, arranges the *menu du jour,* and gives to the cook the necessary materials, with detailed instructions as to how they are to be prepared. The rest of the morning she devotes to her other household duties.

Towards one o'clock dinner is announced, and Ivan Ivan'ich prepares his appetite by swallowing at a gulp a wineglassful of homemade bitters. Dinner is the great event of the day. The food is abundant and of good quality, but mushrooms, onions, and fat play a rather too important part in the repast, and the whole is prepared with very little attention to the recognized principles of culinary hygiene. Many of the dishes, indeed, would make a British valetudinarian stand aghast, but they seem to produce no bad effect on those Russian organisms which have never been weakened by town life, nervous excitement, or intellectual exertion.

No sooner has the last dish been removed than a death-like stillness falls upon the house: it is the time of the after-dinner siesta. The young folks go into the garden, and all the other members of the household give way to the drowsiness naturally engendered by a heavy meal on a hot summer day. Ivan Ivan'ich retires to his own room, from which the flies have been carefully expelled. Maria Petrovna dozes in an armchair in the sitting room, with a pocket handkerchief spread over her face. The servants snore in the corridors, the garret, or the hay shed; and even the old watchdog in the corner of the yard stretches himself out at full length on the shady side of his kennel.

In about two hours the house gradually reawakens. Doors begin to creak; the names of various servants are bawled out in all tones, from bass to falsetto; and footsteps are heard in the yard. Soon a manservant issues from the kitchen bearing an enormous tea urn, which puffs like a little steam engine. The family assembles for tea. In Russia, as elsewhere, sleep after a heavy meal produces thirst, so that the tea and other beverages are very acceptable. Then some little delicacies are served—such as fruit and wild berries, or cucumbers with honey, or something else of the kind—and the family again disperses. Ivan Ivan'ich takes a turn in the fields on his *begovuiya droshki*—an extremely light vehicle composed of two pairs of wheels joined together by a single board, on which the driver sits stride-legged; and Maria Petrovna probably receives a visit from the *Popadyà* (the priest's wife), who is the chief gossipmonger of the neighborhood. There is not much scandal in the district, but what little there is the *Popadyà* carefully collects, and distributes among her acquaintances with undiscriminating generosity.

In the evening it often happens that a little group of peasants come into the court, and ask to see the "master." The master goes to the door, and generally finds that they have some favor to request. In reply to his question, "Well, children, what do you want?" they tell their story in a confused, rambling way, several of them speaking at a time, and he has to question and cross-question them before he comes to understand clearly what they desire. If he tells them he cannot grant it, they probably do not

accept a first refusal, but endeavor by means of supplica-
tion to make him reconsider his decision. Stepping forward a little, and bowing low, one of the group begins in
a half-respectful, half-familiar, caressing tone: "Little
Father, Ivan Ivan'ich, be gracious; you are our father, and
we are your children"—and so on. Ivan Ivan'ich good-
naturedly listens, and again explains that he cannot grant
what they ask; but they still have hopes of gaining their
point by entreaty, and continue their supplications till at
last his patience is exhausted and he says to them in a
paternal tone, "Now, enough! enough! you are blockheads
—blockheads all round! There's no use talking; it can't be
done." And with these words he enters the house, so as to
prevent all further discussion.

A regular part of the evening's occupation is the inter-
view with the steward. The work that has just been done
and the program for the morrow are always discussed at
great length; and much time is spent in speculating as to
the weather during the next few days. On this latter point
the calendar is always carefully consulted, and great confidence is placed in its predictions, though past experience
has often shown that they are not to be implicitly trusted.
The conversation drags on till supper is announced,
and immediately after that meal, which is an abridged
repetition of dinner, all retire for the night.

Thus pass the days and weeks and months in the house
of Ivan Ivan'ich, and rarely is there any deviation from
the ordinary program. The climate necessitates, of course,
some slight modifications. When it is cold, the doors
and windows have to be kept shut, and after heavy
rains those who do not like to wade in mud have to remain
in the house or garden. In the long winter evenings the
family assembles in the sitting room, and all kill time as
they best can. Ivan Ivan'ich smokes and meditates, or
listens to the barrel organ played by one of the children.
Maria Petrovna knits a stocking. The old aunt, who commonly spends the winter with them, plays patience, and
sometimes draws from the game conclusions as to the
future. Her favorite predictions are that a stranger will
arrive, or that a marriage will take place, and she can
determine the sex of the stranger and the color of the

bridegroom's hair; but beyond this her art does not go, and she cannot satisfy the young ladies' curiosity as to further details.

Books and newspapers are rarely seen in the sitting room, but for those who wish to read there is a bookcase full of miscellaneous literature, which gives some idea of the literary tastes of the family during several generations. The oldest volumes were bought by Ivan Ivan'ich's grandfather—a man who, according to the family traditions, enjoyed the confidence of the great Catherine. Though wholly overlooked by recent historians, he was evidently a man who had some pretensions to culture. He had his portrait painted by a foreign artist of considerable talent —it still hangs in the sitting room—and he bought several pieces of Sèvres ware, the last of which stands on a commode in the corner and contrasts strangely with the rude homemade furniture and squalid appearance of the apartment. Among the books which bear his name are the tragedies of Sumarókov, who imagined himself to be "the Russian Voltaire"; the amusing comedies of Von-Wisin, some of which still keep the stage; the loud-sounding odes of the courtly Derzhávin; two or three books containing the mystic wisdom of Freemasonry as interpreted by Schwarz and Novikov; Russian translations of Richardson's *Pamela, Sir Charles Grandison,* and *Clarissa Harlowe;* Rousseau's *Nouvelle Héloïse,* in Russian garb; and three or four volumes of Voltaire in the original. Among the works collected at a somewhat later period are translations of Ann Radcliffe, of Scott's early novels, and of Ducray Duménil, whose stories, "Lolotte et Fanfan" and "Victor," once enjoyed a great reputation. At this point the literary tastes of the family appear to have died out, for the succeeding literature is represented exclusively by Krylov's Fables, a farmer's manual, a handbook of family medicine, and a series of calendars. There are, however, some signs of a revival, for on the lowest shelf stand recent editions of Pushkin, Lermontov, and Gógol, and a few works by living authors.

Sometimes the monotony of the winter is broken by visiting neighbors and receiving visitors in return, or in a more decided way by a visit of a few days to the capital of the province. In the latter case Maria Petrovna spends nearly all her time in shopping, and brings home a large collection of miscellaneous articles. The inspection of these by the assembled family forms an important domestic event, which completely throws into the shade the occasional visits of pedlars and colporteurs. Then there are the festivities at Christmas and Easter, and occasionally little incidents of a less agreeable kind. It may be that there is a heavy fall of snow, so that it is necessary to cut roads to the kitchen and stables; or wolves enter the courtyard at night and have a fight with the watchdogs; or the news is brought that a peasant who had been drinking in a neighboring village has been found frozen to death on the road.

Altogether the family live a very isolated life, but they have one bond of connection with the great outer world. Two of the sons are officers in the army, and both of them write home occasionally to their mother and sisters. To these two youths is devoted all the little stock of sentimentality which Maria Petrovna possesses. She can talk of them by the hour to anyone who will listen to her, and has related to the *Popadyà* a hundred times every trivial incident of their lives. Though they have never given her much cause for anxiety, and they are now men of middle age, she lives in constant fear that some evil may befall them. What she most fears is that they may be sent on a campaign or may fall in love with actresses. War and actresses are, in fact, the two bugbears of her existence, and whenever she has a disquieting dream she asks the priest to offer up a *molében* for the safety of her absent ones. Sometimes she ventures to express her anxiety to her husband, and recommends him to write to them; but he considers writing a letter a very serious bit of work, and always replies evasively, "Well, well, we must think about it."

During the Crimean War, Ivan Ivan'ich half awoke from his habitual lethargy, and read occasionally the meager official reports published by the Government. He was a little surprised that no great victories were reported, and that the army did not at once advance on Constantinople. As to causes he never speculated. Some of his neighbors told him that the army was disorganized, and the whole system of Nicholas had been proved to be utterly worthless. That might all be very true, but he did not understand military and political matters. No doubt it would all come right in the end. All did come right, after a fashion, and he again gave up reading newspapers; but ere long he was startled by reports much more alarming than any rumors of war. People began to talk about the peasant question, and to say openly that the serfs must soon be emancipated. For once in his life Ivan Ivan'ich asked explanations. Finding one of his neighbors, who had always been a respectable, sensible man, and a severe disciplinarian, talking in this way, he took him aside and asked what it all meant. The neighbor explained that the old order of things had shown itself bankrupt and was doomed, that a new epoch was opening, that everything was to be reformed, and that the Emperor, in accordance with a secret clause of the Treaty with the Allies, was about to grant a Constitution! Ivan Ivan'ich listened for a little in silence, and then, with a gesture of impatience, interrupted the speaker: "Polno duráchitsya!" (Enough of fun and tomfoolery.) "Vassili Petróvich, tell me seriously what you mean."

When Vassili Petróvich vowed that he spoke in all seriousness, his friend gazed at him with a look of intense compassion, and remarked, as he turned away, "So you, too, have gone out of your mind!"

The utterances of Vassili Petróvich, which his lethargic, sober-minded friend regarded as indicating temporary insanity in the speaker, represented fairly the mental condition of very many Russian nobles at that time, and were not without a certain foundation. The idea about a secret clause in the Treaty of Paris was purely imaginary, but it was quite true that the country was entering on an epoch of great reforms, among which the Emancipation question occupied the chief place. Of this even the skeptical Ivan Ivan'ich was soon convinced. Alexander II, the son and successor of Nicholas, declared in a formal speech to the Noblesse of the province of Moscow that the actual state of things could not continue forever, and called on the landed proprietors to consider by what means the

condition of their serfs might be ameliorated. Provincial
committees were accordingly formed for the purpose of
preparing definite projects, and gradually it became apparent that the emancipation of the serfs was really at
hand.

Ivan Ivan'ich was alarmed at the prospect of losing his
authority over his serfs. Though he had never been a cruel
taskmaster, he had not spared the rod when he considered
it necessary, and he believed birch twigs to be a necessary instrument in the Russian system of agriculture. For
some time he drew consolation from the thought that
peasants were not birds of the air, that they must under
all circumstances require food and clothing, and that they
would be ready to serve him as agricultural laborers; but
when he learned that they were to receive a large part of
the estate for their own use, his hopes fell, and he greatly
feared that he would be inevitably ruined.

These dark forebodings were not by any means realized.
His serfs were emancipated and received about a half of
the estate, but in return for the land ceded they paid
him annually a considerable sum, and they were always
ready to cultivate his fields for a fair remuneration. The
yearly outlay was considerably greater, but the price of
grain rose, and this counterbalanced the additional yearly
expenditure. The administration of the estate became
much less patriarchal; much that had been left to custom
and tacit understanding was regulated by express agreement on purely commercial principles; a great deal more
money was paid out and a great deal more received; there
was much less authority in the hands of the master, and
his responsibilities were proportionately diminished; but
in spite of all these changes, Ivan Ivan'ich would have
great difficulty in deciding whether he is a richer or a
poorer man. He has fewer horses and fewer servants, but
he has still more than he requires, and his mode of life has
undergone no perceptible alteration. Maria Petrovna
complains that she is no longer supplied with eggs, chickens, and homespun linen by the peasants, and that everything is three times as dear as it used to be; but somehow
the larder is still full, and abundance reigns in the house
as of old.

Ivan Ivan'ich certainly does not possess transcendent qualities of any kind. It would be impossible to make a hero out of him, even though his own son should be his biographer. Muscular Christians may reasonably despise him, and active, energetic men may fairly condemn him for his indolence and apathy. But, on the other hand, he has no very bad qualities. His vices are of the passive, negative kind. He is a respectable if not distinguished member of society, and appears a very worthy man when compared with many of his neighbors who have been brought up in similar conditions. Take, for instance, his younger brother Dimítri, who lives a short way off.

Dimítri Ivan'ich, like his brother Ivan, had been endowed by Nature with a very decided repugnance to prolonged intellectual exertion, but as he was a man of good parts he did not fear a *Junker's* examination—especially when he could count on the colonel's protection—and accordingly entered the army. In his regiment were a number of jovial young officers like himself, always ready to relieve the monotony of garrison life by boisterous dissipation, and among these he easily acquired the reputation of being a thoroughly good fellow. In drinking bouts he could hold his own with the best of them, and in all mad pranks invariably played the chief part. By this means he endeared himself to his comrades, and for a time all went well. The colonel had himself sown wild oats plentifully in his youth, and was quite disposed to overlook, as far as possible, the bacchanalian peccadilloes of his subordinates. But before many years had passed, the regiment suddenly changed its character. Certain rumors had reached headquarters, and the Emperor Nicholas appointed as colonel a stern disciplinarian of German origin, who aimed at making the regiment a kind of machine that should work with the accuracy of a chronometer.

This change did not at all suit the tastes of Dimítri Ivan'ich. He chafed under the new restraints, and as soon as he had gained the rank of lieutenant retired from the service to enjoy the freedom of country life. Shortly afterwards his father died, and he thereby became owner of an estate, with two hundred serfs. He did not, like his elder brother, marry, and "effeminate himself," but he did worse. In his little independent kingdom—for such was practically a Russian estate in the good old times—he was lord of all he surveyed, and gave full scope to his boisterous humor, his passion for sport, and his love of drinking and dissipation. Many of the mad pranks in which he indulged will long be preserved by popular tradition, but they cannot well be related here.

Dimítri Ivan'ich is now a man long past middle age, and still continues his wild, dissipated life. His house resembles an ill-kept, disreputable tavern. The floor is filthy, the furniture chipped and broken, the servants indolent, slovenly, and in rags. Dogs of all breeds and sizes roam about the rooms and corridors. The master, when not asleep, is always in a more or less complete state of intoxication. Generally he has one or two guests staying with him—men of the same type as himself—and days and nights are spent in drinking and cardplaying. When he cannot have his usual boon companions he sends for one or two small proprietors who live near—men who are legally nobles, but who are so poor that they differ little from peasants. Formerly, when ordinary resources failed, he occasionally had recourse to the violent expedient of ordering his servants to stop the first passing travelers, whoever they might be, and bring them in by persuasion or force, as circumstance might demand. If the travelers refused to accept such rough, undesired hospitality, a wheel would be taken off their *tarantass*, or some indispensable part of the harness would be secreted, and they might consider themselves fortunate if they succeeded in getting away next morning.[1]

In the time of serfage the domestic serfs had much to bear from their capricious, violent master. They lived in an atmosphere of abusive language, and were subjected not infrequently to corporal punishment. Worse than this, their master was constantly threatening to "shave their

[1] This custom has fortunately gone out of fashion even in outlying districts, but an incident of the kind happened to a friend of mine as late as 1871. He was detained against his will for two whole days by a man whom he had never seen before, and at last effected his escape by bribing the servants of his tyrannical host.

forehead"—that is to say, to give them as recruits—and
occasionally he put his threat into execution, in spite of
the wailings and entreaties of the culprit and his relations.
And yet, strange to say, nearly all of them remained with
him as free servants after the Emancipation.

In justice to the Russian landed proprietors I must say
that the class represented by Dimítri Ivan'ich has now
practically disappeared. It was the natural result of serfage
and social stagnation—of a state of society in which there
were few legal and moral restraints, and few inducements
to honorable activity.

Among the other landed proprietors of the district, one
of the best known is Nicolaï Petróvich B——, an old
military man with the rank of general. Like Ivan Ivan'ich,
he belongs to the old school; but the two men must be
contrasted rather than compared. The difference in their
lives and characters is reflected in their outward appearance. Ivan Ivan'ich, as we know, is portly in form and
heavy in all his movements, and loves to loll in his armchair or to loaf about the house in a capacious dressing
gown. The General, on the contrary, is thin, wiry, and
muscular, wears habitually a close-buttoned military tunic,
and always has a stern expression, the force of which is
considerably augmented by a bristly mustache resembling
a shoe brush. As he paces up and down the room, knitting
his brows and gazing at the floor, he looks as if he were
forming combinations of the first magnitude; but those
who know him well are aware that this is an optical delusion, of which he is himself to some extent a victim. He
is quite innocent of deep thought and concentrated intellectual effort. Though he frowns so fiercely he is by no
means of a naturally ferocious temperament. Had he
passed all his life in the country he would probably have
been as good-natured and phlegmatic as Ivan Ivan'ich
himself, but, unlike that worshiper of tranquillity, he had
aspired to rise in the service, and had adopted the stern,
formal bearing which the Emperor Nicholas considered
indispensable in an officer. The manner which he had at
first put on as part of his uniform became by the force of
habit almost a part of his nature, and at the age of thirty
he was a stern disciplinarian and uncompromising formal-

ist, who confined his attention exclusively to drill and other
military duties. Thus he rose steadily by his own merit,
and reached the goal of his early ambition—the rank of
general.

As soon as this point was reached he determined to
leave the service and retire to his estate. Many considerations urged him to take this step. He enjoyed the title of
Excellency, which he had long coveted, and when he put
on his full uniform his breast was bespangled with medals
and decorations. Since the death of his father the revenues of his property had been steadily decreasing, and report said that the best wood in his forest was rapidly disappearing. His wife had no love for the country, and
would have preferred to settle in Moscow or St. Petersburg, but they found that with their small income they
could not live in a large town in a style suitable to their
rank.

The General determined to introduce order into his
estate, and became a practical farmer; but a little experience convinced him that his new functions were much
more difficult than the commanding of a regiment. He
has long since given over the practical management of
the property to a steward, and he contents himself with
exercising what he imagines to be an efficient control.
Though he wishes to do much, he finds small scope for
his activity, and spends his days in pretty much the same
way as Ivan Ivan'ich, with this difference, that he plays
cards whenever he gets an opportunity, and reads regularly the *Moscow Gazette* and the *Russkii Invalid*, the
official military paper. What specially interests him is the
list of promotions, retirements, and Imperial awards for
merit and seniority. When he sees the announcement that
some old comrade has been made an officer of his Majesty's suite or has received a *grand cordon*, he frowns a
little more than usual, and is tempted to regret that he
retired from the service. Had he waited patiently, perhaps
a bit of good fortune might have fallen likewise to his lot.
This idea takes possession of him, and during the remainder of the day he is taciturn and morose. His wife
notices the change, and knows the reason for it, but has

too much good sense and tact to make any allusion to the subject.

Anna Alexándrovna—so the good lady is called—is an elderly dame who does not at all resemble the wife of Ivan Ivan'ich. She was long accustomed to a numerous military society, with dinner parties, dancing, promenades, cardplaying, and all the other amusements of garrison life, and she never contracted a taste for domestic concerns. Her knowledge of culinary affairs is extremely vague, and she has no idea of how to make preserves, *nalivka,* and other homemade delicacies, though Maria Petrovna, who is universally acknowledged to be a great adept in such matters, has proposed a hundred times to give her some choice recipes. In short, domestic affairs are a burden to her, and she entrusts them as far as possible to the housekeeper. Altogether she finds country life very tiresome, but, possessing that placid, philosophical temperament which seems to have some causal connection with corpulence, she submits without murmuring, and tries to lighten a little the unavoidable monotony by paying visits and receiving visitors. The neighbors within a radius of twenty miles are, with few exceptions, more or less of the Ivan Ivan'ich and Maria Petrovna type—decidedly rustic in their manners and conceptions; but their company is better than absolute solitude, and they have at least the good quality of being always able and willing to play cards for any number of hours. Besides this, Anna Alexándrovna has the satisfaction of feeling that amongst them she is almost a great personage, and unquestionably an authority in all matters of taste and fashion; and she feels especially well disposed towards those of them who frequently address her as "Your Excellency."

The chief festivities take place on the "name days" of the General and his spouse—that is to say, the days sacred to St. Nicholas and St. Anne. On these occasions all the neighbors come to offer their congratulations, and remain to dinner as a matter of course. After dinner the older visitors sit down to cards, and the young people extemporize a dance. The fête is especially successful when the eldest son comes home to take part in it, and

brings a brother officer with him. He is now a general like
his father.[2] In days gone by one of his comrades was expected to offer his hand to Olga Nikolaevna, the second
daughter, a delicate young lady who had been educated
in one of the great "Instituts"—gigantic boarding schools,
founded and kept up by the Government, for the daughters of those who are supposed to have deserved well of
their country. Unfortunately the expected offer was never
made, and she and her sister live at home as old maids,
bewailing the absence of "civilized" society, and killing
time in a harmless, elegant way by means of music, needle-
work, and light literature.

At those "name day" gatherings one used to meet
still more interesting specimens of the old school. One of
them I remember particularly. He was a tall, corpulent old
man, in a threadbare frock coat which wrinkled up about
his waist. His shaggy eyebrows almost covered his small,
dull eyes, his heavy mustache partially concealed a large
mouth, strongly indicating sensuous tendencies. His hair
was cut so short that it was difficult to say what its color
would have been if it had been allowed to grow. He always arrived in his *tarantass* just in time for the *zakuska*
—the appetizing collation that is served shortly before
dinner—grunted out a few congratulations to the host
and hostess and monosyllabic greetings to his acquaintances, ate a copious meal, and immediately afterwards
placed himself at a card table, where he sat in silence as
long as he could get anyone to play with him. People did
not like, however, to play with Andrei Vassil'ich, for his
society was not agreeable, and he always contrived to go
home with a well-filled purse.

Andrei Vassil'ich was a noted man in the neighborhood.
He was the center of a whole cycle of legends, and I
have often heard that his name was used with effect by
nurses to frighten naughty children. I never missed an
opportunity of meeting him, for I was curious to see and
study a legendary monster in the flesh. How far the nu-

[2] Generals are much more common in Russia than in other
countries. A few years ago there was an old lady in Moscow who
had a family of ten sons, all of whom were generals! The rank
may be obtained in the civil as well as the military service.

merous stories told about him were true 1 cannot pretend
to say, but they were certainly not without foundation.
In his youth he had served for some time in the army, and
was celebrated, even in an age when martinets had always
a good chance of promotion, for his brutality to his subordinates. His career was cut short, however, when he
had only the rank of captain. Having compromised himself in some way, he found it advisable to send in his resignation and retire to his estate. Here he organized his house
on Mahometan rather than Christian principles, and ruled
his servants and peasants as he had been accustomed to
rule his soldiers—using corporal punishment in merciless
fashion. His wife did not venture to protest against the
Mahometan arrangements, and any peasant who stood in
the way of their realization was at once given as a recruit,
or transported to Siberia, in accordance with his master's
demand.[3] At last his tyranny and extortion drove his serfs
to revolt. One night his house was surrounded and set on
fire, but he contrived to escape the fate that was prepared
for him, and caused all who had taken part in the revolt
to be mercilessly punished. This was a severe lesson, but it
had no effect upon him. Taking precautions against a similar surprise, he continued to tyrannize and extort as before, until in 1861 the serfs were emancipated and his
authority came to an end.

A very different sort of man was Pavel Trophim'ich, who
likewise came regularly to pay his respects and present his
congratulations to the General and "Gheneralsha." [4] It was
pleasant to turn from the hard, wrinkled, morose features
of the legendary monster to the soft, smooth, jovial face of
this man, who had been accustomed to look at the bright
side of things till his face had caught something of their
brightness. "A good, jovial, honest face!" a stranger might
exclaim as he looked at him. Knowing something of his

[3] When a proprietor considered any of his serfs unruly he
could, according to law, have them transported to Siberia without trial, on condition of paying the expenses of transport.
Arrived at their destination, they received land, and lived as free
colonists, with the single restriction that they were not allowed
to leave the locality where they settled.

[4] The female form of the word General.

character and history, I could not endorse such an opinion. Jovial he certainly was, for few men were more capable of making and enjoying mirth. Good he might be also called, if the word were taken in the sense of good-natured, for he never took offense, and was always ready to do a kindly action if it did not cost him any trouble. But as to his honesty, that required some qualification. Wholly untarnished his reputation certainly could not be, for he had been a judge in the District Court before the time of the judicial reforms; and, not being a Cato, he had succumbed to the usual temptations. He had never studied law, and made no pretensions to the possession of great legal knowledge. To all who would listen to him he declared openly that he knew much more about pointers and setters than about legal formalities. But his estate was very small, and he could not afford to give up his appointment.

. . . Pavel Trophim'ich was by no means a judge of the worst kind. He had been known to protect widows and orphans against those who wished to despoil them, and no amount of money would induce him to give an unjust decision against a friend who had privately explained the case to him; but when he knew nothing of the case or of the parties he readily signed the decision prepared by the secretary, and quietly pocketed the proceeds, without feeling any very disagreeable twinges of conscience. All judges, he knew, did likewise, and he had no pretension to being better than his fellows.

When Pavel Trophim'ich played cards at the General's house or elsewhere, a small, awkward, clean-shaven man, with dark eyes and a Tatar cast of countenance, might generally be seen sitting at the same table. His name was Alexei Petróvich T——. Whether he really had any Tatar blood in him it is impossible to say, but certainly his ancestors for one or two generations were all good Orthodox Christians. His father had been a poor military surgeon in a marching regiment, and he himself had become at an early age a scribe in one of the bureaus of the district town. He was then very poor, and had great difficulty in supporting life on the miserable pittance which he received as a salary; but he was a sharp, clever youth, and soon discovered that even a scribe had a great many opportunities of extorting money from the ignorant public.

These opportunities Alexei Petróvich used with great ability, and became known as one of the most accomplished bribetakers (*vzyátochniki*) in the district. His position, however, was so very subordinate that he would never have become rich had he not fallen upon a very ingenious expedient which completely succeeded. Hearing that a small proprietor, who had an only daughter, had come to live in the town for a few weeks, he took a room in the inn where the new-comers lived, and when he had made their acquaintance he fell dangerously ill. Feeling his last hours approaching, he sent for a priest, confided to him that he had amassed a large fortune, and requested that a will should be drawn up. In the will he bequeathed considerable sums to all his relations, and did not forget the parish church. The whole affair was to be kept a secret till after his death, but his neighbor—the old gentleman with the daughter—was called in to act as a witness. When all this had been done he did not die, but rapidly recovered, and now induced the old gentleman to whom he had confided his secret to grant him his daughter's hand. The daughter had no objections to marrying a man possessed of such wealth, and the marriage was duly celebrated. Shortly after this the father died—without discovering, it is to be hoped, the hoax that had been perpetrated—and Alexei Petróvich became virtual possessor of a very comfortable little estate. With the change in his fortunes he completely changed his principles, or at least his practice. In all his dealings he was now strictly honest. He lent money, it is true, at from ten to fifteen per cent, but that was considered in these parts not a very exorbitant rate of interest, nor was he unnecessarily hard upon his debtors.

It may seem strange that an honorable man like the General should receive in his house such a motley company, including men of decidedly tarnished reputation; but in this respect he was not at all peculiar. One used constantly to meet in Russian provincial society men who were known to be habitually guilty of corrupt practices; and the honest, respectable landed proprietor had no scruples about associating with such neighbors on friendly terms. This social leniency, moral laxity, or whatever else it may be called, was the result of various causes. Several concurrent influences had tended to lower the moral standard of the Noblesse. So long as serfage existed, the noble who lived on his estate could play with impunity the petty tyrant, and could freely indulge his legitimate and illegitimate caprices without any legal or moral restraint. I do not at all mean to assert that all proprietors abused their authority, but I venture to say that no class of men can long possess such enormous arbitrary power over those around them without being thereby more or less demoralized. When the noble entered the service he had not the same immunity from restraint—on the contrary, his position resembled rather that of the serf—but he breathed an atmosphere of peculation and jobbery, little conducive to moral purity and uprightness. If an official had refused to associate with those who were tainted with the prevailing vices, he would have found himself completely isolated, and would have been ridiculed as a modern Don Quixote. Add to this that all classes of the Russian people have a certain kindly, apathetic good nature which makes them very charitable towards their neighbors, and that they do not always distinguish between forgiving private injury and excusing public delinquencies. If we bear all this in mind, we may readily understand that in the time of serfage and maladministration a man could be guilty of very reprehensible practices without incurring social excommunication.

During the period of moral awakening after the Crimean War, society suddenly changed its tune, reveled in virtuous indignation against the prevailing abuses, and placed on the pillory the most prominent delinquents; but the intensity of the moral feeling soon declined, and something of the old apathy returned. This might have been predicted by anyone well acquainted with the character and past history of the Russian people. Russia advances on the road of progress not in that smooth, gradual, prosaic way to which we are accustomed, but by a series of unconnected, frantic efforts, each of which is naturally followed by a period of temporary exhaustion.

CHAPTER VIII

Proprietors of the Modern School

HITHERTO I have presented to the reader old-fashioned types which were common enough when I first resided in Russia, but which are rapidly disappearing. Let me now present a few of the modern school.

In the same district as Ivan Ivan'ich and the General lives Victor Alexandr'ich L——. As we approach his house we can at once perceive that he differs from the majority of his neighbors. The gate is painted and moves easily on its hinges, the fence is in good repair, the short avenue leading up to the front door is well kept, and in the garden we can perceive at a glance that more attention is paid to flowers than to vegetables. The house is of wood, and not large, but it has some architectural pretensions in the form of a great, pseudo-Doric wooden portico that covers three-fourths of the façade. In the interior we remark everywhere the influence of Western civilization. Victor Alexandr'ich is by no means richer than Ivan Ivan'ich, but his rooms are much more luxuriously furnished. The furniture is of a lighter model, more comfortable, and in a much better state of preservation. Instead of the bare, scantily furnished sitting room, with the old-fashioned barrel organ which played only six airs, we find an elegant drawing room, with a piano by one of the most approved makers, and numerous articles of foreign manufacture, including a small buhl table and two bits of genuine old Wedgwood. The servants are clean, and dressed in European costume. The master, too, is very different in appearance. He pays great attention to his toilette, wearing a dressing gown only in the early morning, and a fashionable lounging coat during the rest of the day. The Turkish pipes which his grandfather loved he holds in abhorrence, and habitually smokes cigarettes. With his wife and daughters he always speaks French, and calls them by French or English names.

But the part of the house which most strikingly illustrates the difference between old and new is "le cabinet de monsieur." In the cabinet of Ivan Ivan'ich the furniture consists of a broad sofa which serves as a bed, a few deal chairs, and a clumsy deal table, on which are generally to be found a bundle of greasy papers, an old chipped ink bottle, a pen, and a calendar. The cabinet of Victor Alexandr'ich has an entirely different appearance. It is small, but at once comfortable and elegant. The principal objects which it contains are a library table, with inkstand, presse-papier, paper knives, and other articles in keeping, and in the opposite corner a large bookcase. The collection of books is remarkable, not from the number of volumes or the presence of rare editions, but from the variety of the subjects. History, art, fiction, the drama, political economy, and agriculture are represented in about equal proportions. Some of the works are in Russian, others in German, a large number in French, and a few in Italian. The collection illustrates the former life and present occupations of the owner.

The father of Victor Alexandr'ich was a landed proprietor, who had made a successful career in the civil service, and desired that his son should follow the same profession. For this purpose Victor was first carefully trained at home, and then sent to the University of Moscow, where he spent four years as a student of law. From the University he passed to the Ministry of the Interior in St. Petersburg, but he found the monotonous routine of official life not at all suited to his taste, and very soon sent in his resignation. The death of his father had made him proprietor of an estate, and thither he retired, hoping to find plenty of occupation more congenial than the writing of official papers.

At the University of Moscow he had attended lectures
on history and philosophy, and had got through a large
amount of desultory reading. The chief result of his studies
was the acquisition of many ill-digested general principles, and certain vague, generous, humanitarian aspirations. With this intellectual capital he hoped to lead a
useful life in the country. When he had repaired and
furnished the house he set himself to improve the estate.
In the course of his promiscuous reading he had stumbled
on some descriptions of English and Tuscan agriculture,
and had there learned what wonders might be effected
by a rational system of farming. Why should not Russia
follow the example of England and Tuscany? By proper
drainage, plentiful manure, good ploughs, and the cultivation of artificial grasses, the production might be
multiplied tenfold; and by the introduction of agricultural machines the manual labor might be greatly diminished. All this seemed as simple as a sum in arithmetic,
and Victor Alexandr'ich, *more scholarium rei familiaris
ignarus,* without a moment's hesitation expended his
ready money in procuring from England a threshing machine, ploughs, harrows, and other implements of the
newest model.

The arrival of these was an event that was long remembered. The peasants examined them with attention,
not unmixed with wonder, but said nothing. When the
master explained to them the advantages of the new instruments, they still remained silent. Only one old man,
gazing at the threshing machine, remarked, in an audible
"aside," "A cunning people these Germans!" [1] On being
asked for their opinion, they replied vaguely, "How
should we know? It *ought* to be so." But when their
master had retired, and was explaining to his wife and
the French governess that the chief obstacle to progress
in Russia was the apathetic indolence and conservative
spirit of the peasantry, they expressed their opinions more

[1] The Russian peasant comprehends all the inhabitants of
Western Europe under the term Nyemtsi, which in the language
of the educated designates only Germans. The rest of humanity
is composed of Pravoslavniye (Greek Orthodox), Busurmanye
(Mahometans), and Poliacki (Poles).

freely. "These may be all very well for the Germans, but
they won't do for us. How are our little horses to drag
these big ploughs? And as for that (the threshing machine), it's of no use." Further examination and reflection
confirmed this first impression, and it was unanimously
decided that no good would come of the newfangled inventions.

These apprehensions proved to be only too well founded.
The ploughs were much too heavy for the peasants' small
horses, and the threshing machine broke down at the first
attempt to use it. For the purchase of lighter implements
or stronger horses there was no ready money, and for the
repairing of the threshing machine there was not an engi-
neer within a radius of a hundred and fifty miles. The experiment was, in short, a complete failure, and the new
purchases were put away out of sight.

For some weeks after this incident Victor Alexandr'ich
felt very despondent, and spoke more than usual about the
apathy and stupidity of the peasantry. His faith in infallible science was somewhat shaken, and his benevolent
aspirations were for a time laid aside. But this eclipse of
faith was not of long duration. Gradually he recovered
his normal condition, and began to form new schemes.
From the study of certain works on political economy he
learned that the system of Communal property was ruinous to the fertility of the soil, and that free labor was
always more productive than serfage. By the light of these
principles he discovered why the peasantry in Russia were
so poor, and by what means their condition could be
ameliorated. The Communal land should be divided into
family lots, and the serfs, instead of being forced to work
for the proprietor, should pay a yearly sum as rent. The
advantages of this change he perceived clearly—as clearly
as he had formerly perceived the advantages of English
agricultural implements—and he determined to make the
experiment on his own estate.

His first step was to call together the more intelligent
and influential of his serfs, and to explain to them his
project; but his efforts at explanation were eminently unsuccessful. Even with regard to ordinary current affairs
he could not express himself in that simple, homely

language with which alone the peasants are familiar, and when he spoke on abstract subjects he naturally became quite unintelligible to his uneducated audience. The serfs listened attentively, but understood nothing. He might as well have spoken to them, as he often did in another kind of society, about the comparative excellence of Italian and German music. At a second attempt he had rather more success. The peasants came to understand that what he wished was to break up the *Mir*, or Rural Commune, and to put them all "on *obrok*"—that is to say, make them pay a yearly sum instead of giving them a certain amount of agricultural labor. Much to his astonishment, his scheme did not meet with any sympathy. As to being put "on *obrok*," the serfs did not much object, though they preferred to remain as they were; but his proposal to break up the *Mir* astonished and bewildered them. They regarded it as a sea captain might regard the proposal of a scientific wiseacre to knock a hole in the ship's bottom in order to make her sail faster. Though they did not say much, he was intelligent enough to see that they would offer a strenuous passive resistance, and as he did not wish to act tyrannically, he let the matter drop. Thus a second benevolent scheme was shipwrecked. Many other schemes had a similar fate, and Victor Alexandr'ich began to perceive that it was very difficult to do good in this world, especially when the persons to be benefited were Russian peasants.

In reality the fault lay less with the serfs than with their master. Victor Alexandr'ich was by no means a stupid man. On the contrary, he had more than average talents. Few men were more capable of grasping a new idea and forming a scheme for its realization, and few men could play more dexterously with abstract principles. What he wanted was the power of dealing with concrete facts. The principles which he had acquired from University lectures and desultory reading were far too vague and abstract for practical use. He had studied abstract science without gaining any technical knowledge of details, and consequently when he stood face to face with real life he was like a student who, having studied mechanics in textbooks, is suddenly placed in a workshop and ordered to construct a machine. Only there was one difference: Victor Alexandr'ich was not ordered to do anything. Voluntarily, without any apparent necessity, he set himself to work with tools which he could not handle. It was this that chiefly puzzled the peasants. Why should he trouble himself with these new schemes, when he might live comfortably as he was? In some of his projects they could detect a desire to increase the revenue, but in others they could discover no such motive. In these latter they attributed his conduct to pure caprice, and put it into the same category as those mad pranks in which proprietors of jovial humor sometimes indulged.

In the last years of serfage there were a good many landed proprietors like Victor Alexandr'ich—men who wished to do something beneficent, and did not know how to do it. When serfage was being abolished the majority of these men took an active part in the great work and rendered valuable service to their country. Victor Alexandr'ich acted otherwise. At first he sympathized warmly with the proposed emancipation and wrote several articles on the advantages of free labor, but when the Government took the matter into its own hands he declared that the officials had deceived and slighted the Noblesse, and he went over to the Opposition. Before the Imperial Edict was signed he went abroad, and traveled for three years in Germany, France, and Italy. Shortly after his return he married a pretty, accomplished young lady, the daughter of an eminent official in St. Petersburg, and since that time he has lived in his country house.

Though a man of education and culture, Victor Alexandr'ich spends his time in almost as indolent a way as the men of the old school. He rises somewhat later, and instead of sitting by the open window and gazing into the courtyard, he turns over the pages of a book or periodical. Instead of dining at midday and supping at nine o'clock, he takes *déjeuner* at twelve and dines at five. He spends less time in sitting on the veranda and pacing up and down with his hands behind his back, for he can vary the operation of time-killing by occasionally writing a letter, or by standing behind his wife at the piano while she plays selections from Mozart and Beethoven. But these peculiarities are merely variations in detail. If there is any essential difference between the lives of Victor Alexandr'-ich and of Ivan Ivan'ich, it is in the fact that the former never goes out into the fields to see how the work is done, and never troubles himself with the state of the weather, the condition of the crops, and cognate subjects. He leaves the management of his estate entirely to his steward, and refers to that personage all peasants who come to him with complaints or petitions. Though he takes a deep interest in the peasant as an impersonal, abstract entity, and loves to contemplate concrete examples of the genus in the works of certain popular authors, he does not like to have any direct relations with peasants in the flesh. If he has to speak with them he always feels awkward, and in winter he suffers from the odor of their sheepskins. Ivan Ivan'ich is ever ready to talk with the peasants, and give them sound, practical advice or severe admonitions; and in the old times he was apt, in moments of irritation, to supplement his admonitions by a free use of his fists. Victor Alexandr'ich, on the contrary, never could give any advice except vague commonplaces, and as to using his fists, he would have shrunk from that, not only from respect to humanitarian principles, but also from motives which belong to the region of aesthetic sensitiveness.

This difference between the two men has an important influence on their pecuniary affairs. The stewards of both steal from their masters; but that of Ivan Ivan'ich steals with difficulty, and to a very limited extent, whereas that of Victor Alexandr'ich steals regularly and methodically, and counts his gains, not by kopeks, but by rubles. Though the two estates are of about the same size and value, they give a very different revenue. The rough, practical man has a much larger income than his elegant, well-educated neighbor, and at the same time spends very much less. The consequences of this, if not at present visible, must some day become painfully apparent. Ivan Ivan'ich will doubtless leave to his children an unencumbered estate and a certain amount of capital. The children of Victor Alexandr'ich have a different prospect. He has already begun to mortgage his property and to cut down the timber, and he always finds a deficit at the end of the year. What will become of his wife and children when the estate comes to be sold for payment of the mortgage, it is difficult to predict. He thinks very little of that eventuality, and when his thoughts happen to wander in that direction, he consoles himself with the thought that before the crash comes he will have inherited a fortune from a rich uncle who has no children.

The proprietors of the old school lead the same uniform, monotonous life year after year, with very little variation. Victor Alexandr'ich, on the contrary, feels the need of a periodical return to "civilized society," and accordingly spends a few weeks every winter in St. Petersburg. During the summer months he has the society of his brother —*un homme tout à fait civilisé*—who possesses an estate a few miles off.

This brother, Vladimir Alexandr'ich, was educated in the School of Law in St. Petersburg, and has since risen rapidly in the service. He holds now a prominent position in one of the Ministries, and has the honorary Court title of "Chambellan de sa Majesté." He is a marked man in the higher circles of the Administration, and will, it is thought, some day become Minister. Though an adherent of enlightened views, and a professed "Liberal," he contrives to keep on very good terms with those who imagine themselves to be "Conservatives." In this he is assisted by his soft, oily manner. If you express an opinion to him he will always begin by telling you that you are quite right; and if he ends by showing you that you are quite wrong, he will at least make you feel that your error is not only excusable, but in some way highly creditable to your intellectual acuteness or goodness of heart. In spite of his Liberalism he is a staunch Monarchist, and considers that the time has not yet come for the Emperor to grant a Constitution. He recognizes that the present order of things has its defects, but thinks that, on the whole, it acts very well, and would act much better if certain high officials were removed, and more energetic men put in their places. Like all genuine St. Petersburg *chinóvniks* (officials), he has great faith in the miraculous power of Imperial ukases and Ministerial circulars, and believes that national progress consists in multiplying these documents, and cen-

tralizing the Administration, so as to give them more effect. As a supplementary means of progress he highly ap-
proves of aesthetic culture, and he can speak with some
eloquence on the humanizing influence of the fine arts.
For his own part he is well acquainted with French and
English classics, and particularly admires Macaulay, whom
he declares to have been not only a great writer, but also
a great statesman. Among writers of fiction he gives the
palm to George Eliot, and speaks of the novelists of his
own country, and, indeed, of Russian literature as a
whole, in the most disparaging terms.

A very different estimate of Russian literature is held
by Alexander Ivan'ich N——, formerly arbiter in peasant
affairs, and afterwards justice of the peace. Discussions
on this subject often take place between the two. The
admirer of Macaulay declares that Russia has, properly
speaking, no literature whatever, and that the works
which bear the names of Russian authors are nothing but a
feeble echo of the literature of Western Europe. "Imitators," he is wont to say, "skilful imitators, we have produced in abundance. But where is there a man of original
genius? What is our famous poet Zhukóvski? A translator.
What is Pushkin? A clever pupil of the romantic school.
What is Lermontov? A feeble imitator of Byron. What is
Gógol?"

At this point Alexander Ivan'ich invariably intervenes.
He is ready to sacrifice all the pseudo-classic and romantic
poetry, and, in fact, the whole of Russian literature an-
terior to about the year 1840, but he will not allow anything disrespectful to be said of Gógol, who about that
time founded the Russian realistic school. "Gógol," he
holds, "was a great and original genius. Gógol not only
created a new kind of literature; he at the same time transformed the reading public, and inaugurated a new era in
the intellectual development of the nation. By his humor-
ous, satirical sketches he swept away the metaphysical
dreaming and foolish romantic affectation then in fashion,
and taught men to see their country as it was, in all its
hideous ugliness. With his help the young generation perceived the rottenness of the Administration, and the
meanness, stupidity, dishonesty, and worthlessness of the

landed proprietors, whom he made the special butt of his ridicule. The recognition of defects produced a desire for reform. From laughing at the proprietors there was but one step to despising them, and when we learned to despise the proprietors we naturally came to sympathize with the serfs. Thus the Emancipation was prepared by the literature; and when the great question had to be solved, it was the literature that discovered a satisfactory solution."

This is a subject on which Alexander Ivan'ich feels very strongly, and on which he always speaks with warmth. He knows a good deal regarding the intellectual movement which began about 1840, and culminated in the great reforms of the sixties. As a University student he troubled himself very little with serious academic work, but he read with intense interest all the leading periodicals, and adopted the doctrine of Belinski that art should not be cultivated for its own sake, but should be made subservient to social progress. This belief was confirmed by a perusal of some of George Sand's earlier works, which were for him a kind of revelation. Social questions engrossed his thoughts, and all other subjects seemed puny by comparison. When the Emancipation question was raised he saw an opportunity of applying some of his theories, and threw himself enthusiastically into the new movement as an ardent abolitionist. When the law was passed he helped to put it into execution by serving for three years as an Arbiter of the Peace. Now he is an old man, but he has preserved some of his youthful enthusiasm, attends regularly the annual assemblies of the Zemstvo, and takes a lively interest in all public affairs.

As an ardent partisan of local self-government he habitually scoffs at the centralized bureaucracy, which he proclaims to be the great bane of his unhappy country. "These chinóvniks," he is wont to say in moments of excitement, "who live in St. Petersburg and govern the Empire, know about as much of Russia as they do of China. They live in a world of official documents, and are hopelessly ignorant of the real wants and interests of the people. So long as all the required formalities are duly observed they are perfectly satisfied. The people may be allowed to die of starvation if only the fact do not appear in the official reports. Powerless to do any good themselves, they are powerful enough to prevent others from working for the public good, and are extremely jealous of all private initiative. How have they acted, for instance, towards the Zemstvo? The Zemstvo is really a good institution, and might have done great things if it had been left alone, but as soon as it began to show a little independent energy the officials at once clipped its wings and then strangled it. Towards the press they have acted in the same way. They are afraid of the press, because they fear above all things a healthy public opinion, which the press alone can create. Everything that disturbs the habitual routine alarms them. Russia cannot make any real progress so long as she is ruled by these cursed chinóvniks."

Scarcely less pernicious than the *chinóvnik*, in the eyes of our would-be reformer, is the *barich*—that is to say, the pampered, capricious, spoiled child of mature years, whose life is spent in elegant indolence and fine talking. Our friend Victor Alexandr'ich is commonly selected as a representative of this type. "Look at him!" exclaims Alexander Ivan'ich. "What a useless, contemptible member of society! In spite of his generous aspirations he never succeeds in doing anything useful to himself or to others. When the peasant question was raised and there was work to be done, he went abroad and talked Liberalism in Paris and Baden-Baden. Though he reads, or at least professes to read, books on agriculture, and is always ready to discourse on the best means of preventing the exhaustion of the soil, he knows less of farming than a peasant boy of twelve, and when he goes into the fields he can hardly distinguish rye from oats. Instead of babbling about German and Italian music, he would do well to learn a little about practical farming, and look after his estate."

Whilst Alexander Ivan'ich thus censures his neighbors, he is himself not without detractors. Some staid old proprietors regard him as a dangerous man, and quote expressions of his which seem to indicate that his notions of property are somewhat loose. Many consider that his Liberalism is of a very violent kind, and that he has strong republican sympathies. In his decisions as Justice he often leaned, it is said, to the side of the peasants against the proprietors. Then he was always trying to induce the peasants of the neighboring villages to found schools, and he had wonderful ideas about the best method of teaching children. These and similar facts make many people believe that he has very advanced ideas, and one old gentleman habitually calls him—half in joke and half in earnest —"our friend the Communist."

In reality Alexander Ivan'ich has nothing of the communist about him. Though he loudly denounces the *chinóvnik* spirit—or, as we should say, red-tape in all its forms—and is an ardent partisan of local self-government, he is one of the last men in the world to take part in any revolutionary movement. He would like to see the Central Government enlightened and controlled by public opinion and by a national representation, but he believes that this can only be effected by voluntary concessions on the part of the autocratic power. He has, perhaps, a sentimental love of the peasantry, and is always ready to advocate its interests; but he has come too much in contact with individual peasants to accept those idealized descriptions in which some popular writers indulge, and it may safely be asserted that the accusation of his voluntarily favoring peasants at the expense of proprietors is wholly unfounded. Alexander Ivan'ich is, in fact, a quiet, sensible man, who is capable of generous enthusiasm, and is not at all satisfied with the existing state of things; but he is not a dreamer and a *révolutionnaire,* as some of his neighbors assert.

I am afraid I cannot say as much for his younger brother Nikolaï, who lives with him. Nikolaï Ivan'ich is a tall, slender man, about sixty years of age, with emaciated face, bilious complexion and long black hair—evidently a person of excitable, nervous temperament. When he speaks he articulates rapidly, and uses more gesticulation than is common among his countrymen. His favorite subject of conversation, or rather of discourse, for he more frequently preaches than talks, is the lamentable state of the country and the worthlessness of the Government. Against the Government he has a great many causes for complaint, and one or two of a personal kind. In 1861 he was a student in

the University of St. Petersburg. At that time there was a
great deal of public excitement all over Russia, and especially in the capital. The serfs had just been emancipated, and other important reforms had been undertaken.
There was a general conviction among the young generation—and it must be added among many older men—that
the autocratic, paternal system of government was at an
end, and that Russia was about to be reorganized according to the most advanced principles of political and social
science. The students, sharing this conviction, wished to be
freed from all academic authority, and to organize a kind
of academic self-government. They desired especially the
right of holding public meetings for the discussion of their
common affairs. The authorities would not allow this, and
issued a list of rules prohibiting meetings and raising the
class fees, so as practically to exclude many of the poorer
students. This was felt to be a wanton insult to the spirit of
the new era. In spite of the prohibition, indignation meetings were held, and fiery speeches made by male and female orators, first in the classrooms, and afterwards in the
courtyard of the University. On one occasion a long procession marched through the principal streets to the house
of the Curator. Never had such a spectacle been seen before in St. Petersburg. Timid people feared that it was the
commencement of a revolution, and dreamed about barri-
cades. At last the authorities took energetic measures;
about 300 students were arrested, and of these, thirty-two
were expelled from the University.

Among those who were expelled was Nikolaï Ivan'ich.
All his hopes of becoming a professor as he had intended
were thereby shipwrecked, and he had to look out for
some other profession. A literary career now seemed the
most promising, and certainly the most congenial to his
tastes. It would enable him to gratify his ambition of being
a public man, and give him opportunities of attacking and
annoying his persecutors. He had already written occasionally for one of the leading periodicals, and now he became a regular contributor. His stock of positive knowledge was not very large, but he had the power of writing
fluently and of making his readers believe that he had an
unlimited store of political wisdom which the press-censure

prevented him from publishing. Besides this, he had the talent of saying sharp, satirical things about those in authority, in such a way that even a press censor could not easily raise objections. Articles written in this style were sure at that time to be popular, and his had a very great success. He became a known man in literary circles, and for a time all went well. But gradually he became less cautious, whilst the authorities became more vigilant. Some copies of a violent seditious proclamation fell into the hands of the police, and it was generally believed that the document proceeded from the coterie to which he belonged. From that moment he was carefully watched, till one night he was unexpectedly roused from his sleep by a gendarme and conveyed to the fortress.

When a man is arrested in this way for a real or supposed political offense, there are two modes of dealing with him: he may be tried before a regular tribunal, or he may be dealt with "by administrative procedure" (*administrativnym poryadkom*). In the former case he will, if convicted, be condemned to imprisonment for a certain term; or, if the offense be of a graver nature, he may be transported to Siberia either for a fixed period or for life. By the administrative procedure he is simply removed without a trial to some distant town, and compelled to live there under police supervision during his Majesty's pleasure. Nikolaï Ivan'ich was treated "administratively," because the authorities, though convinced that he was a dangerous character, could not find sufficient evidence to procure his conviction before a court of justice. For five years he lived under police supervision in a small town near the White Sea, and then one day he was informed, without any explanation, that he might go and live anywhere he pleased except in St. Petersburg and Moscow.

Since that time he has lived with his brother, and spends his time in brooding over his grievances and bewailing his shattered illusions. He has lost none of that fluency which gained him an ephemeral literary reputation, and can speak by the hour on political and social questions to anyone who will listen to him. It is extremely difficult, however, to follow his discourses, and utterly impossible to retain them in the memory. They belong to what may be called political metaphysics—for though he professes to hold metaphysics in abhorrence, he is himself a thorough metaphysician in his modes of thought. He lives, indeed, in a world of abstract conceptions, in which he can scarcely perceive concrete facts, and his arguments are always a kind of clever juggling with such equivocal, conventional terms as aristocracy, *bourgeoisie*, monarchy, and the like. At concrete facts he arrives, not directly by observation, but by deductions from general principles, so that his facts can never by any possibility contradict his theories. Then he has certain axioms which he tacitly assumes, and on which all his arguments are based; as, for instance, that everything to which the term "Liberal" can be applied must necessarily be good at all times and under all conditions.

Among a mass of vague conceptions which it is impossible to reduce to any clearly defined form he has a few ideas which are perhaps not strictly true, but which are at least intelligible. Among these is his conviction that Russia has let slip a magnificent opportunity of distancing all Europe on the road of progress. She might, he thinks, at the time of the Emancipation, have boldly accepted all the most advanced principles of political and social science, and have completely reorganized the political and social structure in accordance with them. Other nations could not take such a step, because they are old and decrepit, filled with stubborn, hereditary prejudices, and cursed with an aristocracy and a *bourgeoisie;* but Russia is young, knows nothing of social castes, and has no deep-rooted prejudices to contend with. The population is like potter's clay, which can be made to assume any form that science may recommend. Alexander II began a magnificent sociological experiment, but he stopped halfway.

Some day, he believes, the experiment will be completed, but not by the autocratic power. In his opinion, autocracy is "played out," and must give way to Parliamentary institutions. For him a Constitution is a kind of omnipotent fetish. You may try to explain to him that a Parliamentary regime, whatever its advantages may be, necessarily produces political parties and political conflicts, and is not nearly so suitable for grand sociological experiments as a good paternal despotism. You may try to convince him that, though it may be difficult to convert an autocrat, it is infinitely more difficult to convert a House of Commons. But all your efforts will be in vain. He will assure you that a Russian Parliament would be something quite different from what Parliaments commonly are. It would contain no parties, for Russia has no social castes, and would be guided entirely by scientific considerations—as free from prejudice and personal influences as a philosopher speculating on the nature of the Infinite! In short, he evidently imagines that a national Parliament would be composed of himself and his friends, and that the nation would calmly submit to their ukases as it has hitherto submitted to the ukases of the Tsars.

Pending the advent of this political millennium, when unimpassioned science is to reign supreme, Nikolaï Ivan-'ich allows himself the luxury of indulging in some very decided political animosities, and he hates with the fervor of a fanatic. Firstly and chiefly, he hates what he calls the *bourgeoisie*—he is obliged to use the French word, because his native language does not contain an equivalent term—and especially capitalists of all sorts and dimensions. Next, he hates aristocracy, especially a form of aristocracy called Feudalism. To these abstract terms he does not attach a very precise meaning, but he hates the entities which they are supposed to represent quite as heartily as if they were personal enemies. Among the things which he hates in his own country, the autocratic power holds the first place. Next as an emanation from the autocratic power, come the *chinóvniks,* and especially the gendarmes. Then come the landed proprietors. Though he is himself a landed proprietor, he regards the class as cumberers of the ground, and thinks that all their land should be confiscated and distributed among the peasantry.

All proprietors have the misfortune to come under his sweeping denunciations, because they are inconsistent with his ideal of a peasant Empire, but he recognizes amongst them degrees of depravity. Some are simply obstructive, whilst others are actively prejudicial to the public welfare. Among these latter a special object of aversion is Prince S——, because he not only possesses very large estates, but at the same time has aristocratic pretensions, and calls himself a Conservative.

Prince S—— is by far the most important man in the district. His family is one of the oldest in the country; but he does not owe his influence to his pedigree, for pedigree pure and simple does not count for much in Russia. He is influential and respected because he is a great landholder with a high official position, and belongs by birth to that group of families which forms the permanent nucleus of the ever changing Court society. His father and grandfather were important personages in the administration and at Court, and his sons and grandsons will probably in this respect follow in the footsteps of their ancestors. Though in the eye of the law all nobles are equal, and, theoretically speaking, promotion is gained exclusively by personal merit, yet, in reality, those who have friends at Court rise more easily and more rapidly.

The Prince has had a prosperous but not very eventful life. He was educated, first at home, under an English tutor, and afterwards in the *Corps des Pages*. On leaving this institution he entered a regiment of the Guards, and rose steadily to high military rank. His activity, however, has been chiefly in the civil administration, and he now has a seat on the Council of State. Though he has always taken a certain interest in public affairs, he did not play an important part in any of the great reforms. When the peasant question was raised he sympathized with the idea of emancipation, but did not at all sympathize with the idea of giving land to the emancipated serfs and preserving the Communal institutions. What he desired was that the proprietors should liberate their serfs without any pecuniary indemnity, and should receive in return a certain share of political power. His scheme was not adopted, but he has not relinquished the hope that the great landed proprietors may somehow obtain a social and political position similar to that of the great landowners in England.

Official duties and social relations compel the Prince to live for a large part of the year in the capital. He spends only a few weeks yearly on his estate. The house is large, and fitted up in the English style, with a view to combining elegance and comfort. It contains several spacious apartments, a library, and a billiard room. There is an extensive park, an immense garden with hothouses, numerous horses and carriages, and a legion of servants. In the drawing room is a plentiful supply of English and French books, newspapers, and periodicals, including the *Journal de St. Pétersbourg*, which gives the news of the day. The family have, in short, all the conveniences and comforts which money and refinement can procure, but it cannot be said that they greatly enjoy the time spent in the country. The Princess has no decided objection to it. She is devoted to a little grandchild, is fond of reading and correspondence, amuses herself with a school and hospital which she has founded for the peasantry, and occasionally drives over to see her friend, the Countess N——, who lives about fifteen miles off.

The Prince, however, finds country life excessively dull. He does not care for riding or shooting, and he finds nothing else to do. He knows nothing about the management of his estate, and holds consultations with the steward merely *pro forma*—this estate, and the others which he possesses in different provinces, being ruled by a head steward in St. Petersburg, in whom he has the most complete confidence. In the vicinity there is no one with whom he cares to associate. Naturally he is not a sociable man, and he has acquired a stiff, formal, reserved manner that is rarely met with in Russia. This manner repels the neighboring proprietors—a fact that he does not at all regret, for they do not belong to his *monde,* and they have in their manners and habits a free-and-easy rusticity which is positively disagreeable to him. His relations with them are therefore confined to formal calls. The greater part of the day he spends in listless loitering, frequently yawning, regretting the routine of St. Petersburg life—the pleasant chats with his colleagues, the opera, the ballet, the French theater, and the quiet rubber at the Club Anglais. His spirits rise as the day of his departure approaches, and when he drives off to the station he looks bright and cheerful. If he consulted merely his own tastes he would never visit his estates at all, and would spend his summer holidays in Germany, France, or Switzerland, as he did in his bachelor days; but as a large landowner he considers it right to sacrifice his personal inclinations to the duties of his position.

There is, by the way, another princely magnate in the district, and I ought perhaps to introduce him to my readers, because he represents worthily a new type. Like Prince S——, of whom I have just spoken, he is a great landowner and a descendant of the half-mythical Rurik; but he has no official rank, and does not possess a single *grand cordon*. In that respect he has followed in the footsteps of his father and grandfather, who had something of the *frondeur* spirit, and preferred the position of a *grand seigneur* and a country gentleman to that of a *chinóvnik* and a courtier. In the Liberal camp he is regarded as a Conservative, but he has little in common with the Reactionaries (*Krepostniki*), who declare that the reforms of the last half-century were a mistake, that everything is going to the bad, that the emancipated serfs are all sluggards, drunkards, and thieves, that the local self-government is an ingenious machine for wasting money, and that the reformed law courts have conferred benefits only on the lawyers. On the contrary, he recognizes the necessity and beneficent results of the reforms, and with regard to the future he has none of the despairing pessimism of the incorrigible old Tory.

But in order that real progress should be made, he thinks that certain current and fashionable errors must be avoided, and among these errors he places, in the first rank, the views and principles of the advanced Liberals, who have a blind admiration for Western Europe, and for what they are pleased to call the results of science. Like the Liberals of the West, these gentlemen assume that the best form of government is constitutionalism, monarchical or republican, on a broad democratic basis, and towards the realization of this ideal all their efforts are directed. Not so our Conservative friend. While admitting that democratic parliamentary institutions may be the best form of government for the more advanced nations of the West, he maintains that the only firm foundation for the Russian Empire, and the only solid guarantee of its future prosperity, is the autocratic power, which is the sole genuine representative of the national spirit. Looking at the past from this point of view, he perceives that the Tsars have ever identified themselves with the nation, and have always understood, in part instinctively and in part by reflection, what the nation really required. Whenever the infiltration of Western ideas threatened to swamp the national individuality, the autocratic power intervened and averted the danger by timely precautions. Something of the kind may be observed, he believes, at present, when the Liberals are clamoring for extreme democratic institutions; but the autocratic power is on the alert, and will as usual do what is necessary.

With the efforts of the Zemstvo in this direction, and with the activity of the Zemstvo generally, the Prince has little sympathy, partly because the institution is in the hands of the Liberals and is guided by their unpractical ideas, and partly because it enables some ambitious outsiders to acquire the influence in local affairs which ought to be exercised by the old-established noble families of the district. What he would like to see is an enlightened, influential gentry working in conjunction with the autocratic power for the good of the country; but he recognizes that his ideal has little prospect of being realized.

The Prince belongs to the highest rank of the Russian Noblesse. If we wish to get an idea of the lowest rank, we can find in the neighborhood a number of poor, uneducated nobles, who live in small, squalid houses, and are not easily to be distinguished from peasants. In other parts of the country we might find men in this condition bearing the title of prince! This is the natural result of the Russian law of inheritance, which does not recognize the principle of primogeniture with regard to titles and estates.

CHAPTER IX

The Landed Proprietors
Since the Emancipation

WHEN the Emancipation question was raised there was a considerable diversity of opinion as to the effect which the abolition of serfage would have on the material interests of the two classes directly concerned. The press and "the young generation" took an optimistic view, and endeavored to prove that the proposed change would be beneficial alike to proprietors and to peasants. Science, it was said, has long since decided that free labor is immensely more productive than slavery or serfage, and the principle has been already proved by demonstration in the countries of Western Europe. In all those countries modern agricultural progress began with the emancipation of the serfs, and increased productivity was everywhere the immediate result of improvements in the methods of culture. Thus the poor, light soils of Germany, France, and Holland have been made to produce more than the vaunted "black earth" of Russia. And from these ameliorations the landowning class has everywhere derived the chief advantages. Are not the landed proprietors of England—the country in which serfage was first abolished—the richest in the world? And is not the proprietor of a few hundred *morgen* in Germany often richer than the Russian noble who has thousands of *dessyatins?*

By these and similar plausible arguments the press endeavored to prove to the proprietors that they ought, even in their own interest, to undertake the emancipation of the serfs. Many proprietors, however, showed little faith in the abstract principles of political economy and the vague teachings of history as interpreted by the contemporary periodical literature. They could not always refute the ingenious arguments adduced by the men of more sanguine temperament, but they felt convinced that their prospects were not nearly so bright as these men represented them to be. They believed that Russia was a peculiar country, and the Russians a peculiar people. The lower classes in England, France, Holland, and Germany were well known to be laborious and enterprising, while the Russian peasant was notoriously lazy, and would certainly, if left to himself, not do more work than was absolutely necessary to keep him from starving. Free labor might be more profitable than serfage in countries where the upper classes possessed traditional practical knowledge and abundance of capital, but in Russia the proprietors had neither the practical knowledge nor the ready money necessary to make the proposed ameliorations in the system of agriculture. To all this it was added that a system of emancipation by which the peasants should receive land and be made completely independent of the landed proprietors had nowhere been tried on such a large scale.

There were thus two diametrically opposite opinions regarding the economic results of the abolition of serfage, and we have now to examine which of these two opinions has been confirmed by experience.

Let us look at the question first from the point of view of the landowners.

The reader who has never attempted to make investigations of this kind may naturally imagine that the question can be easily decided by simply consulting a large number of individual proprietors, and drawing a general conclusion from their evidence. In reality I found the task much more difficult. After roaming about the country for five years (1870-75), collecting information from the best available sources, I hesitated to draw any sweeping conclusions, and my state of mind at that time was naturally reflected in the early editions of this work. As a rule the proprietors could not state clearly how much they had lost or gained, and when definite information was obtained from them, it was not always trustworthy. In the time of serfage very few of them had been in the habit of keeping accurate accounts, or accounts of any kind, and when they lived on their estates there were a very large number of items which could not possibly be reduced to figures. Of course, each proprietor had a general idea as to whether his position was better or worse than it had been in the old times, but the vague statements made by individuals regarding their former and their actual revenues had little or no scientific value. So many considerations which had nothing to do with purely agrarian relations entered into the calculations that the conclusions did not help me much to estimate the economic results of the Emancipation as a whole.

Nor, it must be confessed, was the testimony by any means always unbiased. Not a few spoke of the great reform in an epic or dithyrambic tone, and among these I easily distinguished two categories: the one desired to prove that the measure was a complete success in every way, and that all classes were benefited by it, not only morally, but also materially; whilst the others strove to represent the proprietors in general, and themselves in particular, as the self-sacrificing victims of a great and necessary patriotic reform—as martyrs in the cause of liberty and progress. I do not for a moment suppose that these two groups of witnesses had a clearly conceived intention of deceiving or misleading, but as a cautious investigator I had to make allowance for their idealizing and sentimental tendencies.

Since that time the situation has become much clearer, and during recent visits to Russia I have been able to arrive at much more definite conclusions. These I now proceed to communicate to the reader.

The Emancipation caused the proprietors of all classes to pass through a severe economic crisis. Periods of transition always involve much suffering, and the amount of suffering is generally in the inverse ratio of the precautions taken beforehand. In Russia the precautions had been neglected. Not one proprietor in a hundred had made any serious preparations for the inevitable change. On the eve of the Emancipation there were about 10,000,000 male serfs on private properties, and of these nearly 7,000,000 remained under the old system of paying their dues in labor. Of course, everybody knew that Emancipation must come sooner or later, but forethought, prudence, and readiness to take time by the forelock are not among the prominent traits of the Russian character. Hence most of the landowners were taken unawares. But while all suffered, there were differences of degree. Some were completely shipwrecked. So long as serfage existed all the relations of life were ill defined and extremely elastic, so that a man who was hopelessly insolvent might contrive, with very little effort, to keep his head above water for half a lifetime. For such men the Emancipation, like a crisis in the commercial world, brought a day of reckoning. It did not really ruin them, but it showed them and the world at large that they were ruined, and they could no longer continue their old mode of life. For others the crisis was merely temporary. These emerged with a larger income than they ever had before, but I am not prepared to say that their material condition has improved, because the social habits have changed, the cost of living has become much greater, and the work of administering estates is incomparably more complicated and laborious than in the old patriarchal times.

We may greatly simplify the problem by reducing it to two definite questions:

1. How far were the proprietors *directly* indemnified for the loss of serf labor and for the transfer in perpetual usufruct of a large part of their estates to the peasantry?

2. What have the proprietors done with the remainder of their estates, and how far have they been *indirectly* indemnified by the economic changes which have taken place since the Emancipation?

With the first of these questions I shall deal very briefly, because it is a controversial subject involving very complicated calculations which only a specialist can understand. The conclusion at which I have arrived, after much patient research, is that in most provinces the compensation was inadequate, and this conclusion is confirmed by excellent native authorities. M. Bekhteyev, for example, one of the most laborious and conscientious investigators in this field of research, and the author of an admirable work on the economic results of the Emancipation,[1] told me recently, in course of conversation, that in his opinion the peasant dues fixed by the Emancipation Law represented, throughout the Black-Earth Zone, only about a half of the value of the labor previously supplied by the serfs. To this I must add that the compensation was in reality not nearly so great as it seemed to be according to the terms of the law. As the proprietors found it extremely difficult to collect the dues from the emancipated serfs, and as they required a certain amount of capital to reorganize the estate on the new basis of free labor, most of them were practically compelled to demand the obligatory redemption of the land (*obiazátelny vuíkup*), and in adopting this expedient they had to make considerable sacrifices. Not only had they to accept as full payment four-fifths of the normal sum, but of this amount the greater portion was paid in Treasury bonds, which fell at once to 80 per cent of their nominal value.

Let us now pass to the second part of the problem: What have the proprietors done with the part of their estates which remained to them after ceding the required amount of land to the Communes? Have they been indirectly indemnified for the loss of serf labor by subsequent economic changes? How far have they succeeded in making the transition from serfage to free labor, and what revenues do they now derive from their estates? The answer to these questions will necessarily contain some account of the present economic position of the proprietors.

On all proprietors the Emancipation had at least one good effect: it dragged them forcibly from the old path of indolence and routine, and compelled them to think and calculate regarding their affairs. The hereditary listlessness and apathy, the traditional habit of looking on the estate with its serfs as a kind of self-acting machine which must always spontaneously supply the owner with the means of living, the inveterate practice of spending all ready money, and of taking little heed for the morrow—all this, with much that resulted from it, was rudely swept away and

[1] *Khozaistvenniye Itogi istekshago Sorokolêtiya.* St. Petersburg, 1902.

became a thing of the past. The broad, easy road on which
the proprietors had hitherto let themselves be borne along
by the force of circumstances suddenly split up into a
number of narrow, arduous, thorny paths. Each one had to
use his judgment to determine which of the paths he
should adopt, and, having made his choice, he had to
struggle along as he best could. I remember once asking a
proprietor what effect the Emancipation had had on the
class to which he belonged, and he gave me an answer
which is worth recording. "Formerly," he said, "we kept
no accounts and drank champagne; now we keep accounts and content ourselves with *kvass*." Like all epigrammatic sayings, this laconic reply is far from giving a complete description of reality, but it indicates in a graphic
way a change that has unquestionably taken place. As
soon as serfage was abolished it was no longer possible to
live like "the flowers of the field." Many a proprietor who
had formerly vegetated in apathetic ease had to ask himself the question: How am I now to gain a living? All had
to consider what was the most profitable way of employing the land that remained to them.

The ideal solution of the problem was that as soon as
the peasant land had been demarcated, the proprietor
should take to farming the remainder of his estate by
means of hired labor and agricultural machines in West
European or American fashion. Unfortunately, this solution could not be generally adopted, because the great
majority of the landlords, even when they had the requisite practical knowledge of agriculture, had not the requisite capital, and could not easily obtain it. Where were
they to find money for buying cattle, horses, and agricultural implements, for building stables and cattle sheds, and
for defraying all the other initial expenses? And supposing
they succeeded in starting the new system, where was the
working capital to come from? The old Government institution in which estates could be mortgaged according to the
number of serfs was permanently closed, and the new
land-credit associations had not yet come into existence.
To borrow from private capitalists was not to be thought
of, for money was so scarce that 10 per cent was considered a "friendly" rate of interest. Recourse might be

had, it is true, to the redemption operation, but in that
case the Government would deduct the unpaid portion of
any outstanding mortgage, and would pay the balance in
depreciated Treasury bonds. In these circumstances the
proprietors could not, as a rule, adopt what I have called
the ideal solution, and had to content themselves with
some simpler and more primitive arrangement. They could
employ the peasants of the neighboring villages to prepare
the land and reap the crops either for a fixed sum per acre
or on the *métayage* system, or they could let their land
to the peasants for one, three, or six years at a moderate
rent.

In the northern agricultural zone, where the soil is poor
and primitive farming with free labor can hardly be made
to pay, the proprietors had to let their land at a small rent,
and those of them who could not find places in the rural
administration migrated to the towns and sought employment in the public service or in the numerous commercial
and industrial enterprises which were springing up at that
time. There they have since remained. Their country
houses, if inhabited at all, are occupied only for a few
months in summer, and too often present a melancholy
spectacle of neglect and dilapidation. In the Black-Earth
Zone, on the contrary, where the soil still possesses enough
of its natural fertility to make farming on a large scale
profitable, the estates are in a very different condition. The
owners cultivate at least a part of their property, and can
easily let to the peasants at a fair rent the land which they
do not wish to farm themselves. Some have adopted the
métayage system; others get the field work done by the
peasants at so much per acre. The more energetic, who
have capital enough at their disposal, organize farms with
hired laborers on the European model. If they are not so
well off as formerly, it is because they have adopted a less
patriarchal and more expensive style of living. Their land
has doubled and trebled in value during the last thirty
years, and their revenues have increased, if not in proportion, at least considerably. In 1903 I visited a number of
estates in this region and found them in a very prosperous
condition, with agricultural machines of the English or
American types, an increasing variety in the rotation of

crops, greatly improved breeds of cattle and horses, and all the other symptoms of a gradual transition to a more intensive and more rational system of agriculture.

It must be admitted, however, that even in the Black-Earth Zone the proprietors have formidable difficulties to contend with, the chief of which are the scarcity of good farm laborers, the frequent droughts, the low price of cereals, and the delay in getting the grain conveyed to the seaports. On each of these difficulties and the remedies that might be applied I could write a separate chapter, but I fear to overtax the reader's patience, and shall therefore confine myself to a few remarks about the labor question. On this subject the complaints are loud and frequent all over the country. The peasants, it is said, have become lazy, careless, addicted to drunkenness, and shamelessly dishonest with regard to their obligations, so that it is difficult to farm even in the old primitive fashion, and impossible to introduce radical improvements in the methods of culture. In these sweeping accusations there is a certain amount of truth. That the muzhik, when working for others, exerts himself as little as possible; that he pays little attention to the quality of the work done; that he shows a reckless carelessness with regard to his employer's property; that he is capable of taking money in advance and failing to fulfill his contract; that he occasionally gets drunk; and that he is apt to commit certain acts of petty larceny when he gets the chance—all this is undoubtedly true, whatever biased theorists and sentimental peasant-worshipers may say to the contrary.[2]

It would be a mistake, however, to suppose that the fault is entirely on the side of the peasants, and equally erroneous to believe that the evils might be remedied, as

[2] Amongst themselves the peasants are not addicted to thieving, as is proved by the fact that they habitually leave their doors unlocked when the inmates of the house are working in the fields; but if the muzhik finds in the proprietor's farmyard a piece of iron or a bit of rope, or any of those little things that he constantly requires and has difficulty in obtaining, he is very apt to pick it up and carry it home. Gathering firewood in the landlord's forest he does not consider as theft, because "God planted the trees and watered them," and in the time of serfage he was allowed to supply himself with firewood in this way.

is often suggested, by greater severity on the part of the tribunals, or by an improved system of passports. Farming with free labor, like every other department of human activity, requires a fair amount of knowledge, judgment, prudence, and tact, which cannot be replaced by ingenious legislation or judicial severity. In engaging laborers or servants it is necessary to select them carefully and make such conditions that they feel it to be to their interest to fulfill their contract loyally. This is too often overlooked by the Russian landowners. From false views of economy they are inclined to choose the cheapest laborer without examining closely his other qualifications, or they take advantage of the peasant's pecuniary embarrassments and make with him a contract which it is hardly possible for him to fulfill. In spring, for instance, when his store of provisions is exhausted and he is being hard pressed by the tax collector, they supply him with rye meal or advance him a small sum of money on condition of his undertaking to do a relatively large amount of summer work. He knows that the contract is unfair to him, but what is he to do? He must get food for himself and his family, and a little ready money for his taxes, for the Communal authorities will probably sell his cow if he does not pay his arrears. In desperation he accepts the conditions and puts off the evil day—consoling himself with the reflection that perhaps (*avos'*) something may turn up in the meantime— but when the time comes for fulfilling his engagements the dilemma revives. According to the contract he ought to work nearly the whole summer for the proprietor; but he has his own land to attend to, and he has to make provision for the winter. In such circumstances the temptation to evade the terms of the contract is often too strong to be resisted.

In Russia, as in other countries, the principle holds true that for good labor a fair price must be paid. Several large proprietors of my acquaintance who habitually act on this principle assure me that they always obtain as much good labor as they require. I must add, however, that these fortunate proprietors have the advantage of possessing a comfortable amount of working capital, and are therefore not compelled, as so many of their less fortunate neighbors are, to manage their estates on the hand-to-mouth principle.

It is only, I fear, a minority of the landed proprietors that have grappled successfully with these and other difficulties of their position. As a class they are impoverished and indebted, but this state of things is not due entirely to serf emancipation. The indebtedness of the Noblesse is a hereditary peculiarity of much older date. By some authorities it is attributed to the laws of Peter the Great, by which all nobles were obliged to spend the best part of their lives in the military or civil service, and to leave the management of their estates to incompetent stewards. However that may be, it is certain that from the middle of the eighteenth century downwards the fact has frequently occupied the attention of the Government, and repeated attempts have been made to alleviate the evil. The Empress Elizabeth, Catherine II, Paul, Alexander I, Nicholas I, Alexander II, and Alexander III tried successively, as one of the older ukases expressed it, "to free the Noblesse from debt and from greedy moneylenders, and to prevent hereditary estates from passing into the hands of strangers." The means commonly adopted was the creation of mortgage banks founded and controlled by the Government for the purpose of advancing money to landed proprietors at a comparatively low rate of interest.

These institutions may have been useful to the few who desired to improve their estates, but they certainly did not cure, and rather tended to foster, the inveterate improvidence of the many. On the eve of the Emancipation the proprietors were indebted to the Government for the sum of 425 millions of rubles, and 69 per cent of their serfs were mortgaged. A portion of this debt was gradually extinguished by the redemption operation, so that in 1880 over 300 millions had been paid off, but in the meantime new debts were being contracted. In 1873-4 nine private land-mortgage banks were created, and there was such a rush to obtain money from them that their paper was a glut in the market, and became seriously depreciated. When the prices of grain rose in 1875-80 the mortgage debt was diminished, but when they began to fall in 1880 it again increased, and in 1881 it stood at 396 millions. As the rate of interest was felt to be very burdensome there was a strong feeling among the landed proprietors at that time that the Government ought to help them, and in 1883 the nobles of the province of Orel ventured to address the Emperor on the subject. In reply to the address, Alexander III, who had strong Conservative leanings, was graciously pleased to declare in an ukase that "it was really time to do something to help the Noblesse," and accordingly a new land-mortgage bank for the Noblesse was created. The favorable terms offered by it were taken advantage of to such an extent that in the first four years of its activity (1886-90) it advanced to the proprietors over 200 million rubles. Then came two famine years, and in 1894 the mortgage debt of the Noblesse in that and other credit establishments was estimated at 994 millions.

By means of mortgages some proprietors succeeded in weathering the storm, but many gave up the struggle in despair and migrated to the towns. During the first thirty years after the Emancipation 20,000 estates were sold, and the area of land owned by the Noblesse was thereby diminished by 30 per cent.

This "expropriation of the Noblesse," as it has been called, has gone on with ever increasing rapidity. During the first twenty years after the abolition of serfage (1861-81) the average amount of Noblesse land sold yearly was under one and a half million acres, and it rose steadily until 1906-8, when it reached an average of over three and a half millions. In the short period of these three years (1906-8) the proportion of land owned by nobles in Russia proper sank from 52.2 to 48 per cent of the whole area.

The downward movement indicated by these figures was naturally strongest among the landed proprietors of the barren northern regions, who were not in the habit of living on their estates. In the province of Olónets, for example, these gentlemen have divested themselves of about 90 per cent of their land, and consequently that kind of property has almost entirely disappeared. On the other hand, in the black-soil region, estates with resident proprietors are still plentiful, and there is no province in which more than 35 per cent of the Noblesse-land has been alienated. In one province of this region (Tula) the amount alienated is only about 19 per cent.

The habit of mortgaging and selling estates does not necessarily mean the impoverishment of the landlords as a class. If the capital raised in that way is devoted to agricultural improvements, the result may be an increase of wealth. Unfortunately, in Russia the realized capital was usually not so employed. A very large proportion of it was spent unproductively, partly in luxuries and living abroad, and partly in unprofitable commercial and industrial speculations. The industrial and railway fever which raged at the time induced many to risk and lose their capital, and it had indirectly an injurious effect on all by making money plentiful in the towns, and creating a more expensive style of living from which the landed gentry could not hold entirely aloof.

So far I have dwelt on the dark shadows of the picture, but it is not all shadow. In the last forty years the production and export of grain, which constitute the chief source of revenue for the landed proprietors, have increased enormously, thanks mainly to the improved means of transport. In the first decade after the Emancipation (1860-70) the average annual export of grain did not exceed one and a half million tons; in the second decade (1870-80) it leapt up to three and a half millions; in the last decade of the century it reached six millions; and in the latest period for which we have statistical data (1903-9) it was about eight millions, representing a value of fifty million pounds sterling. At the same time the home trade increased in consequence of the rapidly growing population of the towns. All this must have enriched the landed proprietors, and we can hardly suppose that the gains were all squandered on luxuries and unprofitable speculations.

The pessimists, however—and in Russia their name is legion—will not admit that any permanent advantage has been derived from this enormous increase in exports. On the contrary, they maintain that it is a national misfortune, because it is leading rapidly to a state of permanent impoverishment. It quickly exhausted, they say, the large reserves of grain in the villages, so that as soon as there was a very bad harvest the Government had to come to the rescue and feed the starving peasantry. Worse than this, it compromised the future prosperity of the country. Being in pecuniary difficulties, and consequently impatient to make money, the proprietors increased inordinately the area of grain-producing land at the expense of pasturage and forests, with the result that the livestock and the manuring of the land were diminished, the fertility of the soil impaired, and the necessary quantity of moisture in the atmosphere greatly lessened. There is some truth in this contention; but it would seem that the soil and climate have not been affected so much as the pessimists suppose, because in recent years there have been some very good harvests.

On the whole, then, I think it may be justly said that the efforts of the landed proprietors to work their estates without serf labor have not as yet been brilliantly successful. Those who have failed are in the habit of complaining that they have not received sufficient support from the Government, which is accused of having systematically sacrificed the interests of agriculture, the mainstay of the national resources, to the creation of artificial and unnecessary manufacturing industries. How far such complaints and accusations are well founded I shall not attempt to decide. It is a complicated polemical question, into which the reader would probably decline to accompany me. . . .

3 : *Urban Life*

CHAPTER X

The Towns and the Mercantile Classes

THOSE who wish to enjoy the illusions produced by scene painting and stage decorations should never go behind the scenes. In like manner he who wishes to preserve the delusion that Russian provincial towns are picturesque should never enter them, but content himself with viewing them from a distance.

However imposing they may look when seen from the outside, they will be found on closer inspection, with very few exceptions, to be little more than villages in disguise. If they have not a positively rustic, they have at least a suburban appearance. The streets are straight and wide, and are either miserably paved or not paved at all. *Trottoirs* are not considered indispensable. The houses are built of wood or brick, generally one-storied, and separated from each other by spacious yards. Many of them do not condescend to turn their façades to the street. The general impression produced is that the majority of the burghers have come from the country, and have brought their country houses with them. There are few or no shops with merchandise tastefully arranged in the window to tempt the passer-by. If you wish to make purchases you must go to the Gostinny Dvor,[1] or Bazaar, which consists of long

[1] These words mean literally the Guests' Court or Yard. The Gosti—a word which is etymologically the same as our "host" and "guest"—were originally the merchants who traded with other towns or other countries.

symmetrical rows of low-roofed, dimly lighted stores, with
a colonnade in front. This is the place where merchants
most do congregate, but it presents nothing of that bustle
and activity which we are accustomed to associate with
commercial life. The shopkeepers stand at their doors or
loiter about in the immediate vicinity waiting for custom-
ers. From the scarcity of these latter I should say that
when sales are effected the profits must be enormous.

In the other parts of the town the air of solitude and
languor is still more conspicuous. In the great square, or
by the side of the promenade—if the town is fortunate
enough to have one—cows or horses may be seen grazing
tranquilly, without being at all conscious of the incongruity of their position. And, indeed, it would be strange if
they had any such consciousness, for it does not exist in
the minds either of the police or of the inhabitants. At
night the streets may be lighted merely with a few oil
lamps, which do little more than render the darkness visible, so that cautious citizens returning home late often
provide themselves with lanterns. As late as the sixties the
learned historian, Pogódin, then a town councillor of Moscow, opposed the lighting of the city with gas on the
ground that those who chose to go out at night should
carry their lamps with them. The objection was overruled,
and Moscow is now fairly well lit, but the provincial towns
are still far from being on the same level. Some retain their
old primitive arrangements, while others enjoy the luxury
of electric lighting.

The scarcity of large towns in Russia is not less remarkable than their rustic appearance. According to the latest
statistics the number of towns, officially so-called, is 1,321,
but about three-fifths of them have under 5,000 inhabitants, only 104 have over 25,000, and only 19 over 100,000.
These figures indicate plainly that the urban element of
the population is relatively small, and it is declared by the
statisticians to be only 14 per cent, as against 72 per cent
in Great Britain; but it is now increasing. When the first
edition of this work was published, in 1877, European
Russia in the narrower sense of the term—excluding Finland, the Baltic Provinces, Lithuania, Poland, and the
Caucasus—had only eleven towns with a population of

over 50,000, and now there are thirty-five: that is to say, the number of such towns has more than trebled. In the other portions of the country a similar increase has taken place. The towns which have become important industrial and commercial centers have naturally grown most rapidly. For example, in a period of twelve years (1885-97) the populations of Lodz, of Ekaterinoslav, of Baku, of Yaroslavl, and of Libau, more than doubled. In the five largest towns of the Empire—St. Petersburg, Moscow, Warsaw, Odessa and Lodz—the aggregate population has risen during the last twenty-five years from 2,423,000 to over 5,000,000. In ten other thriving towns, with populations varying from 50,000 to 282,000, the recent increase in the number of inhabitants has been almost equally rapid.

That Russia should have taken so long to assimilate herself in this respect to Western Europe is to be explained by the geographical and political conditions. Her population was not hemmed in by natural or artificial frontiers strong enough to restrain their expansive tendencies. To the north, the east, and the southeast there was a boundless expanse of fertile, uncultivated land, offering a tempting field for emigration; and the peasantry have ever shown themselves ready to take advantage of their opportunities. Instead of improving their primitive system of agriculture, which requires an enormous area and rapidly exhausts the soil, they have always found it easier and more profitable to emigrate and take possession of the virgin land beyond. Thus the territory—sometimes with the aid of, and sometimes in spite of, the Government—has constantly expanded, and has already reached the Polar Ocean, the Pacific, and the northern offshoots of the Himalayas. The little district around the sources of the Dnieper has grown into a mighty empire, comprising one-seventh of the land surface of the globe. Prolific as the Russian race is, its powers of reproduction could not keep pace with its territorial expansion, and consequently the country is still very thinly peopled. According to the most recent statistics (1910), in the whole empire there are about 164 millions of inhabitants, and the average density of population is only about nineteen to the English square mile.

Even European Russia, which is, of course, much more densely populated than the Asiatic provinces, cannot show, as a whole, more than 63 to the English square mile, whereas the United Kingdom has about 374. A people that has such an abundance of land, and can support itself by agriculture, is naturally not disposed to devote itself to manufacturing industry and congregate largely in cities.

For many generations there were other powerful influences working in the same direction. Of these the most important was serfage, which was not abolished till 1861. That institution, and the administrative system of which it formed an essential part, tended to prevent the growth of the towns by hemming the natural movements of the population. Peasants, for example, who learned trades, and who ought to have drifted naturally into the burgher class, were mostly retained by the master on his estate, where artisans of all sorts were daily wanted, and the few who were sent to seek work in the towns were not allowed to settle there permanently.

Thus the insignificance of the Russian towns is to be attributed mainly to two causes. The abundance of land tended to prevent the development of industry, and the little industry which did exist was prevented by serfage from collecting in the towns. But this explanation is evidently incomplete. The same causes existed during the Middle Ages in Central Europe, and yet, in spite of them, flourishing cities grew up and played an important part in the social and political history of Germany. In these cities collected traders and artisans, forming a distinct social class, distinguished from the nobles on the one hand, and the surrounding peasantry on the other, by peculiar occupations, peculiar aims, peculiar intellectual physiognomy, and peculiar moral conceptions. Why did these important towns and this burgher class not likewise come into existence in Russia, in spite of the two preventive causes above mentioned?

To discuss this question fully it would be necessary to enter into certain debated points of medieval history. All I can do here is to indicate what seems to me the true explanation.

In Central Europe, all through the Middle Ages, a perpetual struggle went on between the various political factors of which society was composed, and the important towns were in a certain sense the products of this struggle. They were preserved and fostered by the mutual rivalry of the Sovereign, the feudal nobility, and the Church; and those who desired to live by trade or industry settled in them in order to enjoy the protection and immunities which they afforded. In Russia there was never any political struggle of this kind. As soon as the Grand Princes of Moscow, in the sixteenth century, threw off the yoke of the Tatars, and made themselves Tsars of all Russia, their power was irresistible and uncontested. Complete masters of the situation, they organized their country as they thought fit. At first their policy was favorable to the development of the towns. Perceiving that the mercantile and industrial classes might be made a rich source of revenue, they separated them from the peasantry, gave them the exclusive right of trading, prevented the other classes from competing with them, and freed them from the authority of the landed proprietors. Had they carried out this policy in a cautious, rational way, they might have created a rich burgher class; but they acted with true Oriental short-sightedness, and defeated their own purpose, by imposing inordinately heavy taxes, and treating the urban population as their serfs. The richer merchants were forced to serve as custom-house officers—often at a great distance from their domiciles[2]—and artisans were yearly summoned to Moscow to do work for the Tsars without remuneration.

Besides this, the system of taxation was radically defective and the members of the local administration, who received no pay and were practically free from control, were merciless in their exactions. In a word, the Tsars used their power so stupidly and so recklessly that the industrial and trading population, instead of fleeing to the towns to secure protection, fled from them to escape oppression. At length this emigration from the towns assumed such dimensions that it was found necessary to prevent it by

[2] Merchants from Yaroslavl, for instance, were sent to Astrakhan to collect the custom dues.

administrative and legislative measures; and the urban
population were legally fixed in the towns as the rural
population were fixed to the soil. Those who fled were
brought back as runaways, and those who attempted flight
a second time were ordered to be flogged and transported
to Siberia.[3]

With the eighteenth century began a new era in the
history of the towns and of the urban population. Peter
the Great observed, during his travels in Western Europe,
that national wealth and prosperity reposed chiefly on the
enterprising, educated middle classes, and he attributed
the poverty of his own country to the absence of this
burgher element. Might not such a class be created in
Russia? Peter unhesitatingly assumed that it might, and
set himself at once to create it in a simple, straightfor-
ward way. Foreign artisans were imported into his dominions, and foreign merchants were invited to trade with his
subjects; young Russians were sent abroad to learn the
useful arts; efforts were made to disseminate practical
knowledge by the translation of foreign books and the
foundation of schools; all kinds of trade were encouraged,
and various industrial enterprises were organized. At the
same time the administration of the towns was thoroughly
reorganized after the model of the ancient free towns of
Germany. In place of the old organization, which was a
slightly modified form of the rural Commune, they received German municipal institutions, with burgomasters,
town councils, courts of justice, guilds for the merchants,
trade corporations (*tsekhi*) for the artisans, and an endless list of instructions regarding the development of
trade and industry, the building of hospitals, sanitary precautions, the founding of schools, the dispensation of justice, the organization of the police, and similar matters.

Catherine II followed in the same track. If she did less
for trade and industry, she did more in the way of legislating and writing grandiloquent manifestoes. In the course
of her historical studies she had learned, as she proclaims
in one of her manifestoes, that "from remotest antiquity we
everywhere find the memory of town builders elevated to

[3] *See* the "Ulozhenié" (i.e. the laws of Alexis, father of Peter
the Great), cap. xix., § 13.

the same level as the memory of legislators, and we see that heroes, famous for their victories, hoped by town building to give immortality to their names." As the securing of immortality for her own name was her chief aim in life, she acted in accordance with historical precedent, and created 216 towns in the short space of twenty-three years. This seems a great work, but it did not satisfy her ambition. She was not only a student of history, but was at the same time a warm admirer of the fashionable political philosophy of her time. That philosophy paid much attention to the *tiers-état,* which was then acquiring in France great political importance, and Catherine thought that, as she had created a noblesse on the French model, she might also create a *bourgeoisie.* For this purpose she modified the municipal organization created by her great predecessor, and granted to all the towns an Imperial Charter. This charter remained without essential modification until the publication of the new Municipality Law in 1870.

The efforts of the Government to create a rich, intelligent *tiers-état* were not attended with much success. Their influence was always more apparent in official documents than in real life. The great mass of the population remained serfs, fixed to the soil, whilst the nobles—that is to say, all who possessed a little education—were required for the military and civil services. Those who were sent abroad to learn the useful arts learned little, and made little use of the knowledge which they acquired. On their return to their native country they very soon fell victims to the soporific influence of the surrounding social atmosphere. The "town building" had as little practical result. It was an easy matter to create any number of towns in the official sense of the term. To transform a village into a town, it was necessary merely to prepare an *izbá,* or log house, for the district court, another for the police office, a third for the prison, and so on. On an appointed day the Governor of the province arrived in the village, collected the officials appointed to serve in the newly constructed or newly arranged log houses, ordered a simple religious ceremony to be performed by the priest, caused a formal act to be drawn up, and then declared the town to be "opened." All this required very little creative effort; to

create a spirit of commercial and industrial enterprise
among the population was a more difficult matter, and
could not be effected by Imperial ukase.

To animate the newly imported municipal institutions,
which had no root in the traditions and habits of the people, was a task of equal difficulty. In the West these institutions had been slowly devised in the course of centuries to meet real, keenly felt, practical wants. In Russia
they were adopted for the purpose of creating those wants
which were not yet felt. Let the reader imagine our Board
of Trade supplying the masters of fishing smacks with accurate charts, learned treatises on navigation, and detailed
instructions for the proper ventilation of ships' cabins,
and he will have some idea of the effect which Peter's
legislation had upon the towns. The office bearers, elected
against their will, were hopelessly bewildered by the complicated procedure, and were incapable of understanding
the numerous ukases, which prescribed to them their
multifarious duties, and threatened the most merciless
punishments for sins of omission and commission. Soon,
however, it was discovered that the threats were not nearly
so dreadful as they seemed; and accordingly those municipal authorities who were to protect and enlighten the
burghers "forgot the fear of God and the Tsar," and ex-
torted so unblushingly that it was found necessary to place
them under the control of Government officials.

The chief practical result of the efforts made by Peter
and Catherine to create a *bourgeoisie* was that the inhabitants of the towns were more systematically arranged
in categories for the purpose of taxation, and that the
taxes were increased. All those parts of the new administration which had no direct relation to the fiscal interests
of the Government had very little vitality in them. The
whole system had been arbitrarily imposed on the people,
and had as motor only the Imperial will. Had that motor
power been withdrawn and the burghers left to regulate
their own municipal affairs, the system would immediately
have collapsed. *Rathhaus,* burgomasters, guilds, aldermen,
and all the other lifeless shadows which had been called
into existence by Imperial ukase, would instantly have
vanished into space. In this fact we have one of the

characteristic traits of Russian historical development compared with that of Western Europe. In the West, monarchy had to struggle with municipal institutions to prevent them from becoming too powerful; in Russia, it had to struggle with them to prevent them from committing suicide or dying of inanition.

According to Catherine's legislation, which remained in force until 1870, and still exists in some of its main features, the towns were divided into three categories: (1) government towns (*gubernskiye gorodá*)—that is to say, the chief towns of provinces or "governments" (*gubernii*)—in which are concentrated the various organs of provincial administration; (2) district towns (*uyezdniye gorodá*), in which resides the administration of the districts (*uyezdi*) into which the provinces are divided; and (3) supernumerary towns (*zashtatniye gorodá*), which have no particular significance in the territorial administration.

In all these the municipal organization is the same. Leaving out of consideration those persons who happen to reside in the towns but in reality belong to the noblesse, the clergy, or the lower ranks of officials, we may say that the town population is composed of three groups: the merchants (*kuptsi*), the burghers in the narrower sense of the term (*meshtchanye*), and the artisans (*tsekhoviye*). These categories are not hereditary castes, like the nobles, the clergy, and the peasantry. A noble may become a merchant, or a man may be one year a burgher, the next year an artisan, and the third year a merchant, if he changes his occupation and pays the necessary dues. But the categories form, for the time being, distinct corporations, each possessing a peculiar organization and peculiar privileges and obligations.

Of these three groups, the first in the scale of dignity is that of the merchants. It is chiefly recruited from the burghers and the peasantry. Anyone who wishes to engage in commerce inscribes himself in one of the three guilds, according to the amount of his capital and the nature of the operations in which he wishes to embark, and as soon as he has paid the required dues he becomes officially a merchant. As soon as he ceases to pay these dues he ceases to be a merchant in the legal sense of the term, and returns to the class to which he formerly belonged. There are some families whose members have belonged to the merchant class for several generations, and the law speaks about a certain "velvet book" (*bárkhatnaya kniga*) in which their names should be inscribed, but in reality they do not form a distinct category, and they descend at once from their privileged position as soon as they cease to pay the annual guild dues.

The artisans form the connecting link between the town population and the peasantry, for peasants often enrol themselves in the trades corporations or *tsekhi,* without severing temporarily their connection with the rural Communes to which they belong. Each trade or handicraft constitutes a *tsekh,* at the head of which stands an elder and two assistants, elected by the members; and all the *tsekhi* together form a corporation under an elected head (*Reméslenny Golová*), assisted by a council composed of the elders of the various *tsekhi.* It is the duty of this council and its president to regulate all matters connected with the *tsekhi,* and to see that the multifarious regulations regarding masters, journeymen, and apprentices are duly observed. So much for the theory; in reality, the *tsekhi* have been practically abolished by recent legislation.

The nondescript class, composed of those who are inscribed as permanent inhabitants of the towns but who do not belong to any guild or *tsekh,* constitutes what is called the burghers in the narrower sense of the term. Like the other two categories, they form a separate corporation with an elder and an administrative bureau.

Such is in theory the organization of the urban population; in reality it differs in different localities, and everywhere in recent years it has been slowly divesting itself of medieval forms and adapting itself to modern requirements.

In 1870 the entire municipal administration was reorganized, and the Town Council (*Gorodskáya Dúma*), which formed under the previous system the connecting link between the old-fashioned corporations, and was composed exclusively of members of these bodies, became a genuine representative body composed of householders, irrespective of the social class to which they might belong.

A noble, provided he was a house proprietor, could become Town Councillor or Mayor, and in this way a certain amount of vitality and a progressive spirit were infused into the municipal administration. As a consequence of this change the schools, hospitals, and other benevolent institutions were much improved, the streets were kept cleaner and somewhat better paved, and for a time it seemed as if the towns in Russia might gradually rise to the level of those of Western Europe. But the charm of novelty, which so often works wonders in Russia, soon wore off. After a few years of strenuous effort the best citizens no longer came forward as candidates, and the office bearers selected no longer displayed so much zeal and intelligence in the discharge of their duties.

In these circumstances the Government felt called upon again to intervene. By a decree dated 11th June, 1892, it introduced a new series of reforms, by which the municipal self-government was placed more under the direction and control of the centralized bureaucracy, and the attendance of the Town Councillors at the periodical meetings was declared to be obligatory, recalcitrant members being threatened with reprimands and fines.

This last fact speaks volumes for the low vitality of the institutions and the prevalent popular apathy with regard to municipal affairs. Nor was the unsatisfactory state of things much improved by the new reforms; on the contrary, the increased interference of the regular officials tended rather to weaken the vitality of the urban self-government, and the so-called reform was pretty generally condemned as a needlessly reactionary measure. We have here, in fact, a case of what has often occurred in the administrative history of the Russian Empire since the time of Peter the Great, and to which I shall again have occasion to refer. The central authority, finding itself incompetent to do all that is required of it, and wishing to make a display of liberalism, accords large concessions in the direction of local autonomy; and when it discovers that the new institutions do not accomplish all that was expected of them, and are not quite so subservient and obsequious as is considered desirable, it returns in a certain measure to the old principles of centralized bureaucracy.

The great development of trade and industry in recent years has, of course, enriched the mercantile classes, and has introduced into them a more highly educated element, drawn chiefly from the noblesse, which formerly eschewed such occupations; but it has not yet affected very deeply the mode of life of those who have sprung from the old merchant families and the peasantry. When a merchant, contractor, or manufacturer of the old type becomes wealthy he builds for himself a fine house, or buys and thoroughly repairs the house of some ruined noble, and spends money freely on parquet floors, large mirrors, malachite tables, grand pianos by the best makers, and other articles of furniture made of the most costly materials. Occasionally—especially on the occasion of a marriage or a death in the family—he will give magnificent banquets, and expend enormous sums on gigantic sterlets, choice caviar, foreign fruits, champagne, and all manner of costly delicacies. But this lavish, ostentatious expenditure does not affect the ordinary current of his daily life. As you enter those gaudily furnished rooms you can perceive at a glance that they are not for ordinary use. You notice a rigid symmetry and an indescribable bareness which inevitably suggest that the original arrangements of the upholsterer have never been modified or supplemented. The truth is that by far the greater part of the house is used only on state occasions. The host and his family live downstairs in small, dirty rooms, furnished in a very different, and for them more comfortable, style. At ordinary times the fine rooms are closed, and the fine furniture carefully covered.

If you make a *visite de digestion* after an entertainment, you will probably have some difficulty in gaining admission by the front door. When you have knocked or rung several times, someone will come round from the back regions and ask you what you want. Then follows another long pause, and at last footsteps are heard approaching from within. The bolts are drawn, the door is opened, and you are led up to a spacious drawing room. At the wall opposite the windows, there is sure to be a sofa, and before it an oval table. At each end of the table, and at right-angles to the sofa, there will be a row of three arm-chairs. The other chairs will be symmetrically arranged round the room. In a few minutes the host will appear, in his long double-breasted black coat and well-polished long boots. His hair is parted in the middle, and his beard shows no trace of scissors or razor.

After the customary greetings have been exchanged, glasses of tea, with slices of lemon and preserves, or perhaps a bottle of champagne, are brought in by way of refreshment. The female members of the family you must not expect to see, unless you are an intimate friend; for the old-fashioned merchants still retain something of that female seclusion which was in vogue among the upper classes before the time of Peter the Great. The host himself will probably be an intelligent, but totally uneducated and decidedly taciturn, man. About the weather and the crops he may talk fluently enough, but he will not show much inclination to go beyond these topics. You may, perhaps, desire to converse with him on the subject with which he is best acquainted—the trade in which he is himself engaged; but if you make the attempt, you will certainly not gain much information, and you may possibly meet with such an incident as once happened to my traveling companion, a Russian gentleman who had been commissioned by two learned societies to collect information regarding the grain trade. When he called on a merchant who had promised to assist him in his investigations, he was hospitably received; but when he began to speak about the grain trade of the district, the merchant suddenly interrupted him, and proposed to tell him a story. The story was as follows:

Once on a time a rich landed proprietor had a son, who was a thoroughly spoilt child; and one day the boy said to his father that he wished all the young serfs to come and sing before the door of the house. After some attempts at dissuasion the request was granted, and the young people assembled; but as soon as they began to sing, the boy rushed out and drove them away.

When the merchant had told this apparently pointless story at great length, and with much circumstantial detail, he paused a little, poured some tea into his saucer, drank it off, and then inquired, "Now what do you think was the reason of this strange conduct?"

My friend replied that the riddle surpassed his powers of divination.

"Well," said the merchant, looking hard at him, with a knowing grin, "there was no reason; and all the boy could say was, 'Go away, go away! I've changed my mind; I've changed my mind'" (*poshli von; otkhotyél*).

There was no possibility of mistaking the point of the story. My friend took the hint and departed.

The Russian merchant's love of ostentation is of a peculiar kind—something entirely different from English snobbery. He may delight in gaudy reception rooms, magnificent dinners, fast trotters, costly furs; or he may display his riches by princely donations to churches, monasteries, or benevolent institutions; but in all this he never affects to be other than he really is. He habitually wears a costume which designates plainly his social position; he makes no attempt to adopt fine manners or elegant tastes; and he never seeks to gain admission to what is called in Russia *la société*. Having no desire to seem what he is not, he has a plain, unaffected manner, and sometimes a quiet dignity, which contrasts favorably with the affected manner of those nobles of the lower ranks who make pretensions to being highly educated and strive to adopt the outward forms of French culture. At his great dinners, it is true, the merchant likes to see among his guests as many "generals"—that is to say, official personages—as possible, and especially those who happen to have a *grand cordon;* but he never dreams of thereby establishing an intimacy with these personages, or of being invited by them in return. It is perfectly understood by both parties that nothing of the kind is meant. The invitation is given and accepted from quite different motives. The merchant has the satisfaction of seeing at his table men of high official rank, and feels that the consideration which he enjoys among people of his own class is thereby augmented. If he succeeds in obtaining the presence of three generals, he obtains a victory over a rival who cannot obtain more than two. The general, on his side, gets a first-rate dinner, *à la russe,* and ac-

quires an undefined right to request subscriptions for public objects or benevolent institutions.

Of course this undefined right is commonly nothing
more than a mere tacit understanding, but in certain cases
the subject is expressly mentioned. I know of one case in
which a regular bargain was made. A Moscow magnate
was invited by a merchant to a dinner, and consented to
go in full uniform, with all his decorations, on condition
that the merchant should subscribe a certain sum to a
benevolent institution in which he was particularly interested. It is whispered that such bargains are sometimes
made, not on behalf of benevolent institutions, but simply
in the interest of the gentleman who accepts the invitation.
I cannot believe that there are many official personages
who would consent to let themselves out as table decorations, but that it may happen is proved by the following
incident, which accidentally came to my knowledge. A
rich merchant of the town of T—— once requested the
Governor of the Province to honor a family festivity with
his presence, and added that he would consider it a special
favor if the "Governoress" would enter an appearance. To
this latter request his Excellency made many objections,
and at last let the petitioner understand that her Excellency could not possibly be present because she had no velvet dress that could bear comparison with those of several
merchants' wives in the town. Two days after the inter-
view a piece of the finest velvet that could be procured in
Moscow was received by the Governor from an unknown
donor, and his wife was thus enabled to be present at the
festivity, to the complete satisfaction of all parties concerned.

It is worthy of remark that the merchants recognize no
aristocracy but that of official rank. Many merchants
would willingly give twenty pounds for the presence of an
"actual State-Councillor," who perhaps never heard of his
grandfather, but who can show a *grand cordon;* whilst
they would not give twenty pence for the presence of an
undecorated Prince without official rank, though he might
be able to trace his pedigree up to the half-mythical Rurik.
Of the latter they would probably say, "Kto ikh znaet?"
—who knows what sort of a fellow he is? The former, on

the contrary, whoever his father and grandfather may
have been, possesses unmistakable marks of the Tsar's favor, which, in the merchant's opinion, is infinitely more
important than any rights or pretensions founded on hereditary titles or long pedigrees.

Some marks of Imperial favor the old-fashioned merchants strive to obtain for themselves. They do not dream
of *grands cordons*—that is far beyond their most sanguine
expectations—but they do all in their power to obtain
those lesser decorations which are granted to the mercantile class. For this purpose the most common expedient is a
liberal subscription to some benevolent institution, and occasionally a regular bargain is made. I know of at least one
instance where the kind of decoration was expressly stipulated. The affair illustrates so well the commercial character of these transactions that I venture to state the facts
as related to me by the official chiefly concerned. A merchant subscribed to a society which enjoyed the patronage
of a Grand Duchess a considerable sum of money, under
the express condition that he should receive in return a
St. Vladimir Cross. Instead of the desired decoration,
which was considered too much for the sum subscribed, a
cross of St. Stanislas was granted; but the donor was dis-
satisfied with the latter, and demanded that his money
should be returned to him. The demand had to be complied with, and as an Imperial gift cannot be retracted
the merchant had his Stanislas Cross for nothing.

This traffic in decorations has had its natural result. Like
paper money issued in too large quantities, the decorations
have fallen in value. The gold medals which were formerly
much coveted and worn with pride by the rich merchants
—suspended by a ribbon round the neck—are now little
sought after. In like manner the inordinate respect for official personages has considerably diminished. Fifty years
ago the provincial merchants vied with each other in their
desire to entertain any great dignitary who honored their
town with a visit, but now they seek rather to avoid this
expensive and barren honor. When they do accept the
honor, they fulfill the duties of hospitality in a most liberal
spirit. I have sometimes, when living as an honored guest

in a rich merchant's house, found it difficult to obtain anything simpler than sterlet, caviar, and champagne.

The two great blemishes on the character of the Russian
merchants as a class are, according to general opinion,
their ignorance and their dishonesty. As to the former of
these there cannot be much difference of opinion. In the
last generation many of the merchants could neither read
nor write, and were forced to keep their accounts in their
memory, or by means of ingenious hieroglyphics, intelligible only to the inventor. Others could decipher the calendar and the lives of the saints, could sign their names
with tolerable facility, and could make the simpler arith-
metical calculations with the help of the *shchety*, a little
calculating instrument composed of wooden balls strung
on brass wires, which resembles the "abaca" of the old Ro-
mans, and is universally used in Russia. It was only the
minority who understood the mysteries of regular book-
keeping, and of these very few could make any pretensions to being educated men.

All this is rapidly undergoing a radical change. Children are now much better educated than their parents,
and the next generation will doubtless make further progress, so that the old-fashioned type above described has
almost disappeared. Already there are not a few of the
younger generation—especially among the wealthy manufacturers of Moscow—who have been educated abroad,
who may be described as "*tout à fait civilisés,*" and whose
mode of life differs little from that of the richer nobles;
but they remain outside fashionable society, and constitute a "set" of their own.

As to the dishonesty which is said to be so common
among the Russian commercial classes, it is more difficult
to form an accurate judgment. That an enormous amount
of unfair dealing does exist there can be no possible doubt,
but in this matter a foreigner is likely to be unduly severe.
We are apt to apply unflinchingly our own standard of
commercial morality, and to forget that trade in Russia is
only emerging from that primitive condition in which fixed
prices and moderate profits are entirely unknown. And
when we happen to detect positive dishonesty, it seems to

us especially heinous, because the trickery employed is
more primitive and awkward than that to which we are
accustomed. Trickery in weighing and measuring, for instance, which is by no means unknown in Russia, is likely
to make us more indignant than those ingenious methods
of adulteration which are practiced nearer home, and are
regarded by many as almost legitimate. Besides this, foreigners who go to Russia and embark in speculations without possessing any adequate knowledge of the character,
customs, and language of the people positively invite
spoliation, and ought to blame themselves rather than the
people who profit by their ignorance.

All this, and much more of the same kind, may be
fairly urged in mitigation of the severe judgments which
foreign merchants commonly pass on Russian commercial
morality, but these judgments cannot be reversed by such
argumentation. The dishonesty and rascality which exist
among the merchants are fully recognized by the Russians
themselves. In all moral affairs the lower classes in Russia
are very lenient in their judgments, and are strongly disposed, like the Americans, to admire what is called in
transatlantic phraseology "a smart man," though the
smartness is known to contain a large admixture of dishonesty; and yet the *vox populi* in Russia emphatically declares that the merchants as a class are unscrupulous and
dishonest. There is a rude popular play, in which the
Devil, as principal *dramatis persona,* succeeds in cheating
all manner and conditions of men, but is finally over-
reached by a genuine Russian merchant. When this play
used to be acted in the Carnival Theater in St. Petersburg,
the audience invariably agreed with the moral of the plot.

It must not be supposed that the unsatisfactory organization of the Russian commercial world is the result of any
radical peculiarity of the Russian character. All new countries have to pass through a similar state of things, and in
Russia there are already premonitory symptoms of a
change for the better. For the present, it is true, the extensive construction of railways and the rapid development of
banks and limited liability companies have opened up a
new and wide field for all kinds of commercial swindling;
but, on the other hand, there are now in every large town

a certain number of merchants who carry on business in the West European manner, and have learned by experience that honesty is the best policy. The success which many of these have obtained will doubtless cause their example to be followed. The old spirit of caste and routine which has long animated the merchant class is rapidly disappearing, and not a few nobles are now exchanging country life and the service of the State for industrial and commercial enterprises. In this way is being formed the nucleus of that wealthy, enlightened *bourgeoisie* which Catherine endeavored to create by legislation; but many years must elapse before this class acquires sufficient social and political significance to deserve the title of a *tiers-état*.

CHAPTER · XI

Moscow and the Slavophils

In . . . the preceding [chapter] . . . , the reader must have observed that at one moment there was a sudden break, almost a solution of continuity, in Russian national life. The Tsardom of Muscovy, with its ancient Oriental costumes and Byzantine traditions, unexpectedly disappears, and the Russian Empire, clad in modern garb and animated with the spirit of modern progress, steps forward uninvited into European history. Of the older civilization, if civilization it can be called, very little survived the political transformation, and that little is generally supposed to hover ghostlike around Kiev and Moscow. To one or other of these towns, therefore, the student who desires to learn something of genuine old Russian life, untainted by foreign influences, naturally wends his way.

For my part I thought first of settling for a time in Kiev, the oldest and most revered of Russian cities, where missionaries from Byzantium first planted Christianity on Russian soil, and where thousands of pilgrims still assemble yearly from far and near, to prostrate themselves before the Holy Icons in the churches and to venerate the relics of the blessed saints and martyrs in the catacombs of the great monastery. I soon discovered, however, that Kiev, though it represents in a certain sense the Byzantine traditions so dear to the Russian people, is not a good point of observation for studying the Russian character. It was early exposed to the ravages of the nomadic tribes of the Steppe, and when it was liberated from those incursions it was seized by the Poles and Lithuanians, and remained for centuries under their domination. Only in compara-

tively recent times did it begin to recover its Russian character—a university having been created there for that purpose after the Polish insurrection of 1830. Even now the
process of Russification is far from complete, and the Russian elements in the population are far from being pure
in the nationalist sense.

The city and the surrounding country are, in fact, Little
Russian rather than Great Russian, and between these two
sections of the population there are profound differences—
differences of language, costume, traditions, popular songs,
proverbs, folklore, domestic arrangements, mode of life,
and communal organization. In these and other respects
the Little Russians, South Russians, Ruthenes, or Khokhlý,
as they are variously designated, differ from the Great
Russians of the North, who form the predominant factor in
the Empire, and who have given to that wonderful structure its essential characteristics. Indeed, if I did not fear to
ruffle unnecessarily the patriotic susceptibilities of my
Great Russian friends who have a pet theory on this subject, I should say that we have here two distinct nationalities, farther apart from each other than the English and
the Scotch. The differences are due, I believe, partly to
ethnographical peculiarities and partly to historic conditions.

As it was the energetic Great Russian empire builders
and not the half-dreamy, half-astute, sympathetic descendants of the Free Cossacks that I wanted to study, I soon
abandoned my idea of settling in the Holy City on the
Dnieper, and chose Moscow as my point of observation;
and here, during several years, I spent regularly some of
the winter months.

The first few weeks of my stay in the ancient capital or
the Tsars were spent in the ordinary manner of intelligent
tourists. After mastering the contents of a guidebook I
carefully inspected all the officially recognized objects of
interest—the Kremlin, with its picturesque towers and six
centuries of historical associations; the Cathedrals, containing the venerated tombs of martyrs, saints, and Tsars; the
old churches, with their quaint, archaic, richly decorated
Icons; the "Patriarchs' Treasury," rich in jeweled ecclesiastical vestments and vessels of silver and gold; the ancient

and the modern palace; the Ethnological Museum showing the costumes and physiognomy of all the various races
in the Empire; the archaeological collections, containing
many objects that recall the barbaric splendor of old Muscovy; the picture gallery, with Ivanov's gigantic picture,
in which patriotic Russian critics discover occult merits
that place it above anything that Western Europe has yet
produced! Of course I climbed up to the top of the tall
belfry which rejoices in the name of "Ivan the Great," and
looked down on the "gilded domes" [1] of the churches, and
bright green roofs of the houses, and, far away beyond
these, the gently undulating country with the "Sparrow
Hills," from which Napoleon is said, in cicerone language,
to have "gazed upon the doomed city." Occasionally I
walked about the bazaars in the hope of finding interesting specimens of genuine native art-industry, and was urgently invited to purchase every conceivable article which
I did not want. At midday or in the evening I visited the
most noted *traktirs,* and made the acquaintance of the
caviar, sturgeons, sterlets, and other native delicacies for
which these institutions are famous—deafened the while
by the deep tones of the colossal barrel organ, out of all
proportion to the size of the room; and in order to see
how the common people spent their evenings I looked in
at some of the more modest *traktirs,* and gazed with wonder, not unmixed with fear, at the enormous quantity of
weak tea which the inmates consumed.

Since these first weeks of my sojourn in Moscow forty
years have passed, and many of my early impressions have
been blurred by time, but one scene remains deeply graven
on my memory. It was Easter Eve, and I had gone with a
friend to the Kremlin to witness the customary religious
ceremonies. Though the rain was falling heavily, an immense number of people had assembled in and around the
Cathedral of the Assumption. The crowd was of the most
mixed kind. There stood the patient bearded muzhik in
his well-worn sheepskin; the big, burly, self-satisfied mer-

---

[1] Allowance must be made here for poetical license. In reality,
very few of the domes are gilt. The great majority of them are
painted green, like the roofs of the houses.

chant in his long black glossy *kaftan;* the noble with fashionable greatcoat and umbrella; thinly clad old women shivering in the cold, and bright-eyed young damsels with their warm cloaks drawn closely round them; old men with long beard, wallet, and pilgrim's staff; and mischievous urchins with faces for the moment preternaturally demure. Each right hand, of old and young alike, held a lighted taper, and these myriads of flickering little flames produced a curious illumination, giving to the surrounding buildings a weird picturesqueness which they do not possess in broad daylight. All stood patiently waiting for the announcement of the glad tidings: "He is risen!"

As midnight approached, the hum of voices gradually ceased, till, as the clock struck twelve, the deep-toned bell on "Ivan the Great" began to toll, and in answer to this signal all the bells in Moscow suddenly sent forth a merry peal. Each bell—and their name is legion—seemed frantically desirous of drowning its neighbor's voice, the solemn boom of the great one overhead mingling curiously with the sharp, fussy "ting-a-ting-ting" of diminutive rivals. If demons dwell in Moscow and dislike bell ringing, as is generally supposed, then there must have been at that moment a general stampede of the powers of darkness such as is described by Milton in his poem on the Nativity; and as if this deafening din were not enough, big guns were fired in rapid succession from a battery of artillery close at hand! The noise seemed to stimulate the religious enthusiasm, and the general excitement had a wonderful effect on a Russian friend who accompanied me. When in his normal condition that gentleman was a quiet, undemonstrative person, devoted to science, an ardent adherent of Western civilization in general and of Darwinism in particular, and a thorough skeptic with regard to all forms of religious belief; but the influence of the surroundings was too much for his philosophical equanimity. For a moment his orthodox Muscovite soul awoke from its skeptical, cosmopolitan lethargy. After crossing himself repeatedly— an act of devotion which I had never before seen him perform—he grasped my arm, and pointing to the crowd, said in an exultant tone of voice, "Look there! There is a sight

that you can see nowhere but in the 'White-Stone City.' [2]
Are not the Russians a religious people?"

To this unexpected question I gave a monosyllabic assent, and refrained from disturbing my friend's new-born enthusiasm by any discordant note; but I must confess that this sudden outburst of deafening noise and the dazzling light aroused in my heretical breast feelings of a warlike rather than a religious kind. For a moment I could imagine myself in ancient Moscow, and could fancy the people being called out to repel a Mongol horde already thundering at the gates!

The service lasted two or three hours, and terminated with the curious ceremony of blessing the Easter cakes, which were ranged—each one with a lighted taper stuck in it—in long rows outside the cathedral. A not less curious custom practiced at this season is that of exchanging kisses of fraternal love. Theoretically one ought to embrace and be embraced by all present—indicating thereby that all are brethren in Christ—but the refinements of modern life have made innovations in the practice, and most people confine their salutations to their friends and acquaintances. When two friends meet during that night or on the following day, the one says, "Christós voskrés!" ("Christ hath risen!"); and the other replies, "Vo ístinê voskrés!" ("In truth He hath risen!"). They then kiss each other three times on the right and left cheek alternately. The custom is more or less observed in all classes of society, and the Emperor himself conforms to it.

This reminds me of an anecdote which is related of the Emperor Nicholas I, tending to show that he was not so devoid of kindly human feelings as his imperial and imperious exterior suggested. On coming out of his cabinet one Easter morning, he addressed to the soldier who was mounting guard at the door the ordinary words of salutation, "Christ hath risen!" and received, instead of the ordinary reply, a flat contradiction—"Not at all, your Imperial Majesty!" Astounded by such an unexpected answer —for no one ventured to dissent from Nicholas even in the most guarded and respectful terms—he instantly de-

[2] Bêlokámenny, meaning "of white stone," is one of the popular names of Moscow.

manded an explanation. The soldier, trembling at his own
audacity, explained that he was a Jew, and could not conscientiously admit the fact of the resurrection. This bold-
ness for conscience' sake so pleased the Tsar that he gave
the man a handsome Easter present.

Quarter of a century after the Easter Eve above mentioned—or, to be quite accurate, on the 26th of May,
1896—I again find myself in the Kremlin on the occasion
of a great religious ceremony—a ceremony which shows
that the "White-stone City" on the Moskvá is still in some
respects the capital of Holy Russia. This time my post of
observation is inside the cathedral, which is artistically
draped with purple hangings, and crowded with the most
distinguished personages of the Empire, all arrayed in
gorgeous apparel—Grand Dukes and Grand Duchesses,
Imperial Highnesses and High Excellencies, Metropolitans
and Archbishops, Senators and Councillors of State, Generals and Court dignitaries. In the center of the building,
on a high, richly decorated platform, sits the Emperor
with his Imperial Consort, and his mother, the widowed
Consort of Alexander III. Though Nicholas II has not the
colossal stature which has distinguished so many of the
Románovs, he is well built, holds himself erect, and shows
a quiet dignity in his movements; while his face, which
resembles that of his cousin King George V, wears a
kindly, sympathetic expression. The Empress looks even
more than usually beautiful, in a low dress cut in the ancient fashion, her thick brown hair, dressed most simply
without jewelry or other ornaments, falling in two long
ringlets over her white shoulders. For the moment, her attire is much simpler than that of the Empress Dowager,
who wears a diamond crown, and a great mantle of gold
brocade, lined and edged with ermine, the long train displaying in bright-colored embroidery the heraldic double-
headed eagle of the Imperial arms.

Each of these august personages sits on a throne of curious workmanship, consecrated by ancient historic associations. That of the Emperor, the gift of a Shah of Persia to
Ivan the Terrible, and commonly called the Throne of
Tsar Michael, the founder of the Románov dynasty, is covered with gold plaques, and studded with hundreds of

big, roughly cut precious stones, mostly rubies, emeralds,
and turquoises. Of still older date is the throne of the
young Empress, for it was given by Pope Paul II to Tsar
Ivan III, grandfather of the Terrible, on the occasion of
his marriage with a niece of the last Byzantine Emperor.
More recent but not less curious is that of the Empress
Dowager. It is the throne of Tsar Alexis, the father of Peter
the Great, covered with countless and priceless diamonds,
rubies, and pearls, and surmounted by an Imperial eagle
of solid gold, together with golden statuettes of St. Peter
and St. Nicholas the miracleworker. Over each throne is a
canopy of purple velvet fringed with gold, out of which
rise stately plumes representing the national colors.

Their Majesties have come hither, in accordance with
time-honored custom, to be crowned in this old Cathedral
of the Assumption, the central point of the Kremlin, within
a stone-throw of the Cathedral of the Archangel Michael,
in which lie the remains of the old Grand Dukes and Tsars
of Muscovy. Already the Emperor has read aloud, in a
clear, unfaltering voice, from a richly bound parchment
folio, held by the Metropolitan of St. Petersburg, the
Orthodox creed; and his Eminence, after invoking on his
Majesty the blessing of the Holy Spirit, has performed the
mystic rite of placing his hands in the form of a cross on
the Imperial forehead. Thus all is ready for the most important part of the solemn ceremony. Standing erect, the
Emperor doffs his small diadem and puts on with his own
hands the great diamond crown, offered respectfully by
the Metropolitan; then he reseats himself on his throne,
holding in his right hand the Scepter and in his left the
Orb of Dominion. After sitting thus in state for a few minutes, he stands up and proceeds to crown his august
spouse kneeling before him. First he touches her forehead
with his own crown, and then he places on her head a
smaller one, which is immediately attached to her hair by
four ladies in waiting, dressed in the old Muscovite Court
costume. At the same time her Majesty is invested with a
mantle of heavy gold brocade, similar to those of the Emperor and Empress Dowager, lined and bordered with ermine.

Thus crowned and robed, their Majesties sit in state,

while a proto-deacon reads, in a loud, stentorian voice, the
long list of sonorous hereditary titles belonging of right to
the Imperator and Autocrat of All the Russias, and the
choir chants a prayer invoking long life and happiness—
"Many years! Many years! Many years!"—on the high and
mighty possessor of the titles aforesaid. And now begins
the Mass, celebrated with a pomp and magnificence that
can be witnessed only once or twice in a generation. Sixty
gorgeously robed ecclesiastical dignitaries of the highest
orders fulfill their various functions with due solemnity
and unction; but the magnificence of the vestments and the
pomp of the ceremonial are soon forgotten in the exquisite
solemnizing music, as the deep double-bass tones of the
adult singers in the background—carefully selected for
the occasion in all parts of the Empire—peal forth as from
a great organ, and blend marvelously with the clear, soft,
gentle notes of the red-robed chorister boys in front of the
Iconostase.

Listening with intense emotion, I involuntarily recall to
mind Fra Angelico's pictures of angelic choirs, and cannot
help thinking that the pious old Florentine, whose soul
was attuned to all that was sacred and beautiful, must
have heard in imagination such music as this. So strong is
the impression that the subsequent details of the long ceremony, including the anointing with the holy chrism, fail
to engrave themselves on my memory. One incident, however, remains; and if it had happened in an earlier and
more superstitious age it would doubtless have been chron-
icled as an omen full of significance. As the Emperor is on
the point of descending from the dais, duly crowned and
anointed, a straggling ray of sunshine steals through one of
the narrow upper windows and, traversing the dimly lit
edifice, falls full on the Imperial crown, lighting up for a
moment the great mass of diamonds with a hundredfold
brilliance.

In a detailed account of the Coronation which I wrote
on leaving the Kremlin, I find the following: "The magnificent ceremony is at an end, and now Nicholas II is
the crowned Emperor and anointed Autocrat of All the
Russias. May the cares of Empire rest lightly on him!
That must be the earnest prayer of every loyal subject

and every sincere well-wisher, for of all living mortals he
is perhaps the one who has been entrusted by Providence
with the greatest power and the greatest responsibilities."
In writing those words I did not foresee how heavy his responsibilities would one day weigh upon him, when his
Empire would be sorely tried by foreign war and internal
discontent.

One more of these old Moscow reminiscences and I
have done. A day or two after the Coronation I saw the
Khodinskoye Polye, a great plain in the outskirts of Moscow, strewn with hundreds of corpses! During the previous night enormous crowds from the city and the surrounding districts had collected here in order to receive at
sunrise, by the Tsar's command, a little memento of the
coronation ceremony, in the form of a packet containing
a metal cup and a few eatables; and as day dawned, in
their anxiety to get near the row of booths from which the
distribution was to be made, about two thousand had
been crushed to death. It was a sight more horrible than a
battlefield, because among the dead were a large proportion of women and children, terribly mutilated in the struggle. Altogether, "a sight to shudder at, not to see!"

To return to the remark of my friend in the Kremlin on
Easter Eve, the Russians in general, and the Muscovites in
particular, as the quintessence of all that is Russian, are
certainly a religious people, but their piety sometimes finds
modes of expression which rather shock the Protestant
mind. As an instance of these, I may mention the domiciliary visits of the Iberian Madonna. This celebrated Icon,
for reasons which I have never heard satisfactorily explained, is held in peculiar veneration by the Muscovites,
and occupies in popular estimation a position analogous to
the tutelary deities of ancient pagan cities. Thus when
Napoleon was about to enter the city in 1812, the popu-
lace clamorously called upon the Metropolitan to take the
Madonna, and lead them out armed with hatchets against
the hosts of the infidel; and when the Tsar visits Moscow,
he generally drives straight from the railway station to the
little chapel where the Icon resides—near one of the en-
trances to the Kremlin—and there offers up a short prayer.
Every Orthodox Russian, as he passes this chapel, un-

covers and crosses himself, and whenever a religious
service is performed in it there is always a considerable
group of worshipers.

Some of the richer inhabitants, however, are not content
with thus performing their devotions in public before the
Icon. They like to have the holy picture from time to time
in their houses, and the ecclesiastical authorities think fit to
humor this strange fancy. Accordingly every morning the
Iberian Madonna may be seen driving about the city from
one house to another in a carriage and four! The carriage
may be at once recognized, not from any peculiarity in its
structure, for it is an ordinary landau such as may be
obtained at livery stables, but by the fact that the coachman sits bare-headed, and all the people in the street un-
cover and cross themselves as it passes. Arrived at the
house to which it has been invited, the Icon is carried
through all the rooms, and in the principal apartment a
short religious service is performed before it. As it is being
brought in or taken away, female servants may sometimes
be seen to kneel on the floor so that it may be carried over
them. During its absence from its chapel it is replaced by a
copy not easily distinguishable from the original, and thus
the devotions of the faithful and the flow of pecuniary contributions do not suffer interruption. These contributions,
together with the sums paid for the domiciliary visits,
amount to a considerable yearly sum, and go—if I am
rightly informed—to swell the revenues of the Metropolitan.

A single drive or stroll through Moscow will suffice to
convince the traveler, even if he knows nothing of Russian
history, that the city is not, like its modern rival on the
Neva, the artificial creation of a far-seeing, self-willed
autocrat, but rather a natural product which has grown up
slowly and been modified according to the constantly
changing wants of the population. A few of the streets
have been Europeanized—in all except the paving, which
is everywhere execrably Asiatic—to suit the tastes of those
who have adopted European culture, but the great majority of them still retain much of their ancient character and
primitive irregularity. As soon as we diverge from the principal thoroughfares, we find one-storied houses—some of

them still of wood—which appear to have been transported bodily from the country, with courtyard, garden,
stables, and other appurtenances. The whole is no doubt a
little compressed, for land has here a certain value, but the
character is in no way changed, and we have some difficulty in believing that we are not in the suburbs but near
the center of a great city. There is nothing that can by any
possibility be called street architecture. Though there is
unmistakable evidence of the streets having been laid out
according to a preconceived plan, many of them show
clearly that in their infancy they had a wayward will of
their own, and they still bend to the right or left without
any topographical justification.

The houses, too, display considerable individuality of
character, having evidently during the course of their construction paid no attention to their neighbors. Hence we
find no regularly built terraces, crescents, or squares.
There is, it is true, a double circle of boulevards, but the
houses which flank them have none of that regularity
which we commonly associate with the term. Dilapidated
buildings which in West European cities would hide themselves in some narrow lane or back slum here stand
composedly in the face of day by the side of a palatial residence, without having the least consciousness of the incongruity of their position, just as the unsophisticated muzhik
in his unsavory sheepskin can stand in the midst of a
crowd of well-dressed people without feeling at all awkward or uncomfortable.

All this incongruity, however, is speedily disappearing.
Moscow has become the center of a great network of railways, and the commercial and industrial capital of the
Empire, with a rapidly increasing population of about a
million and a half. The value of land and property is being
doubled and trebled, and building speculations, with the
aid of credit institutions of various kinds, are being carried
on with feverish rapidity. Well may the men of the old
school complain that the world is turned upside down,
and regret the old times of traditional somnolence and
comfortable routine! Those good old times are gone now,
never to return. The ancient capital, which long gloried in
its past historical associations, now glories in its present

commercial prosperity, and looks forward with confidence
to the future. Even the Slavophils, the obstinate champions of the ultra-Muscovite spirit, have changed with
the times and descended to the level of ordinary prosaic
life. These men, who formerly spent years in seeking to
determine the place of Moscow in the past and future history of humanity, have—to their honor be it said—become in these latter days town councillors, and have devoted much of their time to devising ways and means of
improving the drainage and the street paving! But I am
anticipating in a most unjustifiable way. I ought first to
tell the reader who the early Slavophils were, and why
they sought to correct the commonly received conceptions
of universal history.

The reader may have heard of the Slavophils as a set of
fanatics who, about the middle of last century, were wont
to go about in what they considered the ancient Russian
costume, who wore beards in defiance of Peter the Great's
celebrated ukase and Nicholas I's clearly expressed wish
anent shaving, who gloried in Muscovite barbarism, and
had solemnly "sworn a feud" against European civilization
and enlightenment. By the tourists of the time who visited
Moscow they were regarded as among the most note-
worthy lions of the place, and were commonly depicted
in not very flattering colors. At the beginning of the Crimean War they were among the extreme Chauvinists who
urged the necessity of planting the Greek cross on the
desecrated dome of St. Sophia in Constantinople, and
hoped to see the Emperor proclaimed "Panslavonic Tsar";
and after the termination of the war they were frequently
accused of inventing Turkish atrocities, stirring up discontent among the Slav subjects of the Sultan, and secretly
plotting for the overthrow of the Ottoman Empire. All
this was known to me before I went to Russia, and I had
consequently invested the Slavophils with a halo of romance. Shortly after my arrival in St. Petersburg I heard
something more which tended to increase my interest in
them—they had caused, I was told, great trepidation in
the highest official circles by petitioning the Emperor to
resuscitate a certain ancient institution, called a *Zemski
Sobór*, which might be made to serve the purposes of a

Parliament! This threw a new light upon them; under the disguise of archaeological Conservatives they were evidently aiming at important Liberal reforms.

As a foreigner and a heretic, I expected a very cold and distant reception from these uncompromising champions of Russian nationality and the Orthodox faith; but in this I was agreeably disappointed. By all of them I was received in the most amiable and friendly way, and I soon discovered that my preconceived ideas of them were very far from the truth. Instead of wild fanatics I found quiet, extremely intelligent, highly educated gentlemen, speaking foreign languages with ease and elegance, and deeply imbued with that Western culture which they were commonly supposed to despise. One of them, and not the least remarkable, had been partly educated in Germany, and was the most thoroughgoing Hegelian I have ever known. On the whole I was very favorably impressed by them, and this first impression was amply confirmed by subsequent experience during several years of friendly intercourse. They always showed themselves men of earnest character and strong convictions, but they never said or did anything that could justify the appellation of fanatics. Like all philosophical theorists, they often allowed their logic to blind them to facts, but their reasonings were very plausible—so plausible, indeed, that, had I been a Russian, they would have almost persuaded me to be a Slavophil, at least during the time they were talking to me.

To understand their doctrine we must know something of its origin and development.

The origin of the Slavophil sentiment, which must not be confounded with the Slavophil doctrine, is to be sought in the latter half of the seventeenth century, when the Tsars of Muscovy were introducing innovations in Church and State. These innovations were profoundly displeasing to the people. A large portion of the lower classes, as I have related in another chapter, sought refuge in Old Ritualism or sectarianism, and imagined that Tsar Peter, who called himself by the heretical title of "Imperator," was an emanation of the Evil Principle. The nobles did not go quite so far. They remained members of the official Church, and restricted themselves to hinting that Peter

was the son, not of Satan, but of a German surgeon—a
lineage which, according to the conceptions of the time,
was a little less objectionable; but most of them were very
hostile to the changes, and complained bitterly of the new
burdens which these changes entailed. Under Peter's immediate successors, when not only the principles of administration but also many of the administrators were
German, their hostility greatly increased.

So long as the innovations appeared only in the official
activity of the Government, the patriotic, conservative
spirit was obliged to keep silence; but when the foreign
influence spread to the social life of the Court aristocracy,
the opposition began to find a literary expression. In the
time of Catherine II, when Gallomania was at its height
in Court circles, comedies and satirical journals ridiculed
those who, "blinded by some externally brilliant gifts of
foreigners, not only prefer foreign countries to their native
land, but even despise their fellow countrymen, and think
that a Russian ought to borrow all—even personal character. As if Nature, arranging all things with such wisdom,
and bestowing on all regions the gifts and customs which
are appropriate to the climate, had been so unjust as to
refuse to the Russians a character of their own! As if she
condemned them to wander over all regions, and to adopt
by bits the various customs of various nations, in order to
compose out of the mixture a new character appropriate to
no nation whatever!" Numerous passages of this kind
might be quoted, attacking the "monkeyism" and "par-
rotism" of those who indiscriminately adopted foreign
manners and customs—those who

> "Sauntered Europe round,
> And gathered ev'ry vice in ev'ry ground."

Sometimes the terms and metaphors employed were more
forcible than refined. One satirical journal, for instance,
related an amusing story about certain little Russian pigs
that went to foreign lands to enlighten their understanding, and came back to their country full-grown swine. The
national pride was wounded by the thought that Russians
could be called "clever apes who feed on foreign intelligence," and many writers, stung by such reproaches, fell

into the opposite extreme, discovering unheard-of excellences in the Russian mind and character, and vociferously decrying everything foreign in order to place these imagined excellences in a stronger light by contrast. Even when they recognized that their country was not quite so advanced in civilization as certain other nations, they congratulated themselves on the fact, and invented by way of justification an ingenious theory, which was afterwards developed by the Slavophils. "The nations of the West," they said, "began to live before us, and are consequently more advanced than we are; but we have on that account no reason to envy them, for we can profit by their errors, and avoid those deep-rooted evils from which they are suffering. He who has just been born is happier than he who is dying."

Thus, we see, a patriotic reaction against the introduction of foreign institutions and the inordinate admiration of foreign culture already existed in Russia in the eighteenth century. It did not, however, take the form of a philosophical theory till a much later period, when a similar movement was going on in various countries of Western Europe.

After the overthrow of the great Napoleonic Empire a reaction against cosmopolitanism took place in Germany and a romantic enthusiasm for nationality spread over Europe like an epidemic. Blind enthusiastic patriotism became the fashionable sentiment of the time. Each nation took to admiring itself complacently, to praising its own character and achievements, and to idealizing its historical and mythical past. National peculiarities, "local color," ancient customs, traditional superstitions—in short, everything that a nation believed to be specially and exclusively its own—now raised an enthusiasm similar to that which had been formerly excited by cosmopolitan conceptions founded on the law of Nature. The movement produced good and evil results. In serious minds it led to a deep and conscientious study of history, national literature, popular mythology, and the like; whilst in frivolous, inflammable spirits it gave birth merely to a torrent of patriotic fervor and rhetorical exaggeration. The Slavophils were the Russian representatives of this nationalistic reaction, and displayed both its serious and its frivolous elements.

Among the most important products of this movement in Germany was the Hegelian theory of universal history. According to Hegel's views, which were generally accepted by those who occupied themselves with philosophical questions, universal history was described as "Progress in the consciousness of freedom" (*Fortschritt im Bewusstsein der Freiheit*). In each period of the world's history, it was explained, some one nation or race had been entrusted with the high mission of enabling the Absolute Reason, or Weltgeist, to express itself in objective existence, while the other nations and races had for the time no metaphysical justification for their existence, and no higher duty than to imitate slavishly the favored rival in which the Weltgeist had for the moment chosen to incorporate itself. The incarnation had taken place first in the Eastern Monarchies, then in Greece, next in Rome, and lastly in the Germanic race; and it was generally assumed, if not openly asserted, that this mystical Metempsychosis of the Absolute was now at an end. The cycle of existence was complete. In the Germanic peoples the Weltgeist had found its highest and final expression.

Russians in general knew nothing about German philosophy, and were consequently not in any way affected by these ideas, but there was in Moscow a small group of young men who ardently studied German literature and metaphysics, and they were much shocked by Hegel's views. Ever since the brilliant reign of Catherine II, who had defeated the Turks and had dreamed of resuscitating the Byzantine Empire, and especially since the memorable events of 1812-15, when Alexander I appeared as the liberator of enthralled Europe and the arbiter of her destinies, Russians were firmly convinced that their country was destined to play a most important part in human history. Already the great Russian historian Karamzín had declared that henceforth Clio must be silent, or accord to Russia a prominent place in the history of the nations. Now, by the Hegelian theory, the whole of the Slav race was left out in the cold, with no high mission, with no new truths to divulge, with nothing better to do, in fact, than to imitate the Germans.

The patriotic philosophers of Moscow could not, of course, adopt this view. Whilst accepting the fundamental principles, they declared the theory to be incomplete. The incompleteness lay in the assumption that humanity had already entered on the final stages of its development. The Teutonic nations were perhaps for the moment the leaders in the march of civilization, but there was no reason to suppose that they would always retain that privileged position. On the contrary, there were already symptoms that their ascendancy was drawing to a close. "Western Europe," it was said, "presents a strange, saddening spectacle. Opinion struggles against opinion, power against power, throne against throne. Science, Art, and Religion, the three chief motors of social life, have lost their force. We venture to make an assertion which to many at present may seem strange, but which will be in a few years only too evident: Western Europe is on the high road to ruin! We Russians, on the contrary, are young and fresh, and have taken no part in the crimes of Europe. We have a great mission to fulfill. Our name is already inscribed on the tablets of victory, and now we have to inscribe our spirit in the history of the human mind. A higher kind of victory—the victory of Science, Art, and Faith—awaits us on the ruins of tottering Europe!" [2]

This conclusion was supported by arguments drawn from history—or, at least, what was believed to be history. The European world was represented as being composed of two hemispheres—the Eastern, or Graeco-Slavonic, on the one hand, and the Western, or Roman Catholic and Protestant, on the other. These two hemispheres, it was said, are distinguished from each other by many fundamental characteristics. In both of them Christianity formed originally the basis of civilization, but in the West it became distorted and gave a false direction to the intellectual development. By placing the logical reason of the learned above the conscience of the whole Church, Roman Catholicism produced Protestantism, which proclaimed the right of private judgment and consequently

[2] These words were written by Prince Odóevski.

became split up into innumerable sects. The dry, logical spirit which was thus fostered created a purely intellectual, one-sided philosophy, which must end in pure skepticism, by blinding men to those great truths which lie above the sphere of reasoning and logic. The Graeco-Slavonic world, on the contrary, having accepted Christianity not from Rome, but from Byzantium, received pure Orthodoxy and true enlightenment, and was thus saved alike from Papal tyranny and from Protestant free-thinking. Hence the Eastern Christians have preserved faithfully not only the ancient dogmas, but also the ancient spirit of Christianity—that spirit of pious humility, resignation, and brotherly love which Christ taught by precept and example. If they have not yet a philosophy, they will create one, and it will far surpass all previous systems; for in the writings of the Greek Fathers are to be found the germs of a broader, a deeper, and a truer philosophy than the dry, meager rationalism of the West —a philosophy founded not on the logical faculty alone, but on the broader basis of human nature as a whole.

The fundamental characteristics of the Graeco-Slavonic world—so runs the Slavophil theory—have been displayed in the history of Russia. Throughout Western Christendom the principles of individual judgment and reckless individual egotism have exhausted the social forces and brought society to the verge of incurable anarchy and inevitable dissolution, whereas the social and political history of Russia has been harmonious and peaceful. It presents no struggles between the different social classes, and no conflicts between Church and State. All the factors have worked in unison, and the development has been guided by the spirit of pure Orthodoxy. But in this harmonious picture there is one big, ugly black spot— Peter, falsely styled "the Great," and his so-called reforms. Instead of following the wise policy of his ancestors, Peter rejected the national traditions and principles, and applied to his country, which belonged to the Eastern world, the principles of Western civilization. His reforms, conceived in a foreign spirit, and elaborated by men who did not possess the national instincts, were forced upon the nation against its will, and the result was precisely what

might have been expected. The "broad Slavonic nature'
could not be controlled by institutions which had been
invented by narrow-minded, pedantic German bureau-
crats, and, like another Samson, it pulled down the building in which foreign legislators sought to confine it.

The attempt to introduce foreign culture had a still
worse effect. The upper classes, charmed and dazzled by
the glare and glitter of Western science, threw themselves
impulsively on the newly found treasures, and thereby
condemned themselves to moral slavery and intellectual
sterility. Fortunately—and herein lay one of the fundamental principles of the Slavophil doctrine—the imported
civilization had not at all infected the common people.
Through all the changes which the Administration and
the Noblesse underwent the peasantry preserved re-
ligiously in their hearts "the living legacy of antiquity,"
the essence of Russian nationality, "a clear spring welling
up living waters, hidden and unknown, but powerful." [3]
To recover this lost legacy by studying the character,
customs, and institutions of the peasantry, to lead the educated classes back to the path from which they had
strayed, and to re-establish that intellectual and moral
unity which had been disturbed by the foreign importations—such was the task which the Slavophils proposed to
themselves.

Deeply imbued with that romantic spirit which distorted all the intellectual activity of the time, the Slavophils often indulged in the wildest exaggerations, condemning everything foreign and praising everything Russian.
When in this mood they saw in the history of the West
nothing but violence, slavery, and egotism, and in that
of their own country free will, liberty, and peace. The
fact that Russia did not possess free political institutions was adduced as a precious fruit of that spirit of
Christian resignation and self-sacrifice which places the
Russian at such an immeasurable height above the proud,
selfish European; and because Russia possessed few of the

[3] This was one of the favorite themes of Khomiakóv, the
Slavophil poet and theologian, father of Mr. Khomiakóv, who
was president of the Duma.

comforts and conveniences of common life, the West was accused of having made comfort its God!

We need not, however, dwell on these puerilities, which only gained for their authors the reputation of being ignorant, narrow-minded men, imbued with a hatred of enlightenment and desirous of leading their country back to its primitive barbarism. What the Slavophils really condemned, at least in their calmer moments, was not European culture, but the uncritical, indiscriminate adoption of it by their countrymen. Their tirades against foreign culture must appear excusable when we remember that many Russians of the upper ranks could speak and write French more correctly than their native language, and that even the great national poet Pushkin was not ashamed to confess—what was not true, and a mere piece of affectation—that "the language of Europe" was more familiar to him than his mother tongue!

The Slavophil doctrine, though it made a great noise in the world, never found many adherents. The society of St. Petersburg regarded it as one of those harmless provincial eccentricities which are always to be found in Moscow. In the modern capital, with its foreign name, its streets and squares on the European model, its palaces and churches in the Renaissance style, and its passionate love of everything French, any attempt to resuscitate the old Boyaric times would have been eminently ridiculous. Indeed, hostility to St. Petersburg and to "the Petersburg period of Russian history" is one of the characteristic traits of genuine Slavophilism. In Moscow the doctrine found a more appropriate home. There the ancient churches, with the tombs of Grand Princes and holy martyrs, the palace in which the Tsars of Muscovy had lived, the Kremlin which had resisted—not always successfully—the attacks of savage Tatars and heretical Poles, the venerable Icons that had many a time protected the people from danger, the block of masonry from which, on solemn occasions, the Tsar and the Patriarch had addressed the assembled multitude—these, and a hundred other monuments sanctified by tradition, have kept alive in the popular memory some vague remembrance of the olden time, and are still capable of awakening antiquarian patriotism.

The inhabitants, too, have preserved something of the old Muscovite character. Whilst successive sovereigns were striving to make the country a progressive European empire, Moscow remained the home of passive conservatism and an asylum for the discontented, especially for the disappointed aspirants to Imperial favor. Abandoned by the modern Emperors, she could glory in her ancient Tsars. But even the Muscovites were not prepared to accept the Slavophil doctrine in the extreme form which it assumed, and were not a little perplexed by the eccentricities of those who professed it. Plain, sensible people, though they might be proud of being citizens of the ancient capital, and might thoroughly enjoy a joke at the expense of St. Petersburg, could not understand a little coterie of enthusiasts who sought neither official rank nor lucrative official appointments, who slighted many of the conventionalities of the higher classes to which by birth and education they belonged, who loved to fraternize with the common people, and who occasionally dressed in the national costume which had been discarded by the nobles since the time of Peter the Great.

The Slavophils thus remained merely a small literary party, which probably did not count more than a dozen members, but their influence was out of all proportion to their numbers. They preached successfully the doctrine that the historical development of Russia has been peculiar, that her present social and political organization is radically different from that of the countries of Western Europe, and that consequently the social and political evils from which she suffers are not to be cured by the remedies which have proved efficacious in France and Germany. These truths, which now appear commonplace, were formerly by no means generally recognized, and the Slavophils deserve credit for directing attention to them. Besides this, they helped to awaken in the upper classes a lively sympathy with the poor, oppressed, and despised peasantry. So long as the Emperor Nicholas lived they had to confine themselves to a purely literary activity; but during the great reforms initiated by his successor, Alexander II, they descended into the arena of practical politics, and played a most useful and honorable part in the emancipation of the serfs. In the new local self-government, too—the Zemstvo and the new municipal institutions—they labored energetically and to good purpose. . . .

But what of their Panslavist aspirations? By their theory they were constrained to pay attention to the Slav race as a whole, but they were more Russian than Slav, and more Muscovite than Russian. The Panslavist element consequently occupied a secondary place in Slavophil doctrine. Though they did much to stimulate popular sympathy with the Southern Slavs, and always cherished the hope that the Serbs, Bulgarians, and cognate Slav nationalities would one day throw off the bondage of the German and the Turk, they never proposed any elaborate project for the solution of the Eastern Question. So far as I was able to gather from their conversation, they seemed to favor the idea of a grand Slavonic Confederation, in which the hegemony would, of course, belong to Russia. In ordinary times the only steps which they took for the realization of this idea consisted in contributing money for schools and churches among the Slav population of Austria and Turkey, and in educating young Bulgarians in Russia. During the Cretan insurrection they sympathized warmly with the insurgents as co-religionists, but afterwards—especially during the crisis of the Eastern Question which culminated in the Treaty of San Stefano and the Congress of Berlin (1878)—their Hellenic sympathies cooled, because the Greeks showed that they had political aspirations of their own, inconsistent with the designs of Russia, and that they were likely to be the rivals rather than the allies of the Slavs in the struggle for the Sick Man's inheritance.

Since the time when I was living in Moscow in constant intercourse with the leading Slavophils some five-and-thirty years have passed, and of those with whom I spent so many pleasant evenings, discussing the past history and future destinies of the Slav races, not one remains alive. All the great prophets of the old Slavophil doctrine—Yuri Samárin, Prince Cherkaski, Ivan Aksákov, Koshelév— have departed without leaving behind them any genuine disciples. The present generation of Muscovite *frondeurs,*

who continue to rail against Western Europe and the
pedantic officialism of St. Petersburg, are of a more modern and less academic type. Their philippics are directed
not against Peter the Great and his reforms, but rather
against recent Ministers of Foreign Affairs, who are
thought to have shown themselves too subservient to
foreign Powers, and against Count Witte, who, as Minister
of Finance, "favored the introduction of foreign capital
and enterprise, and sacrificed to unhealthy industrial
development the interests of the agricultural classes."
These laments and diatribes find free expression in private
conversation and in the press, but they do not influence
very deeply the policy of the Government or the natural
course of events; for the Ministry of Foreign Affairs continues to cultivate friendly relations with the Cabinets of
the West, and Moscow is rapidly becoming, by the force
of economic conditions, the great industrial and commercial center of the Empire.

Perhaps I ought to say here a few words about a new
kind of Slavophilism, which has its headquarters in St.
Petersburg and differs somewhat from its Muscovite predecessor. Unlike my old reactionary friends who held that
the greatness of Russia could be developed only on the
basis of autocracy and Eastern Orthodoxy, the Slavophils
of this new school declare that their doctrines are quite
consistent with Liberal, Constitutional principles and with
religious freedom in the widest sense of the term. In
foreign policy they disclaim all territorial conquests, but
they maintain, like their predecessors, that Russia must
exercise a certain predominance in the Slav world, and
must resist strenuously any extension of German influence
in the Balkan Peninsula. In accordance with this principle
they protested vigorously against the annexation of Bosnia
and Herzegovina by Austria in 1908, and they thereby
attracted for a time a good deal of public attention; but
as the Cabinet of Vienna would not yield to mere diplomatic pressure, and Russia was not prepared to appeal to
arms, their protests led to no practical result, and they
retired into the political background. There is no doubt,
however, that we shall hear more about them in the next
crisis of the Eastern Question.

Moscow may well pride herself on being, in a certain sense, the capital of Russia, but the administrative and bureaucratic center of the Empire—if anything on the frontier of a country can be called its center—has long been, and is likely to remain, Peter's stately city at the mouth of the Neva, to which I now invite the reader to accompany me.

CHAPTER · XII

৶৽ ৽৶

St. Petersburg and
European Influence

FROM whatever side the traveler approaches St. Petersburg, unless he goes thither by sea, he must traverse several hundred miles of forest and morass, presenting few
traces of human habitation or agriculture. This fact adds
powerfully to the first impression which the city makes
on his mind. In the midst of a waste howling wilderness,
he suddenly comes on a magnificent artificial oasis.

Of all the great European cities, the one that most resembles the capital of the Tsars is Berlin. Both are built on
perfectly level ground; both have wide, regularly arranged
streets; in both there is a general look of stiffness and symmetry which suggests military discipline and German
bureaucracy. But there is at least one profound difference.
Though Berlin is said by geographers to be built on the
Spree, we might live a long time in the city without no-
ticing the sluggish little stream on which the name of a
river has been undeservedly conferred. St. Petersburg, on
the contrary, is built on a magnificent river, which forms
the main feature of the place. By its breadth, and by the
enormous volume of its clear, blue, cold water—somewhat polluted of late by manufacturing industry—the
Neva is certainly one of the noblest rivers of Europe. A
few miles before reaching the Gulf of Finland it breaks up
into several streams and forms a delta. It is here that St.
Petersburg stands.

Like the river, everything in St. Petersburg is on a

colossal scale. The streets, the squares, the palaces, the
public buildings, the churches, whatever may be their defects, have at least the attribute of greatness, and seem to
have been designed for the countless generations to come,
rather than for the practical wants of the present inhabitants. In this respect the city well represents the Empire
of which it is the capital. Even the private houses are built
in enormous blocks and divided into many separate apartments. Those built for the working classes sometimes contain, I am assured, more than a thousand inhabitants.
How many cubic feet of air is allowed to each person I
do not know; not so many, I fear, as is recommended by
the most advanced sanitary authorities.

For a detailed description of the city I must refer the
reader to the guidebooks. Among its numerous monuments,
of which the Russians are justly proud, I confess that the
one which interested me most was neither St. Isaac's
Cathedral, with its majestic gilded dome, its colossal mon-
olithic columns of red granite, and its gaudy interior; nor
the Hermitage, with its magnificent collection of Dutch
pictures; nor the gloomy, frowning fortress of St. Peter
and St. Paul, containing the tombs of the Emperors. These
and other "sights" may deserve all the praise which enthusiastic tourists have lavished upon them, but what made a
far deeper impression on me was the little wooden house
in which Peter the Great lived whilst his future capital was
being built. In its style and arrangement it looks more like
the hut of a navvy than the residence of a Tsar, but it was
quite in keeping with the character of the illustrious man
who occupied it. Peter could and did occasionally work
like a navvy without feeling that his Imperial dignity was
thereby impaired. When he determined to build a new
capital on a Finnish marsh, inhabited chiefly by wild-
fowl, he did not content himself with exercising his autocratic power in a comfortable armchair. Like the old Greek
gods, he went down from his Olympus, and took his place
in the ranks of ordinary mortals, superintending the work
with his own eyes, and taking part in it with his own
hands. If he was as arbitrary and oppressive as any of the
pyramid-building Pharaohs, he could at least say in self-
justification that he did not spare himself any more than

his people, but exposed himself freely to the discomforts
and dangers under which thousands of his fellow laborers
succumbed.

In reading the account of Peter's life, written in part by
his own pen, we can easily understand how the piously
Conservative section of his subjects failed to recognize in
him the legitimate successor of the orthodox Tsars. The
old Tsars had been men of grave, pompous demeanor,
deeply imbued with the consciousness of their semireligious dignity. Living habitually in Moscow or its immediate neighborhood, they spent their time in attending long
religious services, in consulting with their *Boyárs,* in being
present at ceremonious hunting parties, in visiting the
monasteries, and in holding edifying conversations with ecclesiastical dignitaries or revered ascetics. If they undertook a journey, it was probably to make a pilgrimage to
some holy shrine; and, whether in Moscow or elsewhere,
they were always protected from contact with ordinary
humanity by a formidable barricade of Court ceremonial.
In short, they combined the characters of a Christian
monk and of an Oriental potentate.

Peter was a man of an entirely different type, and
played in the calm, dignified, orthodox ceremonious world
of Moscow the part of the bull in the china shop, outraging ruthlessly and wantonly all the time-honored traditional conceptions of propriety and etiquette. Utterly re-
gardless of public opinion and popular prejudices, he
swept away the old formalities, avoided ceremonies of all
kinds, scoffed at ancient usage, preferred foreign secular
books to edifying conversations, chose profane heretics as
his boon companions, traveled in foreign countries, dressed
in heretical costume, defaced the image of God and put
his soul in jeopardy by shaving off his beard, compelled
his nobles to dress and shave like himself, rushed about the
Empire as if goaded on by the demon of unrest, employed
his sacred hands in carpentering and other menial occupations, took part openly in the uproarious orgies of his foreign soldiery, and, in short, did everything that "the Lord's
anointed" might reasonably be expected not to do. No
wonder the Muscovites were scandalized by his conduct,
and that some of them suspected he was not the Tsar at

all, but Antichrist in disguise. And no wonder he felt the atmosphere of Moscow oppressive, and preferred living in the new capital which he had himself created.

His avowed object in building St. Petersburg was to have "a window by which the Russians might look into civilized Europe"; and well has the city fulfilled its purpose. From its foundation may be dated the European period of Russian history. Before Peter's time Russia belonged to Asia rather than to Europe, and was doubtless regarded by Englishmen and Frenchmen pretty much as we nowadays regard Bokhara or Kashgar; since that time she has formed an integral part of the European political system, and her intellectual history has been a reflection of the intellectual history of Western Europe, modified and colored by national character and by peculiar local conditions.

When we speak of the intellectual history of a nation we generally mean in reality the intellectual history of the progressive upper classes. With regard to Russia, more perhaps than with regard to any other country, this distinction must always carefully be borne in mind. Peter succeeded in forcing European civilization on the nobles, but the people remained unaffected. The nation was, as it were, cleft in two, and with each succeeding generation the cleft widened. Whilst the masses clung obstinately to their time-honored customs and beliefs, the nobles came to look on the objects of popular veneration as the relics of a barbarous past, of which a civilized nation ought to be ashamed.

The intellectual movement inaugurated by Peter had a purely practical character. He was himself a thorough utilitarian, and perceived clearly that what his people needed was not theological or philosophical enlightenment, but plain practical knowledge suitable for the requirements of everyday life. He wanted neither theologians nor philosophers, but military and naval officers, administrators, artisans, miners, manufacturers, and merchants, and for this purpose he introduced secular technical education. For the young generation primary schools were founded, and for more advanced pupils the best foreign works on fortification, architecture, navigation, metallurgy, engineering and

cognate subjects, were translated into the native tongue.
Scientific men and cunning artificers were brought into the
country, and the young Russians were sent abroad to learn
foreign languages and the useful arts. In a word, everything was done that seemed likely to raise the Russians to
the level of material well-being already attained by the
more advanced nations.

We have here an important peculiarity in the intellectual development of Russia. In Western Europe the modern scientific spirit, being the natural offspring of numerous concomitant historical causes, was born in the natural
way, and society had, consequently, before giving birth to
it, to endure the pains of pregnancy and the throes of prolonged labor. In Russia, on the contrary, this spirit appeared suddenly as an adult foreigner adopted by a
despotic pater familias. Thus Russia made the transition
from medieval to modern times without any violent struggle between the old and the new conceptions, such as had
taken place in the West. The Church, effectually restrained from all active opposition by the Imperial power,
preserved unmodified her ancient beliefs; whilst the nobles, casting their traditional conceptions and beliefs to
the winds, marched forward unfettered on that path
which their fathers and grandfathers had regarded as the
direct road to perdition.

During the first part of Peter's reign Russia was not subjected to the exclusive influence of any one particular
country. Thoroughly cosmopolitan in his sympathies, the
great reformer, like the modern Japanese, was ready to
borrow from any foreign nation—German, Dutch, Danish,
or French—whatever seemed to him to suit his purpose.
But soon the geographical proximity to Germany, the annexation of the Baltic Provinces in which the civilization
was German, and intermarriages between the Imperial
family and various German dynasties, gave to German influence a decided preponderance. When the Empress
Anne, Peter's niece, who had been Duchess of Courland,
entrusted the whole administration of the country to her
favorite Biron, the German influence became almost exclusive, and the Court, the official world, and the schools
were Germanized.

The harsh, cruel, tyrannical rule of Biron produced a strong reaction, ending in a revolution, which raised to the throne the Princess Elizabeth, Peter's unmarried daughter, who had lived in retirement and neglect during the German regime. She was expected to rid the country of foreigners, and she did what she could to fulfill the expectations that were entertained of her. With loud protestations of patriotic feelings, she removed the Germans from all important posts, demanded that in future the members of the Academy should be chosen from among born Russians, and gave orders that the Russian youth should be carefully prepared for all kinds of official activity.

This attempt to throw off the German bondage did not lead to intellectual independence. During Peter's violent reforms Russia had ruthlessly thrown away her own historic past with whatever germs it contained, and now she possessed none of the elements of a genuine national culture. She was in the position of a fugitive who has escaped from slavery, and, finding himself in danger of starvation, looks about for a new master. The upper classes, who had acquired a taste for foreign civilization, no sooner threw off everything German than they sought some other civilization to put in its place. And they could not long hesitate in making a choice, for at that time all who thought of culture and refinement turned their eyes to Paris and Versailles. All that was most brilliant and refined was to be found at the Court of the French kings, under whose patronage the art and literature of the Renaissance had attained their highest development. Even Germany, which had resisted the ambitious designs of Louis XIV, imitated the manners of his Court. Every petty German potentate strove to ape the pomp and dignity of the Grand Monarque; and the courtiers, affecting to look on everything German as rude and barbarous, adopted French fashions, and spoke a hybrid jargon which they considered much more elegant than the plain mother tongue. In a word, Gallomania had become the prevailing social epidemic of the time, and it could not fail to attack and metamorphose such a class as the Russian Noblesse, which possessed few stubborn deep-rooted national convictions.

At first the French influence was manifested chiefly in external forms—that is to say, in dress, manners, language, and upholstery—but gradually, and very rapidly after the accession of Catherine II, the friend of Voltaire and the Encyclopédistes, it sank deeper. Every noble who had pretensions to being "civilized" learned to speak French fluently, and gained some superficial acquaintance with French literature. The tragedies of Corneille and Racine and the comedies of Molière were played regularly at the Court theater in presence of the Empress, and awakened a real or affected enthusiasm among the audience. For those who preferred reading in their native language, numerous translations were published, a simple list of which would fill several pages. Among them we find not only Voltaire, Rousseau, Lesage, Marmontel, and other favorite French authors, but also all the masterpieces of European literature, ancient and modern, which at that time enjoyed a high reputation in the French literary world—Homer and Demosthenes, Cicero and Virgil, Ariosto and Camoens, Milton and Locke, Sterne and Fielding.

It is related of Byron that he never wrote a description whilst the scene was actually before him; and this fact points to an important psychological principle. The human mind, so long as it is compelled to strain the receptive faculties, cannot engage in that "poetic" activity—to use the term in its Greek sense—which is commonly called "original creation." And as with individuals, so with nations. By accepting in a lump a foreign culture a nation inevitably condemns itself for a time to intellectual sterility. So long as it is occupied in receiving and assimilating a flood of new ideas, unfamiliar conceptions, and foreign modes of thought, it will produce nothing original, and the result of its highest efforts will be merely successful imitation. We need not be surprised therefore to find that the Russians, in becoming acquainted with foreign literature, became imitators and plagiarists. In this kind of work their natural pliancy of mind and powerful histrionic talent made them wonderfully successful. Odes, pseudo-classical tragedies, satirical comedies, epic poems, elegies, and all the other recognized forms of poetical composition, appeared in great profusion, and many of the writers acquired a remarkable command over their native language, which had hitherto been regarded as uncouth and barbarous. But in all this mass of imitative literature, which has since fallen into well-merited oblivion, there are very few traces of genuine originality. To obtain the title of the Russian Racine, the Russian Lafontaine, the Russian Pindar, or the Russian Homer, was at that time the highest aim of Russian literary ambition.

Together with the fashionable literature the Russian educated classes adopted something of the fashionable philosophy. They were peculiarly unfitted to resist that hurricane of "enlightenment" which swept over Europe during the latter half of the eighteenth century, first breaking or uprooting the received philosophical systems, theological conceptions, and scientific theories, and then shaking to their foundations the existing political and social institutions. The Russian Noblesse had neither the traditional conservative spirit nor the firm, well-reasoned, logical beliefs which in England and Germany formed a powerful barrier against the spread of French influence. They had been too recently metamorphosed, and were too eager to acquire a foreign civilization, to have even the germs of a conservative spirit. The rapidity and violence with which Peter's reforms had been effected, together with the peculiar spirit of Greek Orthodoxy and the low intellectual level of the clergy, had prevented theology from associating itself with the new order of things. The upper classes had become estranged from the beliefs of their forefathers without acquiring other beliefs to supply the place of those which had been lost. The old religious conceptions were inseparably interwoven with what was recognized as antiquated and barbarous, whilst the new philosophical ideas were associated with all that was modern and civilized. Besides this, the sovereign, Catherine II, who enjoyed the unbounded admiration of the upper classes, openly professed allegiance to the new philosophy, and sought the advice and friendship of its high priests. If we bear in mind these facts we shall not be surprised to find among the Russian nobles of that time a considerable number of so-called "Voltaireans" and numerous unquestioning believers in the infallibility of the Encyclopédie.

What is a little more surprising is that the new philosophy
sometimes found its way into the ecclesiastical seminaries.
The famous Speranski relates that in the seminary of St.
Petersburg, one of his professors, when not in a state of
intoxication, was in the habit of preaching the doctrines
of Voltaire and Diderot!

The rise of the sentimental school in Western Europe
produced an important change in Russian literature, by
undermining the inordinate admiration for the French
pseudo-classical school. Florian, Richardson, Sterne, Rousseau, and Bernardin de St. Pierre found first translators,
and then imitators, and soon the loud-sounding declamation and wordy ecstatic despair of the stage heroes were
drowned in the deep-drawn sighs and plaintive wailings of
amorous swains and peasant maids forsaken. The mania
seems to have been in Russia even more severe than in
the countries where it originated. Full-grown, bearded
men wept because they had not been born in peaceful
primitive times, "when all men were shepherds and brothers." Hundreds of sighing youths and maidens visited the
scenes described by the sentimental writers, and wandered
by the rivers and ponds in which despairing heroines had
drowned themselves. People talked, wrote, and meditated
about "the sympathy of hearts created for each other,"
"the soft communion of sympathetic souls," and much
more of the same kind. Sentimental journeys became a
favorite amusement, and formed the subject of very popular books, containing maudlin absurdities likely to produce
nowadays mirth rather than tears. One traveler, for instance, throws himself on his knees before an old oak and
makes a speech to it; another weeps daily on the grave of
a favorite dog, and constantly longs to marry a peasant
girl; a third talks love to the moon, sends kisses to the stars,
and wishes to press the heavenly orbs to his bosom! For
a time the public would read nothing but absurd productions of this sort, and Karamzín, the great literary authority of the time, expressly declared that the true function
of Art was "to disseminate agreeable impressions in the region of the sentimental."

The love of French philosophy vanished as suddenly as
the inordinate admiration of the French pseudo-classical

literature. When the great Revolution broke out in Paris, the fashionable philosophic literature in St. Petersburg disappeared. Men who talked about political freedom and the rights of man, without thinking for a moment of limiting the autocratic power or of emancipating their serfs, were naturally surprised and frightened on discovering what the liberal principles could effect when applied to real life. Horrified by the awful scenes of the Terror, they hastened to divest themselves of the principles which led to such results, and sank into a kind of optimistic conservatism that harmonized well with the virtuous sentimentalism in vogue. In this the Empress herself gave the example. The Imperial disciple and friend of the Encyclopédistes became in the last years of her reign a decided *réactionnaire.*

During the Napoleonic wars, when the patriotic feelings were excited, there was a violent hostility to foreign intellectual influence; and feeble intermittent attempts were made to throw off the intellectual bondage. The invasion of the country in 1812 by the Grande Armée, and the burning of Moscow, added abundant fuel to this patriotic fire. For some time anyone who ventured to express even a moderate admiration for French culture incurred the risk of being stigmatized as a traitor to his country and a renegade to the national faith. But this patriotic fanaticism soon evaporated, and the exaggerations of the ultra-national party became the object of satire and parody. When the political danger was past, and people resumed their ordinary occupations, those who loved foreign literature returned to their old favorites—or, as the ultra-patriots called it, to their "wallowing in the mire"—simply because the native literature did not supply them with what they desired. "We are quite ready," they said to their upbraiders, "to admire your great works as soon as they appear, but in the meantime please allow us to enjoy what we possess." Thus in the last years of the reign of Alexander I the patriotic opposition to West European literature gradually ceased, and a new period of unrestricted intellectual importation began.

The intellectual merchandise now brought into the country was very different from that which had been imported in the time of Catherine. The French Revolution, the Napoleonic domination, the patriotic wars, the restoration of the Bourbons, and the other great events of that memorable epoch, had in the interval produced profound changes in the intellectual as well as the political condition of Western Europe. During the Napoleonic wars Russia had become closely associated with Germany; and now the peculiar intellectual fermentation which was going on among the German educated classes was reflected in the society of St. Petersburg. It did not appear, indeed, in the printed literature, for the press censure had been recently organized on the principles laid down by Metternich, but it was none the less violent on that account. Whilst the periodicals were filled with commonplace meditations on youth, spring, the love of art, and similar innocent topics, the young generation was discussing in the salons all the burning questions which Metternich and his adherents were endeavoring to extinguish.

These discussions, if discussions they might be called, were not of a very serious kind. In true dilettante style the fashionable young philosophers culled from the newest books the newest thoughts and theories, and retailed them in the salon or the ballroom. And they were always sure to find attentive listeners. The more astounding the idea or dogma, the more likely was it to be favorably received. No matter whether it came from the Rationalists, the Mystics, the Freemasons, or the Methodists, it was certain to find favor, provided it was novel and presented in an elegant form. The eclectic minds of that curious time could derive equal satisfaction from the brilliant discourses of the reactionary jesuitical De Maistre, the revolutionary odes of Pushkin, and the mysticism of Frau von Krüdener. For the majority the vague theosophic doctrines and the projects for a spiritual union of governments and peoples had perhaps the greatest charm, being specially commended by the fact that they enjoyed the protection and sympathy of the Emperor. Pious souls discovered in the mystical lucubrations of Jung-Stilling and Baader the final solution of all existing difficulties—political, social, and philosophical. Men of less dreamy temperament put their faith in political economy and constitutional theories, and sought a foundation for their favorite schemes in the past history of the country and in the supposed fundamental peculiarities of the national character. Like the young German democrats, who were then talking enthusiastically about Teutons, Cheruskers, Skalds, the shade of Arminius, and the heroes of the Nibelungen, these young Russian savants recognized in early Russian history—when reconstructed according to their own fancy—lofty political ideals, and dreamed, in their new-born enthusiasm, of resuscitating the ancient institutions in all their pristine imaginary splendor.

Each age has its peculiar social and political panaceas. One generation puts its trust in religion, another in philanthropy, a third in written constitutions, a fourth in universal suffrage, a fifth in popular education. In the Epoch of the Restoration, as it is called, the favorite panacea all over the Continent was secret political association. Very soon after the overthrow of Napoleon, the peoples who had risen in arms to obtain political independence discovered that they had merely changed masters. The Princes reconstructed Europe according to their own convenience, without paying much attention to patriotic aspirations, and forgot their promises of liberal institutions as soon as they were again firmly seated on their thrones. This was naturally for many a bitter deception. The young generation, excluded from all share in political life and gagged by the stringent police supervision, sought to realize its political aspirations by means of secret societies, resembling more or less the masonic brotherhoods. There were the Burschenschaften in Germany; the Union, and the "Aide toi et le ciel t'aidera," in France; the Order of the Hammer in Spain; the Carbonari in Italy; and the Hetairai in Greece. In Russia the young nobles followed the prevailing fashion. Secret societies were formed, and in December, 1825, an attempt was made to raise a military insurrection in St. Petersburg, for the purpose of deposing the Imperial family and proclaiming a republic; but the attempt failed, and the vague Utopian dreams of the romantic would-be reformers were swept away by grapeshot.

This "December catastrophe," still vividly remembered,

was for the society of St. Petersburg like the giving way of
the floor in a crowded ballroom. But a moment before, all
had been animated, careless, and happy; now consternation was depicted on every face. The salons that but yesterday had been ringing with lively discussions on morals,
aesthetics, politics, and theology, were now silent and de-
serted. Many of those who had been wont to lead the
causeries had been removed to the cells of the fortress, and
those who had not been arrested trembled for themselves
or their friends; for nearly all had of late dabbled more or
less in the theory and practice of revolution. The announcement that five of the conspirators had been condemned to the gallows and the others sentenced to transportation did not tend to calm the consternation. Society
was like a discomfited child who amidst the delight and
excitement of letting off fireworks has had his fingers severely burned.

The sentimental, wavering Alexander I had been succeeded by his stern, energetic brother Nicholas, and the
command went forth that there should be no more fireworks, no more dilettante philosophizing or political aspirations. There was, however, little need for such an order.
Society had been, for the moment at least, effectually
cured of all tendencies to political dreaming. It had discovered, to its astonishment and dismay, that these new
ideas, which were to bring temporal salvation to humanity, and to make all men happy, virtuous, refined, and
poetical, led in reality to exile and the scaffold! The pleasant dream was at an end, and the fashionable world, giving up its former habits, took to harmless occupations—
card-playing, dissipation, and the reading of French light
literature. "The French quadrille," as a writer of the time
tersely expresses it, "has taken the place of Adam Smith."

When the storm had passed, the life of the salons began
anew, but it was very different from what it had been.
There was no longer any talk about political economy,
theology, popular education, administrative abuses, social
and political reforms. Everything that had any relation to
politics in the wider sense of the term was by tacit consent
avoided. Discussions there were as of old, but they were

now confined to literary topics, theories of art, and similar innocent subjects.

This indifference or positive repugnance to philosophy and political science, strengthened and prolonged by the repressive system of administration adopted by Nicholas, was of course fatal to the many-sided intellectual activity which had flourished during the preceding reign, but it was by no means unfavorable to the cultivation of imaginative literature. On the contrary, by excluding those practical interests which tend to disturb artistic production and to engross the attention of the public, it fostered what was called in the phraseology of that time "the pure-hearted worship of the Muses." We need not, therefore, be surprised to find that the reign of Nicholas, which is commonly and not unjustly described as an epoch of social and intellectual stagnation, may be called in a certain sense the Golden Age of Russian literature.

Already in the preceding reign the struggle between the Classical and the Romantic school—between the adherents of traditional aesthetic principles and the partisans of untrammeled poetic inspiration—which was being carried on in Western Europe, was reflected in Russia. A group of young men belonging to the aristocratic society of St. Petersburg embraced with enthusiasm the new doctrines, and declared war against "classicism," under which term they understood all that was antiquated, dry, and pedantic. Discarding the stately, lumbering, unwieldy periods which had hitherto been in fashion, they wrote a light, elastic, vigorous style, and formed a literary society for the express purpose of ridiculing the most approved classical writers. The new principles found many adherents, and the new style many admirers, but this only intensified the hostility of the literary Conservatives. The staid, respectable leaders of the old school, who had all their lives kept the fear of Boileau before their eyes and considered his precepts as the infallible utterances of aesthetic wisdom, thundered against the impious innovations as unmistakable symptoms of literary decline and moral degeneracy—representing the boisterous young iconoclasts as dissipated Don Juans and dangerous free-thinkers.

Thus for some time in Russia, as in Western Europe, "a terrible war raged on Parnassus." At first the Government frowned at the innovators, on account of certain revolutionary odes which one of their number had written; but when the Romantic Muse, having turned away from the present as essentially prosaic, went back into the distant past and soared into the region of sublime abstractions, the most keen-eyed press censors found no reason to condemn her worship, and the authorities placed almost no restrictions on free poetic inspiration. Romantic poetry acquired the protection of the Government and the patronage of the Court, and the names of Zhukovski, Pushkin, and Lermontov—the three chief representatives of the Russian Romantic school—became household words in all ranks of the educated classes.

These three great luminaries of the literary world were of course attended by a host of satellites of various magnitudes, who did all in their power to refute the Romantic principles by *reductiones ad absurdum.* Endowed for the most part with considerable facility of composition, the poetasters poured forth their feelings with torrential recklessness, demanding freedom for their inspiration, and cursing the age that fettered them with its prosaic cares, its cold reason, and its dry science. At the same time the dramatists and novelists created heroes of immaculate character and angelic purity, endowed with all the cardinal virtues in the superlative degree; and, as a contrast to these, terrible Satanic personages with savage passions, gleaming daggers, deadly poisons, and all manner of aimless melodramatic villainy. These stilted productions, interspersed with light satirical essays, historical sketches, literary criticism, and amusing anecdotes, formed the contents of the periodical literature, and completely satisfied the wants of the reading public. Almost no one at that time took any interest in public affairs or foreign politics. The acts of the Government which were watched most attentively were the promotions in the service and the conferring of decorations. The publication of a new tale by Zagóskin or Marlínski—two writers now well-nigh forgotten—seemed of much greater importance than any amount of legislation, and such events as the French Revo-

lution of 1830 paled before the publication of a new poem
by Pushkin.

The Transcendental philosophy, which in Germany
went hand in hand with the Romantic literature, found
likewise a faint reflection in Russia. A number of young
professors and students in Moscow, who had become ardent admirers of German literature, passed from the works
of Schiller, Goethe, and Hoffmann to the writings of
Schelling and Hegel. Trained in the Romantic School,
these young philosophers found at first a special charm in
Schelling's mystical system, teeming with hazy poetical
metaphors, and presenting a misty grandiose picture of
the universe; but gradually they felt the want of some
logical basis for their speculations, and Hegel became their
favorite. Gallantly they struggled with the uncouth terminology and epigrammatic paradoxes of the great thinker,
and strove to force their way through the intricate mazes
of his logical formulas. With the ardor of neophytes they
looked at every phenomenon—even the most trivial incident of common life—from the philosophical point of view,
talked day and night about principles, ideas, subjectivity,
Weltauffassung, and similar abstract entities, and habitually attacked the "hydra of unphilosophy" by analyzing the
phenomena presented and relegating the ingredient elements to the recognized categories. In ordinary life they
were men of quiet, grave, contemplative demeanor, but
their faces could flush and their blood boil when they discussed the all-important question whether it is possible to
pass logically from Pure Being through Nonentity to the
conception of Development and Definite Existence!

We know how in Western Europe Romanticism and
Transcendentalism, in their various forms, sank into oblivion, and were replaced by a literature which had a closer
connection with ordinary prosaic wants and plain everyday life. The educated public became weary of the Romantic writers, who were always "sighing like a furnace,"
delighting in solitude, cold eternity, and moonshine, delug-
ing the world with their heart-gushings, and calling on
the heavens and the earth to stand aghast at their Prome-
thean agonizing or their Wertherean despair. Healthy human nature revolted against the poetical enthusiasts, who

had lost the faculty of seeing things in their natural light, and who constantly indulged in that morbid self-analysis which is fatal to genuine feeling and vigorous action. And in this healthy reaction the philosophers fared no better than the poets, with whom, indeed, they had much in common. Shutting their eyes to the visible world around them, they had busied themselves with burrowing in the mysterious depths of Absolute Being, grappling with the *ego* and the *non-ego*, constructing the great world, visible and invisible, out of their own puny internal self-consciousness, endeavoring to appropriate all departments of human thought, and imparting to every subject they touched the dryness and rigidity of an algebraical formula. Gradually men with real human sympathies began to perceive that from all this philosophical turmoil little real advantage was to be derived. It became only too evident that the philosophers were perfectly reconciled with all the evil in the world, provided it did not contradict their theories; that they were men of the same type as the physician in Molière's comedy, whose chief care was that his patients should die *selon les ordonnances de la médecine*.

In Russia the reaction first appeared in the aesthetic literature. Its first influential representative was Gógol (b. 1808, d. 1852), who may be called, in a certain sense, the Russian Dickens. A minute comparison of those two great humorists would perhaps show as many points of contrast as of similarity, but there is a strong superficial resemblance between them. They both possessed an inexhaustible supply of broad humor and an imagination of singular vividness. Both had the power of seeing the ridiculous side of common things, and the talent of producing caricatures that had a wonderful semblance of reality. A little calm reflection would suffice to show that the characters presented are for the most part psychological impossibilities; but on first making their acquaintance we are so struck with one or two lifelike characteristics and various little details dexterously introduced, and at the same time we are so carried away by the overflowing fun of the narrative, that we have neither time nor inclination to use our critical faculties. In a very short time Gógol's fame spread throughout the length and breadth of the

Empire, and many of his characters became as familiar to his countrymen as Sam Weller and Mrs. Gamp were to Englishmen. His descriptions were so graphic—so like the world which everybody knew! The characters seemed to be old acquaintances hit off to the life; and readers reveled in that peculiar pleasure which most of us derive from seeing our friends successfully mimicked. Even the Iron Tsar could not resist the fun and humor of "The Inspector" (*Revizór*), and not only laughed heartily, but also protected the author against the tyranny of the literary censors, who considered that the piece was not written in a sufficiently "well-intentioned" tone. In a word, the reading public laughed as it had never laughed before, and this wholesome, genuine merriment did much to destroy the morbid appetite for Byronic heroes and Romantic affectation.

The Romantic Muse did not at once abdicate, but with the spread of Gógol's popularity her reign was practically at an end. In vain some of the conservative critics decried the new favorite as talentless, prosaic, and vulgar. The public were not to be robbed of their amusement for the sake of any abstract aesthetic considerations; and young authors, taking Gógol for their model, chose their subjects from real life, and endeavored to delineate with minute truthfulness.

This new intellectual movement was at first purely literary, and affected merely the manner of writing novels, tales, and poems. The critics who had previously demanded beauty of form and elegance of expression now demanded accuracy of description, condemned the aspirations towards so-called high art, and praised loudly those who produced the best literary photographs. But authors and critics did not long remain on this purely aesthetic standpoint. The authors, in describing reality, began to indicate moral approval and condemnation, and the critics began to pass from the criticism of the representations to the criticism of the realities represented. A poem or a tale was often used as a peg on which to hang a moral lecture, and the fictitious characters were soundly rated for their sins of omission and commission. Much was said about the defense of the oppressed, female emancipation, honor, and humanitarianism; and ridicule was unsparingly launched against all forms of ignorance, apathy, and the spirit of routine. The ordinary refrain was that the public ought now to discard what was formerly regarded as poetical and sublime, and to occupy itself with practical concerns —with the real wants of social life.

The literary movement was thus becoming a movement in favor of social and political reform when it was suddenly arrested by political events in the West. The February Revolution in Paris, and the political fermentation which appeared during 1848-49 in almost every country of Europe, alarmed the Emperor Nicholas and his counsellors. A Russian army was sent into Austria to suppress the Hungarian insurrection and save the Hapsburg dynasty, and the most stringent measures were taken to prevent disorders at home. One of the first precautions for the preservation of domestic tranquillity was to muzzle the press more firmly than before, and to silence the aspirations towards reform and progress; thenceforth nothing could be printed which was not in strict accordance with the ultrapatriotic theory of Russian history, as expressed by a leading official personage: "The past has been admirable, the present is more than magnificent, and the future will surpass all that the human imagination can conceive!" The alarm caused by the revolutionary disorders spread to the nonofficial world, and gave rise to much patriotic self-congratulation. "The nations of the West," it was said, "envy us, and if they knew us better— if they could see how happy and prosperous we are— they would envy us still more. We ought not, however, to withdraw from Europe our solicitude; its hostility should not deprive us of our high mission of saving order and restoring rest to the nations; we ought to teach them to obey authority as we do. It is for us to introduce the saving principle of order into a world that has fallen a prey to anarchy. Russia ought not to abandon that mission which has been entrusted to her by the heavenly and by the earthly Tsar." [1]

[1] These words were written by Chaadáév, who, a few years before, had vigorously attacked the Slavophils for enouncing similar views.

Men who saw in the significant political eruption of 1848 nothing but an outburst of meaningless, aimless anarchy, and who believed that their country was destined to restore order throughout the civilized world, had of course little time or inclination to think of putting their own house in order. No one now spoke of the necessity of social reorganization; the recently awakened aspirations and expectations seemed to be completely forgotten. The critics returned to their old theory that art and literature should be cultivated for their own sake and not used as a vehicle for the propagation of ideas foreign to their nature. It seemed, in short, as if all the prolific ideas which had for a time occupied the public attention had been merely "writ in water," and had now disappeared without leaving a trace behind them.

In reality the new movement was destined to reappear very soon with tenfold force . . . Ever since the time of Peter the Great there has been such a close connection between Russia and Western Europe that every intellectual movement which has appeared in France and Germany has been reflected—albeit in an exaggerated, distorted form—in the educated society of St. Petersburg and Moscow. Thus the window which Peter opened in order to enable his subjects to look into Europe has well served its purpose.

CHAPTER XIII

Lord Novgorod the Great

COUNTRY life in Russia is pleasant enough in summer or in winter, but between summer and winter there is an intermediate period of several weeks, when the rain and mud transform a country house into something very like a prison. To escape this durance vile I determined in the month of October to leave Ivánovka, and chose as my headquarters for the next few months the town of Novgorod—the old town of that name, not to be confounded with Nizhni Novgorod, i.e. Lower Novgorod, on the Volga, where the great annual fair is held.

For this choice there were several reasons. I did not wish to go to St. Petersburg or Moscow, because I foresaw that in either of those cities my studies would certainly be interrupted. In a quiet, sleepy provincial town I should have much more chance of coming in contact with people who could not speak fluently any West European languages, and much better opportunities for studying native life and local administration. Of the provincial capitals, Novgorod was the nearest, and more interesting than most of its rivals; for it has had a curious history, much older than that of St. Petersburg or even of Moscow, and some traces of its former greatness are still visible. Though now a town of third-rate importance—a mere shadow of its former self—it still contains about 27,000 inhabitants, and is the administrative center of a large province.

About eighty miles from St. Petersburg the Moscow railway crosses the Volkhov, a rapid, muddy river which connects Lake Ilmen with Lake Ladoga. At the point of intersection I got on board a small steamer and sailed up

stream towards Lake Ilmen for about fifty miles.[1] The
journey was tedious, for the country is flat and monotonous, and the steamer, though it puffed and snorted inordinately, did not make more than nine knots. Towards
sunset Novgorod appeared on the horizon. Seen thus at a
distance in the soft twilight, it seemed decidedly picturesque. On the east bank lay the greater part of the town,
the skyline of which was agreeably broken by the green
roofs and pear-shaped cupolas of many churches. On the
opposite bank rose the Kremlin. Spanning the river was a
long, venerable stone bridge, half hidden by a temporary
wooden one, which was doing duty for the older structure
while the latter was being repaired. A cynical fellow pas-
senger assured me that the temporary structure was destined to become permanent because it yielded a comfortable revenue to certain officials, but this sinister prediction
has not been fulfilled.

That part of Novgorod which lies on the eastern bank of
the river, and in which I took up my abode for several
months, contains nothing that is worthy of special attention. As is the case in most Russian towns, the streets are
straight, wide, and ill-paved, and all run parallel or at
right angles to each other. At the end of the bridge is a
spacious market place, flanked on one side by the Town-
house. Near the other side stand the houses of the Governor and of the chief military authority of the district. The
only other buildings of note are the numerous churches,
which are mostly small, and offer nothing that is likely to
interest the student of architecture. Altogether this part of
the town is unquestionably commonplace. The learned
archeologist may detect in it some traces of the distant
past, but the ordinary traveler will find little to arrest his
attention.

If now we cross over to the west bank of the river, we
are at once confronted by something which very few Russian towns possess—a kremlin, or citadel. This is a large
and slightly elevated enclosure, surrounded by high brick
walls, and in part by the remains of a moat. Before the

[1] The journey would now be made by rail, but the branch line
which runs near the bank of the river had not been constructed
at that time.

days of heavy artillery these walls must have presented a
formidable barrier to any besieging force, but they have
long ceased to have any military significance, and are now
nothing more than an historical monument. Passing
through the gateway which faces the bridge, we find ourselves in a large open space. To the right stands the cathedral—a small, much-venerated church, which can make
no pretensions to architectural beauty—and an irregular
group of buildings containing the consistory and the residence of the Archbishop. To the left is a long symmetrical
range of buildings containing the Government offices and
the law courts. Midway between this and the cathedral,
in the center of the great open space, stands a colossal
monument, composed of a massive circular stone pedestal
and an enormous globe, on and around which cluster a
number of emblematic and historical figures. This curious
monument, which has at least the merit of being original in
design, was erected in 1862, in commemoration of Russia's thousandth birthday, and is supposed to represent
the history of Russia in general and of Novgorod in particular during the last thousand years. It was placed here
because Novgorod is the oldest of Russian towns, and because somewhere in the surrounding country occurred the
incident which is commonly recognized as the foundation
of the Russian Empire. The incident in question is thus
described in the oldest chronicle:

"At that time, as the southern Slavonians paid tribute
to the Kozars, so the Novgorodian Slavonians suffered
from the attacks of the Variags. For some time the Variags
extracted tribute from the Novgorodian Slavonians and
the neighboring Finns; then the conquered tribes, by unit-
ing their forces, drove out the foreigners. But among the
Slavonians arose strong internal dissensions; the clans rose
against each other. Then, for the creation of order and
safety, they resolved to call in princes from a foreign land.
In the year 862 Slavonic legates went away beyond the sea
to the Variag tribe called Rūs, and said, 'Our land is great
and fruitful, but there is no order in it; come and reign
and rule over us.' Three brothers accepted the invitation,
and appeared with their armed followers. The eldest of
these, Rurik, settled in Novgorod; the second, Sineus, at

Byeloózero; and the third, Truvor, in Isborsk. From them our land is called Rūs. After two years the brothers of Rurik died. He alone began to rule over the Novgorod district, and confided to his men the administration of the principal towns."

This simple legend has given rise to a vast amount of learned controversy, and historical investigators have fought valiantly with each other over the important question, Who were those armed men of Rūs? For a long time the commonly received opinion was that they were Normans from Scandinavia. The Slavophils accepted the legend literally in this sense, and constructed upon it an ingenious theory of Russian history. The nations of the West, they said, were conquered by invaders, who seized the country and created the feudal system for their own benefit; hence the history of Western Europe is a long tale of bloody struggles between conquerors and conquered, and at the present day the old enmity still lives in the political rivalry of the different social classes. The Russo-Slavonians, on the contrary, were not conquered, but voluntarily invited a foreign prince to come and rule over them; hence the whole social and political development of Russia has been essentially peaceful, and the Russian people know nothing of social castes or feudalism. Though this theory afforded some nourishment for patriotic self-satisfaction, it displeased extreme patriots, who did not like the idea that order was first established in their country by men of Teutonic race. These preferred to adopt the theory that Rurik and his companions were Slavonians from the shores of the Baltic.

Though I devoted to the study of this question more time and labor than perhaps the subject deserved, I have no intention of inviting the reader to follow me through the tedious controversy. Suffice it to say that, after careful consideration, and with all due deference to recent historians, I am inclined to adopt the old theory, and to regard the Normans of Scandinavia as in a certain sense the founders of the Russian Empire. We know from other sources that during the ninth century there was a great exodus from Scandinavia. Greedy of booty, and fired with the spirit of adventure, the Northmen, in their light, open boats, swept along the coasts of Germany, France, Spain, Greece, and Asia Minor, pillaging the towns and villages near the sea, and entering into the heart of the country by means of the rivers. At first they were mere marauders, and showed everywhere such ferocity and cruelty that they came to be regarded as something akin to plagues and famines, and the faithful added a new petition to the Litany, "From the wrath and malice of the Normans, O Lord, deliver us!" But towards the middle of the century the movement changed its character. The raids became military invasions, and the invaders sought to conquer the lands which they had formerly plundered, "ut acquirant sibi spoliando regna quibus possent vivere pace perpetua." The chiefs embraced Christianity, married the daughters or sisters of the reigning princes, and obtained the con-quered territories as feudal grants. Thus arose Norman principalities in the Low Countries, in France, in Italy, and in Sicily; and the Northmen, rapidly blending with the native population, soon showed as much political talent as they had formerly shown reckless and destructive valor.

It would have been strange indeed if these adventurers, who succeeded in reaching Asia Minor and the coasts of North America, should have overlooked Russia, which lay, as it were, at their very doors. The Volkhov, flowing through Novgorod, formed part of a great waterway, which afforded almost uninterrupted water communica-tion between the Baltic and the Black Sea; and we know that some time afterwards the Scandinavians used this route in their journeys to Constantinople. The change which the Scandinavian movement underwent elsewhere is clearly indicated by the Russian chronicles: first, the Variags came as collectors of tribute, and raised so much popular opposition that they were expelled, and then they came as rulers, and settled in the country. Whether they really came on invitation may be doubted, but that they adopted the language, religion, and customs of the native population does not militate against the assertion that they were Normans. On the contrary, we have here rather an additional confirmation, for elsewhere the Nor-mans did likewise. In the North of France they adopted almost at once the French language and religion, and the son and successor of the famous Rollo was sometimes reproached with being more French than Norman.[2]

Though it is difficult to decide how far the legend is literally true, there can be no possible doubt that the event which it more or less accurately describes had an important influence on Russian history. From that time dates the rapid expansion of the Russo-Slavonians—a movement that is still going on at the present day. To the north, the east, and the south, new principalities were formed and governed by men who all claimed to be descendants of Rurik, and down to the end of the sixteenth century no Russian outside of this great family ever attempted to establish independent sovereignty.

For six centuries after the so-called invitation of Rurik, the city on the Volkhov had a strange, checkered history. Rapidly it conquered the neighboring Finnish tribes, and grew into a powerful independent state, with a territory extending to the Gulf of Finland, and northwards to the White Sea. At the same time its commercial importance increased, and it became an outpost of the Hanseatic League. In this work the descendants of Rurik played an important part, but they were always kept in strict subordination to the popular will. Political freedom kept pace with commercial prosperity. What means Rurik employed for establishing and preserving order we know not, but the chronicles show that his successors in Novgorod possessed merely such authority as was freely granted them by the people. The supreme power resided, not in the prince, but in the assembly of the citizens called together in the market place by the sound of the great bell. This assembly made laws for the prince as well as for the people, entered into alliances with foreign powers, declared war, and concluded peace, imposed taxes, raised troops, and not only elected the magistrates, but also judged and deposed them when it thought fit. The prince was little more than the hired commander of the troops and the president of the judicial administration. When entering on his functions he had to take a solemn oath that he would faithfully observe the ancient laws and usages, and if he failed to fulfill his

[2] Strinnholm, *Die Vikingerzüge* (Hamburg, 1839), I., p. 135.

promise he was sure to be summarily deposed and expelled. The people had an old rhymed proverb, "Koli khud knyaz, tak v gryaz!" ("If the prince is bad, into the mud with him!"), and they habitually acted according to it. So unpleasant, indeed, was the task of ruling those sturdy, stiff-necked burghers, that some princes refused to undertake it, and others, having tried it for a time, voluntarily laid down their authority and departed. But these frequent depositions and abdications—as many as thirty took place in the course of a single century—did not permanently disturb the existing order of things. The descendants of Rurik were numerous, and there were always plenty of candidates for the vacant post. The municipal republic continued to grow in strength and in riches, and during the thirteenth and fourteenth century it proudly styled itself "Lord Novgorod the Great" (*Gospodin Veliki Novgorod*).

"Then came a change, as all things human change." To the east arose the principality of Moscow—not an old, rich municipal republic, but a young, vigorous State, ruled by a line of crafty, energetic, ambitious, and unscrupulous princes of the Rurik stock, who were freeing the country from the Tatar yoke and gradually annexing by fair means and foul the neighboring principalities to their own dominions. At the same time, and in a similar manner, the Lithuanian princes to the westward united various small principalities, and formed a large independent state. Thus Novgorod found itself in a critical position. Under a strong government it might have held its own against these rivals and successfully maintained its independence, but its strength was already undermined by internal dissensions. Political liberty had led to anarchy. Again and again on that great open space where the national monument now stands, and in the market place on the other side of the river, scenes of disorder and bloodshed took place, and more than once on the bridge battles were fought by contending factions. Sometimes it was a contest between rival families, and sometimes a struggle between the municipal aristocracy, who sought to monopolize the political power, and the common people, who wished to have a large share in the administration. A state thus divided against itself could not long resist the aggressive tendencies of powerful neighbors. Artful diplomacy could but postpone the evil day, and it required no great political foresight to predict that sooner or later Novgorod must become Lithuanian or Muscovite. The great families inclined to Lithuania, but the popular party and the clergy, disliking Roman Catholicism, looked to Moscow for assistance, and the Grand Princes of Muscovy ultimately won the prize.

The barbarous way in which the Grand Princes effected the annexation shows how thoroughly they had imbibed the spirit of Tatar statesmanship. Thousands of families were transported to Moscow, and Muscovite families put in their place; and when, in spite of this, the old spirit revived, Ivan the Terrible determined to apply the method of physical extermination, which he had found so effectual in breaking the power of his own nobles. Advancing with a large army, which met with no resistance, he devastated the country with fire and sword, and during a residence of five weeks in the town, he put the inhabitants to death with a ruthless ferocity which has perhaps never been surpassed even by Oriental despots. If those old walls could speak they would have many a horrible tale to tell. Enough has been preserved in the chronicles to give us some idea of this awful time. Monks and priests were subjected to the Tatar punishment called *pravezh,* which consisted in tying the victim to a stake, and flogging him daily until a certain sum of money was paid for his release. The merchants and officials were tortured with fire, and then thrown from the bridge with their wives and children into the river. Lest any of them should escape by swimming, boatfuls of soldiers despatched those who were not killed by the fall. At the present day there is a curious bubbling immediately below the bridge, which prevents the water from freezing in winter, and according to popular belief this is caused by the spirits of the terrible Tsar's victims. Of those who were murdered in the villages there is no record, but in the town alone no less than 60,000 human beings are said to have been butchered—an awful hecatomb on the altar of national unity and autocratic power!

This tragic scene, which occurred in 1570, closes the

history of Novgorod as an independent state. Its real independence had long since ceased to exist, and now the last spark of the old spirit was extinguished. The Tsars could not suffer even a shadow of political independence to exist within their dominions.

In the old days, when many Hanseatic merchants annually visited the city, and when the market place, the bridge, and the Kremlin were often the scene of violent political struggles, Novgorod must have been an interesting place to live in; but now its glory has departed, and in respect of social resources it is not even a first-rate provincial town. Kiev, Kharkov, and other towns which are situated at a greater distance from the capital, in districts fertile enough to induce the nobles to farm their own land, are in their way little semi-independent centers of civilization. They contain a theater, a library, two or three clubs, and large houses belonging to rich landed proprietors, who spend the summer on their estates and come into town for the winter months. These proprietors, together with the resident officials, form a numerous society, and during the winter, dinner parties, balls, and other social gatherings are by no means infrequent. In Novgorod the society is much more limited. It does not, like Kiev, Kharkov, and Kazan, possess a university, and it contains no houses belonging to wealthy nobles. The few proprietors of the province who live on their estates, and are rich enough to spend part of the year in town, prefer St. Petersburg for their winter residence. The society, therefore, is composed exclusively of officials and of the officers who happen to be quartered in the town or the immediate vicinity.

Of all the people whose acquaintance I made at Novgorod, I can recall only two men who did not occupy some official position, civil or military. One of these was a retired doctor, who was attempting to farm on scientific principles, and who, I believe, soon afterwards gave up the attempt and migrated elsewhere. The other was a Polish Roman Catholic bishop, who had been compromised in the insurrection of 1863, and was condemned to live here under police supervision. This latter could scarcely be said to belong to the society of the place;

though he sometimes appeared at the unceremonious weekly receptions given by the Governor, and was invariably treated by all present with marked respect, he could not but feel that he was in a false position, and he was rarely or never seen in other houses.

The official circle of a town like Novgorod is sure to contain a good many people of average education and agreeable manners, but it is sure to be neither brilliant nor interesting. Though it is constantly undergoing a gradual renovation by the accepted system of frequently transferring officials from one locality to another, it preserves faithfully, in spite of the new blood which it thus receives, its essentially languid character. When a new official arrives he exchanges visits with all the notables, and for a few days he produces quite a sensation in the little community. If he appears at social gatherings he is much talked to, and if he does not appear he is much talked about. His former history is repeatedly narrated, and his various merits and defects assiduously discussed.

If he is married, and has brought his wife with him, the field of comment and discussion is very much enlarged. The first time that madame appears in society she is "the cynosure of neighboring eyes." Her features, her complexion, her hair, her dress, and her jewelry are carefully noted and criticized. Perhaps she has brought with her, from the capital or from abroad, some dresses of the newest fashion. As soon as this is discovered she at once becomes an object of special curiosity to the ladies, and of envious jealousy to those who regard as a personal grievance the presence of a toilet finer or more fashionable than their own. Her demeanor, too, is very carefully observed. If she is friendly and affable in manner, she is patronized; if she is distant and reserved, she is condemned as proud and pretentious. In either case she is pretty sure to form a close intimacy with some one of the older female residents, and for a few weeks the two ladies are inseparable, till some incautious word or act disturbs the new-born friendship, and the devoted friends become bitter enemies. Voluntarily or involuntarily the husbands get mixed up in the quarrel. Highly undesirable qualities are discovered in the characters of all parties concerned, and are made the

subject of unfriendly comment. Then the feud subsides,
and some new feud of a similar kind comes to occupy the
public attention. Mrs. A. wonders how her friends Mr.
and Mrs. B. can afford to lose considerable sums every
evening at cards, and suspects that they are getting into
debt or starving themselves and their children; in her humble opinion they would do well to give fewer supper parties, and to refrain from poisoning their guests. The bosom
friend to whom this is related retails it directly or indirectly to Mrs. B., and Mrs. B. naturally retaliates. Here is
a new quarrel, which for some time affords material for
conversation.

When there is no quarrel, there is sure to be a bit of
scandal afloat. Though Russian provincial society is not at
all prudish, and leans rather to the side of extreme leniency, it cannot entirely overlook *les convenances*. Madame C. has always a large number of male admirers, and
to this there can be no reasonable objection so long as her
husband does not complain, but really she parades her
preference for Mr. X. at balls and parties a little too conspicuously. Then there is Madame D., with the big
dreamy eyes. How can she remain in the place after her
husband was killed in a duel by a brother officer? Ostensibly the cause of the quarrel was a trifling incident at the
card table, but everyone knows that in reality she was the
cause of the deadly encounter. And so on, and so on. In
the absence of graver interests society naturally bestows
inordinate attention on the private affairs of its members;
and quarreling, backbiting, and scandalmongery help indolent people to kill the time that hangs heavily on their
hands.

Potent as these instruments are, they are not sufficient
to kill all the leisure hours. In the forenoons the gentlemen
are occupied with their official duties, whilst the ladies go
out shopping or pay visits, and devote any time that remains to their household duties and their children; but
the day's work is over about four o'clock, and the long
evening remains to be filled up. The siesta may dispose of
an hour or an hour and a half, but about seven o'clock
some definite occupation has to be found. As it is impossible to devote the whole evening to discussing the ordi-

nary news of the day, recourse is almost invariably had
to cardplaying, which is indulged in to an extent that we
had no conception of in England until bridge was imported. Hour after hour the Russians of both sexes will sit
in a hot room, filled with a constantly renewed cloud of
tobacco smoke—in the production of which most of the
ladies take part—and silently play "Préference" or "Yarolash," a game resembling whist.[3] Those who for some
reason are obliged to be alone can amuse themselves with
"Patience," in which no partner is required. In the other
games the stakes are commonly very small, but the sittings
are often continued so long that a player may win or lose
two or three pounds sterling. It is no unusual thing for
gentlemen to play for eight or nine hours at a time. At the
weekly club dinners, before coffee had been served, nearly
all present used to rush off impatiently to the card room,
and sit there placidly from five o'clock in the afternoon till
one or two o'clock in the morning! When I asked my
friends why they devoted so much time to this unprofitable occupation, they always gave me pretty much the
same answer: "What are we to do? We have been reading
or writing official papers all day, and in the evening we
like to have a little relaxation. When we come together we
have very little to talk about, for we have all read the daily
papers and nothing more. The best thing we can do is to
sit down at the card table, where we can spend our time
pleasantly, without the necessity of talking."

In addition to the daily papers, some people read the
monthly periodicals—big, thick volumes, containing several serious articles on historical and social subjects, sections of one or two novels, satirical sketches, and a long review of home and foreign politics on the model of those
in the *Revue des Deux Mondes*. Several of these periodicals are very ably conducted, and offer to their readers a
large amount of valuable information; but I have noticed
that the leaves of the more serious part often remain uncut.
The translation of a sensational novel by the latest French
or English favorite finds many more readers than an article
by an historian or a political economist. As to books, they

[3] Since the time of my residence in Novgorod, "Yarolash" has
been replaced by bridge.

seem to be very little read, for during all the time I lived in Novgorod I never discovered a bookseller's shop, and when I required books I had to get them sent from St. Petersburg. The local administration, it is true, conceived the idea of forming a museum and circulating library, but in my time the project was never realized. Of all the magnificent projects that are formed in Russia, only a very small percentage come into existence, and these are too often very short-lived. The Russians have learned theoretically what are the wants of the most advanced civilization, and are ever ready to rush into the grand schemes which their theoretical knowledge suggests; but very few of them really and permanently feel these wants, and consequently the institutions artificially formed to satisfy them very soon languish and die. In the provincial towns the shops for the sale of gastronomic delicacies spring up and flourish, whilst shops for the sale of intellectual food are rarely to be met with.

About the beginning of December the ordinary monotony of Novgorod life is a little relieved by the annual Provincial Assembly, which sits daily for two or three weeks and discusses the economic wants of the province. During this time a good many landed proprietors, who habitually live on their estates or in St. Petersburg, collect in the town, and enliven a little the ordinary society. But as Christmas approaches the deputies disperse, and again the town becomes enshrouded in that "eternal stillness" (*véchnaya tishiná*) which a native poet has declared to be the essential characteristic of Russian provincial life.

4 : *The Peasants*

CHAPTER · XIV

❧ ☙

A Peasant Family
of the Old Type

IVAN [Petrov] must have been about sixty years of age, but was still robust and strong, and had the reputation of being able to mow more hay in a given time than any other peasant in the village. His head would have made a fine study for a portrait painter. Like Russian peasants in general, he wore his hair parted in the middle—a custom which perhaps owes its origin to the religious pictures. The reverend appearance given to his face by his long fair beard, slightly tinged with gray, was in part counteracted by his eyes, which had a strange twinkle in them— whether of humor or of roguery, it was difficult to say. Under all circumstances—whether in his light, nondescript summer costume, or in his warm sheepskin, or in the long, glossy, dark-blue, double-breasted coat which he put on occasionally on Sundays and holidays—he always looked a well-fed, respectable, prosperous member of society; whilst his imperturbable composure, and the entire absence of obsequiousness or truculence in his manner, indicated plainly that he possessed no small amount of calm, deep-rooted self-respect. A stranger, on seeing him, might readily have leaped to the conclusion that he must be the Village Elder, but in reality he was a simple member of the Commune, like his neighbor, poor Zakhar Leshkov, who never let slip an opportunity of getting drunk, was always in debt, and, on the whole, possessed a more than dubious reputation.

Ivan had, it is true, been Village Elder some years before. When elected by the Village Assembly, against his own wishes, he had said quietly, "Very well, children; I will serve my three years"; and at the end of that period, when the Assembly wished to re-elect him, he had answered firmly, "No, children; I have served my term. It is now the turn of someone who is younger, and has more time. There's Peter Alekseyev, a good fellow, and an honest: you may choose him." And the Assembly chose the peasant indicated; for Ivan, though a simple member of the Commune, had more influence in Communal affairs than any other half-dozen members put together. No grave matter was decided without his being consulted, and there was at least one instance on record of the Village Assembly postponing deliberations for a week because he happened to be absent in St. Petersburg.

No stranger casually meeting Ivan would ever for a moment have suspected that that big man, of calm, commanding aspect, had been during a great part of his life a serf. And yet a serf he had been from his birth till he was about thirty years of age—not merely a serf of the State, but the serf of a proprietor who had lived habitually on his property. For thirty years of his life he had been dependent on the arbitrary will of a master who had the legal power to have him flogged as often and as severely as he considered desirable. In reality he had never been subjected to corporal punishment, for the proprietor to whom he had belonged had been, though in some respects severe, a just and intelligent master.

Ivan's bright, sympathetic face had early attracted the master's attention, and it was decided that he should learn a trade. For this purpose he was sent to Moscow, and apprenticed there to a carpenter. After four years of apprenticeship he was able not only to earn his own bread, but to help the household in the payment of their taxes, and to pay annually to his master a fixed yearly sum—first ten, then twenty, then thirty, and ultimately, for some years immediately before the Emancipation, seventy rubles. In return for this annual sum he was free to work and wander about as he pleased, and for some years he had made ample use of his conditional liberty. I never succeeded in extracting from him a chronological account of his travels, but I could gather from his occasional remarks that he had wandered over a great part of European Russia. Evidently he had been in his youth what is colloquially termed "a roving blade," and had by no means confined himself to the trade which he had learned during his four years of apprenticeship. Once he had helped to navigate a raft from Vetluga to Astrakhan, a distance of about two thousand miles. At another time he had been at Archangel and Onega, on the shores of the White Sea. St. Petersburg and Moscow were both well known to him, and he had visited Odessa.

The precise nature of Ivan's occupations during these wanderings I could not ascertain; for, with all his openness of manner, he was extremely reticent regarding his commercial affairs. To all my inquiries on this topic he was wont to reply vaguely, "Lesnóe dyelo"—that is to say, "Timber business"; and from this I concluded that his chief occupation had been that of a timber merchant. Indeed, when I knew him, though he was no longer a regular trader, he was always ready to buy any bit of forest that could be bought in the vicinity for a reasonable price.

During all this nomadic period of his life Ivan had never entirely severed his connection with his native village or with agricultural life. When about the age of twenty he had spent several months at home, taking part in the field labor, and had married a wife—a strong, healthy young woman, who had been selected for him by his mother, and strongly recommended to him on account of her good character and her physical strength. In the opinion of Ivan's mother, beauty was a kind of luxury which only nobles and rich merchants could afford, and ordinary comeliness was a very secondary consideration—so secondary as to be left almost entirely out of sight. This was likewise the opinion of Ivan's wife. She had never been comely herself, she used to say, but she had been a good wife to her husband. He had never complained about her want of good looks, and had never gone after those who were considered good-looking. In expressing this opinion she always first bent forward, then drew herself up to her full height, and finally gave a little jerky nod sideways, so as to clench the statement. Then Ivan's bright eye would twinkle more brightly than usual, and he would ask her how she knew that—reminding her that he was not always at home. This was Ivan's stereotyped mode of teasing his wife, and every time he employed it he was called an "old scare-crow," or something of the kind.

Perhaps, however, Ivan's jocular remark had more significance in it than his wife cared to admit, for during the first years of their married life they had seen very little of each other. A few days after the marriage, when according to our notions the honeymoon should be at its height, Ivan had gone to Moscow for several months, leaving his young bride to the care of his father and mother. The young bride did not consider this an extraordinary hardship, for many of her companions had been treated in the same way, and according to public opinion in that part of the country there was nothing abnormal in the proceeding. Indeed, it may be said in general that there is very little romance or sentimentality about Russian peasant marriages. In this as in other respects the Russian peasantry are, as a class, extremely practical and matter-of-fact in their conceptions and habits, and are not at all prone to indulge in sublime, ethereal sentiments of any kind. They have little or nothing of what may be termed the Hermann and Dorothea element in their composition, and consequently know very little about those sentimental, romantic ideas which we habitually associate with the preliminary steps to matrimony. Even those authors who endeavor to idealize peasant life have rarely ventured to make their story turn on a sentimental love affair. Certainly in real life the wife is taken as a helpmate, or in plain language a worker, rather than as a companion, and the mother-in-law leaves her very little time to indulge in fruitless dreaming.

As time wore on, and his father became older and frailer, Ivan's visits to his native place became longer and more frequent, and when the old man was at last incapable of work, Ivan settled down permanently and undertook the direction of the household. In the meantime his own children had been growing up. When I knew the family it comprised—besides two daughters who had married early and gone to live with their parents-in-law—Ivan and his wife, two sons, three daughters-in-law, and an indefinite and frequently varying number of grandchildren. The fact that there were three daughters-in-law and only two sons was the result of the Conscription, which had taken away the youngest son shortly after his marriage. The two who remained spent only a small part of the year at home. The one was a carpenter and the other a bricklayer, and both wandered about the country in search of employment, as their father had done in his younger days. There was, however, one difference. The father had always shown a leaning towards commercial transactions, rather than the simple practice of his handicraft, and consequently he had usually lived and traveled alone. The sons, on the contrary, confined themselves to their handicrafts, and were always during the working season members of an *artél*.

The *artél* in its various forms is a curious institution. Those to which Ivan's sons belonged were simply temporary, itinerant associations of workmen, who during the summer lived together, fed together, worked together, and periodically divided amongst themselves the profits. This is the primitive form of the institution, and is now not very often met with. Here, as elsewhere, capital has made itself felt and destroyed that equality which exists among the members of an *artél* in the above sense of the word. Instead of forming themselves into a temporary association, the workmen now generally make an arrangement with a contractor who has a little capital, and receive from him fixed monthly wages. The only association which exists in this case is for the purchase and preparation of provisions, and even these duties are very often left to the contractor.

In some of the larger towns there are *artéls* of a much more complex kind—permanent associations, possessing a large capital, and pecuniarily responsible for the acts of the individual members. Of these, by far the most celebrated is that of the Bank Porters. These men have unlimited opportunities of stealing, and are often entrusted with the guarding or transporting of enormous sums; but the banker has no cause for anxiety, because he knows that if any defalcations occur they will be made good to him by the *artél*. Such accidents very rarely happen, and the fact is by no means so extraordinary as many people suppose. The *artél*, being responsible for the individuals of which it is composed, is very careful in admitting new members, and a man when admitted is closely watched, not only by the regularly constituted office bearers, but also by all his fellow members who have an opportunity of observing him. If he begins to spend money too freely or to neglect his duties, though his employer may know nothing of the fact, suspicions are at once aroused among his fellow members, and an investigation ensues—ending in summary expulsion if the suspicions prove to have been well founded. Mutual responsibility, in short, creates a very efficient system of mutual supervision.

Of Ivan's sons, the one who was a carpenter visited his family only occasionally, and at irregular intervals; the bricklayer, on the contrary, as building is impossible in Russia during the cold weather, spent the greater part of the winter at home. Both of them paid a large part of their earnings into the family treasury, over which their father exercised uncontrolled authority. If he wished to make any considerable outlay, he consulted his sons on the subject; but, as he was a prudent, intelligent man, and enjoyed the respect and confidence of the family, he never met with any strong opposition. All the field work was performed by him with the assistance of his daughters-in-law; only at harvest time he hired one or two laborers to help him.

Ivan's household was a good specimen of the Russian peasant family of the old type. Previous to the Emancipation in 1861 there were many households of this kind, containing the representatives of three generations. All the members, young and old, lived together in patriarchal fashion under the direction and authority of the Head of the House, called usually the *Khozaïn*—that is to say, the Administrator; or, in some districts, the *Bolshák*, which means literally "the Big One." Generally speaking, this important position was occupied by the grandfather, or, if he was dead, by the eldest brother, but the rule was not very strictly observed. If, for instance, the grandfather be-

came infirm, or if the eldest brother was incapacitated by
disorderly habits or other cause, the place of authority
was taken by some other member—it might be by a
woman—who was a good manager and possessed the
greatest moral influence.

The relations between the Head of the Household and
the other members depended on custom and personal
character, and they consequently varied greatly in different families. If the Big One was an intelligent man, of decided, energetic character, like my friend Ivan, there was
probably perfect discipline in the household, except perhaps in the matter of female tongues, which do not readily
submit to the authority even of their owners; but very
often it happened that the Big One was not thoroughly
well fitted for his post, and in that case endless quarrels
and bickerings inevitably took place. Those quarrels were
generally caused and fomented by the female members of
the family—a fact which will not seem strange if we try to
realize how difficult it must be for several sisters-in-law
to live together, with their children and a mother-in-law,
within the narrow limits of a peasant's household. The
complaints of the young bride, who finds that her mother-
in-law puts all the hard work on her shoulders, form a
favorite theme in the popular poetry.

The house, with its appurtenances, the cattle, the agricultural implements, the grain and other products, the
money gained from the sale of these products—in a word,
the house and nearly everything it contained—were the
joint property of the family. Hence, nothing was bought
or sold by any member—not even by the Big One himself, unless he possessed an unusual amount of authority
—without the express or tacit consent of the other
grown-up males, and all the money that was earned was
put into the common purse. When one of the sons left
home to work elsewhere, he was expected to bring or send
home all his earnings, except what he required for food,
lodgings, and other *necessary* expenses; and if he understood the word "necessary" in too lax a sense, he had to
listen to very plain-spoken reproaches when he returned.
During his absence, which might last for a whole year or

several years, his wife and children remained in the house as before, and the money which he earned could be devoted to the payment of the family taxes.

The peasant household of the old type was thus a primitive labor association, of which the members had all things in common, and it is not a little remarkable that the peasant conceived it as such rather than as a family. This was shown by the customary terminology, for the Head of the Household was not called by any word corresponding to Paterfamilias, but was termed, as he is still, *Khozaïn,* or Administrator—a word that is applied equally to a farmer, a shopkeeper, or the head of an industrial undertaking, and does not at all convey the idea of blood relationship. It was likewise shown by what took place when a household was broken up. On such occasions the degree of blood-relationship was not taken into consideration in the distribution of the property. All the adult male members shared equally. Illegitimate and adopted sons, if they had contributed their share of labor, had the same rights as the sons born in lawful wedlock. The married daughter, on the contrary—being regarded as belonging to her husband's family—and the son who had previously separated himself from the household were excluded from the succession. Strictly speaking, the succession or inheritance was confined to the wearing apparel and any little personal effects of a deceased member. The house and all that it contained belonged to the little household community; and, consequently, when it was broken up, by the death of the *Khozaïn* or other cause, the members did not inherit, but merely appropriated individually what they had hitherto possessed collectively. Thus there was properly no inheritance or succession, but simply liquidation and distribution of the property among the members. The written law of inheritance, founded on the conception of personal property, was quite unknown to the peasantry, and quite inapplicable to their mode of life. Thus a large and most important section of the Code remained a dead letter for about four-fifths of the population.

This predominance of practical economic considerations was exemplified also by the way in which marriages were arranged in these large families. In the primitive system of agriculture usually practiced in Russia, the natural labor unit—if I may use such a term—comprised a man, a woman, and a horse. As soon, therefore, as a boy became an able-bodied laborer he had to be provided with the two accessories necessary for the completion of the labor unit. To procure a horse, either by purchase or by rearing a foal, was the duty of the Head of the House; to procure a wife for the youth was the duty of "the female Big One" (*Bolshúkha*). And the chief consideration in determining the choice was in both cases the same. Prudent domestic administrators were not to be tempted by showy horses or beautiful brides; what they sought was not beauty, but physical strength and capacity for work. When the youth reached the age of eighteen he was informed that he ought to marry at once, and as soon as he gave his consent negotiations were opened with the parents of some eligible young person. In the larger villages the negotiations were sometimes facilitated by certain old women called *svakhi*, who occupied themselves specially with this kind of mediation; but very often the affair was arranged directly, or through the agency of, some common friend of the two houses.

Care had, of course, to be taken that there was no legal obstacle, and these obstacles were not always easily avoided in a small village, the inhabitants of which had been long in the habit of intermarrying. According to Russian ecclesiastical law, not only is marriage between first cousins illegal, but affinity is considered as equivalent to consanguinity—that is to say, a mother-in-law and a sister-in-law are regarded as a mother and a sister—and even the fictitious relationship created by standing together at the baptismal font as godfather and godmother is legally recognized, and may constitute a bar to matrimony. If all the preliminary negotiations were successful, the marriage took place, and the bridegroom brought his bride home to the house of which he was a member. She brought nothing with her as a dowry except her trousseau, but she brought a pair of good strong arms, and thereby enriched her adopted family. Of course it happened occasionally—for human nature is everywhere essentially the same—that a young peasant fell in love with one of his former playmates, and brought his little romance to a happy conclusion at the altar; but such cases were very rare, and as a rule it may be said that the marriages of the Russian peasantry were arranged under the influence of economic rather than sentimental considerations.

The custom of living in large families has many economic advantages. We all know the edifying fable of the dying man who showed to his sons by means of a piece of wickerwork the advantages of living together and assisting each other. In ordinary times the necessary expenses of a large household of ten members are considerably less than the combined expenses of two households comprising five members each, and when a "black day" comes a large family can bear temporary adversity much more successfully than a small one. These are principles of world-wide application, but in the life of the Russian peasantry they have a peculiar force. Each adult peasant possesses, as I shall hereafter explain, a share of the Communal land, but this share is not sufficient to occupy all his time and working power. One married pair can easily cultivate two shares—at least in all provinces where the peasant allotments are not very large. Now, if a family is composed of two married couples, one of the men can go elsewhere and earn money, whilst the other, with his wife and sister-in-law, can cultivate the two combined shares of land. If, on the contrary, a family consists merely of one pair with young children, the man must either remain at home—in which case he may have difficulty in finding work for the whole of his time—or he must leave home, and entrust the cultivation of his share of the land to his wife, whose time must be in great part devoted to domestic affairs.

In the time of serfage the proprietors clearly perceived these and similar advantages, and compelled their serfs to live together in large families. No family could be broken up without the proprietor's consent, and this consent was not easily obtained unless the family had assumed quite abnormal proportions and was permanently disturbed by domestic dissension. In the matrimonial affairs of the serfs, too, the majority of the proprietors systematically exercised a certain supervision, not necessarily from any paltry meddling spirit, but because their own material interests were thereby affected. A proprietor would not, for instance, allow the daughter of one of his serfs to marry a serf belonging to another proprietor—because he would thereby lose a female laborer—unless some compensation were offered. The compensation might be a sum of money, or the affair might be arranged on the principle of reciprocity by the master of the bridegroom allowing one of his female serfs to marry a serf belonging to the master of the bride.

However advantageous the custom of living in large families may appear when regarded from the economic point of view, it has very serious defects, both theoretical and practical.

That families connected by the ties of blood relationship and marriage can easily live together in harmony is one of those social axioms which are accepted universally and believed by nobody. We all know by our own experience, or by that of others, that the friendly relations of two such families are greatly endangered by proximity of habitation. To live in the same street is not advisable; to occupy adjoining houses is positively dangerous; and to live under the same roof is certainly fatal to prolonged amity. There may be the very best intentions on both sides, and the arrangement may be inaugurated by the most gushing expressions of undying affection and by the discovery of innumerable secret affinities, but neither affinities, affection, nor good intentions can withstand the constant friction and occasional jerks which inevitably ensue.

Now the reader must endeavor to realize that Russian peasants, even when clad in sheepskins, are human beings like ourselves. Though they are often represented as abstract entities—as figures in a table of statistics or dots on a diagram—they have in reality "organs, dimensions, senses, affections, passions." If not exactly "fed with the same food," they are at least "hurt with the same weapons, subject to the same diseases, healed by the same means," and liable to be irritated by the same annoyances, as we are. And those of them who live in large families are subjected to a kind of probation that most of us have never dreamed of. The families comprising a large household not only live together, but have nearly all things in common. Each member works, not for himself, but for the household, and all that he earns is expected to go into the family treasury. The arrangement almost inevitably leads to one of two results—either there are continual dissensions, or order is preserved by a powerful domestic tyranny.

It was quite natural, therefore, that when the authority of the landed proprietors was abolished by the Emancipation Edict of 1861, the large peasant families almost all crumbled to pieces. The arbitrary rule of the *Khozaïn* was based on, and maintained by, the arbitrary rule of the proprietor, and both naturally fell together. In 1870, when I spent the autumn at Ivánovka, large households like that of our friend Ivan were preserved only in exceptional cases, where the Head of the House happened to possess an unusual amount of moral influence over the other members; and since that time they have been rapidly disappearing.

This change has unquestionably had a prejudicial influence on the material welfare of the peasantry, but it must have added considerably to their domestic comfort, and may perhaps produce good moral results. For the present, however, the evil consequences are by far the most prominent. Every married peasant strives to have a house of his own, and many of them, in order to defray the necessary expenses, have recourse to the moneylenders. This is a very serious matter. Even if the peasants could obtain money at five or six per cent, the position of the debtors would be bad enough, but it is in reality much worse, for the village usurers consider twenty or twenty-five per cent a by no means exorbitant rate of interest. A laudable attempt has been made to remedy this state of things by village banks, but these have proved successful only in certain exceptional localities. As a rule the peasant who contracts debts has a hard struggle to pay the interest in ordinary times, and when some misfortune overtakes him—when, for instance, the harvest is bad or his horse is stolen—he probably falls hopelessly into pecuniary embarrassments. I have seen peasants not specially addicted to drunkenness or other ruinous habits sink to a helpless state of insolvency. Fortunately for such insolvent debtors, they are treated by the law with extreme leniency. Their house, their share of the common land, their agricultural implements, their horse—in a word, all that is necessary for their subsistence, is exempt from sequestration. The Commune, however, may bring strong pressure to bear on those who do not pay their taxes. When I lived among the peasantry in the seventies, corporal punishment, inflicted by order of the Commune, was among the means usually employed; and though the custom has been prohibited by an Imperial decree of Nicholas II, I am not at all sure that it has entirely disappeared in real life. Traditional usage in Russia sometimes resists successfully even the Imperial power

CHAPTER XV

The Mir, or Village Community

When I had gained a clear notion of the family life and occupations of the peasantry, I turned my attention to the constitution of the village. This was a subject which specially interested me, because I was aware that the *Mir* is the most peculiar of Russian institutions. Long before visiting Russia I had looked into Haxthausen's celebrated work, by which the peculiarities of the Russian village system were first made known to Western Europe, and during my stay in St. Petersburg I had often been informed by intelligent, educated Russians that the rural Commune presented a practical solution of many difficult social problems with which the philosophers and statesmen of the West had long been vainly struggling. "The nations of the West"—such was the substance of innumerable discourses which I had heard—"are at present on the high road to political and social anarchy, and England has the unenviable distinction of being foremost in the race. The natural increase of population, together with the expropriation of the small landholders by the great landed proprietors, has created a dangerous and ever-increasing proletariat—a great disorganized mass of human beings, without homes, without permanent domicile, without property of any kind, without any stake in the existing institutions. Part of these gain a miserable pittance as agricultural laborers, and live in a condition infinitely worse than serfage. The others have been forever uprooted

from the soil, and have collected in the large towns, where
they earn a precarious living in the factories and workshops, or swell the ranks of the criminal classes. In England you have no longer a peasantry in the proper sense
of the term, and unless some radical measures be very
soon adopted, you will never be able to create such a class,
for men who have been long exposed to the unwholesome
influences of town life are physically and morally incapable of becoming agriculturists.

"Hitherto," the disquisition proceeded, "England has
enjoyed, in consequence of her geographical position, her
political freedom, and her vast natural deposits of coal
and iron, a wholly exceptional position in the industrial
world. Fearing no competition, she has proclaimed the
principles of Free Trade, and has inundated the world
with her manufactures—using unscrupulously her powerful navy and all the other forces at her command for
breaking down every barrier which might check the flood
sent forth from Manchester and Birmingham. In that way
her hungry proletariat has been fed. But the industrial
supremacy of England is drawing to a close. The nations
have discovered the perfidious fallacy of Free Trade principles, and are now learning to manufacture for their own
wants, instead of paying England enormous sums to manufacture for them. Very soon English goods will no longer
find foreign markets, and how will the hungry proletariat
then be fed? Already the grain production of England is
far from sufficient for the wants of the population, so that,
even when the harvest is exceptionally abundant, enormous quantities of wheat are imported from all quarters of
the globe. Hitherto this grain has been paid for by the
manufactured goods annually exported, but how will it be
procured when these goods are no longer wanted by foreign consumers? And what then will the hungry proletariat do?" [1]

This somber picture of England's future had often been
presented to me, and on nearly every occasion I had been

[1] This passage was written, precisely as it stands, long before
the fiscal question was raised by Mr. Chamberlain. It will be
found in the first edition of this work, published in 1877. (Vol.
I, pp. 179-81.)

assured that Russia had been saved from these terrible
evils by the rural Commune—an institution which, in spite
of its simplicity and incalculable utility, West-Europeans
seemed utterly incapable of understanding and appreciat-
ing.

The reader will now easily conceive with what interest
I took to studying this wonderful institution, and with
what energy I prosecuted my researches. An institution
which professes to solve satisfactorily the most difficult
social problems of the future is not to be met with every
day, even in Russia, which is specially rich in material for
the student of social science.

On my arrival at Ivánovka my knowledge of the institution was of that vague, superficial kind which is commonly derived from men who are fonder of sweeping generalizations and rhetorical declamation than of serious,
patient study of phenomena. I knew that the chief personage in a Russian village is the *Sélski Stárosta,* or Village
Elder, and that all important Communal affairs are regulated by the *Sélski Skhod,* or Village Assembly. Further, I
was aware that the land in the vicinity of the village belongs to the Commune, and is distributed periodically
among the members in such a way that every able-bodied
peasant possesses a share sufficient, or nearly sufficient,
for his maintenance. Beyond this elementary information
I knew little or nothing.

My first attempt at extending my knowledge was not
very successful. Hoping that my friend Ivan might be
able to assist me, and knowing that the popular name for
the Commune is *Mir,* which means also "the world," I put
to him the direct, simple question, "What is the Mir?"

Ivan was not easily disconcerted, but for once he
looked puzzled, and stared at me vacantly. When I endeavored to explain to him my question, he simply knitted
his brows and scratched the back of his head. This latter
movement is the Russian peasant's method of accelerating
cerebral action; but in the present instance it had no practical result. In spite of his efforts, Ivan could not get much
farther than the "Kak vam skazat'?" that is to say, "How
am I to tell you?"

It was not difficult to perceive that I had adopted an

utterly false method of investigation, and a moment's reflection sufficed to show me the absurdity of my question.
I had asked from an uneducated man a philosophical
definition, instead of extracting from him material in the
form of concrete facts, and constructing therefrom a definition for myself. These concrete facts Ivan was both able
and willing to supply; and as soon as I adopted a rational
mode of questioning, I obtained from him all I wanted.
This information he gave me, together with the results of
much subsequent conversation and reading, I now propose
to present to the reader in my own words.

The peasant family of the old type is, as we have just
seen, a kind of primitive labor association, in which the
members have nearly all things in common. The village
may be roughly described as a primitive labor association on a larger scale.

Between these two social units there are many points of
analogy. In both there are common interests and common
responsibilities. In both there is a principal personage,
who is in a certain sense ruler within, and representative
as regards the outside world: in the one case called
Khozaïn, or Head of the Household, and in the other
Stárosta, or Village Elder. In both the authority of the
ruler is limited: in the one case by the adult members of
the family, and in the other by the Heads of Households.
In both there is a certain amount of common property:
in the one case the house and nearly all that it contains,
and in the other the arable land and possibly a little pasturage. In both cases there is a certain amount of common responsibility: in the one case for all the debts,
and in the other for all the taxes and Communal obligations. And both are protected to a certain extent against
the ordinary legal consequences of insolvency, for the family cannot be deprived of its house or necessary agricultural
implements, and the Commune cannot be deprived of its
land, by importunate creditors.

On the other hand, there are many important points of
contrast. The Commune is, of course, much larger than
the family, and the mutual relations of its members are
by no means so closely interwoven. The members of a
family all farm together, and those of them who earn

money from other sources are expected to put their savings into the common purse; whilst the households composing a Commune farm independently, and pay into the common treasury only a certain fixed sum.

From these brief remarks the reader will at once perceive that a Russian village is something very different from a village in our sense of the term, and that the villagers are bound together by ties quite unknown to the English rural population. A family living in an English village has little reason to take an interest in the affairs of its neighbors. The isolation of the individual families is never quite perfect, for man, being a social animal, takes necessarily a certain interest in the affairs of those around him, and this social duty is sometimes fulfilled by the weaker sex with more zeal than is absolutely indispensable to the public welfare; but families may live for many years in the same village without ever becoming conscious of common interests. So long as the Jones family do not commit any culpable breach of public order, such as putting obstructions on the highway or habitually setting their house on fire, their neighbor Brown takes probably no interest in their affairs, and has no ground for interfering with their perfect liberty of action. Amongst the families composing a Russian village such a state of isolation is impossible. The Heads of Households must often meet together and consult in the Village Assembly, and their daily occupations must be influenced by the Communal decrees. They cannot begin to mow the hay or plough the fallow field until the Village Assembly has passed a resolution on the subject. Under the old system, if a peasant became a drunkard, or took some equally efficient means to become insolvent, every family in the village had a right to complain, not merely in the interests of public morality, but from selfish motives, because all the families were collectively responsible for his taxes. This common responsibility for the taxes was abolished by the Emperor in 1903, on the advice of M. Witte, and the other Communal fetters were afterwards gradually relaxed by the Duma, under the influence of M. Stolypin, who was an energetic opponent of the old Communal system. A peasant may now, if he wishes, cease to be a member of the Commune altogether, as soon as he has defrayed all his outstanding obligations, or he may insist on his share of the Communal land being converted into private property.

For the reason given above no peasant could permanently leave the village without the consent of the Commune, and this consent would not be granted until the applicant gave satisfactory security for the fulfillment of his actual and future liabilities. If a peasant wished to go away for a short time, in order to work elsewhere, he had to obtain a written permission, which served him as a passport during his absence; and he might be recalled at any moment by a Communal decree. In reality he was rarely recalled so long as he sent home regularly the full amount of his taxes—including the dues which he had to pay for the temporary passport—but sometimes the Commune used the power of recall for purposes of extortion. If it became known, for instance, that an absent member was receiving a good salary or otherwise making money, he might one day receive a formal order to return at once to his native village, but he was probably informed at the same time, unofficially, that his presence would be dispensed with if he would send to the Commune a certain specified sum. The money thus sent was generally used by the Commune for convivial purposes. With the relaxing of the Communal fetters already referred to, and of which I shall have occasion to speak later, this abuse should disappear.

In all countries the theory of government and administration differs considerably from the actual practice. Nowhere is this difference greater than in Russia, and in no Russian institution is it greater than in the Village Commune. It is necessary, therefore, to know both theory and practice; and it is well to begin with the former, because it is the simpler of the two. When we have once thoroughly mastered the theory, it is easy to understand the deviations that are made to suit peculiar local conditions.

According, then, to theory, all male peasants in every part of the Empire are inscribed in census lists, which form the basis of the direct taxation. These lists are revised at irregular intervals, and all males alive at the time

of the "revision," from the new-born babe to the cen-
tenarian, are duly inscribed. Each Commune has a list of
this kind, and pays to the Government an annual sum
proportionate to the number of names which the list contains, or, in popular language, according to the number of
"revision souls." During the intervals between the revisions
the financial authorities take no notice of the births and
deaths. A Commune which has a hundred male members
at the time of the revision may have in a few years considerably more or considerably less than that number,
but it has to pay taxes for a hundred members all the
same until a new revision is made for the whole Empire.

Now, in Russia, so far at least as the rural population is
concerned, the payment of taxes is inseparably connected with the possession of land. Every peasant who
pays taxes is supposed to have a share of the land belonging to the Commune. If the Communal revision lists
contain a hundred names, the Communal land ought to be
divided into a hundred shares, and each "revision soul"
should enjoy his share in return for the taxes which he
pays.

The reader who has followed my explanations up to
this point may naturally conclude that the taxes paid by
the peasants are in reality a species of rent for the land
which they enjoy. Such a conclusion would not be altogether justified. When a man rents a bit of land he acts
according to his own judgment, and makes a voluntary
contract with the proprietor; but the Russian peasant is
obliged to pay his taxes whether he desires to enjoy land
or not. The theory, therefore, that the taxes are simply
the rent of the land will not bear even superficial examination. Equally untenable is the theory that they are a
species of land tax. In any reasonable system of land dues
the yearly sum imposed bears some kind of proportion
to the quantity and quality of the land enjoyed; but in
Russia it may be that the members of one Commune possess six acres of bad land, and the members of the neighboring Commune seven acres of good land, and yet the
taxes in both cases are the same. The truth is that the
taxes are personal, and are calculated according to

the number of male "souls," and the Government does
not take the trouble to inquire how the Communal land is
distributed. The Commune has to pay into the Imperial
Treasury a fixed yearly sum, according to the number of
its "revision souls," and distributes the land among its
members as it thinks fit.

How, then, does the Commune distribute the land? To
this question it is impossible to reply in brief, general
terms, because each Commune acts as it pleases.[2] Some
act strictly according to the theory. These divide their
land at the time of the revision into a number of portions
or shares corresponding to the number of revision souls,
and give to each family a number of shares corresponding
to the number of revision souls which it contains. This is
from the administrative point of view by far the simplest
system. The census list determines how much land each
family will enjoy, and the existing tenures are disturbed
only by the revisions which take place at irregular intervals.[3] But, on the other hand, this system has serious
defects. The revision list represents merely the numerical
strength of the families, and the numerical strength is
often not at all in proportion to the working power. Let
us suppose, for example, two families, each containing at
the time of the revision five male members. According to
the census list these two families are equal, and ought to
receive equal shares of the land; but in reality it may
happen that the one contains a father in the prime of life
and four able-bodied sons, whilst the other contains a
widow and five little boys. The wants and working power
of these two families are, of course, very different, and if
the above system of distribution be applied, the man with
four sons and a goodly supply of grandchildren will prob-

[2] A long list of the various systems of allotment to be found in
individual Communes in different parts of the country is given in
the opening chapter of a valuable work by Karélin, entitled
Obshchinnoye Vladênié v Rossii (St. Petersburg, 1893). As my
object is to convey to the reader merely a general idea of the
institution, I refrain from confusing him by an enumeration of
the endless divergences from the original type.

[3] Since 1719 eleven revisions have been made, the last in
1897. The intervals varied from six to forty-one years.

ably find that he has too little land, whilst the widow
with her five little boys will find it difficult to cultivate the
five shares allotted to her, and utterly impossible to pay
the corresponding amount of taxation—for in all cases, it
must be remembered, the Communal burdens are distributed in the same proportion as the land.

But why, it may be said, should the widow not accept
provisionally the five shares, and let to others the part
which she does not require? The balance of rent after payment of taxes might help her to bring up her young family.

So it seems to one acquainted only with the rural
economy of England, where land is scarce, and always
gives a revenue more than sufficient to defray the taxes.
But in Russia the possession of a share of Communal land
is often not a privilege, but a burden. In some Communes
the land is so poor and abundant that it cannot be let at
any price. In others the soil will repay cultivation, but a
fair rent will not suffice to pay the taxes and dues.

To obviate these inconvenient results of the simpler
system, many Communes have adopted the expedient of
allotting the land, not according to the number of revision souls, but according to the working power of the
families. Thus, in the instance above supposed, the widow
would receive perhaps two shares, and the large household, containing five workers, would receive perhaps
seven or eight. Since the breaking up of the large families,
such inequality as I have supposed is, of course, rare; but
inequality of a less extreme kind does still occur, and
justifies a departure from the system of allotment according to the revision lists.

Even if the allotment be fair and equitable at the time
of the revision, it may soon become unfair and burdensome
by the natural fluctuations of the population. Births and
deaths may in the course of a very few years entirely alter
the relative working power of the various families. The
sons of the widow may grow up to manhood, whilst two
or three able-bodied members of the other family may be
cut off by an epidemic. Thus, long before a new revision
takes place, the distribution of the land may be no longer
in accordance with the wants and capacities of the various families composing the Commune. To correct this, vari-

ous expedients are employed. Some Communes transfer particular lots from one family to another, as circumstances demand; whilst others make from time to time, during the intervals between the revisions, a complete redistribution and reallotment of the land. Of these two systems the former is now the more frequently employed.

The system of allotment adopted depends entirely on the will of the particular Commune. In this respect the Communes enjoy the most complete autonomy, and no peasant ever dreams of appealing against a Communal decree.[4] The higher authorities not only abstain from all interference in the allotment of the Communal lands, but remain in profound ignorance as to which system the Communes habitually adopt. Though the Imperial Administration has a most voracious appetite for symmetrically constructed statistical tables—many of them formed chiefly out of materials supplied by the mysterious inner consciousness of the subordinate officials—no attempt has yet been made, so far as I know, to collect statistical data which might throw light on this important subject. In spite of the systematic and persistent efforts of the centralized bureaucracy to regulate minutely all departments of the national life, the rural Communes, which contain about five-sixths of the population, remain in many respects entirely beyond its influence, and even beyond its sphere of vision! But let not the reader be astonished overmuch. He will learn in time that Russia is the land of paradoxes; and meanwhile he is about to receive a still more startling bit of information. In "the great stronghold of Caesarian despotism and centralized bureaucracy," these Village Communes, containing about five-sixths of the population, are capital specimens of representative Constitutional government of the extreme democratic type!

When I say that the rural Commune is a good specimen of Constitutional government, I use the phrase in the

---

[4] This has been somewhat modified by recent legislation. According to the Emancipation Law of 1861, redistribution of the land could take place at any time provided it was voted by a majority of two-thirds at the Village Assembly. By a law of 1893 redistribution cannot take place oftener than once in twelve years, and must receive the sanction of certain local authorities.

English, and not in the Continental sense. In the Continental languages a Constitutional regime implies the existence of a long, formal document, in which the functions of the various institutions, the powers of the various authorities, and the methods of procedure are carefully defined. Such a document was never heard of in Russian Village Communes, except those belonging to the Imperial Domains, and the special legislation which formerly regulated their affairs was repealed at the time of the Emancipation. At the present day the Constitution of all the Village Communes is of the English type—a body of unwritten, traditional conceptions, which have grown up and modified themselves under the influence of ever changing practical necessity. No doubt certain definitions of the functions and mutual relations of the Communal authorities might be extracted from the Emancipation Law and subsequent official documents, but as a rule neither the Village Elder nor the members of the Village Assembly ever heard of such definitions; and yet every peasant knows, as if by instinct, what each of these authorities can do and cannot do. The Commune is, in fact, a living institution, whose spontaneous vitality enables it to dispense with the assistance and guidance of the written law, and its constitution is thoroughly democratic. The Elder represents merely the executive power. The real authority resides in the Assembly, of which all Heads of Households are members.[5]

The simple procedure, or rather the absence of all formal procedure, at the Assemblies, illustrates admirably the essentially practical character of the institution. The meetings are held in the open air, because in the village there is no building—except the church, which can be used only for religious purposes—large enough to contain all the members; and they almost always take place on Sundays or holidays, when the peasants have plenty of leisure. Any open space may serve as a forum. The discussions are occasionally very animated, but there is rarely

[5] An attempt was made by Alexander III in 1884 to bring the Rural Communes under supervision and control by the appointment of rural officials called *Zémskiye Nachálniki*. Of this so-called reform I shall have occasion to speak later.

any attempt at speechmaking. If any young member
should show an inclination to indulge in oratory, he is sure
to be unceremoniously interrupted by some of the older
members, who have never any sympathy with fine talking. The assemblage has the appearance of a crowd of
people who have accidentally come together, and are discussing in little groups subjects of local interest. Gradually some one group, containing two or three peasants
who have more moral influence than their fellows, attracts
the others, and the discussion becomes general. Two or
more peasants may speak at a time, and interrupt each
other freely—using plain, unvarnished language, not at
all parliamentary—and the discussion may become a confused, unintelligible din; but at the moment when the
spectator imagines that the consultation is about to be
transformed into a free fight, the tumult spontaneously
subsides, or perhaps a general roar of laughter announces
that someone has been successfully hit by a strong *argu-
mentum ad hominem* or biting personal remark. In any
case there is no danger of the disputants coming to blows.
No class of men in the world are more good-natured and
pacific than the Russian peasantry. When sober they
never fight, and even when under the influence of alcohol
they are more likely to be violently affectionate than disagreeably quarrelsome. If two of them take to drinking
together, the probability is that in a few minutes, though
they may never have seen each other before, they will be
expressing in very strong terms their mutual regard and
affection, confirming their words with an occasional
friendly embrace.

Theoretically speaking, the Village Parliament has a
Speaker, in the person of the Village Elder. The word
Speaker is etymologically less objectionable than the term
President, for the personage in question never sits down,
but mingles in the crowd like the ordinary members. Objection may be taken to the word on the ground that the
Elder speaks much less than many other members, but
this may likewise be said of the Speaker of the House of
Commons. Whatever we may call him, the Elder is
officially the principal personage in the crowd, and wears
the insignia of office in the form of a small medal sus-

pended from his neck by a thin brass chain. His duties, however, are extremely light. To call to order those who interrupt the discussion is no part of his functions. If he calls an honorable member "Durák!" (blockhead), or interrupts an orator with a laconic "Molchi!" (hold your tongue!), he does so in virtue of no special prerogative, but simply in accordance with a time-honored privilege, which is equally enjoyed by all present, and may be employed with impunity against himself. Indeed, it may be said in general that the phraseology and the procedure are not subjected to any strict rules. The Elder comes prominently forward only when it is necessary to take the sense of the meeting. On such occasions he may stand back a little from the crowd and say, "Well, Orthodox, have you decided so?" and the crowd will probably shout, "Ládno! ládno!" that is to say, "Agreed! agreed!"

Communal measures are generally carried in this way by acclamation; but it sometimes happens that there is such a diversity of opinion that it is difficult to tell which of the two parties has a majority. In this case the Elder requests the one party to stand to the right and the other to the left. The two groups are then counted, and the minority submits, for no one ever dreams of opposing openly the will of the *Mir*.

During the reign of Nicholas I an attempt was made to regulate by the written law the procedure of Village Assemblies amongst the peasantry of the State Domains, and among other reforms voting by ballot was introduced; but the new custom never struck root. The peasants did not regard with favor the new method, and persisted in calling it, contemptuously, "playing at marbles." Here, again, we have one of those wonderful and apparently anomalous facts which frequently meet the student of Russian affairs: the Emperor Nicholas I, the Incarnation of Autocracy and the champion of the Reactionary Party throughout Europe, tries to force the ballot-box, the ingenious invention of extreme radicals, on several millions of his subjects!

In the northern provinces, where a considerable portion of the male population is always absent, the Village Assembly generally includes a good many female members. These are women who, on account of the absence or death of their husbands, happen to be for the moment Heads of Households. As such they are entitled to be present, and their right to take part in the deliberations is never called in question. In matters affecting the general welfare of the Commune they rarely speak, and if they do venture to enounce an opinion on such occasions they have little chance of commanding attention, for the Russian peasantry are as yet little imbued with the modern doctrines of female equality, and express their opinion of female intelligence by the homely adage: "The hair is long, but the mind is short." According to one proverb, seven women have collectively but one soul, and according to a still more ungallant popular saying, women have no souls at all, but only a vapor. Woman, therefore, as woman, is not deserving of much consideration, but a particular woman, as Head of a Household, is entitled to speak on all questions directly affecting the household under her care. If, for instance, it be proposed to increase or diminish her household's share of the land and the burdens, she will be allowed to speak freely on the subject, and even to indulge in personal invective against her male opponents. She thereby exposes herself, it is true, to uncomplimentary remarks; but any which she happens to receive she is pretty sure to repay with interest—referring, perhaps, with pertinent virulence to the domestic affairs of those who attack her. And when argument and invective fail, she can try the effect of pathetic appeal, supported by copious tears.

As the Village Assembly is really a representative institution in the full sense of the term, it reflects faithfully the good and the bad qualities of the rural population. Its decisions are therefore usually characterized by plain, practical common sense, but it is subject to occasional unfortunate aberrations in consequence of pernicious influences, chiefly of an alcoholic kind. An instance of this fact occurred during my sojourn at Ivánovka. The question under discussion was whether a *kabák*, or gin-shop, should be established in the village. A trader from the district town desired to establish one, and offered to pay to the Commune a yearly sum for the necessary permission. The more industrious, respectable members of the Commune, backed by the whole female population, were strongly opposed to the project, knowing full well that a *kabák* would certainly lead to the ruin of more than one household; but the enterprising trader had strong arguments wherewith to seduce a large number of the members, and succeeded in obtaining a decision in his favor.

The Assembly discusses all matters affecting the Communal welfare, and, as these matters have never been legally defined, its recognized competence is very wide. It fixes the time for making the hay, and the day for commencing the ploughing of the fallow field; it decrees what measures shall be employed against those who do not punctually pay their taxes; it decides whether a new member shall be admitted into the Commune, and whether an old member shall be allowed to change his domicile; it gives or withholds permission to erect new buildings on the Communal land; it prepares and signs all contracts which the Commune makes with one of its own members or with a stranger; it interferes whenever it thinks necessary in the domestic affairs of its members; it elects the Elder—as well as the Communal tax collector and watchman, where such offices exist—and the Communal herd boy; above all, it divides and allots the Communal land among the members as it thinks fit.

Of all these various proceedings the English reader may naturally assume that the elections are the most noisy and exciting. In reality this is a mistake. The elections produce little excitement, for the simple reason that, as a rule, no one desires to be elected. Once, it is said, a peasant who had been guilty of some misdemeanor was informed by an Arbiter of the Peace—a species of official of which I shall have occasion to speak in the sequel—that he would be no longer capable of filling any Communal office; and instead of regretting this diminution of his civil rights, he bowed very low, and respectfully expressed his thanks for the new privilege which he had acquired. This anecdote may not be true, but it illustrates the undoubted fact that the Russian peasant regards office as a burden rather than as an honor. There is no civic ambition in those little rural Commonwealths, whilst the privilege of wearing a bronze medal, which commands no respect, and the reception of a few rubles as salary, afford no adequate compensation for the trouble, annoyance, and responsibility which a Village Elder has to bear. The elections are therefore generally very tame and uninteresting. The following description may serve as an illustration.

It is a Sunday afternoon. The peasants, male and female, have turned out in Sunday attire, and the bright costumes of the women help the sunshine to put a little rich color into the scene, which is at ordinary times monotonously gray. Slowly the crowd collects on the open space at the side of the church. All classes of the population are represented. On the extreme outskirts are a band of fair-haired, merry children—some of them standing or lying on the grass and gazing attentively at the proceedings, and others running about and amusing themselves. Close to these stand a group of young girls, convulsed with half-suppressed laughter. The cause of their merriment is a youth of some seventeen summers, evidently the wag of the village, who stands beside them with an accordion in his hand, and relates to them in a half-whisper how he is about to be elected Elder, and what mad pranks he will play in that capacity. When one of the girls happens to laugh outright, the matrons who are standing near turn round and scowl; and one of them, stepping forward, orders the offender, in a tone of authority, to go home at once if she cannot behave herself. Crestfallen, the culprit retires, and the youth who is the cause of the merriment makes the incident the subject of a new joke. Meanwhile the deliberations have begun. The majority of the members are chatting together, or looking at a little group composed of three peasants and a woman, who are standing a little apart from the others. Here alone the matter in hand is being really discussed. The woman is explaining, with tears in her eyes, and a vast amount of useless repetition, that her "old man," who is

Elder for the time being, is very ill, and cannot fulfill his duties.

"But he has not yet served a year, and he'll get better," remarks one peasant, evidently the youngest of the little group.

"Who knows?" replies the woman, sobbing. "It is the will of God, but I don't believe that he'll ever put his foot to the ground again. The Feldsher has been four times to see him, and the doctor himself came once, and said that he must be brought to the hospital."

"And why has he not been taken there?"

"How could he be taken? Who is to carry him? Do you think he's a baby? The hospital is forty versts off. If you put him in a cart he would die before he had gone a verst. And then, who knows what they do with people in the hospital?" This last question contained probably the true reason why the doctor's orders had been disobeyed.

"Very well; that's enough; hold your tongue," says the graybeard of the little group to the woman; and then, turning to the other peasants, remarks, "There is nothing to be done. The Stanovoi (officer of rural police) will be here one of these days, and will make a row again if we don't elect a new Elder. Whom shall we choose?"

As soon as this question is asked, several peasants look down to the ground, or try in some other way to avoid attracting attention, lest their names should be suggested. When the silence has continued a minute or two, the graybeard says, "There is Alexei Ivánov; he has not served yet!"

"Yes, yes, Alexei Ivánov!" shout half a dozen voices, belonging probably to peasants who fear they may be elected.

Alexei protests in the strongest terms. He cannot say that he is ill, because his big ruddy face would give him the lie direct, but he finds half a dozen other reasons why he should not be chosen, and accordingly requests to be excused. But his protestations are not listened to, and the proceedings terminate. A new Village Elder has been duly elected.

Far more important than the elections is the redistribu-

tion of the Communal land. It can matter but little to the
Head of a Household how the elections go, provided he
himself is not chosen. He can accept with perfect equanimity Alexei, or Ivan, or Nikolaï, because the office bearers
have very little influence in Communal affairs. But he
cannot remain a passive, indifferent spectator when the
division and allotment of the land come to be discussed,
for the material welfare of every household depends to a
great extent on the amount of land and of burdens which
it receives.

In the southern provinces, where the soil is fertile, and
the taxes do not exceed the normal rent, the process of
division and allotment is comparatively simple. Here each
peasant desires to get as much land as possible, and consequently each household demands all the land to which it
is entitled—that is to say, a number of shares equal to the
number of its members inscribed in the last revision list.
The Assembly has therefore no difficult questions to decide. The Communal revision list determines the number
of shares into which the land must be divided, and the
number of shares to be allotted to each family. The only
difficulty likely to arise is as to which particular shares a
particular family shall receive, and this difficulty is commonly obviated by the custom of drawing lots. There
may be, it is true, some difference of opinion as to when a
redistribution should be made, but this question is easily
decided by a vote of the Assembly.

Very different is the process of division and allotment
in many Communes of the northern provinces. Here the
soil is often very unfertile and the taxes exceed the normal rent, and consequently it may happen that the peasants strive to have as little land as possible. In these cases
such scenes as the following may occur.

Ivan is being asked how many shares of the Communal
land he will take, and replies in a slow, contemplative
way, "I have two sons, and there is myself, so I'll take
three shares, or somewhat less if it is your pleasure."

"Less!" exclaims a middle-aged peasant, who is not the
Village Elder, but merely an influential member, and takes
the leading part in the proceedings. "You talk nonsense.

Your two sons are already old enough to help you, and
soon they may get married, and so bring you two new
female laborers."

"My eldest son," explains Ivan, "always works in
Moscow, and the other often leaves me in summer."

"But they both send or bring home money, and when
they get married, the wives will remain with you."

"God knows what will be," replies Ivan, passing over
in silence the first part of his opponent's remark. "Who
knows if they will marry?"

"You can easily arrange that!"

"That I cannot do. The times are changed now. The
young people do as they wish, and when they do get
married they all wish to have houses of their own. Three
shares will be heavy enough for me!"

"No, no. If they wish to separate from you, they will
take some land from you. You must take at least four.
The old wives there who have little children cannot take
shares according to the number of souls."

"He is a rich muzhik!" says a voice in the crowd. "Lay
on him five souls!" (that is to say, give him five shares of
the land and of the burdens).

"Five souls I cannot! By God, I cannot!"

"Very well, you shall have four," says the leading spirit
to Ivan; and then, turning to the crowd, inquires, "Shall
it be so?"

"Four! four!" murmurs the crowd; and the question is
settled.

Next comes one of the old wives just referred to. Her
husband is a permanent invalid, and she has three little
boys, only one of whom is old enough for field labor. If
the number of souls were taken as the basis of distribution, she would receive four shares; but she would never
be able to pay four shares of the Communal burdens. She
must therefore receive less than that amount. When asked
how many she will take, she replies with downcast eyes,
"As the Mir decides, so be it!"

"Then you must take three."

"What do you say, little father?" cries the woman,
throwing off suddenly her air of submissive obedience.
"Do you hear that, ye Orthodox? They want to lay upon

me three souls! Was such a thing ever heard of? Since St.
Peter's Day my husband has been bedridden—bewitched,
it seems, for nothing does him good. He cannot put a foot
to the ground—all the same as if he were dead; only he
eats bread!"

"You talk nonsense," says a neighbor; "he was in the
kabák (gin-shop) last week."

"And you!" retorts the woman, wandering from the subject in hand; "what did *you* do last parish fête? Was it
not you who got drunk and beat your wife till she roused
the whole village with her shrieking? And no further gone
than last Sunday—pfu!"

"Listen!" says the old man sternly, cutting short the
torrent of invective. "You must take at least two shares and
a half. If you cannot manage it yourself, you can get
someone to help you."

"How can that be? Where am I to get the money to pay
a laborer?" asks the woman, with much wailing and a
flood of tears. "Have pity, ye Orthodox, on the poor
orphans! God will reward you"; and so on, and so on.

I need not weary the reader with a further description
of these scenes, which are always very long and sometimes violent. All present are deeply interested, for the allotment of the land is by far the most important event in
Russian peasant life, and the arrangement cannot be made
without endless talking and discussion. After the number
of shares for each family has been decided, the distribution of the lots gives rise to new difficulties. The families
who have plentifully manured their land strive to get back
their old lots, and the Commune respects their claims so
far as these are consistent with the new arrangement; but
often it happens that it is impossible to conciliate private
rights and Communal interests, and in such cases the
former are sacrificed in a way that would not be tolerated
by men of Anglo-Saxon race. This leads, however, to no
serious consequences. The peasants are accustomed to
work together in this way, to make concessions for the
Communal welfare, and to bow unreservedly to the will of
the *Mir.* I know of many instances where the peasants
have set at defiance the authority of the police, of the provincial governor, and of the central Government itself, but

I have never heard of any instance where the will of the *Mir* was openly opposed by one of its members.

In the preceding pages I have repeatedly spoken about "shares of the Communal land." To prevent misconception I must explain carefully what this expression means. A share does not mean simply a plot or parcel of land; on the contrary, it always contains at least four, and may contain a large number of distinct plots. We have here a new point of difference between the Russian village and the villages of Western Europe.

Communal land in Russia is of three kinds: the land on which the village is built, the arable land, and the meadow or hay field, if the village is fortunate enough to possess one. On the first of these each family possesses a house and garden, which are the hereditary property of the family, and are never affected by the periodical redistributions. The other two kinds are both subject to redistribution, but on somewhat different principles.

The whole of the Communal arable land is first of all divided into three fields, to suit the triennial rotation of crops, and each field is then divided into a number of long, narrow strips—corresponding to the number of male members in the Commune—as nearly as possible equal to each other in area and quality. Sometimes it is necessary to divide the field into several portions, according to the quality of the soil, and then to subdivide each of these portions into the requisite number of strips. Thus in all cases every household possesses at least one strip in each field; and in those cases where subdivision is necessary, every household possesses a strip in each of the portions into which the field is subdivided. It often happens, therefore, that the strips are very narrow, and the portions belonging to each family very numerous. Strips six feet wide are by no means rare. In 124 villages of the province of Moscow, regarding which I have special information, they varied in width from three to 45 yards, with an average of 11 yards. Of these narrow strips a household may possess as many as thirty in a single field! The complicated process of division and subdivision is accomplished by the peasants themselves, with the aid of simple measuring rods, and the accuracy of the result is truly marvelous.

The meadow, which is reserved for the production of hay, is divided into the same number of shares as the arable land. There, however, the division and distribution take place, not at irregular intervals, but annually. Every year, on a day fixed by the Assembly, the villagers proceed in a body to this part of their property, and divide it into the requisite number of portions. Lots are then cast, and each family at once mows the portion allotted to it. In some Communes the meadow is mown by all the peasants in common, and the hay afterwards distributed by lot among the families; but this system is by no means so frequently used.

As the whole of the Communal land thus resembles to some extent a big farm, it is necessary to make certain rules concerning cultivation. A family may sow what it likes in the land allotted to it, but all families must at least conform to the accepted system of rotation. In like manner, a family cannot begin the autumn ploughing before the appointed time, because it would thereby interfere with the rights of the other families, who use the fallow field as pasturage.

It is not a little strange that this primitive system of land tenure should have succeeded in living into the twentieth century, and still more remarkable that the institution of which it forms an essential part should be regarded by many intelligent people as one of the great institutions of the future, and almost as a panacea for social and political evils. The explanation of these facts will form the subject of the next chapter.

CHAPTER · XVI

The Serfs

BEFORE proceeding to describe the Emancipation, it may be well to explain briefly how the Russian peasants became serfs, and what serfage in Russia really was.

In the earliest period of Russian history the rural population was composed of three distinct classes. At the bottom of the scale stood the slaves, who were very numerous. Their numbers were continually augmented by prisoners of war, by freemen who voluntarily sold themselves as slaves, by insolvent debtors, and by certain categories of criminals. Immediately above the slaves were the free agricultural laborers, who had no permanent domicile, but wandered about the country and settled temporarily where they happened to find work and satisfactory remuneration. In the third place, distinct from these two classes, and in some respects higher in the social scale, were the peasants properly so called.[1]

These peasants proper, who may be roughly described as small farmers or cottiers, were distinguished from the free agricultural laborers in two respects: they were possessors of land in property or usufruct, and they were members of a rural Commune. The Communes were free primitive corporations which elected their office bearers from among the heads of families, and sent delegates to act as judges or assessors in the Prince's Court. Some of the Communes possessed land of their own, whilst others were settled on the estates of the landed proprietors or on the extensive

[1] My chief authority for the early history of the peasantry has been Bêláev, *Krestyánye na Rusí*, Moscow, 1860; a most able and conscientious work.

domains of the monasteries. In the latter case the peasant paid a fixed yearly rent in money, in produce, or in labor, according to the terms of his contract with the proprietor or the monastery; but he did not thereby sacrifice in any way his personal liberty. As soon as he had fulfilled the engagements stipulated in the contract and had settled accounts with the owner of the land, he was free to change his domicile as he pleased.

If we turn now from these early times to the eighteenth century, we find that the position of the rural population has entirely changed in the interval. The distinction between slaves, agricultural laborers, and peasants has completely disappeared. All three categories have melted together into a common class, called serfs, who are regarded as the property of the landed proprietors or of the State. "The proprietors sell their peasants and domestic servants not even in families, but one by one, like cattle, as is done nowhere else in the whole world, from which practice there is not a little wailing." [2] And yet the Government, whilst professing to regret the existence of the practice, takes no energetic measures to prevent it. On the contrary, it deprives the serfs of all legal protection, and expressly commands that if any serf shall dare to present a petition against his master, he shall be punished with the knout and transported for life to the mines of Nerchinsk. (Ukase of August 22nd, 1767.) [3]

How did this important change take place, and how is it to be explained?

If we ask any educated Russian who has never specially occupied himself with historical investigations regarding the origin of serfage in Russia, he will probably reply somewhat in this fashion: "In Russia slavery has never existed(!), and even serfage in the West European sense has never been recognized by law! In ancient times the rural population was completely free, and every peasant might change his domicile on St. George's Day—that is to

[2] These words are taken from an Imperial ukase of April 15th, 1721. Pólnoye Sobránye Zakónov, No. 3,770.

[3] This is an ukase of the liberal and tolerant Catherine! How she reconciled it with her respect and admiration for Beccaria's humane views on criminal law she does not explain.

say, at the end of the agricultural year. This right of migration was abolished by Tsar Boris Godunóv—who, by the way, was half a Tatar and more than half a usurper—and herein lies the essence of serfage in the Russian sense. The peasants have never been the property of the landed proprietors, but have always been personally free; and the only legal restriction on their liberty was that they were not allowed to change their domicile without the permission of the proprietor. If so-called serfs were sometimes sold, the practice was simply an abuse not justified by legislation."

This simple explanation, in which may be detected a note of patriotic pride, is almost universally accepted in Russia; but it contains, like most popular conceptions of the distant past, a curious mixture of fact and fiction. Serious historical investigation tends to show that the power of the proprietors over the peasants came into existence, not suddenly, as the result of an ukase, but gradually, as a consequence of permanent economic and political causes, and that Boris Godunóv was no more to blame than many of his predecessors and successors.

Although the peasants in ancient Russia were free to wander about as they chose, there appeared at a very early period—long before the reign of Boris Godunóv—a decided tendency in the princes, in the proprietors, and in the Communes, to prevent migration. This tendency will be easily understood if we remember that land without laborers is useless, and that in Russia at that time the population was small in comparison with the amount of reclaimed and easily reclaimable land. The prince desired to have as many inhabitants as possible in his principality, because the amount of his regular revenues depended on the number of the population. The landed proprietor desired to have as many peasants as possible on his estate, to till for him the land which he reserved for his own use, and to pay him for the remainder a yearly rent in money, produce, or labor. The free Communes desired to have a number of members sufficient to keep the whole of the Communal land under cultivation, because each Commune had to pay yearly to the prince a fixed sum in money or agricultural produce, and the greater the number of able-bodied members, the less each individual had to pay. To use the language of political economy, the princes, the landed proprietors, and the free Communes all appeared as buyers in the labor market; and the demand was far in excess of the supply.

Nowadays, when young colonies or landed proprietors in an outlying corner of the world are similarly in need of labor, they seek to supply the want by organizing a regular system of importing laborers—using illegal violent means, such as kidnaping expeditions, merely as an exceptional expedient. In old Russia any such regularly organized system was impossible, and consequently illegal or violent measures were not the exception, but the rule. The chief practical advantage of the frequent military expeditions for those who took part in them was the acquisition of prisoners of war, who were commonly transformed into slaves by their captors. If it be true, as some assert, that only unbaptized prisoners were legally considered lawful booty, it is certain that in practice before the unification of the principalities under the Tsars of Moscow, little distinction was made in this respect between unbaptized foreigners and Orthodox Russians. A similar method was sometimes employed for the acquisition of free peasants: the more powerful proprietors organized kidnaping expeditions, and carried off by force the peasants settled on the land of their weaker neighbors.

Under these circumstances it was only natural that those who possessed this valuable commodity should do all in their power to keep it. Many, if not all, of the free Communes adopted the simple measure of refusing to allow a member to depart until he had found someone to take his place. The proprietors never, so far as we know, laid down formally such a principle, but in practice they did all in their power to retain the peasants actually settled on their estates. For this purpose some simply employed force, whilst others acted under cover of legal formalities. The peasant who accepted land from a proprietor rarely brought with him the necessary implements, cattle, and capital to begin at once his occupations, and to feed himself and his family till the ensuing harvest. He was ob-

liged, therefore, to borrow from his landlord, and the debt
thus contracted was easily converted into a means of preventing his departure if he wished to change his domicile.
We need not enter into further details. The proprietors
were the capitalists of the time. Frequent bad harvests,
plagues, fires, military raids, and similar misfortunes, often
reduced even prosperous peasants to beggary. The muzhik
was probably then, as now, only too ready to accept a
loan without taking the necessary precautions for repaying it. The laws relating to debt were terribly severe, and
there was no powerful judicial organization to protect the
weak. If we remember all this, we shall not be surprised
to learn that a considerable part of the peasantry were
practically serfs before serfage was recognized by law.

So long as the country was broken up into independent
principalities, and each landowner was almost an independent prince on his estate, the peasants easily found a
remedy for these abuses in flight. They fled to a neighboring proprietor who could protect them from their former
landlord and his claims, or they took refuge in a neighboring principality, where they were, of course, still safer. All
this was changed when the independent principalities
were transformed into the Tsardom of Muscovy. The Tsars
had new reasons for opposing the migration of the peasants and new means for preventing it. The old princes
had simply given grants of land to those who served them,
and left the grantee to do with his land what seemed good
to him; the Tsars, on the contrary, gave to those who
served them merely the usufruct of a certain quantity of
land, and carefully proportioned the quantity to the rank
and the obligations of the receiver.

In this change there was plainly a new reason for fixing
the peasants to the soil. The real value of a grant depended not so much on the amount of land as on the
number of peasants settled on it, and hence any migration
of the population was tantamount to a removal of the
ancient landmarks—that is to say, to a disturbance of the
arrangements made by the Tsar. Suppose, for instance,
that the Tsar granted to a *Boyár* or some lesser dignitary
an estate on which were settled a hundred peasant families,
and that afterwards fifty of these emigrated to neighbor-

ing proprietors. In this case the recipient might justly complain that he had lost half of his estate—though the amount of land was in no way diminished—and that he was consequently unable to fulfill his obligations. Such complaints would be rarely, if ever, made by the great dignitaries, for they had the means of attracting peasants to their estates; [4] but the small proprietors had good reason to complain, and the Tsar was bound to remove their grievances. The attaching of the peasants to the soil was, in fact, the natural consequence of feudal tenures—an integral part of the Muscovite political system. The Tsar compelled the nobles to serve him, and was unable to pay them in money. He was obliged, therefore, to procure for them some other means of livelihood. Evidently the simplest method of solving the difficulty was to give them land, with a certain number of laborers, and to prevent the laborers from migrating.

Towards the free Communes the Tsars had to act in the same way for similar reasons. The Communes, like the nobles, had obligations to the Sovereign, and could not fulfill them if the peasants were allowed to migrate from one locality to another. They were, in a certain sense, the property of the Tsar, and it was only natural that the Tsar should do for himself what he had done for his nobles.

With these new reasons for fixing the peasants to the soil came, as has been said, new means of preventing migration. Formerly it was an easy matter to flee to a neighboring principality, but now all the principalities were combined under one ruler, and the foundations of a centralized administration were laid. Severe fugitive laws were issued against those who attempted to change their domicile and against the proprietors who should harbor the runaways. Unless the peasant chose to face the difficulties

[4] There are plain indications in the documents of the time that the great dignitaries were at first hostile to the *adscriptio glebae.* We find a similar phenomenon at a much more recent date in Little Russia. Long after serfage had been legalized in that region by Catherine II, the great proprietors, such as Rumyantsev, Razumovski, Bezborodko, continued to attract to their estates the peasants of the smaller proprietors. See the article of Pogódin in the *Rússkaya Beséda,* 1858, No. 4, p. 154.

of "squatting" in the inhospitable northern forests, or resolved to brave the dangers of the Steppe, he could nowhere escape the heavy hand of Moscow.[5]

The indirect consequences of thus attaching the peasants to the soil did not at once become apparent. The
serf retained all the civil rights he had hitherto enjoyed,
except that of changing his domicile. He could still appear
before the courts of law as a free man, freely engage in
trade or industry, enter into all manner of contracts, and
rent land for cultivation.

But as time wore on, the change in the legal relation between the two classes became apparent in real life. In attaching the peasantry to the soil, the Government had
been so thoroughly engrossed with the direct financial aim
that it entirely overlooked, or willfully shut its eyes to, the
ulterior consequences which must necessarily flow from
the policy it adopted. It was evident that as soon as the
relation between proprietor and peasant was removed from
the region of voluntary contract by being rendered indis-
soluble, the weaker of the two parties legally tied together
must fall completely under the power of the stronger unless energetically protected by the law and the Administration. To this inevitable consequence the Government
paid no attention. So far from endeavoring to protect the
peasantry from the oppression of the proprietors, it did not
even determine by law the mutual obligations which ought
to exist between the two classes. Taking advantage of this
omission, the proprietors soon began to impose whatever
obligations they thought fit; and as they had no legal
means of enforcing fulfillment, they gradually introduced a
patriarchal jurisdiction similar to that which they exercised
over their slaves, with fines and corporal punishment as
means of coercion. From this they ere long proceeded a

[5] The above account of the origin of serfage in Russia is
founded on a careful examination of the evidence which we
possess on the subject, but I must not conceal the fact that some
of the statements are founded on inference rather than on direct,
unequivocal documentary evidence. The whole question is one
of great difficulty, and will in all probability not be satisfactorily
solved until a large number of the old local Land Registers
(*Pistsóviya Knigi*) have been published and carefully studied.

step further, and began to sell their peasants without the
land on which they were settled. At first this was merely a
flagrant abuse unsanctioned by law, for the peasant had
never been declared the private property of the landed
proprietor; but the Government tacitly sanctioned the
practice, and even exacted dues on such sales, as on the
sale of slaves. Finally the right to sell peasants without
land was formally recognized by various Imperial ukases.[6]

The old Communal organization still existed on the estates of the proprietors, and had never been legally deprived of its authority, but it was now powerless to protect
the members. The proprietor could easily overcome any
active resistance by selling or converting into domestic
servants the peasants who dared to oppose his will.

The peasantry had thus sunk to the condition of serfs
practically deprived of legal protection and subject to the
arbitrary will of the proprietors; but they were still in some
respects legally and actually distinguished from the slaves
on the one hand and the "free wandering people" on the
other. These distinctions were obliterated by Peter the
Great and his immediate successors.

To effect his great civil and military reforms, Peter required an annual revenue such as his predecessors had
never dreamed of, and he was consequently always on the
lookout for some new object of taxation. When looking
about for this purpose, his eye naturally fell on the slaves,
the domestic servants, and the free agricultural laborers.
None of these classes paid taxes—a fact which stood in
flagrant contradiction to his fundamental principle of pol-
ity, that every subject should in some way serve the State.
He caused, therefore, a national census to be taken, in
which all the various classes of the rural population—
slaves, domestic servants, agricultural laborers, peasants—
should be inscribed in one category; and he imposed
equally on all the members of this category a poll tax, in
lieu of the former land tax, which had lain exclusively on
the peasants. To facilitate the collection of this tax the
proprietors were made responsible for their serfs; and
the "free wandering people" who did not wish to enter the

[6] For instance, the ukases of October 13th, 1675, and June
25th, 1682. See Béláev, pp. 203-209.

army were ordered, under pain of being sent to the galleys,
to inscribe themselves as members of a Commune or as
serfs to some proprietor.

These measures had a considerable influence, if not on
the actual position of the peasantry, at least on the legal
conceptions regarding them. By making the proprietor
pay the poll tax for his serfs, as if they were slaves or cattle,
the law seemed to sanction the idea that they were part of
his goods and chattels. Besides this, it introduced the entirely new principle that any member of the rural population not legally attached to the land or to a proprietor
should be regarded as a vagrant, and treated accordingly.
Thus the principle that every subject should in some way
serve the State had found its complete realization. There
was no longer any room in Russia for free men.

The change in the position of the peasantry, together
with the hardships and oppression by which it was accompanied, naturally increased fugitivism and vagrancy.
Thousands of serfs ran away from their masters, and fled
to the Steppe or sought enrollment in the army. To prevent
this the Government considered it necessary to take severe
and energetic measures. The serfs were forbidden to enlist
without the permission of their masters, and those who
persisted in presenting themselves for enrollment were to
be beaten "cruelly" (*zhestóko*) with the knout, and sent to
the mines.[7] The proprietors, on the other hand, received
the right to transport without trial their unruly serfs to Siberia, and even to send them to the mines for life.[8]

If these stringent measures had any effect it was not of
long duration, for there soon appeared among the serfs a
still stronger spirit of discontent and insubordination,
which threatened to produce a general agrarian rising,
and actually did create a movement resembling in many
respects the Jacquerie in France and the Peasant War in
Germany. A glance at the causes of this movement will
help us to understand the real nature of serfage in Russia.

Up to this point serfage had, in spite of its flagrant
abuses, a certain theoretical justification. It was, as we

[7] Ukase of June 2nd, 1942.

[8] See ukases of January 17th, 1765, and of January 28th,
1766.

have seen, merely a part of a general political system in
which obligatory service was imposed on all classes of the
population. The serfs served the nobles in order that the
nobles might serve the Tsar. In 1762 this theory was entirely overturned by a manifesto of Peter III abolishing the
obligatory service of the Noblesse. According to strict justice this act ought to have been followed by the liberation
of the serfs, for if the nobles were no longer obliged to
serve the State they had no just claim to the service of the
peasants. The Government had so completely forgotten
the original meaning of serfage that it never thought of
carrying out the measure to its logical consequences, but
the peasantry held tenaciously to the ancient conceptions,
and looked impatiently for a second manifesto liberating
them from the power of the proprietors. Reports were
spread that such a manifesto really existed, and was being
concealed by the nobles. A spirit of insubordination accordingly appeared among the rural population, and local
insurrections broke out in several parts of the Empire.

At this critical moment Peter III was dethroned and
assassinated by a Court conspiracy. The peasants, who of
course knew nothing of the real motives of the conspirators
supposed that the Tsar had been assassinated by those
who wished to preserve serfage, and believed him to be a
martyr in the cause of Emancipation. At the news of the
catastrophe their hopes of Emancipation fell, but soon they
were revived by new rumors. The Tsar, it was said, had
escaped from the conspirators and was in hiding. Soon he
would appear among his faithful peasants, and with their
aid would regain his throne and punish the wicked oppressors. Anxiously he was awaited, and at last the glad
tidings came that he had appeared in the Don country,
that thousands of Cossacks had joined his standard, that
he was everywhere putting the proprietors to death without mercy, and that he would soon arrive in the ancient
capital!

Peter III was in reality in his grave, but there was a terrible element of truth in these reports. A pretender, a Cossack called Pugachév, had really appeared on the Don,
and had assumed the role which the peasants expected the
late Tsar to play. Advancing through the country of the

Lower Volga, he took several places of importance, put to death all the proprietors he could find, defeated on more than one occasion the troops sent against him, and threatened to advance into the heart of the Empire. It seemed as if the old troublous times were about to be renewed—as if the country was once more to be pillaged by those wild Cossacks of the Southern Steppe. But the pretender showed himself incapable of playing the part he had assumed. His inhuman cruelty estranged many who would otherwise have followed him, and he was too deficient in decision and energy to take advantage of favorable circumstances. If it be true that he conceived the idea of creating a peasant empire (*muzhítskoé tsárstvo*) he was not the man to realize such a scheme. After a series of mistakes and defeats he was taken prisoner, and the insurrection was quelled.

Meanwhile Peter III had been succeeded by his consort, Catherine II. As she had no legal right to the throne, and was by birth a foreigner, she could not gain the affections of the common people, and was obliged to court the favor of the Noblesse. In such a difficult position she could not venture to apply her humane principles to the question of serfage. Even during the first years of her reign, when she had no reason to fear agrarian disturbances, she increased rather than diminished the power of the proprietors over their serfs, and the Pugachév affair confirmed her in this line of policy. During her reign serfage may be said to have reached its climax. The serfs were regarded by the law as part of the master's immovable property[9]—as part of the working capital of the estate—and as such they were bought, sold, and given as presents[10] in hundreds and thousands, sometimes with the land, and sometimes without it, sometimes in families, and sometimes individually. The only legal restriction was that they should not be offered for sale at the time of the con-

[9] See Ukase of October 7th, 1792.

[10] As an example of making presents of serfs, the following may be cited: Count Panin presented some of his subordinates for an Imperial recompense, and on receiving a refusal, made them a present of 4,000 serfs from his own estates.—Bêláev, p. 320.

scription, and that they should at no time be sold publicly by auction, because such a custom was considered as "unbecoming in a European State." In all other respects the serfs might be treated as private property; and this view is to be found not only in the legislation, but also in the popular conceptions. It became customary—a custom that continued down to the year 1861—to compute a noble's fortune, not by his yearly revenue or the extent of his estate, but by the number of his serfs. Instead of saying that a man had so many hundreds or thousands a year, or so many acres, it was commonly said that he had so many hundreds or thousands of "souls." And over these "souls" he exercised the most unlimited authority. The serfs had no legal means of self-defense. The Government feared that the granting to them of judicial or administrative protection would inevitably awaken in them a spirit of insubordination, and hence it was ordered that those who presented complaints should be punished with the knout and sent to the mines.[11] It was only in extreme cases, when some instance of atrocious cruelty happened to reach the ears of the Sovereign, that the authorities interfered with the proprietor's jurisdiction, and these cases had not the slightest influence on the proprietors in general.[12]

The last years of the eighteenth century may be regarded as the turning point in the history of serfage. Up till that time the power of the proprietors had steadily increased, and the area of serfage had rapidly expanded.

[11] See the ukases of August 22nd, 1767, and March 30th, 1781.

[12] Perhaps the most horrible case on record is that of a certain lady called Saltykóv, who was brought to justice in 1768. According to the ukase regarding her crimes, she had killed by inhuman tortures in the course of ten or eleven years about a hundred of her serfs, chiefly of the female sex, and among them several young girls of eleven and twelve years of age. According to popular belief her cruelty proceeded from cannibal propensities, but this was not confirmed by the judicial investigation. Details in the *Rússki Arkhiv*, 1865, pp. 644–652. The atrocities practiced on the estate of Count Arakchéyev, the favorite of Alexander I, at the commencement of last century, have been frequently described, and are scarcely less revolting.

Under the Emperor Paul (1796-1801) we find the first decided symptoms of a reaction. He regarded the proprietors as his most efficient officers of police, but he desired to limit their authority, and for this purpose issued an ukase to the effect that the serfs should not be forced to work for their masters more than three days in the week. With the accession of Alexander I, in 1801, commenced a long series of abortive projects for a general emancipation, and endless attempts to correct the more glaring abuses; and during the reign of Nicholas no fewer than six committees were formed at different times to consider the question. But the practical result of these efforts was extremely small. The custom of giving grants of land with peasants was abolished; certain slight restrictions were placed on the authority of the proprietors; a number of the worst specimens of the class were removed from the administration of their estates; a few who were convicted of atrocious cruelty were exiled to Siberia;[13] and some thousands of serfs were actually emancipated; but no decisive radical measures were attempted, and the serfs did not receive even the right of making formal complaints. Serfage had, in fact, come to be regarded as a vital part of the State organization, and the only sure basis for autocracy. It was therefore treated tenderly, and the rights and protection accorded by various ukases were almost entirely illusory.

If we compare the development of serfage in Russia and in Western Europe, we find very many points in common, but in Russia the movement had certain peculiarities. One of the most important of these was caused by the rapid development of the autocratic power. In feudal Europe, where there was no strong central authority to control the Noblesse, the free rural Communes entirely, or almost entirely, disappeared. They were either appropriated by the nobles or voluntarily submitted to powerful landed pro-

[13] Speranski, for instance, when Governor of the province of Penza, brought to justice, among others, a proprietor who had caused one of his serfs to be flogged to death, and a lady who had murdered a serf boy by pricking him with a penknife because he had neglected to take proper care of a tame rabbit committed to his charge!—Korff, "Zhizn Speránskago," II, p. 127, note.

prietors or to monasteries, and in this way the whole of the
reclaimed land, with a few rare exceptions, became the
property of the nobles or of the Church. In Russia we find
the same movement, but it was arrested by the Imperial
power before all the land had been appropriated. The
nobles could reduce to serfage the peasants settled on
their estates, but they could not take possession of the free
Communes, because such an appropriation would have infringed the rights and diminished the revenues of the Tsar.
Down to the commencement of the last century, it is true,
large grants of land with serfs were made to favored individuals among the Noblesse, and in the reign of Paul
(1796-1801) a considerable number of estates were affected to the use of the Imperial family under the name of
appanages (*Udyélniya iméniya*); but on the other hand,
the extensive Church lands, when secularized by Catherine II, were not distributed among the nobles, as in many
other countries, but were transformed into State Domains.
Thus, at the date of the Emancipation (1861), by far the
greater part of the territory belonged to the State, and
one-half of the rural population were so-called State Peasants (*Gosudárstvenniye krestyanye*).

Regarding the condition of these State Peasants, or
Peasants of the Domains, as they are sometimes called, I
may say briefly that they were, in a certain sense, serfs
being attached to the soil like the others; but their condition was, as a rule, somewhat better than the serfs in the
narrower acceptation of the term. They had to suffer
much from the tyranny and extortion of the special administration under which they lived, but they had more land
and more liberty than was commonly enjoyed on the estates of resident proprietors, and their position was much
less precarious. It is often asserted that the officials of the
Domains were worse than the serf owners, because they
had not the same personal interest in the prosperity of the
peasantry; but this *à priori* reasoning does not stand the
test of experience.

It is not a little interesting to observe the numerical proportion and geographical distribution of these two rural
classes. In European Russia, as a whole, about three-
eighths of the population were composed of serfs belonging

to the nobles;[14] but if we take the provinces separately we find great variations from this average. In five provinces the serfs were less than 3 per cent, whilst in others they formed more than 70 per cent of the population! This is not an accidental phenomenon. In the geographical distribution of serfage we can see reflected the origin and history of the institution.

If we were to construct a map showing the geographical distribution of the serf population, we should at once perceive that serfage radiated from Moscow. Starting from that city as a center and traveling in any direction towards the confines of the Empire, we find that, after making allowance for a few disturbing local influences, the proportion of serfs regularly declines in the successive provinces traversed. In the region representing the old Muscovite Tsardom they form considerably more than half of the rural population. Immediately to the south and east of this, in the territory that was gradually annexed during the seventeenth century and first half of the eighteenth, the proportion varies from 25 to 50 per cent, and in the more recently annexed provinces it steadily decreases till it almost reaches zero.

We may perceive, too, that the percentage of serfs decreases towards the north much more rapidly than towards the east and south. This points to the essentially agricultural nature of serfage in its infancy. In the south and east there was abundance of rich "black earth" celebrated for its fertility, and the nobles in quest of estates naturally preferred this region to the inhospitable north, with its poor soil and severe climate.

A more careful examination of the supposed map would bring out other interesting facts. Let me notice one by way

[14] The exact numbers, according to official data, were—

Entire Population	....	....	....	....	60,909,309
Peasantry of all Classes	....	....	....	49,486,665

Of these latter there were—

State Peasants	....	....	....	....	....	23,138,191
Peasants on the Lands of Proprietors	....	23,022,390
Peasants of the Appanages and other Departments	....	....	....	....	....	3,326,084
					49,486,665

of illustration. Had serfage been the result of conquest we should have found the Slavonic race settled on the State Domains, and the Finnish and Tatar tribes supplying the serfs of the nobles. In reality we find quite the reverse; the Finns and Tatars were nearly all State Peasants, and the serfs of the proprietors were nearly all of Slavonic race. This is to be accounted for by the fact that the Finnish and Tatar tribes inhabit chiefly the outlying regions, in which serfage never attained such dimensions as in the center of the Empire.

The dues paid by the serfs were of three kinds: labor, money, and farm produce. The last-named is so unimportant that it may be dismissed in a few words. It consisted chiefly of eggs, chickens, lambs, mushrooms, wild berries, and linen cloth. The amount of these various products depended entirely on the will of the master. The other two kinds of dues, as more important, we must examine more closely.

When a proprietor had abundance of fertile land and wished to farm on his own account, he commonly demanded from his serfs as much labor as possible. Under such a master the serfs were probably free from money dues, and fulfilled their obligations to him by laboring in his fields in summer and transporting his grain to market in winter. When, on the contrary, a landowner had more serf labor at his disposal than he required for the cultivation of his fields, he put the superfluous serfs "on *obrók*"—that is to say, he allowed them to go and work where they pleased on condition of paying him a fixed yearly sum. Sometimes the proprietor did not farm at all on his own account, in which case he put all the serfs "on *obrók*," and generally gave to the Commune in usufruct the whole of the arable land and pasturage. In this way the *Mir* played the part of a tenant.

We have here the basis for a simple and important classification of estates in the time of serfage: (1) estates on which the dues were exclusively in labor; (2) estates on which the dues were partly in labor and partly in money; and (3) estates on which the dues were exclusively in money.

In the manner of exacting the labor dues there was

considerable variety. According to the famous manifesto of
Paul I, the peasant could not be compelled to work more
than three days in the week; but this law was by no means
universally observed, and those who did observe it had
various methods of applying it. A few took it literally, and
laid down a rule that the serfs should work for them three
definite days in the week—for example, every Monday,
Tuesday, and Wednesday—but this was an extremely inconvenient method, for it prevented the field labor from
being carried on regularly. A much more rational system
was that according to which one-half of the serfs worked
the first three days of the week, and the other half the remaining three. In this way there was, without any contravention of the law, a regular and constant supply of
labor. It seems, however, that the great majority of the
proprietors followed no strict method, and paid no attention whatever to Paul's manifesto, which gave to the peasant no legal means of making formal complaints. They simply summoned daily as many laborers as they required.
The evil consequences of this for the peasants' crops were
in part counteracted by making the peasants sow their
own grain a little later than that of the proprietor, so that
the master's harvest work was finished, or nearly finished,
before their grain was ripe. This combination did not, however, always succeed, and in cases where there was a conflict of interests, the serf was, of course, the losing party.
All that remained for him to do in such cases was to work
a little in his own fields before six o'clock in the morning
and after nine o'clock at night, and in order to render this
possible he economized his strength, and worked as little
as possible in his master's fields during the day.

It has frequently been remarked, and with much truth
—though the indiscriminate application of the principle
has often led to unjustifiable legislative inactivity—that
the practical result of institutions depends less on the intrinsic abstract nature of the institutions themselves than
on the character of those who work them. So it was with
serfage. When a proprietor habitually acted towards his
serfs in an enlightened, rational, humane way, they had
little reason to complain of their position, and their life was
much easier than that of many men who live in a state of

complete individual freedom and unlimited, unrestricted competition. However paradoxical the statement may seem to those who are in the habit of regarding all forms of slavery from the sentimental point of view, it is unquestionable that the condition of serfs under such a proprietor as I have supposed was more enviable than that of the majority of English agricultural laborers. Each family had a house of its own, with a cabbage garden, one or more horses, one or two cows, several sheep, poultry, agricultural implements, a share of the Communal land, and everything else necessary for carrying on its small farming operations; and in return for this it had to supply the proprietor with an amount of labor which was by no means oppressive. If, for instance, a serf had three adult sons— and the households, as I have said, were at that time generally numerous—two of them might work for the proprietor, whilst the father himself and the remaining son could attend exclusively to the family affairs. By the events which used to be called "the visitations of God" he had no fear of being permanently ruined. If his house were burned, or his cattle died from the plague, or a series of "bad years" left him without seed for his fields, he could always count upon temporary assistance from his master. He was protected, too, against all oppression and exactions on the part of the officials: for the police, when there was any cause for its interference, applied to the proprietor, who was to a certain extent responsible for his serfs. Thus the serf might live a tranquil, contented life, and die at a ripe old age, without ever having been conscious that serfage was a grievous burden.

If all the serfs had lived in this way we might, perhaps, regret that the emancipation was ever undertaken. In reality there was, as the French say, *le revers de la médaille,* and serfage generally appeared under a form very different from that which I have just depicted. The proprietors were, unfortunately, not all of the enlightened, humane type. Amongst them were many who demanded from their serfs an inordinate amount of labor, and treated them in a very inhumane fashion.

These oppressors of their serfs may be divided into four categories. First, there were the proprietors who managed their own estates, and oppressed simply for the purpose of increasing their revenues. Secondly, there were a number of retired officers, who wished to establish a certain order and discipline on their estates, and who employed for this purpose the barbarous measures which were at that time used in the army, believing that merciless corporal punishment was the only means of curing laziness, disorderliness and other vices. Thirdly, there were the absentees who lived beyond their means, and demanded from their steward, under pain of giving him or his son as a recruit, a much greater yearly sum than the estate could be reasonably expected to yield. Lastly, in the latter years of serfage, there were a number of men who bought estates as a mercantile speculation, and made as much money out of them as they could in the shortest possible space of time.

Of all hard masters, the last-named were the most terrible. Utterly indifferent to the welfare of the serfs and the ultimate fate of the property, they cut down the timber, sold the cattle, exacted heavy money dues under threats of giving the serfs or their children as recruits, presented to the military authorities a number of conscripts greater than was required by law—selling the conscription receipts (*zachétniya kvitántsii*) to the merchants and burghers who were liable to the conscription but did not wish to serve—compelled some of the richer serfs to buy their liberty at an enormous price, and, in a word, used every means, legal and illegal, for extracting money. By this system of management they ruined the estate completely in the course of a few years; but by that time they had realized probably the whole sum paid, with a very fair profit from the operation; and this profit could be considerably augmented by selling a number of the peasant families for transportation to another estate (*na svoz*), or by mortgaging the property in the Opekúnski Sovêt—a Government institution which lent money on landed property without examining carefully the nature of the security.

As to the means which the proprietors possessed of oppressing their peasants, we must distinguish between the legal and the actual. The legal were almost as complete as anyone could desire. "The proprietor," it is said in the Laws (Vol. IX., § 1045, ed. an. 1857), "may impose on his

serfs every kind of labor, may take from them money dues
(*obrók*) and demand from them personal service, with
this one restriction, that they should not be thereby ruined,
and that the number of days fixed by law should be left to
them for their own work." [15] Besides this, he had the right
to transform peasants into domestic servants, and might,
instead of employing them in his own service, hire them
out to others who had the rights and privileges of Noblesse
(§§1047-48). For all offenses committed against himself
or against anyone under his jurisdiction he could subject
the guilty ones to corporal punishment not exceeding forty
lashes with the birch or fifteen blows with the stick
(§ 1052); and if he considered any of his serfs as incorrigible he could have them drafted into the army or transported to Siberia, as he might desire (§§ 1053-55). In
cases of insubordination, where the ordinary domestic
means of discipline did not suffice, he could call in the
police and the military to support his authority.

Such were the legal means by which the proprietor
might oppress his peasants, and it will be readily understood that they were very considerable and very elastic. By
the law he had the power to impose any dues in labor or
money which he might think fit, and in all cases the serfs
were ordered to be docile and obedient (§ 1027). Corporal punishment, though restricted by law, he could in reality apply to any extent. Certainly none of the serfs, and
very few of the proprietors, were aware that the law
placed any restriction on this right. All the proprietors
were in the habit of using corporal punishment as they
thought proper, and unless a proprietor became notorious
for inhuman cruelty, the authorities never thought of interfering. But in the eyes of the peasants, corporal punishment was not the worst. What they feared infinitely more
than the birch or the stick was the proprietor's power of
giving them or their sons as recruits. The law assumed that
this extreme means would be employed only against those
serfs who showed themselves incorrigibly vicious or in-

[15] I give here the references to the Code, because Russians
commonly believe and assert that the hiring out of serfs, the in-
fliction of corporal punishment, and similar practices were
merely abuses unauthorized by law.

subordinate; but the authorities accepted those presented without making any investigations, and consequently the proprietor might use this power as an effective means of extortion.

Against these means of extortion and oppression the serfs had no legal protection. The law provided them with no means of resisting any injustice to which they might be subjected, or of bringing to punishment the master who oppressed and ruined them. The Government, notwithstanding its sincere desire to protect them from inordinate burdens and cruel treatment, rarely interfered between the master and his serfs, being afraid of thereby undermining the authority of the proprietors, and awakening among the peasantry a spirit of insubordination. The serfs were left, therefore, to their own resources, and had to defend themselves as they best could. The simplest way was open mutiny; but this was rarely employed, for they knew by experience that any attempt of the kind would be at once put down by the military and mercilessly punished. Much more favorite and efficient methods were passive resistance, flight, and fire-raising or murder. . . .

In speaking of the serfs I have hitherto confined my attention to the members of the *Mir*, or rural Commune—that is to say, the peasants in the narrower sense of the term; but besides these there were the *Dvoróvuye*, or domestic servants, and of these I must add a word or two.

The *Dvoróvuye* were domestic slaves rather than serfs in the proper sense of the term. Let us, however, avoid wounding unnecessarily Russian sensibilities by the use of the ill-sounding word. We may call the class in question "domestics"—remembering, of course, that they were not quite domestic servants in the ordinary sense. They received no wages, were not at liberty to change masters, possessed almost no legal rights, and might be punished, hired out, or sold by their owners without any infraction of the written law.

These "domestics" were very numerous—out of all proportion to the work to be performed—and could consequently lead a very lazy life;[16] but the peasant considered

[16] Those proprietors who kept orchestras, large packs of hounds, etc., had sometimes several hundred domestic serfs.

it a great misfortune to be transferred to their ranks, for
he thereby lost his share of the Communal land and the
little independence which he enjoyed. It very rarely happened, however, that the proprietor took an able-bodied
peasant as domestic. The class generally kept up its
numbers by the legitimate and illegitimate method of
natural increase; and involuntary additions were occasionally made when orphans were left without near
relatives, and no other family wished to adopt them. To
this class belonged the lackeys, servant girls, cooks, coach-
men, stable boys, gardeners, and a large number of nondescript old men and women who had no very clearly defined functions. If the proprietor had a private theater or
orchestra, it was from this class that the actors and musi-
cians were drawn. Those of them who were married and
had children occupied a position intermediate between
the ordinary domestic servant and the peasant. On the one
hand, they received from the master a monthly allowance
of food and a yearly allowance of clothes, and they were
obliged to live in the immediate vicinity of the mansion
house; but, on the other hand, they had each a separate
house or apartment, with a little cabbage garden, and
commonly a small plot of flax. The unmarried ones lived in
all respects like ordinary domestic servants.

The number of these domestic serfs being generally out
of all proportion to the amount of work they had to perform, they were imbued with a hereditary spirit of indolence, and they performed lazily and carelessly what they
had to do. On the other hand, they were often sincerely
attached to the family they served, and occasionally
proved by acts their fidelity and attachment. Here is an
instance out of many for which I can vouch. An old nurse,
whose mistress was dangerously ill, vowed that, in the
event of the patient's recovery, she would make a pilgrimage, first to Kiev, the Holy City on the Dnieper,
and afterwards to Solovetsk, a much revered monastery
on an island in the White Sea. The patient recovered, and
the old woman, in fulfillment of her vow, walked more
than two thousand miles!

This class of serfs might well be called domestic slaves,
but I must warn the reader that he ought not to use the

expression when speaking with Russians, because they are extremely sensitive on the point. Serfage, they say, was something quite different from slavery, and slavery never existed in Russia.

The first part of this assertion is perfectly true, and the second part perfectly false. In old times, as I have said above, slavery was a recognized institution in Russia as in other countries. One can hardly read a few pages of the old chronicles without stumbling on references to slaves; and I distinctly remember—though I cannot at this moment give chapter and verse—that one of the old Russian princes was so valiant and so successful in his wars that during his reign a slave might be bought for a few coppers. As late as the beginning of last century the domestic serfs were sold very much as domestic slaves used to be sold in countries where slavery was recognized as a legal institution. Here is a specimen of the customary advertisements; I take it almost at random from the *Moscow Gazette* of 1801:

> To Be Sold:—Three coachmen, well trained and handsome; and two girls, the one eighteen and the other fifteen years of age, both of them good-looking, and well acquainted with various kinds of handiwork. In the same house there are for sale two hairdressers; the one, twenty-one years of age, can read, write, play on a musical instrument, and act as huntsman; the other can dress ladies' and gentlemen's hair. In the same house are sold pianos and organs.

A little farther on in the same number of the paper, a first-rate clerk, a carver, and a lackey are offered for sale, and the reason assigned is a superabundance of the articles in question (*za izlíshestvom*). In some instances it seems as if the serfs and the cattle were intentionally put in the same category, as in the following announcement: "In this house one can buy a coachman and a Dutch cow about to calve." The style of these advertisements, and the frequent recurrence of the same addresses show that there was at this time in Moscow a regular class of slavedealers. The humane Alexander I prohibited advertisements of this kind, but he did not put down the custom which they

represented, and his successor, Nicholas I, took no effective
measures for its repression.

Of the whole number of serfs belonging to the proprietors, the domestics formed, according to the census of
1857, no less than 6¾ per cent (6.79), and their numbers
were evidently increasing rapidly, for in the preceding
census they represented only 4.79 per cent of the whole.
This fact seems all the more significant when we observe
that during this period the number of peasant serfs had
diminished.

I must now bring this long chapter to an end. My aim
has been to represent serfage in its normal, ordinary forms
rather than in its occasional monstrous manifestations. Of
these latter I have a collection containing ample materials
for a whole series of sensation novels, but I refrain from
quoting them, because I do not believe that the criminal
annals of a country give a fair representation of its real
condition. On the other hand, I do not wish to whitewash
serfage or attenuate its evil consequences. No large body
of men could long wield such enormous uncontrolled
power without abusing it,[17] and no great body of men
could long live under such power without suffering morally and materially from its pernicious influence. If serfage
did not create that moral apathy and intellectual lethargy
which formed, as it were, the atmosphere of Russian provincial life, it did much at least to preserve it. In short,
serfage was the chief barrier to all material and moral
progress, and in a time of moral awakening such as that
which I have described in the preceding chapter, the question of Emancipation naturally came at once to the front.

[17] The number of deposed proprietors—or rather the number
of estates placed under curators in consequence of the abuse of
authority on the part of their owners—amounted in 1859 to 215.
So at least I found in an official MS. document shown to me by
the late Nicholas Milútin.

CHAPTER · XVII

੭ဒ ੩ﻟ

The Emancipation
of the Serfs

IT was a fundamental principle of Russian political organization that all initiative in public affairs should proceed
from the autocratic power. The widespread desire, therefore, for the Emancipation of the serfs did not find free
expression so long as the Emperor kept silence regarding
his intentions. The educated classes watched anxiously for
some sign, and soon a sign was given to them. In March,
1856—a few days after the publication of the manifesto
announcing the conclusion of peace with the Western
Powers—his Majesty said to the Marshals of Noblesse in
Moscow: "For the removal of certain unfounded reports
I consider it necessary to declare to you that I have not at
present the intention of annihilating serfage; but certainly,
as you yourselves know, the existing manner of possessing
serfs cannot remain unchanged. It is better to abolish serfage from above than to await the time when it will begin
to abolish itself from below. I request you, gentlemen, to
consider how this can be put into execution, and to submit
my words to the Noblesse for their consideration."

This announcement was made with a view to ascertain-
ing the sentiments of the landed proprietors and encouraging them to express themselves in favor of Emancipation,
but it had not the desired effect. Abolitionist enthusiasm
was rare among the great nobles, and those who really
wished to see serfage abolished considered the Imperial
utterance too vague and oracular to justify them in taking

the initiative. As no further steps were taken for some time the excitement caused by the incident soon subsided, and many people assumed that the consideration of the problem had been indefinitely postponed. "The Government," it was said, "evidently intended to raise the question, but on perceiving the indifference or hostility of the landed proprietors, it became frightened and drew back."

The Emperor was in reality disappointed. He had expected that his "faithful Moscow Noblesse," of which he was wont to say he was himself a member, would at once respond to his call, and that the ancient capital would have the honor of beginning the work. And if the example were thus given by Moscow he had no doubt that it would soon be followed by the other provinces. He now perceived that the fundamental principles on which the Emancipation should be effected must be laid down by the Government, and for this purpose he created a secret committee composed of several great officers of State.

This "Chief Committee for Peasant Affairs," as it was afterwards called, devoted six months to studying the history of the question. Emancipation schemes were by no means a new phenomenon in Russia. Ever since the time of Catherine II the Government had thought of improving the condition of the serfs, and on more than one occasion a general Emancipation had been contemplated. In this way the question had slowly ripened, and certain fundamental principles had come to be pretty generally recognized. Of these principles the most important was that the State should not consent to any project which would uproot the peasant from the soil and allow him to wander about at will; for such a measure would render the collection of the taxes impossible, and in all probability produce the most frightful agrarian disorders. And to this general principle there was an important corollary: if severe restrictions were to be placed on free migration, it would be necessary to provide the peasantry with land in the immediate vicinity of the villages; otherwise they must inevitably fall back under the power of the proprietors, and a new and worse kind of serfage would thus be created. But in order to give land to the peasantry it would be necessary to take it from the proprietors; and this ex-

propriation seemed to many a most unjustifiable infringe-
ment of the sacred rights of property. It was this consideration that had restrained the Emperor Nicholas from taking
any decisive measures with regard to serfage; and it had
now considerable weight with the members of the committee, who were nearly all great landowners.

Notwithstanding the strenuous exertions of the Grand
Duke Constantine, who had been appointed a member for
the express purpose of accelerating the proceedings, the
committee did not show as much zeal and energy as was
desired, and orders were given to take some decided step.
At that moment a convenient opportunity presented itself.

In the Lithuanian Provinces, where the nobles were
Polish by origin and sympathies, the miserable condition
of the peasantry had induced the Government in the preceding reign to limit the arbitrary power of the serf owners
by so-called Inventories, in which the mutual obligations
of masters and serfs were regulated and defined. These
Inventories had caused great dissatisfaction, and the proprietors now proposed that they should be revised. Of this
the Government determined to take advantage. On the
somewhat violent assumption that these proprietors wished
to emancipate their serfs, an Imperial rescript was prepared approving of their supposed desire, and empower-
ing them to form committees for the preparation of definite
projects.[1] In the rescript itself the word emancipation was
studiously avoided, but there could be no doubt as to the
implied meaning, for it was expressly stated in the supplementary considerations that "the abolition of serfage
must be effected not suddenly, but gradually." Four days
later the Minister of the Interior, in accordance with a
secret order from the Emperor, sent a circular to the Governors and Marshals of Noblesse all over Russia Proper, in-
forming them that the nobles of the Lithuanian Provinces
"had recognized the necessity of liberating the peasants,"
and that "this noble intention" had afforded peculiar satis-

[1] This celebrated document is known as "The Rescript to
Nazímov." More than once in the course of conversation I did
all in my power, within the limits of politeness and discretion,
to extract from General Nazímov a detailed account of this
important episode, but my efforts were unsuccessful.

faction to his Majesty. A copy of the rescript and the fundamental principles to be observed accompanied the circular, "in case the nobles of other provinces should express a similar desire."

This circular produced an immense sensation throughout the country. No one could for a moment misunderstand the suggestion that the nobles of other provinces *might possibly* express a desire to liberate their serfs. Such vague words, when spoken by an autocrat, have a very definite and unmistakable meaning, which prudent loyal subjects have no difficulty in understanding. If any doubted, their doubts were soon dispelled, for the Emperor, a few weeks later, publicly expressed a hope that, with the help of God and the co-operation of the nobles, the work would be successfully accomplished.

The die was cast, and the Government looked anxiously to see the result.

The periodical press—which was at once the product and fomenter of the liberal aspirations—hailed the raising of the question with boundless enthusiasm. The Emancipation, it was said, would certainly open a new and glorious epoch in the national history. Serfage was described as an ulcer that had long been poisoning the national blood; as an enormous weight under which the whole nation groaned; as an insurmountable obstacle, preventing all material and moral progress; as a cumbrous load, which rendered all free, vigorous action impossible, and prevented Russia from rising to the level of the Western nations. If Russia had succeeded in stemming the flood of adverse fortune in spite of this millstone round her neck, what might she not accomplish when free and untrammeled? All sections of the literary world had arguments to offer in support of the foregone conclusion. The moralists declared that all the prevailing vices were the product of serfage, and that moral progress was impossible in an atmosphere of slavery; the lawyers held that the arbitrary authority of the proprietors over the peasants had no legal basis; the economists explained that free labor was an indispensable condition of industrial and commercial prosperity; the philosophical historians showed that the normal historical development of the country demanded the im-

mediate abolition of this superannuated remnant of barbarism; and the writers of the sentimental, gushing type
poured forth endless effusions about brotherly love to the
weak and the oppressed. In a word, the press was for the
moment unanimous, and displayed a feverish excitement
which demanded a liberal use of superlatives.

This enthusiastic tone accorded perfectly with the feelings of a large section of the nobles. Nearly the whole of
the Noblesse was more or less affected by the new-born
enthusiasm for everything just, humanitarian, and liberal.
The aspirations found, of course, their most ardent representatives among the educated youth; but they were by
no means confined to the younger men, who had passed
through the universities and had always regarded serfage
as a stain on the national honor. Many a Saul was found
among the prophets. Many an old man, with gray hairs
and grandchildren, who had all his life placidly enjoyed
the fruits of serf labor, was now heard to speak of serfage
as an antiquated institution which could not be reconciled
with modern humanitarian ideas; and not a few of all
ages, who had formerly never thought of reading books or
newspapers, now perused assiduously the periodical literature, and picked up the liberal and humanitarian phrases
with which it was filled.

This Abolitionist fervor was considerably augmented by
certain political aspirations which did not appear in the
newspapers, but which were at that time very generally
entertained. In spite of the press censure a large section of
the educated classes had become acquainted with the
political literature of France and Germany, and had imbibed therefrom an unbounded admiration for constitutional government. A Constitution, it was thought, would
necessarily remove all political evils and create something
like a political millennium. And it was not to be a Constitution of the ordinary sort—the fruit of compromise between
hostile political parties—but an institution designed calmly
according to the latest results of political science, and so
constructed that all classes would voluntarily contribute to
the general welfare. The necessary prelude to this happy
era of political liberty was, of course, the abolition of serfage. When the nobles had given up their power over their

serfs they would receive a Constitution as an indemnity
and reward.

There were, however, many nobles of the old school
who remained impervious to all these new feelings and
ideas. On them the raising of the Emancipation question
had a very different effect. They had no source of revenue
but their estates, and they could not conceive the possibility of working their estates without serf labor. If the
peasant was indolent and careless even under strict supervision, what would he become when no longer under the
authority of a master? If the profits from farming were already small, what would they be when no one would work
without wages? And this was not the worst, for it was
quite evident from the circular that the land question
was to be raised, and that a considerable portion of each
estate would be transferred, at least for a time, to the
emancipated peasants.

To the proprietors who looked at the question in this
way the prospect of Emancipation was certainly not at all
agreeable, but we must not imagine that they felt as English landowners would feel if threatened by a similar
danger. In England an hereditary estate has for the family
a value far beyond what it would bring in the market. It
is regarded as one and indivisible, and any dismemberment of it would be looked upon as a grave family misfortune. In Russia, on the contrary, estates have nothing
of this semisacred character, and may be at any time dis-
membered without outraging family feeling or traditional
associations. Indeed, it is not uncommon that when a proprietor dies, leaving only one estate and several children,
the property is broken up into fractions and divided among
the heirs. Even the prospect of pecuniary sacrifice did not
alarm the Russians so much as it would alarm Englishmen.
Men who keep no accounts and take little thought for the
morrow are much less averse to making pecuniary sacrifices—whether for a wise or a foolish purpose—than those
who carefully arrange their mode of life according to their
income.

Still, after due allowance has been made for these
peculiarities, it must be admitted that the feeling of dissatisfaction and alarm was very widespread. Even Rus-

sians do not like the prospect of losing a part of their land
and income. No protest, however, was entered, and no opposition was made. Those who were hostile to the measure
were ashamed to show themselves selfish and unpatriotic.
At the same time they knew very well that the Emperor, if
he wished, could effect the Emancipation in spite of them,
and that resistance on their part would draw down upon
them the Imperial displeasure, without affording any com-
pensating advantage. They knew, too, that there was a
danger from below, so that any useless show of opposition
would be like playing with matches in a powder magazine.
The serfs would soon hear that the Tsar desired to set
them free, and they might, if they suspected that the proprietors were trying to frustrate the Tsar's benevolent intentions, use violent measures to get rid of the opposition.
The idea of agrarian massacres had already taken possession of many timid minds. Besides this, all classes of the
proprietors felt that if the work was to be done, it should
be done by the Noblesse and not by the bureaucracy. If it
were effected by the nobles the interests of the landowners would be duly considered, but if it were effected
by the Administration without their concurrence and co-
operation, their interests would be neglected, and there
would inevitably be an enormous amount of jobbery and
corruption. In accordance with this view the Noblesse
corporations of the various provinces successively requested
permission to form committees for the consideration of the
question, and during the year 1858 a committee was
opened in almost every province in which serfage existed.

In this way the question was apparently handed over
for solution to the nobles, but in reality the Noblesse was
called upon merely to advise, and not to legislate. The
Government had not only laid down the fundamental
principles of the scheme; it continually supervised the
work of construction, and it reserved to itself the right of
modifying or rejecting the projects proposed by the committees.

According to these fundamental principles the serfs
should be emancipated gradually, so that for some time
they would remain attached to the glebe and subject to
the authority of the proprietors. During this transition pe-

riod they should redeem by money payments or labor their houses and gardens, and enjoy in usufruct a certain quantity of land, sufficient to enable them to support themselves, and to fulfill their obligations to the State as well as to the proprietor. In return for this land they should pay a yearly rent in money, produce, or labor, over and above the yearly sum paid for the redemption of their houses and gardens. As to what should be done after the expiry of the transition period, the Government seems to have had no clearly conceived intentions. Probably it hoped that by that time the proprietors and their emancipated serfs would have invented some convenient *modus vivendi*, and that nothing but a little legislative regulation would be necessary. But radical legislation is like the letting-out of water. These fundamental principles, adopted at first with a view to mere immediate practical necessity, soon acquired a very different significance. To understand this we must return to the periodical literature.

Until the serf question came to be discussed, the reform aspirations were very vague, and consequently there was a remarkable unanimity among their representatives. The great majority of the educated classes were unanimously of opinion that Russia should at once adopt from the West all those liberal principles and institutions, the exclusion of which had prevented the country from rising to the level of the Western nations. But very soon symptoms of a schism became apparent. Whilst literature in general was still preaching the doctrine that Russia should adopt everything that was "liberal," a few voices began to be heard warning the unwary that much which bore the name of liberal was in reality already antiquated and worthless— that Russia ought not to follow blindly in the footsteps of other nations, but ought rather to profit by their experience, and avoid the errors into which they had fallen.

The chief of these errors was, according to these new teachers, the abnormal development of individualism—the adoption of that principle of *laissez faire* which forms the basis of what may be called the Orthodox School of Political Economists. Individualism and unrestricted competition, it was said, have now reached in the West an abnormal and monstrous development. Supported by the *laissez*

faire principle, they have led—and must always lead—to
the oppression of the weak, the tyranny of capital, the impoverishment of the masses for the benefit of the few, and
the formation of a hungry, dangerous Proletariat! This has
already been recognized by the most advanced thinkers
of France and Germany. If the older countries cannot at
once cure those evils, that is no reason for Russia to inocu-
late herself with them. She is still at the commencement of
her career, and it would be folly for her to wander voluntarily for ages in the Desert, when a direct route to the
Promised Land has been already discovered.

In order to convey some idea of the influence which this
teaching exercised, I must here recall, at the risk of re-
peating myself, what I said in a former chapter. The Russians, as I have there pointed out, have a peculiar way of
treating political and social questions. Having received
their political education from books, they naturally attribute to theoretical considerations an importance which
seems to us exaggerated. When any important or trivial
question arises, they at once launch into a sea of philosophical principles, and pay less attention to the little objects close at hand than to the big ones that appear on
the distant horizon of the future. And when they set to
work at any political reform they begin *ab ovo*. As they
have no traditional prejudices to fetter them, and no traditional principles to lead them, they naturally take for their
guidance the latest conclusions of political philosophy.

Bearing this in mind, let us see how it affected the
Emancipation question. The Proletariat—described as a
dangerous monster which was about to swallow up society in Western Europe, and which might at any moment
cross the frontier unless kept out by vigorous measures—
took possession of the popular imagination, and aroused
the fears of the reading public. To many it seemed that
the best means of preventing the formation of a Proletariat
in Russia was the securing of land for the emancipated
serfs, and the careful preservation of the rural Commune.
"Now is the moment," it was said, "for deciding the important question whether Russia is to fall a prey, like the
Western nations, to this terrible evil, or whether she is to
protect herself forever against it. In the decision of this

question lies the future destiny of the country. If the peasants be emancipated without land, or if those Communal
institutions, which give to every man a share of the soil
and secure this inestimable boon for the generations still
unborn, be now abolished, a Proletariat will be rapidly
formed, and the peasantry will become a disorganized
mass of homeless wanderers like the English agricultural
laborers. If, on the contrary, a fair share of land be
granted to them, and if the Commune be made proprietor
of the land ceded, the danger of a Proletariat is forever
removed, and Russia will thereby set an example to the
civilized world! Never has a nation had such an opportunity of making an enormous leap forward on the road of
progress, and never again will the opportunity occur. The
Western nations have discovered their error when it is too
late—when the peasantry have been already deprived of
their land, and the laboring classes of the towns have already fallen a prey to the insatiable cupidity of the capitalists. In vain their most eminent thinkers warn and exhort. Ordinary remedies are no longer of any avail. But
Russia may avoid these dangers, if she but act wisely and
prudently in this matter. The peasants are still in actual,
if not legal, possession of the land, and there is as yet no
Proletariat in the towns. All that is necessary, therefore,
is to abolish the arbitrary authority of the proprietors
without expropriating the peasants, and without disturbing the existing Communal institutions, which form the
best barrier against pauperism."

These ideas were warmly espoused by many proprietors,
and exercised a very great influence on the deliberations of
the Provincial Committees. In these committees there were
generally two groups. The majorities, whilst making large
concessions to the claims of justice and expediency, endeavored to defend, as far as possible, the interests of their
class; the minorities, though by no means indifferent to the
interests of the class to which they belonged, allowed the
more abstract theoretical considerations to be predominant.
At first the majorities considered the fundamental principles laid down by the Government as much too favorable
to the peasantry, and were inclined to protest; but when
they perceived that public opinion, as represented by the

press, went much farther than the Government, they clung
to these fundamental principles—which secured at least
the fee simple of the estate to the landlord—as their an-
chor of safety. Between the two parties arose naturally a
strong spirit of hostility, and the Government, which
wished to have the support of the minorities, found it advisable that both should present their projects for consideration.

As the Provincial Committees worked independently,
there was considerable diversity in the conclusions at
which they arrived. The task of codifying these conclusions, and elaborating out of them a general scheme of
Emancipation, was entrusted to a special Imperial Commission, composed partly of officials and partly of landed
proprietors named by the Emperor.[2] Those who believed
that the question had really been handed over to the
Noblesse assumed that this Commission would merely
codify the materials presented by the Provincial Committees, and that the Emancipation Law would thereafter be
elaborated by a National Assembly of deputies elected by
the nobles. In reality the Commission, working in St.
Petersburg under the direct guidance and control of the
Government, fulfilled a very different and much more important function. Using the combined projects merely as a
storehouse from which it could draw the proposals it required, it formed a new project of its own, which ultimately received, after undergoing modification in detail,
the Imperial assent. Instead of being a mere *chancellerie*,
as many expected, it became in a certain sense the author
of the Emancipation Law.

There were, as we have seen, in nearly all the Provincial
Committees a majority and a minority, the former of which
strove to defend the interests of the proprietors, whilst the
latter paid more attention to theoretical considerations, and
endeavored to secure for the peasantry a large amount of
land and Communal self-government. In the Commission
there were the same two parties, but their relative strength
was very different. Here the men of theory, instead of

[2] Known as the *Redaktsiónnaya Komissiya*, or Elaboration
Commission. Strictly speaking there were two, but they are commonly spoken of as one.

forming a minority, were more numerous than their opponents, and enjoyed the support of the Government, which regulated the proceedings. In its instructions we see how much the question had ripened under the influence of the theoretical considerations. There is no longer any trace of the idea that the Emancipation should be gradual; on the contrary, it is expressly declared that the immediate effect of the law should be the complete abolition of the proprietor's authority. There is even evidence of a clear intention of preventing the proprietor as far as possible from exercising any influence over his former serfs. The sharp distinction between the land occupied by the village and the arable land to be ceded in usufruct likewise disappears, and it is merely said that efforts should be made to enable the peasants to become proprietors of the land they required.

The aim of the Government had thus become clear and well defined. The task to be performed was to transform the serfs at once, and with the least possible disturbance of the existing economic conditions, into a class of small Communal proprietors—that is to say, a class of free peasants possessing a house and a garden, and a share of the Communal land. To effect this it was merely necessary to declare the serf personally free, to draw a clear line of demarcation between the Communal land and the rest of the estate, and to determine the price or rent which should be paid for this Communal property, inclusive of the land on which the village was built.

The law was prepared in strict accordance with these principles. As to the amount of land to be ceded, it was decided that the existing arrangements, founded on experience, should, as a general rule, be preserved—in other words, the land actually enjoyed by the peasants should be retained by them; and in order to prevent extreme cases of injustice, a maximum and a minimum were fixed for each district. In like manner, as to the dues, it was decided that the existing arrangements should be taken as the basis of the calculation, but that the sum should be modified according to the amount of land ceded. At the same time facilities were to be given for the transforming of the labor dues into yearly money payments, and for

enabling the peasants to redeem them, with the assistance
of the Government in the form of credit.

This idea of redemption created, at first, a feeling of
alarm among the proprietors. It was bad enough to be
obliged to cede a large part of the estates in usufruct,
but it seemed to be much worse to have to sell it. Redemption appeared to be a species of wholesale confiscation.
But very soon it became evident that the redeeming of the
land was profitable for both parties. Cession in perpetual
usufruct was felt to be in reality tantamount to alienation
of the land, whilst the immediate redemption would enable the proprietors, who had generally little or no ready
money, to pay their debts, to clear their estates from mortgages, and to make the outlays necessary for the transition
to free labor. The majority of the proprietors, therefore,
said openly: "Let the Government give us a suitable compensation in money for the land that is taken away from
us, so that we may be at once freed from all further
trouble and annoyance."

When it became known that the Commission was not
merely arranging and codifying the materials, but elaborating a law of its own and regularly submitting its decisions for Imperial confirmation, a feeling of dissatisfaction appeared all over the country. The nobles perceived
that the question was being taken out of their hands, and
was being solved by a small body composed of bureau-
crats and nominees of the Government. After having made
a voluntary sacrifice of their rights, they were being unceremoniously pushed aside! They had still, however, the
means of correcting this. The Emperor had publicly promised that before the project should become law, deputies
from the Provincial Committees should be summoned to
St. Petersburg to make objections and propose amendments.

The Commission and the Government would have willingly dispensed with all further advice from the nobles,
but it was necessary to redeem the Imperial promise.
Deputies were therefore summoned to the capital, but
they were not allowed to form, as they hoped, a public
assembly for the discussion of the question. All their efforts
to hold meetings were frustrated, and they were required

merely to answer in writing a list of printed questions regarding matters of detail. The fundamental principles, they were told, had already received the Imperial sanction, and were consequently removed from discussion. Those who desired to discuss details were invited individually to attend meetings of the Commission, where they found one or two members ready to engage with them in a little dialectical fencing. This, of course, did not give much satisfaction. Indeed, the ironical tone in which the fencing was too often conducted served to increase the existing irritation. It was only too evident that the Commission had triumphed, and some of the members could justly boast that they had drowned the deputies in ink and buried them under reams of paper.

Believing, or at least professing to believe, that the Emperor was being deceived in this matter by the Administration, several groups of deputies presented petitions to his Majesty containing a respectful protest against the manner in which they had been treated. But by this act they simply laid themselves open to "the most unkindest cut of all." Those who had signed the petitions received a formal reprimand through the police!

This treatment of the deputies, and, above all, this gratuitous insult, produced among the nobles a storm of indignation. They felt that they had been entrapped! The Government had artfully induced them to form projects for the emancipation of their serfs, and now, after having been used as a cat's-paw in the work of their own spoliation, they were being unceremoniously pushed aside as no longer necessary! Those who had indulged in the hope of gaining political rights felt the blow most keenly. A first gentle and respectful attempt at remonstrance had been answered by a dictatorial reprimand through the police! Instead of being called to take an active part in home and foreign politics, they were being treated as naughty schoolboys. In view of this insult all differences of opinion were for the moment forgotten, and all parties resolved to join in a vigorous protest against the insolence and arbitrary conduct of the bureaucracy.

A convenient opportunity of making this protest in a legal way was offered by the triennial Provincial Assem-

blies of the Noblesse about to be held in several provinces.
So at least it was thought, but here again the Noblesse was
checkmated by the Administration. Before the opening of
the Assemblies a circular was issued excluding the Emancipation question from their deliberations. Some Assemblies evaded this order, and succeeded in making a little
demonstration by submitting to his Majesty that the time
had arrived for other reforms, such as the separation of
the administrative and judicial powers, and the creation of
local self-government, public judicial procedure, and trial
by jury.

All these reforms were voluntarily effected by the Emperor a few years later, but the manner in which they were
suggested seemed to savor of insubordination, and was a
flagrant infraction of the principle that all initiative in public affairs should proceed from the central Government.
New measures of repression were accordingly used. Some
Marshals of Noblesse were reprimanded and others deposed. Of the conspicuous leaders, two were exiled to
distant provinces and others placed under the supervision
of the police. Worst of all, the whole agitation strengthened
the Commission by convincing the Emperor that the majority of the nobles were hostile to his benevolent plans.[3]

When the Commission had finished its labors, its proposals passed to the two higher instances—the Committee
for Peasant Affairs and the Council of State—and in both
of these the Emperor declared plainly that he could allow
no fundamental changes. From all the members he demanded a complete forgetfulness of former differences and
a conscientious execution of his orders; "for you must remember," he significantly added, "that in Russia laws are
made by the autocratic power." From an historical review
of the question he drew the conclusion that "the autocratic
power created serfage, and the autocratic power ought to
abolish it." On March 3rd (February 19th, old style),
1861, the law was signed, and by that act more than 20,-

[3] This was a misinterpretation of the facts. Very many of those
who joined in the protest sincerely sympathized with the idea
of Emancipation, and were ready to be even more "liberal"
than the Government.

000,000 serfs were liberated.[4] A Manifesto containing the fundamental principles of the law was at once sent all over the country, and an order was given that it should be read in all the churches.

The three fundamental principles laid down by the law were:

1. That the serfs should at once receive the civil rights of the free rural classes, and that the authority of the proprietor should be replaced by Communal self-government.

2. That the rural Communes should as far as possible retain the land they actually held, and should in return pay to the proprietor certain yearly dues in money or labor.

3. That the Government should by means of credit assist the Communes to redeem these dues, or, in other words, to purchase the lands ceded to them in usufruct.

With regard to the domestic serfs, it was enacted that they should continue to serve their masters during two years, and that thereafter they should be completely free, but they should have no claim to a share of the land.

It might be reasonably supposed that the serfs received with boundless gratitude and delight the Manifesto proclaiming these principles. Here at last was the realization of their long-cherished hopes. Liberty was accorded to them; and not only liberty, but a goodly portion of the soil —about half of all the arable land possessed by the proprietors.

In reality the Manifesto created among the peasantry a feeling of disappointment rather than delight. To understand this strange fact we must endeavor to place ourselves at the peasant's point of view.

[4] It is sometimes said that 40,000,000 serfs have been emancipated. The statement is true, if we regard the State Peasants as serfs. They held, as I have already explained, an intermediate position between serfage and freedom. The peculiar administration under which they lived was partly abolished by Imperial Orders of September 7th, 1859, and October 23rd, 1861. In 1866 they were placed, as regards administration, on a level with the emancipated serfs of the proprietors. As a general rule, they received rather more land and had to pay somewhat lighter dues than the emancipated serfs in the narrower sense of the term.

In the first place it must be remarked that all vague, rhetorical phrases about free labor, human dignity, national progress, and the like, which may readily produce among educated men a certain amount of temporary enthusiasm, fall on the ears of the Russian peasant like drops of rain on a granite rock. The fashionable rhetoric of philosophical liberalism is as incomprehensible to him as the flowery circumlocutionary style of an Oriental scribe would be to a keen City merchant. The idea of liberty in the abstract and the mention of rights which lie beyond the sphere of his ordinary everyday life awaken no enthusiasm in his breast. And for mere names he has a profound indifference. What matters it to him that he is officially called, not a "serf," but a "free village-inhabitant," if the change in official terminology is not accompanied by some immediate material advantage? What he wants is a house to live in, food to eat, and raiment wherewithal to be clothed, and to gain these first necessaries of life with as little labor as possible.

He looked at the question exclusively from two points of view—that of historical right and that of material advantage—and from both of these the Emancipation Law seemed to him very unsatisfactory.

On the subject of historical right the peasantry had their own traditional conceptions, which were completely at variance with the written law. According to the positive legislation the Communal land formed part of the estate, and consequently belonged to the proprietor; but according to the conceptions of the peasantry it belonged to the Commune, and the right of the proprietor consisted merely in that personal authority over the serfs which had been conferred on him by the Tsar. The peasants could not, of course, put these conceptions into a strict legal form, but they often expressed them in their own homely laconic way by saying to their master, "Mui vashi no zemlyá nasha"—that is to say, "We are yours, but the land is ours." And it must be admitted that this view, though legally untenable, had a certain historical justification. In old times the nobles had held their land by feudal tenure, and were liable to be ejected as soon as they did not fulfill

their obligations to the State. These obligations had long
since been abolished, and the feudal tenure transformed
into an unconditional right of property, but the peasants
clung to the old ideas in a way that strikingly illustrates
the vitality of deep-rooted popular conceptions. In their
minds the proprietors were merely temporary occupants,
who were allowed by the Tsar to exact labor and dues
from the serfs. What, then, was Emancipation? Certainly
the abolition of all obligatory labor and money dues, and
perhaps the complete ejectment of the proprietors. On this
latter point there was a difference of opinion. All assumed,
as a matter of course, that the Communal land would remain the property of the Commune, but it was not so clear
what would be done with the rest of the estate. Some
thought that it would be retained by the proprietor, but
very many believed that *all* the land would be given to the
Communes. In this way the Emancipation would be in accordance with historical right and with the material advantage of the peasantry, for whose exclusive benefit, it
was assumed, the reform had been undertaken.

Instead of this the peasants found that they were still
to pay dues, even for the Communal land which they regarded as unquestionably their own! So at least said the
expounders of the law. But the thing was incredible. Either
the proprietors must be concealing or misinterpreting the
law, or this was merely a preparatory measure, which
would be followed by the real Emancipation. Thus were
awakened among the peasantry a spirit of mistrust and
suspicion and a widespread belief that there would be a
second Imperial Manifesto, by which all the land would
be divided and all the dues abolished.

On the nobles the Manifesto made a very different impression. The fact that they were to be entrusted with the
putting of the law into execution, and the flattering al-
lusions made to the spirit of generous self-sacrifice which
they had exhibited, kindled amongst them enthusiasm
enough to make them forget for a time their just grievances and their hostility towards the bureaucracy. They
found that the conditions on which the Emancipation was
effected were by no means so ruinous as they had antici-

pated; and the Emperor's appeal to their generosity and patriotism made many of them throw themselves with ardor into the important task confided to them.

Unfortunately they could not at once begin the work. The law had been so hurried through the last stages that the preparations for putting it into execution were by no means complete when the Manifesto was published. The task of regulating the future relations between the proprietors and the peasantry was entrusted to local proprietors in each district, who were to be called Arbiters of the Peace (*Mirovuiye Posrédniki*); but three months elapsed before these Arbiters could be appointed. During that time there was no one to explain the law to the peasants and settle the disputes between them and the proprietors; and the consequence of this was that many cases of insubordination and disorder occurred. The muzhik naturally imagined that, as soon as the Tsar said he was free, he was no longer obliged to work for his old master—that all obligatory labor ceased as soon as the Manifesto was read. In vain the proprietor endeavored to convince him that, in regard to labor, the old relations must continue, as the law enjoined, until a new arrangement had been made. To all explanations and exhortations he turned a deaf ear, and to the efforts of the rural police he too often opposed a dogged, passive resistance. In many cases the simple appearance of the higher authorities sufficed to restore order, for the presence of one of the Tsar's servants convinced many that the order to work for the present as formerly was not a mere invention of the proprietors. But not infrequently the birch had to be applied. Indeed, I am inclined to believe, from the numerous descriptions of this time which I received from eyewitnesses, that rarely, if ever, had the serfs seen and experienced so much flogging as during these first three months after their liberation. Sometimes even the troops had to be called out, and on three occasions they fired on the peasants with ball cartridge. In the most serious case, where a young peasant had set up for a prophet and declared that the Emancipation Law was a forgery, fifty-one peasants were killed and seventy-seven were more or less seriously wounded.

In spite of these lamentable incidents, there was nothing which even the most violent alarmist could dignify with the name of an insurrection. Nowhere was there anything that could be called organized resistance. Even in the case above alluded to, the three thousand peasants on whom the troops fired were entirely unarmed, made no attempt to resist, and dispersed in the utmost haste as soon as they discovered that they were being shot down. Had the military authorities shown a little more judgment, tact and patience, the history of the Emancipation would not have been stained even with those three cases of unnecessary bloodshed.

This interregnum between the eras of serfage and liberty was brought to an end by the appointment of the Arbiters of the Peace. Their first duty was to explain the law, and to organize the new peasant self-government. The lowest instance or primary organ of this self-government, the rural Commune, already existed, and at once recovered much of its ancient vitality as soon as the authority and interference of the proprietors were removed. The second instance, the *Vólost*—a territorial administrative unit comprising several contiguous Communes—had to be created, for nothing of the kind had previously existed on the estates of the nobles. It had existed, however, for nearly a quarter of a century among the peasants of the Domains, and it was therefore necessary merely to copy an existing model.

As soon as all the Vólosts in his district had been thus organized, the Arbiter had to undertake the much more arduous task of regulating the agrarian relations between the proprietors and the Communes—with the individual peasants, be it remembered, the proprietors had no direct relations whatever. It had been enacted by the law that the future agrarian relations between the two parties should be left, as far as possible, to voluntary contract; and accordingly each proprietor was invited to come to an agreement with the Commune or Communes on his estate. On the ground of this agreement a statute-charter (*ustávnaya grámota*) was prepared, specifying the number of male serfs, the quantity of land actually enjoyed by them, any proposed changes in this amount, the dues to be levied, and other details. If the Arbiter found that the conditions were in accordance with the law and clearly understood by the peasants, he confirmed the charter, and the arrangement was complete. When the two parties could not come to an agreement within a year, he prepared a charter according to his own judgment, and presented it for confirmation to the higher authorities.

The dissolution of partnership, if it be allowable to use such a term, between the proprietor and his serfs was sometimes very easy and sometimes very difficult. On many estates the charter did little more than legalize the existing arrangements, but in many instances it was necessary to add to, or subtract from, the amount of Communal land, and sometimes it was even necessary to remove the village to another part of the estate. In all cases there were, of course, conflicting interests and complicated questions, so that the Arbiter had always abundance of difficult work. Besides this, he had to act as mediator in those differences which naturally arose during the transition period, when the authority of the proprietor had been abolished but the separation of the two classes had not yet been effected. The unlimited patriarchal authority which had been formerly wielded by the proprietor or his steward now passed with certain restrictions into the hands of the Arbiters, and these peacemakers had to spend a great part of their time in driving about from one estate to another to put an end to alleged cases of insubordination—some of which, it must be admitted, existed only in the imagination of the proprietors.

At first the work of amicable settlement proceeded slowly. The proprietors generally showed a conciliatory spirit, and some of them generously proposed conditions much more favorable to the peasants than the law demanded; but the peasants were filled with vague suspicions, and feared to commit themselves by "putting pen to paper." Even the highly respected proprietors, who imagined that they possessed the unbounded confidence of the peasantry, were suspected like the others, and their generous offers were regarded as well-baited traps. Often I have heard old men, sometimes with tears in their eyes, describe the distrust and ingratitude of the muzhik at this time. Many peasants still believed that the proprietors were hiding the real Emancipation Law, and imaginative or ill-intentioned persons fostered this belief by professing to know what the real law contained. The most absurd rumors were afloat, and whole villages sometimes acted upon them. In the province of Moscow, for instance, one Commune sent a deputation to the proprietor to inform him that, as he had always been a good master, the *Mir* would allow him to retain his house and garden during his lifetime. In another locality it was rumored that the Tsar sat daily on a golden throne in the Crimea, receiving all peasants who came to him, and giving them as much land as they desired; and in order to take advantage of the Imperial liberality a large body of peasants set out for the place indicated, and had to be stopped by the military!

As an illustration of the illusions in which the peasantry indulged at this time, I may mention here one of the many characteristic incidents related to me by gentlemen who had served as Arbiters of the Peace.

In the province of Riazán there was one Commune which had acquired a certain local notoriety for the obstinacy with which it refused all arrangements with the proprietor. My informant, who was Arbiter for the locality, was at last obliged to make a statute charter for it without its consent. He wished, however, that the peasants should voluntarily accept the arrangement he proposed, and accordingly called them together to talk with them on the subject. After explaining fully the part of the law which related to their case, he asked them what objection they had to making a fair contract with their old master. For some time he received no answer, but gradually by questioning individuals he discovered the cause of their obstinacy: they were firmly convinced that not only the Communal land, but also the rest of the estate, belonged to them. To eradicate this false idea he set himself to reason with them, and the following characteristic dialogue ensued:

Arbiter: "If the Tsar gave all the land to the peasantry, what compensation could he give to the proprietors to whom the land belongs?"

Peasant: "The Tsar will give them salaries according to their service."

Arbiter: "In order to pay these salaries he would require a great deal more money. Where could he get that money? He would have to increase the taxes, and in that way you would have to pay all the same."

Peasant: "The Tsar can make as much money as he likes."

Arbiter: "If the Tsar can make as much money as he likes, why does he make you pay the poll tax every year?"

Peasant: "It is not the Tsar that receives the taxes we pay."

Arbiter: "Who, then, receives them?"

Peasant (after a little hesitation, and with a knowing smile): "The officials, of course!"

Gradually, through the efforts of the Arbiters, the peasants came to know better their real position, and the work began to advance more rapidly. But soon it was checked by another influence. By the end of the first year the "liberal" patriotic enthusiasm of the nobles had cooled. The sentimental, idyllic tendencies had melted away at the first touch of reality, and those who had imagined that liberty would have an immediately salutary effect on the moral character of the serfs confessed themselves disappointed. Many complained that the peasants showed themselves greedy and obstinate, stole wood from the forest, allowed their cattle to wander on the proprietors' fields, failed to fulfill their legal obligations, and broke their voluntary engagements. At the same time the fears of an agrarian rising subsided, so that even the timid were tranquilized. From these causes the conciliatory spirit of the proprietors decreased.

The work of conciliating and regulating became consequently more difficult, but the great majority of the Arbiters showed themselves equal to the task, and displayed an impartiality, tact, and patience beyond all praise. To them Russia is in great part indebted for the peaceful character of the Emancipation. Had they sacrificed the general good to the interests of their class, or had they habitually acted in that stern, administrative, military spirit which caused the instances of bloodshed above referred to, the prophecies of the alarmists would, in all probability, have been realized, and the historian of the Emancipation would have had a terrible list of judicial massacres to record. Fortunately they played the part of mediators, as their name signified, rather than that of administrators in the bureaucratic sense of the term, and they were animated with a just and humane rather than a merely legal spirit. Instead of simply laying down the law, and ordering their decisions to be immediately executed, they were ever ready to spend hours in trying to conquer, by patient and laborious reasoning, the unjust claims of proprietors or the false conceptions and ignorant obstinacy of the peasants. It was a new spectacle for Russia to see a public function fulfilled by conscientious men who had their heart in their work, who sought neither promotion nor decorations, and who paid less attention to the punctilious observance of prescribed formalities than to the real objects in view.

There were, it is true, a few Arbiters to whom this description does not apply. Some of these were unduly under the influence of the feelings and conceptions created by serfage. Some, on the contrary, erred on the other side. Desirous of securing the future welfare of the peasantry and of gaining for themselves a certain kind of popularity, and at the same time animated with a violent spirit of pseudo-liberalism, these latter occasionally forgot that their duty was to be, not generous, but just, and that they had no right to practice generosity at other people's expense. All this I am quite aware of—I could even name one or two Arbiters who were guilty of positive dishonesty —but I hold that these were rare exceptions. The great majority did their duty faithfully and well.

The work of concluding contracts for the redemption of the dues, or, in other words, for the purchase of the land ceded in perpetual usufruct, proceeded slowly. The arrangement was as follows: The dues were capitalized at 6 per cent, and the Government paid at once to the proprietors four-fifths of the whole sum. The peasants were to pay to the proprietor the remaining fifth, either at once or in installments, and to the Government 6 per cent for forty-nine years on the sum advanced. The proprietors

willingly adopted this arrangement, for it provided them
with a sum of ready money, and freed them from the
difficult task of collecting the dues. But the peasants did
not show much desire to undertake the operation. Some
of them still expected a second emancipation, and those
who did not take this possibility into their calculations
were little disposed to make present sacrifices for distant
prospective advantages which would not be realized for
half a century.

In most cases the proprietor was obliged to remit, in
whole or in part, the fifth to be paid by the peasants.
Many Communes refused to undertake the operation on
any conditions, and in consequence of this not a few proprietors demanded the so-called obligatory redemption,
according to which they accepted the four-fifths from the
Government as full payment, and the operation was thus
effected without the peasants being consulted. The total
number of *male* serfs emancipated was about 9,750,000,[5]
and of these, only about 7,250,000 had, at the beginning
of 1875, made redemption contracts. Of the contracts
signed at that time, about 63 per cent were "obligatory."
In 1887 the redemption was made obligatory for both
parties, and in 1905 the redemption dues were remitted
by the Emperor, so that the rural Communes became full
proprietors of the land previously held in perpetual usufruct.

The serfs were thus not only liberated, but also made
Communal proprietors, and the old Communal institutions
were preserved and developed. In answer to the question,
Who effected this gigantic reform? we may say that the
chief merit undoubtedly belongs to Alexander II. Had
he not possessed a very great amount of courage he would
neither have raised the question nor allowed it to be raised
by others, and had he not shown a great deal more decision and energy than was expected, the solution would
have been indefinitely postponed. Among the members of
his own family he found an able and energetic assistant in
his brother, the Grand Duke Constantine, and a warm
sympathizer with the cause in the Grand Duchess Helena,

[5] This does not include the domestic serfs, who did not
receive land.

a German Princess, thoroughly devoted to the welfare of her adopted country. But we must not overlook the important part played by the nobles. Their conduct was very characteristic. As soon as the question was raised, a large number of them adopted the liberal ideas with enthusiasm; and as soon as it became evident that emancipation was inevitable, all made a holocaust of their ancient rights, and demanded to be liberated at once from all relations with their serfs. Moreover, when the law was passed, it was the proprietors who faithfully put it into execution. Lastly, we should remember that praise is due to the peasantry for their patience under disappointment, and for their orderly conduct as soon as they understood the law and recognized it to be the will of the Tsar. Thus it may justly be said that the Emancipation was not the work of one man, or one party, or one class, but of the nation as a whole.

CHAPTER · XVIII

The Emancipated
Peasantry

. . . I [HAVE already] pointed out in general terms the difficulty of describing clearly the immediate consequences of the Emancipation. In beginning now to speak of the influence which the great reform has had on the peasantry, I feel that the difficulty has reached its climax. The foreigner who desires merely to gain a general idea of the subject cannot be expected to take an interest in details, and even if he took the trouble to examine them attentively, he would derive from the labor little real information. What he wishes is a clear, concise, and dogmatic statement of general results. Has the material and moral condition of the peasantry improved since the Emancipation? That is the simple question which he has to put, and he naturally expects a simple, categorical answer.

In beginning my researches in this interesting field of inquiry, I had no adequate conception of the difficulties awaiting me. I imagined that I had merely to question intelligent, competent men who had had abundant opportunities of observation, and to criticize and boil down the information collected; but when I put this method of investigation to the test of experience it proved unsatisfactory. Very soon I came to perceive that my authorities were very far from being impartial observers. Most of them were evidently suffering from shattered illusions. They had expected that the Emancipation would produce instantaneously a wonderful improvement in the life and charac-

ter of the rural population, and that the peasant would
become at once a sober, industrious, model agriculturist.

These expectations were not realized. One year passed,
five years passed, ten years passed, and the expected
transformation did not take place. On the contrary, there
appeared certain very ugly phenomena which were not at
all in the program. The peasants, it was said, began to
drink more and to work less, and the public life which
the Communal institutions produced was by no means of
a desirable kind. The "bawlers" (*gorlopány*) acquired a
prejudicial influence in the Village Assemblies, and in very
many Vólosts the peasant judges, elected by their fellow
villagers, acquired a bad habit of selling their decisions
for vodka. The natural consequence of all this was that
those who had indulged in exaggerated expectations sank
into a state of inordinate despondency, and imagined
things to be much worse than they really were.

For different reasons, those who had not indulged in exaggerated expectations, and had not sympathized with the
Emancipation in the form in which it was effected, were
equally inclined to take a pessimistic view of the situation.
In every ugly phenomenon they found a confirmation of
their opinions. The result was precisely what they had
foretold. The peasants had used their liberty and their
privileges to their own detriment and to the detriment of
others!

The extreme "Liberals" were also inclined, for reasons of
their own, to join in the doleful chorus. They desired that
the condition of the peasantry should be further improved
by legislative enactments, and accordingly they painted
the evils in as dark colors as possible.

Thus, from various reasons, the majority of the educated
classes were unduly disposed to represent to themselves
and to others the actual condition of the peasantry in a
very unfavorable light, and I felt that from them there was
no hope of obtaining the *lumen siccum* which I desired. I
determined, therefore, to try the method of questioning the
peasants themselves. Surely they must know whether their
condition was better or worse than it had been before their
Emancipation.

Again I was doomed to disappointment. A few months'

experience sufficed to convince me that my new method
was by no means so effectual as I had imagined. Uneducated people rarely make generalizations which have no
practical utility, and I feel sure that very few Russian peasants ever put to themselves the question: Am I better off
now than I or my father was in the time of serfage?
When such a question is put to them they feel taken aback.
And in truth it is no easy matter to sum up the two sides of
the account and draw an accurate balance, save in those
exceptional cases in which the proprietor flagrantly abused
his authority. The present money dues and taxes are often
more burdensome than the labor dues in the old times. If
the serfs had a great many ill-defined obligations to fulfill
—such as the carting of the master's grain to market, the
preparing of his firewood, the supplying him with eggs,
chickens, home-made linen, and the like—they had, on
the other hand, a good many ill-defined privileges. They
grazed their cattle during a part of the year on the manor
land; they received firewood and occasionally logs for repairing their huts; sometimes the proprietor lent them or
gave them a cow or a horse when they had been visited
by the cattle plague or the horse stealer; and in times of
famine they could look to their master for support. All this
has now come to an end. Their burdens and their privileges
have been swept away together, and been replaced by
clearly defined, unbending, unelastic legal relations. They
have now to pay the market price for every stick of firewood which they burn, for every log which they require
for repairing their houses, and for every rood of land on
which to graze their cattle. Nothing is now to be had
gratis. The demand to pay is encountered at every step. If
a cow dies or a horse is stolen, the owner can no longer go
to the proprietor with the hope of receiving a present, or at
least a loan without interest, but must, if he has no ready
money, apply to the village usurer, who probably considers 20 or 30 per cent as a by no means exorbitant rate
of interest.

Besides this, from the economic point of view village life
has been completely revolutionized. Formerly the members
of a peasant family obtained from their ordinary domestic
resources nearly all they required. Their food came from

their fields, cabbage garden, and farmyard. Materials for
clothing were supplied by their plots of flax and their
sheep, and were worked up into linen and cloth by the female members of the household. Fuel, as I have said, and
torches wherewith to light the *izbà*—for oil was too expensive and petroleum was unknown—were obtained gratis. Their sheep, cattle, and horses were bred at home, and
their agricultural implements, except in so far as a little
iron was required, could be made by themselves without
any pecuniary expenditure. Money was required only for
the purchase of a few cheap domestic utensils, such as
pots, pans, knives, hatchets, wooden dishes and spoons,
and for the payment of taxes, which were small in amount
and often paid by the proprietor. In these circumstances
the quantity of money in circulation among the peasants
was infinitesimally small, the few exchanges which took
place in a village being generally effected by barter. The
taxes and the vodka required for village festivals, wed-
dings, or funerals were the only large items of expenditure for the year, and they were generally covered by the
sums brought home by the members of the family who
went to work in the towns.

Very different is the present condition of affairs. The
spinning, weaving, and other home industries have been
killed by the big factories, and the flax and wool have to
be sold to raise a little ready money for the numerous new
items of expenditure. Everything has to be bought—
clothes, firewood, petroleum, improved agricultural implements, and many other articles which are now regarded as
necessaries of life—whilst comparatively little is earned by
working in the towns, because the big families have been
broken up, and a household now consists usually of husband and wife, who must both remain at home, and children who are not yet breadwinners. Recalling to mind all
these things and the other drawbacks and advantages of
his actual position, the old muzhik has naturally much
difficulty in striking a balance, and he may well be quite
sincere when, on being asked whether things now are on
the whole better or worse than in the time of serfage, he
scratches the back of his head and replies hesitatingly,
with a mystified expression on his wrinkled face: "How

shall I say to you? They are both better and worse!" ("*Kak vam skazát'? I lútche i khúdzhe!*") If, however, you press him further, and ask whether he would himself like to return to the old state of things, he is pretty sure to answer, with a slow shake of the head and a twinkle in his eye, as if some forgotten item in the account had suddenly recurred to him: "Oh, no!"

What materially increases the difficulty of this general computation is that great changes have taken place in the well-being of the particular households. Some have greatly prospered, while others have become impoverished. That is one of the most characteristic consequences of the Emancipation. In the old times the general economic stagnation and the uncontrolled authority of the proprietor tended to keep all the households of a village on the same level. There was little opportunity for an intelligent, enterprising serf to become rich, and if he contrived to increase his revenue, he had probably to give a considerable share of it to the proprietor, unless he had the good fortune to belong to a *grand seigneur* like Count Sheremétiev, who was proud of having rich men among his serfs.

On the other hand, the proprietor, for evident reasons of self-interest, as well as from benevolent motives, prevented the less intelligent and less enterprising members of the Commune from becoming bankrupt. The Communal equality thus artificially maintained has now disappeared, the restrictions on individual freedom of action have been removed, the struggle for life has become intensified, and, as always happens in such circumstances, the strong men go up in the world while the weak ones go to the wall. All over the country we find on the one hand the beginnings of a village aristocracy—or perhaps we should call it a plutocracy, for it is based on money—and on the other hand an ever-increasing pauperism. Some peasants possess capital, with which they buy land outside the Commune or embark in trade, while others have to sell their livestock, and have sometimes to cede to neighbors their share of the Communal property. This change in rural life is so often referred to that, in order to express it, a new, barbarous word, *differentsiatsia* (differentiation) has been invented.

Hoping to obtain fuller information with the aid of
official protection, I attached myself to one of the traveling sections of an agricultural Commission appointed by
the Government, and during a whole summer I helped to
collect materials in the provinces bordering on the Volga.
The inquiry resulted in a gigantic report of nearly 2,500
folio pages, but the general conclusions were extremely
vague. The peasantry, it was said, were passing, like the
landed proprietors, through a period of transition, in which
the main features of their future normal life had not yet
become clearly defined. In some localities their condition
had decidedly improved, whereas in others it had improved little or not at all. Then followed a long list of
recommendations in favor of Government assistance, better
agronomic education, competitive exhibitions, more varied
rotation of crops, and greater zeal on the part of the clergy
in disseminating among the people moral principles in general and love of work in particular.

Not greatly enlightened by this official activity, I returned to my private studies, and at the end of six years I
published my impressions and conclusions in the first edition of this work. While recognizing that there was much
uncertainty as to the future, I was inclined, on the whole,
to take a hopeful view of the situation. I was unable, however, to maintain permanently that comfortable frame of
mind. After my departure from Russia in 1878, the accounts which reached me from various parts of the country became blacker and blacker, and were partly confirmed by short tours which I made in 1889-96. At last,
in the summer of 1903, I determined to return to some of
my old haunts and look at things with my own eyes. At
that moment some hospitable friends invited me to pay
them a visit at their country house in the province of
Smolensk, and I gladly accepted the invitation because
Smolensk, when I knew it formerly, was one of the poorest
provinces, and I thought it well to begin my new studies
by examining the impoverishment, of which I had heard
so much, at its maximum.

From the railway station at Viazma, where I arrived one
morning at sunrise, I had some twenty miles to drive, and
as soon as I got clear of the little town I began my ob-

servations. What I saw around me seemed to contradict
the somber accounts I had received. The villages through
which I passed had not at all the look of dilapidation and
misery which I expected. On the contrary, the houses
were larger and better constructed than they used to be,
and each of them had a chimney! That latter fact was
important, because formerly a large proportion of the
peasants of this region had no such luxury, and allowed
the smoke to find its exit by the open door. In vain I
looked for a hut of the old type, and my *yamshchik* assured me I should have to go a long way to find one.
Then I noticed a good many iron ploughs of the European
model, and my *yamshchik* informed me that their predecessor, the *sokhá*, with which I had been so familiar, had
entirely disappeared from the district. Next I noticed that
in the neighborhood of the villages flax was grown in large
quantities. That was certainly not an indication of poverty, because flax is a valuable product which requires to
be well manured, and plentiful manure implies a considerable quantity of livestock. Lastly, before arriving at my
destination, I noticed clover being grown in the fields.
This made me open my eyes with astonishment, because
the introduction of artificial grasses into the traditional
rotation of crops indicates the transition to a higher and
more intensive system of agriculture. As I had never seen
clover in Russia except on the estates of very advanced
proprietors, I said to my *yamshchik:*

"Listen, little brother! That field belongs to the landlord?"

"Not at all, Master; it is muzhik land."

On arriving at the country house I told my friends what
I had seen, and they explained it to me. Smolensk is no
longer one of the poorer provinces; it has become comparatively prosperous. In two or three districts large quantities
of flax are produced and give the cultivators a big revenue;
in other districts plenty of remunerative work is supplied
by the forests. Everywhere a considerable proportion of
the younger men go regularly to the towns and bring home
savings enough to pay the taxes and make a little surplus
in the domestic budget. A few days afterwards the village

secretary brought me his books, and showed me that there were practically no arrears of taxation.

Passing on to other provinces, I found similar proofs of progress and prosperity, but at the same time not a few indications of impoverishment; and I was rapidly relapsing into my previous state of uncertainty as to whether any general conclusions could be drawn, when an old friend, himself a first-rate authority, with many years of practical experience, came to my assistance.[1] He informed me that a number of specialists had recently made detailed investigations into the present economic conditions of the rural population, and he kindly placed at my disposal, in his charming country house near Moscow, the voluminous researches of these investigators. Here, during a good many weeks, I reveled in the statistical materials collected, and to the best of my ability I tested the conclusions drawn from them. Many of these conclusions I had to dismiss with the Scottish verdict of "not proven," whilst others seemed to me worthy of acceptance. Of these latter the most important were those drawn from the arrears of taxation.

The arrears in the payment of taxes may be regarded as a pretty safe barometer for testing the condition of the rural population, because the peasant habitually pays his rates and taxes when he has the means of doing so; when he falls seriously and permanently into arrears, it may be assumed that he is becoming impoverished. If the arrears fluctuate from year to year, the causes of the impoverishment may be regarded as accidental and perhaps temporary, but if they steadily accumulate, we must conclude that there is something radically wrong. Bearing these facts in mind, let us hear what the statistics say.

During the first twenty years after the Emancipation (1861-81) things went on in their old grooves. The poor provinces remained poor, and the fertile provinces showed no signs of distress. During the next twenty years (1881-1901) the arrears of the whole of European Russia rose, roughly speaking, from 27 to 144 millions of rubles, and

[1] I hope I am committing no indiscretion when I say that the old friend in question was Prince Alexander Shcherbátov of Vasilievskoe.

the increase, strange to say, took place chiefly in the fertile provinces. In 1890, for example, out of 52 millions, nearly 41 millions, or 78 per cent, fell to the share of the provinces of the Black-Earth Zone. In seven of these the average arrears per male, which had been in 1882 only 90 kopeks, rose in 1893 to 600, and in 1899 to 2,200! And this accumulation had taken place in spite of reductions of taxation to the extent of 37 million rubles in 1881-83, and successive famine grants from the Treasury in 1891-99 to the amount of 203 millions.[2] On the other hand, in the provinces with a poor soil the arrears had greatly decreased. In Smolensk, for example, they had sunk from 202 per cent to 13 per cent of the annual sum to be paid, and in nearly all the other provinces of the west and north a similar change for the better had taken place.

These and many other figures which I might quote show that a great and very curious economic revolution has been gradually effected. The Black-Earth Zone, which was formerly regarded as the inexhaustible granary of the Empire, has become impoverished, whilst the provinces which were formerly regarded as hopelessly poor are now in a comparatively flourishing condition. This fact has been officially recognized. In a classification of the provinces according to their degree of prosperity, drawn up by a special commission of experts in 1903, those with a poor light soil appear at the top, and those with the famous black earth are at the bottom of the list. In the deliberations of the commission, many reasons for this extraordinary state of things are adduced. Most of them have merely a local significance. The big fact, taken as a whole, seems to me to show that, in consequence of certain changes of which I shall speak presently, the peasantry of European Russia can no longer live by the traditional modes of agriculture, even in the most fertile districts, and require for their support some subsidiary occupations such as are practiced in the less fertile provinces.

Another sign of impoverishment is the decrease in the quantity of livestock. According to the very imperfect statistics available, for every hundred inhabitants the number

[2] In 1901 an additional famine grant of 33½ million rubles had to be made by the Government.

of horses has decreased from 26 to 17, the number of cattle from 36 to 25, and the number of sheep from 73 to 40. This is a serious matter, because it means that the land is not so well manured and cultivated as formerly, and is consequently not so productive. Several economists have attempted to fix precisely to what extent the productivity has decreased, but I confess I have little faith in the accuracy of their conclusions. M. Polêno, for example, a most able and conscientious investigator, calculates that between 1861 and 1895, all over Russia, the amount of food produced, in relation to the number of the population, has decreased by seven per cent. His methods of calculation are ingenious, but the statistical data with which he operates are so far from accurate that his conclusions on this point have, in my opinion, little or no scientific value. With all due deference to Russian economists I may say parenthetically that they are very fond of juggling with carelessly collected statistics, as if their data were mathematical quantities.

Several of the Zemstvos have grappled with this question of peasant impoverishment, and the data which they have collected make a very doleful impression. In the province of Moscow, for example, a careful investigation gave the following results: Forty per cent of the peasant households had no longer any horses, fifteen per cent had given up agriculture altogether, and about ten per cent had no longer any land. We must not, however, assume, as is often done, that the peasant families who have no livestock and no longer till the land are utterly ruined. In reality many of them are better off then their neighbors who appear as prosperous in the official statistics, having found profitable occupation in the home industries, in the towns, in the factories, or on the estates of the landed proprietors. It must be remembered that Moscow is the center of one of the regions in which manufacturing industry has progressed with gigantic strides during the last half-century, and it would be strange indeed if, in such a region, the peasantry who supply the labor to the towns and factories remained thriving agriculturists. That many Russians are surprised and horrified at the actual state of things shows to what an extent the educated classes are

still under the illusion that Russia can create for herself a
manufacturing industry capable of competing with that of
Western Europe without uprooting from the soil a portion
of her rural population.

It is only in the purely agricultural regions that families
officially classed as belonging to the peasantry may be regarded as on the brink of pauperism because they have no
livestock, and even with regard to them I should hesitate
to make such an assumption, because the muzhiks, as I
have already had occasion to remark, have strange nomadic habits unknown to the rural population of other
countries. It is a mistake, therefore, to calculate the Russian peasant's budget exclusively on the basis of local
resources.

To the pessimists who assure me that according to their
calculations the peasantry in general *must be* on the brink
of starvation, I reply that there are many facts, even in the
statistical tables on which they rely, which run counter to
their deductions. Let me quote a few by way of illustration. The peasantry have not only redeemed the land
which they received at the time of the Emancipation, but
they have also, of their own free will, greatly added to it
by purchase, with the assistance of a Peasant Land Bank,
which was founded for that purpose by the Government in
1882. During the first twenty years of its activity that institution expended over forty millions sterling on the purchase of nineteen millions of acres, which were resold to
rural communes, peasant associations, and individual peasants on the credit system. In subsequent years these operations were greatly increased and accelerated. During the
three years of 1906, 1907 and 1908 the quantity of land
purchased by the peasants with the assistance of the bank
amounted to 5,827,000 acres, which constituted an addition of about one-twelfth to the land they already possessed. All these purchases remain, of course, mortgaged
until the debt to the bank is extinguished by the sinking
fund, and the fact that the owners willingly pay, as interest and sinking fund, no less than 7½ per cent, shows that
the peasantry as a class are very far from absolute destitution. No doubt there is another side to the medal. While
many peasants are thus increasing their landed property,

others are becoming poorer, but this is merely one of those inevitable results of economic progress of which I have spoken elsewhere.

Another indication that the impoverishment of the peasantry is not so great as is often asserted is to be found in the extension of savings banks and small credit associations. From 1865 to 1909 the branches of the Government Savings Bank increased in number from 47 to 6,752, the number of depositors from 72,000 to over six millions, and the amount of deposits from £564,000 to over 120 millions sterling, of which about one-fourth is believed to belong to the rural population. In addition to this, there are now 3,556 village savings banks, which held in 1910 deposits to the amount of £2,780,000, and a large number of rural credit associations, of which 1,476 held deposits amounting to £6,000,000. This is not much for a big country like Russia, but it is a beginning, and it suggests that the impoverishment is not so severe and so universal as the pessimists would have us believe.

There is thus room for differences of opinion as to how far the peasantry have become impoverished, but there is no doubt that their condition is far from satisfactory, and we have to face the important problem why the abolition of serfage has not produced the beneficent consequences which even moderate men so confidently predicted, and how the present unsatisfactory state of things is to be remedied.

The most common explanation among those who have never seriously studied the subject is that it all comes from the demoralization of the common people. In this view there is a modicum of truth. That the peasantry injure their material welfare by drunkenness and improvidence there can be no reasonable doubt, as is shown by the comparatively flourishing state of certain villages of Old Ritualists and Molokánye in which there is no drunkenness, and in which the community exercises a strong moral control over the individual members. If the Orthodox Church could make the peasantry refrain from the inordinate use of strong drink as effectually as it makes them refrain during a great part of the year from animal food, and if it could instill into their minds a few simple moral principles as suc-

cessfully as it has inspired them with a belief in the efficacy
of the sacraments, it would certainly confer on them an
inestimable benefit. But this is not to be expected. The
great majority of the parish priests are quite unfit for
such a task, and the few who have aspirations in that direction rarely acquire a perceptible moral influence over
their parishioners.

Perhaps more is to be expected from the schoolmaster
than from the priest, but it will be long before the schools
can produce even a partial moral regeneration. Their first
influence, strange as the assertion may seem, is often in a
diametrically opposite direction. When only a few peasants in a village can read and write they have such facilities for overreaching their "dark" neighbors that they are
apt to employ their knowledge for dishonest purposes; and
thus it occasionally happens that the man who has the
most education is the greatest scoundrel in the *Mir*. Such
facts are often used by the opponents of popular education, but in reality they supply a good reason for disseminating primary education as rapidly as possible. When all
the peasants have learned to read and write they will
present a less inviting field for swindling, and the temptations to dishonesty will be proportionately diminished.
Meanwhile it must be admitted that the village schools
sometimes tend to demoralize rather than moralize the
peasantry by disseminating crude Socialist notions. During
the revolutionary movement of 1905-7, for example, the
village schoolmaster sometimes helped the student agitators to foment agrarian disorders.

After drunkenness the besetting sin which is supposed
to explain the impoverishment of the peasantry is incorrigible laziness. On that subject I feel inclined to put in a
plea of extenuating circumstances in favor of the muzhik.
Certainly he is very slow in his movements—slower perhaps than the English rustic—and he has a marvelous
capacity for wasting valuable time without any perceptible qualms of conscience; but he is in this respect, if I
may use a favorite phrase of the social scientists, "the
product of environment." To the proprietors who habitually reproach him with time wasting he might reply with a
very strong *tu quo que* argument, and to other classes of

the population the argument might likewise be addressed.
The St. Petersburg official, for example, who writes edifying disquisitions about peasant indolence, considers that
for himself attendance at his office for four hours, a large
portion of which is devoted to the unproductive labor of
cigarette smoking, constitutes a very fair day's work. The
truth is that in Russia the struggle for life is not nearly so
intense as in more densely populated countries, and society
is so constituted that all can live without very strenuous
exertion. The Russians seem, therefore, to the traveler who
comes from the West, an indolent, apathetic race. If the
traveler happens to come from the East—especially if he
has been living among pastoral races—the Russians will
appear to him energetic and laborious. Their character
in this respect corresponds to their geographical position:
they stand midway between the laborious, painstaking, industrious population of Western Europe and the indolent,
undisciplined, spasmodically energetic populations of Central Asia. They are capable of effecting much by vigorous,
intermittent effort—witness the peasant at harvest time,
or the St. Petersburg official when some big legislative
project has to be submitted to the Emperor before a given
date—but they have not yet learned regular laborious
habits. In short, the Russians might move the world if it
could be done by a jerk, but they are still deficient in
that calm perseverance and dogged tenacity which characterize the Teutonic race.

Without seeking further to determine how far the moral
defects of the peasantry have a deleterious influence on
their material welfare, I proceed to examine the external
causes which are generally supposed to contribute largely
to their impoverishment, and will deal first with the evils
of peasant self-government.

That the peasant self-government is very far from being
in a satisfactory condition must be admitted by any impartial observer. The more laborious and well-to-do peasants, unless they wish to abuse their position directly or
indirectly for their own advantage, try to escape election
as office bearers, and leave the administration in the
hands of the less respectable members. Not infrequently
a *Vólost* Elder trades with the money he collects as dues

or taxes; and sometimes, when he becomes insolvent, the
peasants have to pay their taxes and dues a second time.
The Village Assemblies, too, have become worse than they
were in the days of serfage. At that time the Heads of
Households—who, it must be remembered, have alone a
voice in the decisions—were few in number, laborious, and
well-to-do, and they kept the lazy, unruly members under strict control. Now that the large families have been
broken up, and almost every adult peasant is Head of a
Household, the Communal affairs are sometimes decided
by a noisy majority; and certain Communal decisions may
be obtained by "treating the *Mir*"—that is to say, by supplying a certain amount of vodka. Often I have heard old
peasants speak of these things, and finish their recital by
some such remark as this: "There is no order now; the
people have been spoiled; it was better in the time of the
masters."

These evils are very real, and I have no desire to ex-
tenuate them, but I believe they are by no means so great
as is commonly supposed. If the lazy, worthless members
of the Commune had really the direction of Communal
affairs we should find that in the Northern Agricultural
Zone, where it is necessary to manure the soil, the periodical redistributions of the Communal land would be very
frequent; for in a new distribution the lazy peasant has a
good chance of getting a well-manured lot in exchange for
the lot which he has exhausted. In reality, so far as my
observations extend, these general distributions of the land
are not more frequent than they were before.

Of the various functions of the peasant self-government
the judicial are perhaps the most frequently and the most
severely criticized. And certainly not without reason, for
the *Vólost* Courts are too often accessible to the influence
of alcohol, and in some districts the peasants say that he
who becomes a judge takes a sin on his soul. I am not at
all sure, however, that it would be well to abolish these
courts altogether, as some people propose. In many respects they are better suited to peasant requirements
than the ordinary tribunals. Their procedure is infinitely
simpler, more expeditious, and incomparably less expen-

sive, and they are guided by traditional custom and plain common sense, whereas the ordinary tribunals have to judge according to the civil law, which is unknown to the peasantry and not always applicable to their affairs. Few ordinary judges have a sufficiently intimate knowledge of the minute details of peasant life to be able to decide fairly the cases that are brought before the *Vólost* Courts; and even if a justice had sufficient knowledge he could not adopt the moral and juridical notions of the peasantry. These are often very different from those of the upper classes. In cases of matrimonial separation, for instance, the educated man naturally assumes that, if there is any question of alimony, it should be paid by the husband to the wife. The peasant, on the contrary, assumes as naturally that the wife who ceases to be a member of the family ought to pay compensation for the loss of labor power which the separation involves. In like manner, according to traditional peasant law, if an unmarried son is working away from home, his earnings do not belong to himself, but to his family, and in a *Vólost* Court they could be claimed by the Head of the Household.

Occasionally, it is true, the peasant judges allow their respect for old traditional conceptions in general, and for the authority of parents in particular, to carry them a little too far. I was told lately of one affair which took place not long ago, within a hundred miles of Moscow, in which the judges decided that a respectable young peasant should be flogged because he refused to give his father the money he earned as groom in the service of a neighboring proprietor, though it was notorious in the district that the father was a disreputable old drunkard who carried to the *kabak* (gin shop) all the money he could obtain by fair means and foul. When I remarked to my informant, who was not an admirer of peasant institutions, that the incident reminded me of the respect for the *patria potestas* in old Roman times, he stared at me with a look of surprise and indignation, and exclaimed laconically, "*Patria potestas?* No, no! Simply *Vodka!*" He was evidently convinced that the disreputable old father had got his respectable son flogged by "treating" the judges. In such

cases flogging can no longer be used, for the *Vólost* Courts
were recently deprived of the right to inflict corporal
punishment.

These administrative and judicial abuses gradually
reached the ears of the Government, and in 1889 it attempted to remove them by creating a body of Rural Supervisors (*Zemskiye Nachalniki*). Under their supervision and control some abuses may have been occasionally
prevented or corrected, and some rascally *Vólost* Secretaries may have been punished or dismissed, but the peasant self-government as a whole has not been perceptibly
improved, and the Supervisors, or Land Captains as they
are sometimes called, are extremely unpopular. In the
Duma and elsewhere I have frequently heard them described as simply instruments of bureaucratic tyranny.

Let us glance now at the opinions of those who hold
that the material progress of the peasantry has been prevented chiefly, not by the mere abuses of the Communal
administration, but by the essential principles of the Communal institutions, and especially by the practice of periodically redistributing the Communal land. In the endless
discussions on this subject between abolitionists and Conservatives, there has been a great deal of exaggeration on
both sides. The backward condition of the peasantry cannot really be explained by the influence of one particular
institution or custom; it is the result of the economic, social and political development of the nation as a whole;
and among the numerous causes by which it has been produced, the traditional practice of periodically redistributing the Communal land has played, I believe, a very subordinate part.

As a matter of principle there can be no doubt that it is
much more difficult to farm well on a large number of narrow strips of land, many of which are at a great distance from the farmyard, than on a compact piece of land
which the farmer may divide and cultivate as he pleases;
and there can be as little doubt that the husbandman is
more likely to improve his land if his tenure is secure. All
this, and much more of the same kind, must be accepted
as indisputable truth, but it has little direct bearing on the
concrete practical question as to why the Russian peas-

antry have made so little progress in agriculture. That they were prevented by the Communal institutions from adopting various systems of high farming is a theory which hardly requires serious consideration. They never thought of such radical innovations, and if they had conceived such novel ideas they possessed neither the knowledge nor the capital necessary to realize them. Since the Emancipation, in many villages some of the more intelligent and enterprising peasants purchase land outside the Communal limits, and are free to cultivate it as they please; but on this private property they rarely improve their traditional methods of culture. And in this there is nothing surprising, because the neighboring estates, owned by rich landed proprietors, are farmed precisely in the same primitive fashion.

But is it not true that the Commune prevented good cultivation according to the system of agriculture actually in use? To reply to this question I must make a little digression.

Except in the far north and the Steppe region, where the agriculture is of a peculiar kind, adapted to the local conditions, the peasants invariably till their land according to the ordinary three-field system, in which good cultivation means, practically speaking, the plentiful use of manure. Does, then, the existence of the *Mir* prevent the peasants from manuring their fields well?

Many people who speak on this subject in an authoritative tone seem to imagine that the peasants in general do not manure their fields at all. This idea is an utter mistake. In those regions, it is true, where the rich black soil still retains a large part of its virgin fertility, the manure is used as fuel, or simply thrown away, because the peasants believe that it would not be profitable to put it on their fields, and their conviction is, at least to some extent, well founded;[3] but in the Northern Agricultural Zone, where unmanured soil gives only a very meager harvest, the peasants put upon their fields all the manure

[3] As recently as 1903 I found that one of the most intelligent and energetic landlords of the province of Vorónezh followed in this respect the example of the peasants, and he assured me that he had proved by experience the advantage of doing so.

they possess. If they do not put enough it is simply because they have not sufficient livestock.

It is only in the southern provinces, where no manure is required, that periodical redistributions take place frequently. As we travel northward we find the term lengthens; and in the Northern Agricultural Zone, where manure is indispensable, general redistributions are extremely rare. In the province of Yaroslavl, for example, the Communal land is generally divided into two parts: the manured land lying near the village, and the unmanured land lying beyond. The latter alone is subject to frequent redistribution. On the former the existing tenures are rarely disturbed, and when it becomes necessary to give a share to a new household, the change is effected with the least possible prejudice to vested rights.

The policy of the Government has always been to admit redistributions in principle, but to prevent their too frequent recurrence. For this purpose the Emancipation Law stipulated that they could be decreed only by a three-fourths majority of the Village Assembly, and in 1893 a further obstacle was created by a law providing that the minimum term between two redistributions should be twelve years, and that they should never be undertaken without the sanction of the Rural Supervisor.

Whatever the merits and disadvantages of the Russian Communal system may be, this venerable institution now seems destined to disappear. In official circles it has come to be regarded as one of the greatest obstacles to economic development by hampering the energies of the more industrious and enterprising section of the peasantry; and it is believed to conduce to the spread of revolutionary ideas by preventing the growth of a healthy veneration for the rights of private property. One of its most determined enemies was M. Stolypin. Soon after his accession to power he prepared a bill for its gradual abolition, and this bill was issued as an ukase on November 22, 1906. Since that time local commissions have been busy at work all over the country, making arrangements for the transition from Communal to individual property, and their labors are already bearing fruit abundantly. On May 1, 1911, no less than 1,518,800 Heads of Households had made the transi-

tion, and about 30,000,000 acres of Communal land had
become private property. If the work of these commissions,
which display great zeal and ability, continues to advance
as rapidly as hitherto, it must effect, in a few years, a wonderful revolution in the economic life of the peasantry.
Meanwhile the results are being awaited with intense interest by all serious students of Russian affairs.

Up to this point I have dealt with the so-called causes
of peasant impoverishment which are much talked of, but
which are, in my opinion, only of secondary importance.
I pass now to those which are more tangible and which
have exerted on the condition of the peasantry a more
palpable influence. And, first, inordinate taxation.

This is a very big subject, on which a bulky volume
might be written, but I shall cut it very short, because I
know that the ordinary reader does not like to be troubled
with voluminous financial statistics. Briefly, then, the
emancipated serf had to pay three kinds of direct taxation: Imperial to the Central Government, local to the
Zemstvo, and Communal to the *Mir* and the *Vólost;* and
besides these he had to pay a yearly sum for the redemption of the land allotment which he received at the time
of the Emancipation. Taken together, these sums formed a
heavy burden, but for ten or twelve years they were paid
pretty regularly. Then began to appear symptoms of distress, especially in the provinces with a poor soil, and in
1872 the Government sent into the provinces a Commission
of Inquiry, in which I had the privilege of taking part unofficially. The inquiry showed that something ought to be
done, but at that moment the authorities were so busy with
administrative reforms and with trying to develop industry and commerce that they had little time for studying
and improving the economic position of the silent, long-
suffering muzhik.

It was not till nearly ten years later, when the Government began to feel the pinch of the ever increasing arrears,
that it recognized the necessity for relieving the rural
population. For this purpose it abolished the salt tax and
the poll tax and repeatedly lessened the burden of the redemption payments until they were completely remitted
in 1906-7. Further relief was afforded in 1899 by an im-

portant reform in the mode of collecting the direct taxes. From the police, who often ruined peasant householders by applying distraint indiscriminately, the collection of taxes was transferred to special authorities who took into consideration the temporary pecuniary embarrassments of the taxpayers. Another benefit conferred on the peasantry by this reform was that the individual members of the Commune ceased to be responsible for the fiscal obligations of the Commune as a whole.

After these alleviations had been granted the annual total demanded from the peasantry directly was 173 million rubles, and the average annual sum to be paid by each peasant household varied, according to the locality, from 11½ to 20 rubles (23s. to 40s.). In addition to this annuity there was a heavy burden of accumulated arrears, especially in the central and eastern provinces, which amounted in 1899 to 143 millions. Of the indirect taxes I can say nothing definite, because it is impossible to calculate, even approximately, the share of them which falls on the rural population, but they must not be left out of account. During the ten years of M. Witte's term of office as Minister of Finance (1893-1903) the revenue of the Imperial Treasury was nearly doubled, and though the increase was due partly to improvements in the financial administration, we can hardly believe that the peasantry did not in some measure contribute to it. In any case, it was very difficult, if not impossible, for them, under these conditions, to improve their economic position. On that point all Russian economists are agreed. One of the most competent and sober-minded authorities, the late M. Schwanebach, calculated that the head of a peasant household, after deducting the grain required to feed his family, had to pay into the Imperial Treasury, according to the district in which he resided, from 25 to 100 per cent of his agricultural revenue. If that calculation was even approximately correct, we must conclude that further financial reforms were urgently required, especially in those provinces where the population live exclusively by agriculture.

Since that time the peasant's burden has been somewhat lessened, especially by the remission of the redemption dues, which I have already mentioned, but it is still far too heavy in proportion to his slender resources. With good harvests he can balance his budget and avoid arrears of taxation, but as soon as the harvest is below the average he gets into difficulties; and, as he has too often little or no reserve to fall back upon, a second bad harvest may bring him to the verge of bankruptcy.

Heavy as the burden of taxation undoubtedly is, it might perhaps be borne without very serious inconvenience if the peasant families could utilize productively all their time and strength. Unfortunately, in the existing economic organization a great deal of their time and energy is necessarily wasted. Their economic life was radically dislocated by the Emancipation, and they have not yet succeeded in reorganizing it according to the new conditions.

In the time of serfage an estate formed, from the economic point of view, a co-operative agricultural association, under a manager who possessed unlimited authority, and sometimes abused it, but who was generally wordly-wise enough to understand that the prosperity of the whole required the prosperity of the component parts. By the abolition of serfage the association was dissolved and liquidated, and the strong, compact whole fell into a heap of independent units, with separate and often mutually hostile interests. Some of the disadvantages of this change for the peasantry I have already enumerated above. The most important I have now to mention. In virtue of the Emancipation Law each family received an amount of land which tempted it to continue farming on its own account, but which did not enable it to earn a living and pay its rates and taxes. The peasant thus became a kind of amphibious creature—half farmer and half something else —cultivating his allotment for a portion of his daily bread, and obliged to have some other occupation wherewith to cover the inevitable deficit in his domestic budget. If he was fortunate enough to find near his home a bit of land to be let at a reasonable rent, he might cultivate it in addition to his own, and thereby gain a livelihood; but if he had not the good luck to find such a piece of land in the immediate neighborhood, he had to look for some subsidiary occupation in which to employ his leisure time;

and where was such occupation to be found in an ordinary
Russian village? In former years he might have employed
himself perhaps in carting the proprietor's grain to distant
markets or still more distant seaports, but that means of
making a little money has been destroyed by the extension
of railways. Practically, then, he is now obliged to choose
between two alternatives: either to farm his allotment
and spend a great part of the year in idleness, or to leave
the cultivation of his allotment to his wife and children
and to seek employment elsewhere—often at such a distance that his earnings hardly cover the expenses of the
journey. In either case much time and energy are wasted.

The evil results of this state of things were intensified
by another change which was brought about by the
Emancipation. In the time of serfage the peasant families,
as I have already remarked, were usually very large. They
remained undivided, partly from the influence of patriarchal conceptions, but chiefly because the proprietors,
recognizing the advantage of large units, prevented them
from breaking up. As soon as the proprietor's authority
was removed, the process of disintegration began and
spread rapidly. Everyone wished to be independent, and
in a very short time nearly every able-bodied married
peasant had a house of his own. The economic consequences were disastrous. A large amount of money had to
be expended in constructing new houses and farmstead-
ings; and the old habit of one male member remaining at
home to cultivate the land allotment with the female
members of the family whilst the others went to earn
wages elsewhere had to be abandoned. Many large families, which had been prosperous and comfortable—rich
according to peasant conceptions—dissolved into three or
four small ones, all on the brink of pauperism.

The last cause of peasant impoverishment that I have to
mention is perhaps the most important of all: I mean the
natural increase of population without a corresponding increase in the means of subsistence. Since the Emancipation in 1861 the population has nearly doubled, whilst the
amount of Communal land, in the great majority of Communes, has remained the same. It is not surprising, therefore, that when talking with peasants about their actual

condition, one constantly hears the despairing cry, *"Zemli malo!"* ("There is not enough land"); and one notices that those who look a little ahead ask anxiously: "What is to become of our children? Already the Communal allotment is too small for our wants, and the land outside is doubling and trebling in price! What will it be in the future?"

Must we, then, accept for Russia the Malthus doctrine that population increases more rapidly than the means of subsistence, and that starvation can be avoided only by plague, pestilence, war, and other destructive forces? I think not. It is quite true that, if the amount of land actually possessed by the peasantry and the present system of cultivating it remained unchanged, semistarvation would be the inevitable result within a comparatively short space of time; but the danger can be averted, and the proper remedies are not far to seek. If Russia is suffering from overpopulation it must be her own fault, for she is, with the exception of Norway and Sweden, the most thinly populated country in Europe, and she has more than her share of fertile soil and mineral resources.

A glance at the map showing the density of population in the various provinces suggests an obvious remedy, and I am happy to say it is already being applied. The population of the congested districts of the center is gradually spreading out, like a drop of oil on a sheet of soft paper, towards the more thinly populated regions of the south and east. In this way the vast region containing millions of acres which lies to the north of the Black Sea, the Caucasus, the Caspian, and Central Asia is yearly becoming more densely peopled, and agriculture is steadily encroaching on the pastoral area. Breeders of sheep and cattle, who formerly lived and throve in the western portion of that great expanse, are being pushed eastwards by the rapid increase in the value of land, and their place is being taken by enterprising tillers of the soil. Farther north another stream of emigration is flowing into Central Siberia. It does not flow so rapidly, because in that part of the Empire, unlike the bare, fertile Steppes of the south, the land has to be cleared before the seed can be sown, and the pioneer colonists have to work hard for a year or two before they get any return for their labor; but the Govern-

ment and private societies come to their assistance, and for
the last twenty years their numbers have been steadily increasing. In 1886 the annual contingent was only about
25,000 souls, whereas in 1908 it reached the high figure
of 626,000. Roughly speaking, we may say that during the
last fifteen years more than three and a half million peasants from European Russia have been successfully settled
in the Asiatic provinces.

Even in the European portion of the Empire millions of
acres which are at present unproductive might be utilized.
Anyone who has traveled by rail from Berlin to St. Petersburg must have noticed how the landscape suddenly
changes its character as soon as he has crossed the frontier.
Leaving a prosperous agricultural country, he traverses for
many weary hours a region in which there is hardly a sign
of human habitation, though the soil and climate of that
region resemble closely the soil and climate of East Prussia. The difference lies in the amount of labor and capital
expended. According to official statistics the area of European Russia contains, roughly speaking, 406 millions of
dessyatins, of which 78 millions, or 19 per cent, are classified as *neudobniya,* unfit for cultivation; 157 millions, or
39 per cent, as forest; 106 millions, or 26 per cent, as
arable land; and 65 millions, or 16 per cent, as pasturage.
Thus the arable and pasture land compose only 42 per
cent, or considerably less than half, of the area. Of the
land classed as unfit for cultivation—19 per cent of the
whole—a large portion, including the perennially frozen
tundri of the far north, must ever remain unproductive;
but in latitudes with a milder climate this category of land
is for the most part ordinary morass or swamp, which can
be transformed into pasturage, or even into arable land,
by drainage at a moderate cost. As a proof of this statement I may cite the draining of the great Pinsk swamps,
which was begun by the Government in 1872. If we may
trust an official report of the progress of the work in
1897, an area of 2,855,000 *dessyatins* (more than seven
and a half million acres) had been drained at an average
cost of about three shillings an acre, and the price of land
had risen from four to twenty-eight rubles per *dessyatin.*

Reclamation of marshes might be undertaken elsewhere

on a much more moderate scale. The observant traveler on
the highways and byways of the northern provinces must
have noticed on the banks of almost every stream many
acres of marshy land producing merely reeds or coarse,
rank grass that no well-brought-up animal would look at.
With a little elementary knowledge of engineering and the
expenditure of a moderate amount of manual labor these
marshes might be converted into excellent pasture or even
into highly productive kitchen gardens; but the peasants
have not yet learned to take advantage of such opportunities, and the reformers, who generally deal only in large
projects and scientific panaceas for the cure of impoverishment, consider such trifles as unworthy of their attention.
The Scotch proverb that if the pennies be well looked
after, the pounds will look after themselves, contains a
bit of homely wisdom unknown to the Russian educated
classes.

After the morasses, swamps, and marshes come the
forests, constituting 39 per cent of the whole area, and the
question naturally arises whether some portions of them
might not be advantageously transformed into pasturage
or arable land. In the south and east they have been
diminished to such an extent as to affect the climate in-
juriously, so that the forest area in that part of the country
ought to be increased rather than lessened; but in the
northern provinces the vast expanses of forest, covering
millions of acres, might perhaps be curtailed with advantage. The proprietors prefer, however, to keep them in
their present condition because they give a modest revenue
without any expenditure of capital.

Therein lies the great obstacle to land reclamation in
Russia: it requires an outlay of capital, and capital is
extremely scarce in the Empire of the Tsars. Until it becomes more plentiful, the area of arable land and pasturage is not likely to be largely increased, and other means
of checking the impoverishment of the peasantry must be
adopted.

A less expensive means is suggested by the statistics of
foreign trade. In the preceding chapter we have seen that
from 1860 to 1900 the average annual export of grain rose
steadily from under 1½ millions to over 6 millions of tons.

It is evident, therefore, that in the food supply, so far from there being a deficiency, there has been a large and constantly increasing surplus. If the peasantry have been on short rations, it is not because the quantity of food produced has fallen short of the requirements of the population, but because it has been unequally distributed. The truth is that the large landed proprietors produce more and the peasants less than they consume, and it has naturally occurred to many people that the present state of things might be improved if a portion of the arable land passed, without any socialistic, revolutionary measures, from the one class to the other.

This operation, as we have seen above, has already begun and is proceeding rapidly with the aid of the Peasant Land Bank, but the process is too slow to meet all the requirements of the situation. Some additional expedient, therefore, must be found, and we naturally look for it in the experience of older countries with a denser population.

In the more densely populated countries of Western Europe a safety valve for the inordinate increase of the rural population has been provided by the development of manufacturing industry. High wages and the attractions of town life draw the rural population to the industrial centers, and the movement has increased to such an extent that already complaints are heard of the rural districts' becoming depopulated. In Russia a similar movement is taking place on a smaller scale. During the last fifty years, under the fostering influence of a protective tariff, the manufacturing industry has made gigantic strides, as we shall see in a future chapter, and it has already absorbed about two millions of the redundant hands in the villages; but it cannot keep pace with the rapidly increasing surplus. Two millions constitute but a small factor in a population of 160 millions. The great mass of the people has always been, and must long continue to be, purely agricultural; and it is to their fields that they must look for the means of subsistence. If the fields do not supply enough for their support under the existing primitive methods of cultivation, better methods must be adopted. To use a favorite semiscientific phrase, Russia has now reached the point in her economic development at which she must abandon her traditional *extensive* system of agriculture and adopt a more *intensive* system. So far all competent authorities are agreed. But how is the transition, which requires technical knowledge, a spirit of enterprise, an enormous capital, and a dozen other things which the peasantry do not at present possess, to be effected? Here begin the well-marked differences of opinion.

Hitherto the momentous problem has been dealt with chiefly by the theorists and doctrinaires, who delight in radical solutions by means of panaceas, and who have little taste for detailed local investigation and gradual improvement. I do not refer merely to the so-called "Saviors of the Fatherland" (*Spasíteli Otéchestva*), well-meaning cranks and visionaries who discover ingenious devices for making their native country at once prosperous and happy. I speak of the great majority of reasonable, educated men who devote some attention to the problem. Their favorite method of dealing with it is this: The intensive system of agriculture requires scientific knowledge and a higher level of intellectual culture. What has to be done, therefore, is to create agricultural colleges supplied with all the newest appliances of agronomic research and to educate the peasantry to such an extent that they may be able to use the means which science recommends.

For many years this doctrine prevailed in the press, among the reading public, and even in the official world. The Government was accordingly urged to improve and multiply the agronomic colleges and the schools of all grades and descriptions. Learned dissertations were published on the chemical constitution of the various soils, the action of the atmosphere on the different ingredients, the necessity of making careful meteorological observations, and numerous other topics of a similar kind; and would-be reformers who had no taste for such highly technical researches could console themselves with the idea that they were advancing the vital interests of the country by discussing the relative merits of Communal and personal land tenure—deciding generally in favor of the former as more in accordance with the peculiarities of Russian, as contrasted with West European, principles of economic and social development.

While much valuable time and energy were thus being expended to little purpose, on the assumption that the old system might be left untouched until the preparations for a radical solution had been completed, disagreeable facts which could not be entirely overlooked gradually produced in influential quarters the conviction that the question was much more urgent than was commonly supposed. A sensitive chord in the heart of the Government was struck by the steadily increasing arrears of taxation, and spasmodic attempts have since been made to cure the evil. In the local administration, too, the urgency of the question has come to be recognized, and measures are now being taken by the Zemstvo to help the peasantry in making gradually the transition to that higher system of agriculture which is the only means of permanently saving them from starvation. For this purpose, in many districts, well-trained specialists have been appointed to study the local conditions and to recommend to the villagers such simple improvements as are within their means. These improvements may be classified under the following heads:

(1) Increase of the cereal crops by better seed and improved implements.

(2) Change in the rotation of crops by the introduction of certain grasses and roots which improve the soil and supply food for livestock.

(3) Improvement and increase of livestock, so as to get more labor power, more manure, more dairy produce, and more meat.

(4) Increased cultivation of vegetables and fruit.

With these objects in view the Zemstvo is establishing depots, in which improved implements and better seed are sold at moderate prices, and the payments may be made in installments, so that even the poorer members of the community can take advantage of the facilities offered. Bulls and stallions are kept at central points for the purpose of improving the breed of cattle and horses, and the good results are already visible. Elementary instruction in farming and gardening is being introduced into the primary schools. In some districts the exertions of the Zemstvo are supplemented by small agricultural societies, mutual credit associations, and village banks, and these are to some ex-

tent assisted by the Central Government. But the beneficent action in this direction is not all official. Many proprietors deserve great praise for the good influence which
they exercise on the peasants of their neighborhood and
the assistance they give them; and it must be admitted
that their patience is often sorely tried, for the peasants
have the obstinacy of ignorance, and possess other qualities which are not sympathetic. I know one excellent proprietor who began his civilizing efforts by giving to the
Mir of the nearest village an iron plough as a model and a
fine pedigree ram as a producer, and who found, on returning from a tour abroad, that during his absence the
plough had been sold for vodka, and the pedigree ram
had been eaten before it had time to produce any descendants! In spite of this he continues his efforts, and not
altogether without success.

It need hardly be said that the progress of the peasantry
is not so rapid as could be wished. The muzhik is naturally
conservative, and is ever inclined to regard novelties with
suspicion. Even when he is half convinced of the utility of
some change, he has still to think about it for a long time
and talk it over again and again with his friends and
neighbors, and this preparatory stage of progress may last
for years. Unless he happens to be a man of unusual intelligence and energy, it is only when he sees with his own
eyes that some humble individual of his own condition
in life has actually gained by abandoning the old routine
and taking to new courses, that he makes up his mind to
take the plunge himself. Still, he is beginning to jog on.
E pur si muove! A spirit of progress is beginning to move
on the face of the long-stagnant waters, and progress once
begun is pretty sure to continue with increasing rapidity.
With starvation hovering in the rear, even the most conservative are not likely to stop or turn back.

5 : *Religion*

CHAPTER · XIX

❧ ☙

The Village Priest

In formal introductions it is customary to pronounce in a more or less inaudible voice the names of the two persons introduced. Circumstances compel me in the present case to depart from received custom. The truth is, I do not know the names of the two people whom I wish to bring together! The reader who knows his own name will readily pardon one-half of my ignorance, but he may naturally expect that I should know the name of a man with whom I profess to be acquainted, and with whom I daily held long conversations during a period of several months. Strange as it may seem, I do not. During all the time of my sojourn in Ivánovka I never heard him addressed or spoken of otherwise than as "Bátushka." Now "Bátushka" is not a name at all. It is simply the diminutive form of an obsolete word meaning "father," and is usually applied to all village priests. The *ushka* is a common diminutive termination, and the root *Bat* is evidently the same as that which appears in the Latin *pater*.

Though I do not happen to know what Bátushka's family name was, I can communicate two curious facts concerning it: he had not possessed it in his childhood, and it was not the same as his father's.

The reader whose intuitive powers have been preternaturally sharpened by a long course of sensation novels will probably leap to the conclusion that Bátushka was a mysterious individual, very different from what he seemed —either the illegitimate son of some great personage, or a man of high birth who had committed some great sin, and who now sought oblivion and expiation in the humble

duties of a parish priest. Let me dispel at once all delusions
of this kind. Bátushka was actually as well as legally the
legitimate son of an ordinary parish priest, who was still
living about twenty miles off, and for many generations all
his paternal and maternal ancestors, male and female, had
belonged to the priestly caste. He was thus a Levite of the
purest water, and thoroughly Levitical in his character.
Though he knew by experience something about the weakness of the flesh, he had never committed any sins of the
heroic kind, and had no reason to conceal his origin. The
curious facts above stated were simply the result of a
peculiar custom which exists among the Russian clergy.
According to this custom, when a boy enters the seminary
he receives from the Bishop a new family name. The name
may be Bogoslavski, from a word signifying "Theology,"
or Bogolubov, "the love of God," or some similar term; or
it may be derived from the name of the boy's native village, or from any other word which the Bishop thinks fit
to choose. I know of one instance where a Bishop chose
two French words for the purpose. He had intended to
call the boy *Velikoselski*, after his native place, Velikoe
Seló, which means "big village"; but finding that there
was already a Velikoselski in the seminary, and being in a
facetious frame of mind, he called the new-comer Grand-
villageski—a word that may perhaps sorely puzzle some
philologist of the future.

My reverend teacher was a tall, muscular man of about
forty years of age, with a full dark-brown beard, and long
lank hair falling over his shoulders. The visible parts of
his dress consisted of three articles—a dingy-brown robe
of coarse material buttoned closely at the neck and descending to the ground, a wideawake hat, and a pair of
large, heavy boots. As to the esoteric parts of his attire, I
refrained from making investigations. His life had been an
uneventful one. At an early age he had been sent to the
seminary in the chief town of the province, and had made
for himself the reputation of a good average scholar. "The
seminary of that time," he used to say to me, referring to
that part of his life, "was not what it is now. Nowadays
the teachers talk about humanitarianism, and the boys
would think that a crime had been committed against hu-

man dignity if one of them happened to be flogged. But they don't consider that human dignity is at all affected by their getting drunk, and going to—to—to places that I never went to. I was flogged often enough, and I don't think that I am a worse man on that account; and though I never heard then anything about pedagogical science that they talk so much about now, I'll read a bit of Latin yet with the best of them.

"When my studies were finished," said Bátushka, continuing the simple story of his life, "the Bishop found a wife for me, and I succeeded her father, who was then an old man. In that way I became parish priest of Ivánovka, and I have remained here ever since. It is a hard life, for the parish is big, and my bit of land is not very fertile; but, praise be to God! I am healthy and strong, and get on well enough."

"You said that the Bishop found a wife for you," I remarked. "I suppose, therefore, that he was a great friend of yours."

"Not at all. The Bishop does the same for all the seminarists who wish to be ordained: it is an important part of his pastoral duties."

"Indeed!" I exclaimed in astonishment. "Surely that is carrying the system of paternal government a little too far. Why should his Reverence meddle with things that don't concern him?"

"But these matters do concern him. He is the natural protector of widows and orphans, especially among the clergy of his own diocese. When a parish priest dies, what is to become of his wife and daughters?"

Not perceiving clearly the exact bearing of these last remarks, I ventured to suggest that priests ought to economize in view of future contingencies.

"It is easy to speak," replied Bátushka: " 'A story is soon told,' as the old proverb has it, 'but a thing is not soon done.' How are we to economize? Even without saving we have the greatest difficulty to make the two ends meet."

"Then the widow and daughters might work and gain a livelihood."

"What, pray, could they work at?" asked Bátushka, and paused for a reply. Seeing that I had none to offer him, he continued, "Even the house and land belong not to them, but to the new priest."

"If that position occurred in a novel," I said, "I could foretell what would happen. The author would make the new priest fall in love with and marry one of the daughters, and then the whole family, including the mother-in-law, would live happily ever afterwards."

"That is exactly how the Bishop arranges the matter. What the novelist does with the puppets of his imagination, the Bishop does with real beings of flesh and blood. As a rational being he cannot leave things to chance. Besides this, he must arrange the matter before the young man takes orders, because, by the rules of the Church, the marriage cannot take place after the ceremony of ordination. When the affair is arranged before the charge becomes vacant, the old priest can die with the pleasant consciousness that his family is provided for."

"Well, Bátushka, you certainly put the matter in a very plausible way, but there seem to be two flaws in the analogy. The novelist can make two people fall in love with each other, and make them live happily together with the mother-in-law, but that—with all due respect to his Reverence be it said—is beyond the power of a Bishop."

"I am not sure," said Bátushka, avoiding the point of the objection, "that love marriages are always the happiest ones; and as to the mother-in-law, there are—or at least there were until the emancipation of the serfs—a mother-in-law and several daughters-in-law in almost every peasant household."

"And does harmony generally reign in peasant households?"

"That depends upon the head of the house. If he is a man of the right sort, he can keep the womenfolk in order." This remark was made in an energetic tone, with the evident intention of assuring me that the speaker was himself "a man of the right sort"; but I did not attribute much importance to it, for I have occasionally heard henpecked husbands talk in this grandiloquent way when their wives were out of hearing. Altogether I was by no means convinced that the system of providing for the widows and orphans of the clergy by means of *mariages de convenance* was a good one, but I determined to suspend my judgment until I should obtain fuller information.

An additional bit of evidence came to me a week or two later. One morning, on going into the priest's house, I found that he had a friend with him—the priest of a village some fifteen miles off. Before we had got through the ordinary conventional remarks about the weather and the crops, a peasant drove up to the door in his cart with a message that an old peasant was dying in a neighboring village, and desired the last consolations of religion. Bátushka was thus obliged to leave us, and his friend and I agreed to stroll leisurely in the direction of the village to which he was going, so as to meet him on his way home. The harvest was already finished, so that our road, after emerging from the village, lay through stubble fields. Beyond this we entered the pine forest, and by the time we had reached this point I had succeeded in leading the conversation to the subject of clerical marriages.

"I have been thinking a good deal on this subject," I said, "and I should very much like to know your opinion about the system."

My new acquaintance was a tall, lean, black-haired man, with a sallow complexion and vinegar aspect—evidently one of those unhappy mortals who are intended by Nature to take a pessimistic view of all things, and to point out to their fellows the deep shadows of human life. I was not at all surprised, therefore, when he replied in a deep, decided tone, "Bad, very bad—utterly bad!"

The way in which these words were pronounced left no doubt as to the opinion of the speaker, but I was desirous of knowing on what that opinion was founded—more especially as I seemed to detect in the tone a note of personal grievance. My answer was shaped accordingly.

"I suspected that; but in the discussions which I have had I have always been placed at a disadvantage, not being able to adduce any definite facts in support of my opinion."

"You may congratulate yourself on being unable to find any in your own experience. A mother-in-law living in the house does not conduce to domestic harmony. I don't know how it is in your country, but so it is with us."

I hastened to assure him that this was not a peculiarity of Russia.

"I know it only too well," he continued. "My mother-in-law lived with me for some years, and I was obliged at last to insist on her going to another son-in-law."

"Rather selfish conduct towards your brother-in-law," I said to myself, and then added audibly, "I hope you have thus solved the difficulty satisfactorily."

"Not at all. Things are worse now than they were. I agreed to pay her three rubles a month, and have regularly fulfilled my promise, but lately she has thought it not enough, and she made a complaint to the Bishop. Last week I went to him to defend myself, but as I had not money enough for all the officials in the Consistory, I could not obtain justice. My mother-in-law had made all sorts of absurd accusations against me, and consequently I was laid under an inhibition for six weeks!"

"And what is the effect of an inhibition?"

"The effect is that I cannot perform the ordinary rites of our religion. It is really very unjust," he added, assuming an indignant tone, "and very annoying. Think of all the hardship and inconvenience to which it gives rise."

As I thought of the hardship and inconvenience to which the parishioners must be exposed through the inconsiderate conduct of the old mother-in-law, I could not but sympathize with my new acquaintance's indignation. My sympathy was, however, somewhat cooled when I perceived that I was on a wrong tack, and that the priest was looking at the matter from an entirely different point of view.

"You see," he said, "it is a most unfortunate time of year. The peasants have gathered in their harvest, and can give of their abundance. There are merrymakings and marriages, besides the ordinary deaths and baptisms. Altogether I shall lose by the thing more than a hundred rubles!"

I confess I was a little shocked on hearing the priest thus speak of his sacred functions as if they were an ordinary marketable commodity, and talk of the inhibition as a pushing undertaker might talk of sanitary improvements. My surprise was caused not by the fact that he regarded

the matter from a pecuniary point of view—for I was old
enough to know that clerical human nature is not altogether insensible to pecuniary considerations—but by the
fact that he should thus undisguisedly express his opinions
to a stranger without in the least suspecting that there was
anything unseemly in his way of speaking. The incident
appeared to me very characteristic, but I refrained from
all audible comments, lest I should inadvertently check his
communicativeness. With the view of encouraging it, I
professed to be very much interested, as I really was, in
what he said, and I asked him how in his opinion the
present unsatisfactory state of things might be remedied.

"There is but one cure," he said, with a readiness that
showed he had often spoken on the theme already, "and
that is freedom and publicity. We full-grown men are
treated like children, and watched like conspirators. If I
wish to preach a sermon—not that I often wish to do such
a thing, but there are occasions when it is advisable—I
am expected to show it first to the Blagochinny, and——"

"I beg your pardon, who is the Blagochinny?"

"The Blagochinny is a parish priest, who is in direct
relations with the Consistory of the Province, and who is
supposed to exercise a strict supervision over all the other
parish priests of his district. He acts as the spy of the Consistory, which is filled with greedy, shameless officials,
deaf to anyone who does not come provided with a handful of rubles. The Bishop may be a good, well-intentioned
man, but he always sees and acts through these worthless
subordinates. Besides this, the Bishops and heads of monasteries, who monopolize the higher places in the ecclesiastical Administration, all belong to the Black Clergy—
that is to say, they are all monks—and consequently cannot understand our wants. How can they, on whom celibacy is imposed by the rules of the Church, understand
the position of a parish priest who has to bring up a
family and to struggle with domestic cares of every kind?
What they do is to take all the comfortable places for
themselves, and leave us all the hard work. The monasteries are rich enough, and you see how poor we are. Perhaps you have heard that the parish priests extort money
from the peasants—refusing to perform the rites of baptism

or burial until a considerable sum has been paid. It is only too true, but who is to blame? The priest must live and bring up his family, and you cannot imagine the humiliations to which he has to submit in order to gain a scanty pittance. I know it by experience. When I make the periodical visitation I can see that the peasants grudge every handful of rye and every egg that they give me. I can overhear their sneers as I go away, and I know they have many sayings such as, 'The priest takes from the living and from the dead.' Many of them fasten their doors, pretending to be away from home, and do not even take the precaution of keeping silent till I am out of hearing."

"You surprise me," I said, in reply to the last part of this long tirade; "I have always heard that the Russians are a very religious people—at least, the lower classes."

"So they are; but the peasantry are poor and heavily taxed. They set great importance on the sacraments, and observe rigorously the fasts, which comprise nearly a half of the year; but they show very little respect for their priests, who are almost as poor as themselves."

"But I do not see clearly how you propose to remedy this state of things."

"By freedom and publicity, as I said before." The worthy man seemed to have learned this formula by rote. "First of all, our wants must be made known. In some provinces there have been attempts to do this by means of provincial assemblies of the clergy, but these efforts have always been strenuously opposed by the Consistories, whose members fear publicity above all things. But in order to have publicity we must have more freedom."

Here followed a long discourse on freedom and publicity, which seemed to me very confused. So far as I could understand the argument, there was a good deal of reasoning in a circle. Freedom was necessary in order to get publicity, and publicity was necessary in order to get freedom; and the practical result would be that the clergy would enjoy bigger salaries and more popular respect. We had only got thus far in the investigation of the subject, when our conversation was interrupted by the rumbling of a peasant's cart. In a few seconds our friend Bátushka appeared, and the conversation took a different turn.

Since that time I have frequently spoken on this subject with competent authorities, and nearly all have admitted that the present condition of the clergy is highly unsatisfactory, and that the parish priest rarely enjoys the respect of his parishioners. In a semi-official report, which I once accidentally stumbled upon when searching for material of a different kind, the facts are stated in the following plain language: "The people"—I seek to translate as literally as possible—"do not respect the clergy, but persecute them with derision and reproaches, and feel them to be a burden. In nearly all the popular comic stories the priest, or his wife, or his laborer is held up to ridicule, and in all the proverbs and popular sayings where the clergy are mentioned it is always with derision. The people shun the clergy, and have recourse to them not from the inner impulse of conscience, but from necessity. . . . And why do the people not respect the clergy? Because they form a class apart; because, having received a false kind of education, they do not introduce into the life of the people the teaching of the Spirit, but remain in the mere dead forms of outward ceremonial, at the same time despising these forms even to blasphemy; because the clergy themselves continually present examples of want of respect to religion, and transform the service of God into a profitable trade. Can the people respect the clergy when they hear how one priest stole money from below the pillow of a dying man at the moment of confession, how another was publicly dragged out of a house of ill-fame, how a third christened a dog, how a fourth whilst officiating at the Easter service was dragged by the hair from the altar by the deacon? Is it possible for the people to respect priests who spend their time in the gin shop, write fraudulent petitions, fight with the cross in their hands, and abuse each other in bad language at the altar?

"One might fill several pages with examples of this kind —in each instance naming the time and place—without overstepping the boundaries of the province of Nizhni-Novgorod. Is it possible for the people to respect the clergy when they see everywhere amongst them simony, carelessness in performing the religious rites, and disorder in administering the sacraments? Is it possible for the people to respect the clergy when they see that truth has disappeared from them, and that the Consistories, guided in their decisions not by rules, but by personal friendship and bribery, destroy in them the last remains of truthfulness? If we add to all this the false certificates which the clergy give to those who do not wish to partake of the Eucharist, the dues illegally extracted from the Old Ritualists, the conversion of the altar into a source of revenue, the giving of churches to priests' daughters as a dowry, and similar phenomena, the question as to whether the people can respect the clergy requires no answer."

As these words were written by an orthodox Russian,[1] celebrated for his extensive and intimate knowledge of Russian provincial life, and were addressed in all seriousness to a member of the Imperial family, we may safely assume that they contain a considerable amount of truth. The reader must not, however, imagine that all Russian priests are of the kind above referred to. Many of them are honest, respectable, well-intentioned men, who conscientiously fulfill their humble duties, and strive hard to procure a good education for their children. If they have less learning, culture, and refinement than the Roman Catholic priesthood, they have at the same time infinitely less fanaticism, less spiritual pride, and less intolerance towards the adherents of other faiths.

Both the good and the bad qualities of the Russian priesthood at the present time can be easily explained by its past history, and by certain peculiarities of the national character.

The Russian White Clergy—that is to say, the parish priests, as distinguished from the monks, who are called the Black Clergy—have had a curious history. In primitive times they were drawn from all classes of the population, and freely elected by the parishioners. When a man was elected by the popular vote, he was presented to the Bishop, and if he was found to be a fit and proper person for the office, he was at once ordained. But this custom early fell into disuse. The Bishops, finding that many of the candidates presented were illiterate peasants, gradu-

[1] Mr. Melnikov, in a Secret Report to the Grand Duke Constantine Nikolaievich.

ally assumed the right of appointing the priests, with or
without the consent of the parishioners; and their choice
generally fell on the sons of the clergy as the men best
fitted to take orders. The creation of Bishops' schools,
afterwards called seminaries, in which the sons of the
clergy were educated, naturally led, in the course of time,
to the total exclusion of the other classes. The policy of
the civil Government led to the same end. Peter the Great
laid down the principle that every subject should in some
way serve the State—the nobles as officers in the army or
navy, or as officials in the civil service; the clergy as ministers of religion; and the lower classes as soldiers, sailors, or
taxpayers. Of these three classes, the clergy had by far
the lightest burdens, and consequently many nobles and
peasants would willingly have entered its ranks. But this
species of desertion the Government could not tolerate,
and accordingly the priesthood was surrounded by a legal
barrier, which prevented all outsiders from entering it.
Thus, by the combined efforts of the ecclesiastical and the
civil Administration, the clergy became a separate class or
caste, legally and actually incapable of mingling with the
other classes of the population.

The simple fact that the clergy became an exclusive
caste, with a peculiar character, peculiar habits, and
peculiar ideals, would in itself have had a prejudicial influence on the priesthood; but this was not all. The caste
increased in numbers by the process of natural reproduction much more rapidly than the offices to be filled, so
that the supply of priests and deacons soon far exceeded
the demand; and the disproportion between supply and
demand became every year greater and greater. In this
way was formed an ever-increasing clerical Proletariat,
which—as is always the case with a Proletariat of any kind
—gravitated towards the towns. In vain the Government
issued ukases prohibiting the priests from quitting their
places of domicile, and treated as vagrants and runaways
those who disregarded the prohibition; in vain successive
sovereigns endeavored to diminish the number of these
supernumeraries by drafting them wholesale into the army.
In Moscow, St. Petersburg, and all the larger towns the
cry was "Still they come!" Every morning, in the Kremlin

of Moscow, a large crowd of them assembled for the purpose of being hired to officiate in the private chapels of the rich nobles, and a great deal of hard bargaining took place between the priests and the lackeys sent to hire them—conducted in the same spirit, and in nearly the same forms, as that which simultaneously took place in the bazaar close by between extortionate traders and thrifty housewives. "Listen to me," a priest would say, as an ultimatum, to a lackey who was trying to beat down the price, "if you don't give me seventy-five kopeks without further ado, I'll take a bite of this roll, and that will be an end to it!" And that would have been an end to the bargaining, for, according to the rules of the Church, a priest cannot officiate after breaking his fast. The ultimatum, however, could be used with effect only to country servants who had recently come to town. A sharp lackey, experienced in this kind of diplomacy, would have laughed at the threat, and replied coolly, "Bite away, Bátushka; I can find plenty more of your sort!" Amusing scenes of this kind I have heard described by old people who professed to have been eyewitnesses.

The condition of the priests who remained in the villages was not much better. Those of them who were fortunate enough to find places were raised at least above the fear of absolute destitution, but their position was by no means enviable. They received little consideration or respect from the peasantry, and still less from the nobles. When the church was situated not on the State Domains, but on a private estate, they were practically under the power of the proprietor—almost as completely as his serfs; and sometimes that power was exercised in a most humiliating and shameful way. I have heard, for instance, of one priest who was ducked in a pond on a cold winter day for the amusement of the proprietor and his guests—choice spirits, of rough, jovial temperament; and of another who, having neglected to take off his hat as he passed the proprietor's house, was put into a barrel and rolled down a hill into the river at the bottom!

In citing these incidents, I do not at all mean to imply that they represent the relations which usually existed between proprietors and village priests, for I am quite aware

that wanton cruelty was not among the ordinary vices of
Russian serf owners. My object in mentioning the incidents
is to show how a brutal proprietor—and it must be admitted that there were not a few brutal individuals in the
class—could maltreat a priest without much danger of being called to account for his conduct. Of course such conduct was an offense in the eyes of the criminal law; but
the criminal law of that time was very short-sighted, and
strongly disposed to close its eyes completely when the
offender was an influential proprietor. Had the incidents
reached the ears of the Emperor Nicholas, he would probably have ordered the culprit to be summarily and severely punished; but, as the Russian proverb has it,
"Heaven is high, and the Tsar is far off." A village priest
treated in this barbarous way could have little hope of
redress, and, if he were a prudent man, he would make
no attempt to obtain it; for any annoyance which he
might give the proprietor by complaining to the ecclesiastical authorities would be sure to be paid back to him with
interest in some indirect way.

The sons of the clergy who did not succeed in finding
regular sacerdotal employment were in a still worse position. Many of them served as scribes or subordinate officials in the public offices, where they commonly eked out
their scanty salaries by unblushing extortion and pilfering.
Those who did not succeed in gaining even modest employment of this kind had to keep off starvation by less
lawful means, and not infrequently found their way into
the prisons or to Siberia.

In judging of the Russian priesthood of the present
time, we must call to mind this demoralizing atmosphere
to which it was so long condemned, and we must also take
into consideration the spirit which has been for centuries
predominant in the Eastern Church—I mean the strong
tendency both in the clergy and in the laity to attribute an
inordinate importance to the ceremonial element of religion. Primitive mankind is everywhere and always disposed to regard religion as simply a mass of mysterious
rites, which have a secret magical power of averting evil
in this world and securing felicity in the next. To this
general rule the Russian peasantry are no exception, and

the Russian Church has not done all it might have done
to eradicate this conception and to bring religion into
closer association with ordinary morality. Hence such incidents as the following are still possible: A robber kills
and rifles a traveler, but refrains from eating a piece of
cooked meat which he finds in the cart, because it happens
to be a fast day! A peasant prepares to rob a young *attaché* of the Austrian Embassy in St. Petersburg, and ultimately kills his victim, but before going to the house he
enters a church and commends his undertaking to the
protection of the saints! A housebreaker, when in the act
of robbing a church, finds it difficult to extract the jewels
from an Icon, and makes a vow that if a certain saint assists him he will place a ruble's-worth of tapers before the
saint's image! These facts are within the memory of the
last generation. I knew the young *attaché*, and saw him a
few days before his death.

All these are of course extreme cases, but they illustrate
a tendency which in its milder forms is only too general
amongst the Russian people—the tendency to regard religion as a mass of ceremonies which have a magical rather
than a spiritual significance. The poor woman who kneels
at a religious procession in order that the Icon may be
carried over her head, and the rich merchant who invites
the priests to bring some famous Icon to his house, illustrate this tendency in a more harmless form.

According to a popular saying, "As is the priest, so is
the parish," and the converse proposition is equally true
—as is the parish, so is the priest. The great majority of
priests, like the great majority of men in general, content
themselves with simply striving to perform what is expected of them, and their character is consequently determined to a certain extent by the ideas and conceptions of
their parishioners. This will become more apparent if we
contrast the Russian priest with the Protestant pastor.

According to Protestant conceptions, the village pastor
is a man of grave demeanor and exemplary conduct, and
possesses a certain amount of education and refinement.
He ought to expound weekly to his flock, in simple, impressive words, the great truths of Christianity, and exhort
his hearers to walk in the paths of righteousness. Besides

this, he is expected to comfort the afflicted, to assist the needy, to counsel those who are harassed with doubts, and to admonish those who openly stray from the narrow path. Such is the ideal in the popular mind, and pastors generally seek to realize it, if not in very deed, at least in appearance. The Russian priest, on the contrary, has no such ideal set before him by his parishioners. He is expected merely to conform to certain observances, and to perform punctiliously the rites and ceremonies prescribed by the Church. If he does this without practicing extortion, his parishioners are quite satisfied. He rarely preaches or exhorts, and too often he neither has nor seeks to have a moral influence over his flock. I have occasionally heard of Russian priests who approach to what I have termed the Protestant ideal, and I have even seen one or two of them, but I fear they are not numerous.

In the above contrast I have accidentally omitted one important feature. The Protestant clergy have in all countries rendered valuable service to the cause of popular education. The reason of this is not difficult to find. In order to be a good Protestant it is necessary to "search the Scriptures," and to do this one must be able at least to read. To be a good member of the Greek Orthodox Church, on the contrary, according to popular conceptions, the reading of the Scriptures is not necessary, and therefore primary education has not in the eyes of the Greek Orthodox priest the same importance which it has in the eyes of the Protestant pastor.

It must be admitted that the Russian people are in a certain sense religious. They go regularly to church on Sundays and holy days, cross themselves repeatedly when they pass a church or Icon, take the Holy Communion at stated seasons, rigorously abstain from animal food—not only on Wednesdays and Fridays, but also during Lent and the other long fasts—make occasional pilgrimages to holy shrines, and, in a word, fulfill punctiliously the ceremonial observances which they suppose necessary for salvation. But here their religiousness ends. They are generally profoundly ignorant of religious doctrine, and know little or nothing of Holy Writ. A peasant, it is said, was once asked by a priest if he could name the three Persons of the Trinity, and replied without a moment's hesitation, "How can one not know that, Bátushka? Of course it is the Savior, the Mother of God, and Saint Nicholas the miracleworker!"

That answer represents fairly enough the theological attainments of a very large section of the peasantry. The anecdote is so often repeated that it is probably an invention, but it is not a calumny. Of theology and of what Protestants term the "inner religious life," the orthodox Russian peasant—of Dissenters, to whom these remarks do not apply, I shall speak later—has no conception. For him the ceremonial part of religion suffices, and he has the most unbounded, childlike confidence in the saving efficacy of the rites which he practices. If he has been baptized in infancy, has regularly observed the fasts, has annually partaken of the Holy Communion, and has just confessed and received extreme unction, he feels death approach with the most perfect tranquillity. He is tormented with no doubts as to the efficacy of faith or works, and has no fears that his past life may possibly have rendered him unfit for eternal felicity. Like a man in a sinking ship who has buckled on his life-preserver, he feels perfectly secure. With no fear for the future and little regret for the present or the past, he awaits calmly the dread summons, and dies with a resignation which a Stoic philosopher might envy.

In the above remarks I have used the word Icon, and perhaps the reader may not clearly understand the word. Let me explain then, briefly, what an Icon is—a very necessary explanation, for the Icons play an important part in the religious observances of the Russian people.

Icons are pictorial, usually half-length, representations of the Savior, of the Madonna, or of a saint, executed in archaic Byzantine style, on a yellow or gold ground, and varying in size from a square inch to several square feet. Very often the whole picture, with the exception of the face and hands of the figure, is covered with a metal plaque, embossed so as to represent the form of the figure and the drapery. When this plaque is not used, the crown and costume are often adorned with pearls and other precious stones—sometimes of great price.

In respect of religious significance, Icons are of two kinds: simple, and miraculous or miracleworking (*chudotvorny*). The former are manufactured in enormous quantities—chiefly in the province of Vladimir, where whole villages are employed in this kind of work—and are to be found in every Russian house, from the hut of the peasant to the palace of the Emperor. They are generally placed high up in a corner facing the door, and good orthodox Christians on entering bow in that direction, making at the same time the sign of the cross. Before and after meals the same short ceremony is always performed. On the eve of fête days a small lamp is kept burning before at least one of the Icons in the house.

The wonderworking Icons are comparatively few in number, and are always carefully preserved in a church or chapel. They are commonly believed to have been "not made with hands," and to have appeared in a miraculous way. A monk, or it may be a common mortal, has a vision, in which he is informed that he may find a miraculous Icon in such a place, and on going to the spot indicated he finds it, sometimes buried, sometimes hanging on a tree. The sacred treasure is then removed to a church, and the news spreads like wildfire through the district. Thousands flock to prostrate themselves before the heaven-sent picture, and some are healed of their diseases—a fact that plainly indicates its miracleworking power. The whole affair is then officially reported to the Most Holy Synod, the highest ecclesiastical authority in Russia, in order that the existence of the miracleworking power may be fully and regularly proved. The official recognition of the fact is by no means a mere matter of form, for the Synod is well aware that wonderworking Icons are always a rich source of revenue to the monasteries where they are kept, and that zealous Superiors are consequently apt in such cases to lean to the side of credulity rather than that of over-severe criticism. A regular investigation is therefore made, and the formal recognition is not granted till the testimony of the finder is thoroughly examined and the alleged miracles duly authenticated. If the recognition is granted, the Icon is treated with the greatest veneration, and is sure to be visited by pilgrims from far and near.

Some of the most revered Icons—as, for instance, the
Kazan Madonna—have annual fête days instituted in their
honor; or, more correctly speaking, the anniversary of their
miraculous appearance is observed as a religious holiday.
A few of them have an additional title to popular respect
and veneration: that of being intimately associated with
great events in the national history. The Vladimir Madonna, for example, once saved Moscow from the Tatars;
the Smolensk Madonna accompanied the army in the
glorious campaign against Napoleon in 1812; and when
in that year it was known in Moscow that the French were
advancing on the city, the people wished the Metropolitan to take the Iberian Madonna, which may still be seen
near one of the gates of the Kremlin, and to lead them out
armed with hatchets against the enemy.

If the Russian priests have done little to advance popular education, they have at least never intentionally opposed it. Unlike their Roman Catholic brethren, they do
not hold that "a little learning is a dangerous thing," and
do not fear that faith may be endangered by knowledge.
Indeed, it is a remarkable fact that the Russian Church
regards with profound apathy those various intellectual
movements which cause serious alarm to many thoughtful
Christians in Western Europe. It considers religion as
something so entirely apart that its votaries do not feel the
necessity of bringing their theological beliefs into logical
harmony with their scientific conceptions. A man may remain a good orthodox Christian long after he has adopted
scientific opinions irreconcilable with Eastern Orthodoxy,
or, indeed, with dogmatic Christianity of any kind. In the
confessional the priest never seeks to ferret out heretical
opinions; and I can recall no instance in Russian history of
a man being burnt at the stake on the demand of the
ecclesiastical authorities, as so often happened in the
Roman Catholic world, for his scientific views. This tolerance proceeds partly, no doubt, from the fact that the
Eastern Church in general, and the Russian Church in
particular, have remained for centuries in a kind of intellectual torpor. Even such a fervent orthodox Christian as
the late Ivan Aksákov perceived this absence of healthy
vitality, and he did not hesitate to declare his conviction

that "neither the Russian nor the Slavonic world will be resuscitated . . . so long as the Church remains in such lifelessness (*mertvennost'*), which is not a matter of chance, but the legitimate fruit of some organic defect." [2]

Though the unsatisfactory condition of the parochial clergy is generally recognized by the educated classes, very few people take the trouble to consider seriously how it might be improved. During the Reform enthusiasm which raged for some years after the Crimean War ecclesiastical affairs were entirely overlooked. Many of the reformers of those days were so very "advanced" that religion in all its forms seemed to them an old-world superstition which tended to retard rather than accelerate social progress, and which consequently should be allowed to die as tranquilly as possible; whilst the men of more moderate views found they had enough to do in emancipating the serfs and reforming the corrupt civil and judicial Administration. During the subsequent reactionary period, which culminated in the reign of the Emperor Alexander III, much more attention was devoted to Church matters, and it came to be recognized in official circles that something ought to be done for the parish clergy in the way of improving their material condition so as to increase their moral influence. With this object in view, M. Pobêdonostsev, the Procurator of the Holy Synod, induced the Government in 1893 to make a State grant of about 6,500,-000 rubles, which should be increased every year, but the sum was very inadequate, and a large portion of it was devoted to purposes of political propaganda in the form of maintaining Greek Orthodox priests in districts where the population was Protestant or Roman Catholic. Consequently, of the 35,865 parishes which Russia contained, only 18,936, or a little more than one-half, were enabled to benefit by the grant. In an optimistic, semiofficial statement published as late as 1896 it is admitted that "the means for the support of the parish clergy must even now be considered insufficient and wanting in stability, making the priests dependent on the parishioners, and thereby

[2] Solovyov. *Ocherki iz istorii Russkoi Literatury XIX. vêka.* St. Petersburg, 1903, p. 269.

preventing the establishment of the necessary moral authority of the spiritual father over his flock."

In some places the needs of the Church are attended to by voluntary parish curatorships which annually raise a certain sum of money, and the way in which they distribute it is very characteristic of the Russian people, who have a profound veneration for the Church and its rites, but very little consideration for the human beings who serve at the altar. In 14,564 parishes possessing such curatorships no less than 2,500,000 rubles were collected, but of this sum 2,000,000 were expended on the maintenance and embellishment of churches, and only 174,000 were devoted to the personal wants of the clergy. According to the semiofficial document from which these figures are taken, the whole body of the Russian White Clergy in 1893 numbered 99,391, of whom 42,513 were priests, 12,953 deacons, and 43,925 clerks.

In more recent observations among the parochial clergy, I have noticed premonitory symptoms of important changes. This may be illustrated by an entry in my notebook, written in a village of one of the Southern provinces, under date 30th September, 1903:

"I have made here the acquaintance of two good specimens of the parish clergy, both excellent men in their way, but very different from each other. The elder one, Father Dmitri, is of the old school, a plain, practical man, who fulfills his duties conscientiously according to his lights, but without enthusiasm. His intellectual wants are very limited, and he devotes his attention chiefly to the practical affairs of everyday life, which he manages very successfully. He does not squeeze his parishioners unduly, but he considers that the laborer is worthy of his hire, and insists on his flock providing for his wants according to their means. At the same time he farms on his own account and attends personally to all the details of his farming operations. With the condition and doings of every member of his flock he is intimately acquainted, and, on the whole, as he never idealized anything or anybody, he has not a very high opinion of them.

"The younger priest, Father Alexander, is of a different type, and the difference may be remarked even in his exter-

nal appearance. There is a look of delicacy and refinement
about him, though his dress and domestic surroundings
are of the plainest, and there is not a tinge of affectation in his manner. His language is less archaic and picturesque. He uses fewer Biblical and semi-Slavonic expressions—I mean expressions which belong to the antiquated
language of the Church Service rather than to modern
parlance—and his armory of terse popular proverbs, which
constitute such a characteristic trait of the peasantry, is
less frequently drawn on. When I ask him about the
present condition of the peasantry, his account does not
differ substantially from that of his elder colleague, but he
does not condemn their sins in the same forcible terms. He
laments their shortcomings in an evangelical spirit, and
has apparently aspirations for their future improvement.
Admitting frankly that there is a great deal of lukewarmness among them, he hopes to revive their interest in ecclesiastical affairs and he has an idea of constituting a sort
of church committee for attending to the temporal affairs
of the village church and for works of charity, but he
looks to influencing the younger rather than the older
generation.

"His interest in his parishioners is not confined to their
spiritual welfare, but extends to their material well-being.
Of late an association for mutual credit has been founded
in the village, and he uses his influence to induce the
peasants to take advantage of the benefits it offers, both to
those who are in need of a little ready money and to those
who might invest their savings, instead of keeping them
hidden away in an old stocking or buried in an earthen pot.
The proposal to create a local agricultural society meets
also with his sympathy."

If the number of parish priests of this latter type increase, the clergy may come to exercise great moral influence on the common people.

❧ ☙

CHAPTER XX

Among the Heretics

WHILST traveling on the Steppe I heard a great deal about a peculiar religious sect called the Molokánye, and I felt interested in them because their religious belief, whatever it was, seemed to have a beneficial influence on their material welfare. Of the same race and placed in the same economic conditions as the Orthodox peasantry around them, they were undoubtedly better housed, better clad, more punctual in the payment of their taxes, and, in a word, more prosperous. All my informants agreed in describing them as quiet, decent, sober people; but regarding their religious doctrines the evidence was vague and contradictory. Some considered them to be Protestants or Lutherans, whilst others believed them to be the last remnants of a curious heretical sect which existed in the early Christian Church.

Desirous of obtaining clearer notions on the subject, I determined to investigate the matter for myself. At first I found this to be no easy task. In the villages through which I passed I found numerous members of the sect, but they all showed a decided repugnance to speak about their religious beliefs. Long accustomed to extortion and persecution at the hands of the Administration, and suspecting me to be a secret agent of the Government, they carefully avoided speaking on any subject beyond the state of the weather and the prospects of the harvest, and replied to my questions on other topics as if they had been standing before a Grand Inquisitor.

A few unsuccessful attempts convinced me that it would be impossible to extract from them their religious beliefs by direct questioning. I adopted, therefore, a different system of tactics. From meager replies already received I had discovered that their doctrine had at least a superficial resemblance to Presbyterianism, and from former experience I was aware that the curiosity of intelligent Russian peasants is easily excited by descriptions of foreign countries. On these two facts I based my plan of campaign. When I found a Molokán, or someone whom I suspected to be such, I talked for some time about the weather and the crops, as if I had no ulterior object in view. Having fully discussed this matter, I led the conversation gradually from the weather and crops in Russia to the weather and crops in Scotland, and then passed slowly from Scotch agriculture to the Scotch Presbyterian Church. On nearly every occasion this policy succeeded. When the peasant heard that there was a country where the people interpreted the Scriptures for themselves, had no bishops, and considered the veneration of Icons as idolatry, he invariably listened with profound attention; and when he learned further that in that wonderful country the parishes annually sent deputies to an assembly in which all matters pertaining to the Church were freely and publicly discussed, he almost always gave free expression to his astonishment, and I had to answer a whole volley of questions. "Where is that country?" "Is it to the east, or the west?" "Is it very far away?" "If our Presbyter could only hear all that!"

This last expression was precisely what I wanted, because it gave me an opportunity of making the acquaintance of the Presbyter, or pastor, without seeming to desire it; and I knew that a conversation with that personage, who is always an uneducated peasant like the others, but is generally more intelligent and better acquainted with religious doctrine, would certainly be of use to me. On more than one occasion I spent a great part of the night with a Presbyter, and thereby learned much concerning the religious beliefs and practices of the sect. After these interviews I was sure to be treated with confidence and respect by all the Molokánye in the village, and recommended to the brethren of the faith in the neighboring villages through which I intended to pass. Several of the

more intelligent peasants with whom I spoke advised me
strongly to visit Alexandrov-Haï, a village situated on the
borders of the Kirghiz Steppe. "We are dark (i.e. ignorant)
people here," they were wont to say, "and do not know
anything, but in Alexandrov-Haï you will find those who
know the faith, and they will discuss with you." This prediction was fulfilled in a somewhat unexpected way.

When returning some weeks later from a visit to the
Kirghiz of the Inner Horde, I arrived one evening at this
center of the Molokán faith and was hospitably received by one of the brotherhood. In conversing casually
with my host on religious subjects I expressed to him a
desire to find someone well read in Holy Writ and well
grounded in the faith, and he promised to do what he
could for me in this respect. Next morning he kept his
promise with a vengeance. Immediately after the tea
urn had been removed the door of the room was opened
and twelve peasants were ushered in! After the customary
salutations with these unexpected visitors, my host informed me to my astonishment that his friends had come
to have a talk with me about the faith; and without further
ceremony he placed before me a folio Bible in the old
Slavonic tongue, in order that I might read passages in
support of my arguments. As I was not at all prepared to
open a formal theological discussion, I felt not a little
embarrassed, and I could see that my traveling companions, two Russian friends who cared for none of these
things, were thoroughly enjoying my discomfiture. There
was, however, no possibility of drawing back. I had asked
for an opportunity of having a talk with some of the
brethren, and now I had got it in a way that I certainly
did not expect. My friends withdrew—"leaving me to
my fate," as they whispered to me—and the "talk" began.

My fate was by no means so terrible as had been anticipated, but at first the situation was a little awkward.
Neither party had any clear ideas as to what the other
desired, and my visitors expected that I was to begin the
proceedings. This expectation was quite natural and justifiable, for I had inadvertently invited them to meet me,
but I could not make a speech to them, for the best of all
reasons—that I did not know what to say. If I told them

my real aims, their suspicions would probably be aroused.
My usual stratagem of the weather and the crops was
wholly inapplicable. For a moment I thought of proposing
that a psalm should be sung as a means of breaking the
ice, but I felt that this would give to the meeting a solemnity which I wished to avoid. On the whole it seemed best
to begin at once a formal discussion. I told them, therefore, that I had spoken with many of their brethren in
various villages, and that I had found what I considered
grave errors of doctrine. I could not, for instance, agree
with them in their belief that it was unlawful to eat
pork. This was perhaps an abrupt way of entering on the
subject, but it furnished at least a *locus standi*—something
to talk about—and an animated discussion immediately
ensued. My opponents first endeavored to prove their thesis from the New Testament, and when this argument
broke down they had recourse to the Pentateuch. From a
particular article of the ceremonial law we passed to the
broader question as to how far the ceremonial law is still
binding, and from this to other points equally important.

If the logic of the peasants was not always unimpeach-
able, their knowledge of the Scriptures left nothing to be
desired. In support of their views they quoted long passages from memory, and whenever I indicated vaguely
any text which I needed, they at once supplied it verba-
tim, so that the big folio Bible served merely as an ornament. Three or four of them seemed to know the whole of
the New Testament by heart. The course of our informal
debate need not here be described; suffice it to say that,
after four hours of uninterrupted conversation, we agreed
to differ on questions of detail, and parted from each other
without a trace of that ill feeling which religious discussion
commonly engenders. Never have I met men more honest
and courteous in debate, more earnest in the search after
truth, or more careless of dialectical triumphs, than
these simple, uneducated muzhiks. If at one or two
points in the discussion a little undue warmth was displayed, I must do my opponents the justice to say that
they were not the offending party.

This long discussion, as well as numerous discussions

which I had had before and have had since with
Molokánye in various parts of the country, confirmed my
first impression that their doctrines have a strong resemblance to Presbyterianism. There is, however, an important difference. Presbyterianism has an ecclesiastical organization and a written creed, and its doctrines have
long since become clearly defined by means of public discussion, polemical literature, and General Assemblies. The
Molokánye, on the contrary, have had no means of developing their fundamental principles and formulating
their vague religious beliefs into a clearly defined logical
system. Their theology is, therefore, still in a half-fluid
state, so that it is impossible to predict what form it will
ultimately assume. "We have not yet thought about that,"
I have frequently been told when I inquired about some
abstruse doctrine; "we must talk about it at the meeting
next Sunday. What is your opinion?" Besides this, their
fundamental principles allow great latitude for individual
and local differences of opinion. They hold that Holy
Writ is the only rule of faith and conduct, but that it must
be taken in the spiritual, and not in the literal, sense. As
there is no terrestrial authority to which doubtful points
can be referred, each individual is free to adopt the interpretation which commends itself to his own judgment.
This will no doubt ultimately lead to a variety of sects,
and already there is a considerable diversity of opinion
between different communities; but this diversity has not
yet been recognized, and I may say that I nowhere found
that fanatically dogmatic quibbling spirit which is usually
the soul of sectarianism.

For their ecclesiastical organization the Molokánye take
as their model the early Apostolic Church, as depicted in
the New Testament, and uncompromisingly reject all
later authorities. In accordance with this model they have
no hierarchy and no paid clergy, but choose from among
themselves a Presbyter and two assistants—men well
known among the brethren for their exemplary life and
their knowledge of the Scriptures—whose duty it is to
watch over the religious and moral welfare of the flock.
As they have no churches, they hold meetings in private
houses, and on Sundays they usually spend two or three

hours in psalm singing, prayer, reading the Scriptures, and friendly conversation on religious subjects. If anyone has a doctrinal difficulty which he desires to have cleared up, he states it to the congregation, and some of the others give their opinions, with the texts on which the opinions are founded. If the question seems clearly solved by the texts, it is decided; if not, it is left open.

As in many young sects, there exists among the Molokánye a system of severe moral supervision. If a member has been guilty of drunkenness or any act unbecoming a Christian, he is first admonished by the Presbyter in private or before the congregation; and if this does not produce the desired effect, he is excluded for a longer or shorter period from the meetings and from all intercourse with the members. In extreme cases expulsion is resorted to. On the other hand, if any one of the members happens to be, from no fault of his own, in pecuniary difficulties, the others will assist him. This system of mutu ' control and mutual assistance has no doubt something to do with the fact that the Molokánye are distinguished from the surrounding population by their sobriety, uprightness, and material prosperity.

Of the history of the sect my friends in Alexandrov-Haï could tell me very little, but I have obtained from other quarters some interesting information. The founder was a peasant of the province of Tambóv called Uklein, who lived in the reign of Catherine II, and gained his living as an itinerant tailor. For some time he belonged to the sect of the Dukhobortsi—who are sometimes called the Russian Quakers, and who have since become known in Western Europe through the efforts of Count Tolstoy on their behalf—but he soon seceded from them, because he could not admit their doctrine that God dwells in the human soul, and that consequently the chief source of religious truth is internal enlightenment. To him it seemed that religious truth was to be found only in the Scriptures. With this doctrine he soon made many converts, and one day he unexpectedly entered the town of Tambóv, surrounded by seventy "apostles" chanting psalms. They were all quickly arrested and imprisoned, and when the affair was reported to St. Petersburg the Empress Catherine ordered that they should be handed over to the ecclesiastical authorities, and that in the event of their proving obdurate to exhortation they should be tried by the Criminal Courts. Uklein professed to recant, and was liberated; but he continued his teaching secretly in the villages, and at the time of his death he was believed to have no fewer than five thousand followers.

As to the actual strength of the sect it is difficult to form even a conjecture. Certainly it has many thousand members—probably several hundred thousand. Formerly the Government transported them from the central provinces to the thinly populated outlying districts, where they had less opportunity of contaminating Orthodox neighbors; and accordingly we find them in the southeastern districts of Samára, on the north coast of the Sea of Azov, in the Crimea, in the Caucasus, and in Siberia. There are still, however, very many of them in the central region, especially in the province of Tambóv.

The readiness with which the Molokánye modify their opinions and beliefs in accordance with what seems to them new light saves them effectually from bigotry and fanaticism, but it at the same time exposes them to evils of a different kind, from which they might be preserved by a few stubborn prejudices. "False prophets arise among us," said an old, sober-minded member to me on one occasion, "and lead many away from the faith."

In 1835, for example, great excitement was produced among them by rumors that the Second Advent of Christ was at hand, and that the Son of Man, coming to judge the world, was about to appear in the New Jerusalem, somewhere near Mount Ararat. As Elijah and Enoch were to appear before the opening of the Millennium, they were anxiously awaited by the faithful, and at last Elijah appeared, in the person of a Melitopol peasant called Bêlozvorov, who announced that on a given day he would ascend into heaven. On the appointed day a great crowd collected, but he failed to keep his promise, and was handed over to the police as an impostor by the Molokánye themselves. Unfortunately they were not always so sensible as on that occasion. In the very next year many of them were persuaded by a certain Lukian

Petróv to put on their best garments and start for the Promised Land in the Caucasus, where the Millennium was about to begin.[1]

Of the Molokán false prophets the most remarkable in recent times was a man who called himself Ivan Grigoriev, a mysterious personage who had at one time a Turkish and at another an American passport, but who seemed in all other respects a genuine Russian. Some years previously to my visit he appeared at Alexandrov-Haï. Though he professed himself to be a good Molokán and was received as such, he enounced at the weekly meetings many new and startling ideas. At first he simply urged his hearers to live like the early Christians, and have all things in common. This seemed sound doctrine to the Molokánye, who profess to take the early Christians as their model, and some of them thought of at once abolishing personal property; but when the teacher intimated pretty plainly that this communism should include free love, a decided opposition arose, and it was objected that the early Church did not recommend wholesale adultery and cognate sins. This was a formidable objection, but "the prophet" was equal to the occasion. He reminded his friends that in accordance with their own doctrine the Scriptures should be understood, not in the literal, but in the spiritual, sense—that Christianity had made men free, and every true Christian ought to use his freedom.

This account of the new doctrine was given to me by an intelligent Molokán, who had formerly been a peasant and was now a trader, as I sat one evening in his house in Novouzensk, the chief town of the district in which Alexandrov-Haï is situated. It seemed to me that the author of this ingenious attempt to conciliate Christianity with extreme Utilitarianism must be an educated man

[1] It may be remembered that a few years ago a similar movement took place among the Russian Dukhobortsi settled in Northern Canada, and that the authorities had to interfere, because the pilgrims journeying southwards towards Winnipeg where the Second Advent was expected, instead of putting on their best garments like the adherents of Lukian Petróv, insisted on wearing no garments at all.

in disguise. This conviction I communicated to my host, but he did not agree with me.

"No, I think not," he replied; "in fact, I am sure he is a peasant, and I strongly suspect he was at some time a soldier. He has not much learning, but he has a wonderful gift of talking. Never have I heard anyone speak like him. He would have talked over the whole village, had it not been for an old man who was more than a match for him. And then he went to Orlóv-Haï, and there he did talk the people over." What he really did in this latter place I never could clearly ascertain. Report said that he founded a communistic association, of which he was himself president and treasurer, and converted the members to an extraordinary theory of prophetic succession, invented apparently for his own sensual gratification. For further information my host advised me to apply either to the prophet himself, who was at that time confined in the jail on a charge of using a forged passport, or to one of his friends, a certain Mr. I——, who lived in the town. As it was a difficult matter to gain admittance to the prisoner, and I had little time at my disposal, I adopted the latter alternative.

Mr. I—— was himself a somewhat curious character. He had been a student in Moscow, and in consequence of some youthful indiscretions during the University disturbances, had been exiled to this place. After waiting in vain some years for a release, he gave up the idea of entering one of the learned professions, married a peasant girl, rented a piece of land, bought a pair of camels, and settled down as a small farmer.[2] He had a great deal to tell about the prophet.

Grigoriev, it seemed, was really a simple Russian peasant, but he had been from his youth upwards one of those restless people who can never long work in harness. Where his native place was, and why he left it, he never divulged, for reasons best known to himself. He had traveled much, and had been an attentive observer. Whether he had ever been in America was doubtful, but he had

[2] Here for the first time I saw camels used for agricultural purposes. When yoked to a small four-wheeled cart, the "ships of the desert" seemed decidedly out of place.

certainly been in Turkey, and had fraternized with various Russian sectarians, who are to be found in considerable number near the Danube. Here, probably, he acquired many of his peculiar religious ideas, and conceived his grand scheme of founding a new religion—of rivaling the Founder of Christianity! He aimed at nothing less than this, as he on one occasion confessed, and he did not see why he should not be successful. He believed that the Founder of Christianity had been simply a man like himself, who understood better than others the people around him and the circumstances of the time, and he was convinced that he himself had these qualifications. One qualification, however, for becoming a prophet he certainly did not possess: he had no genuine religious enthusiasm in him—nothing of the martyr spirit about him. Much of his own preaching he did not himself believe, and he had a secret contempt for those who naïvely accepted it all. Not only was he cunning, but he knew he was cunning, and he was conscious that he was playing an assumed part. And yet perhaps it would be unjust to say that he was merely an impostor exclusively occupied with his own personal advantage. Though he was naturally a man of sensual tastes, and could not resist convenient opportunities of gratifying them, he seemed to believe that his communistic schemes would, if realized, be beneficial not only to himself, but also to the people. Altogether a curious mixture of the prophet, the social reformer, and the cunning impostor!

Besides the Molokánye, there are in Russia many other heretical sects. Some of them are simply Evangelical Protestants, like the "Stundisti," who have adopted the religious conceptions of their neighbors, the German colonists; whilst others are composed of wild enthusiasts, who give a loose rein to their excited imagination, and revel in what the Germans aptly term "der höhere Blödsinn." I cannot here attempt to convey even a general idea of these fantastic sects with their doctrinal and ceremonial absurdities, but I may offer the following classification of them for the benefit of those who may desire to study the subject:

1. Sects which take the Scriptures as the basis of their belief, but interpret and complete the doctrines therein

contained by means of the occasional inspiration or internal
enlightenment of their leading members.

2. Sects which reject interpretation and insist on certain
passages of Scripture being taken in the literal sense. In
one of the best known of these sects—the Skoptsi, or
Eunuchs—fanaticism has led to physical mutilation.

3. Sects which pay little or no attention to Scripture,
and derive their doctrine from the supposed inspiration
of their living teachers.

4. Sects which believe in the reincarnation of Christ.

5. Sects which confound religion with nervous excitement, and are more or less erotic in their character. The
excitement necessary for prophesying is commonly produced by dancing, jumping, pirouetting, or self-castiga-
tion; and the absurdities spoken at such times are regarded
as the direct expression of Divine wisdom. The religious
exercises resemble more or less closely those of the "dancing dervishes" and "howling dervishes," with which all who
have visited Constantinople are familiar. There is, however, one important difference: these dervishes practice
their religious exercises in public, and consequently observe a certain decorum, whilst the Russian sects to which
I refer assemble in secret, and give free scope to their
excitement, so that the most disgusting orgies sometimes
take place at their meetings.

To illustrate the general character of the sects belonging to this last category, I may quote here a short extract
from a description of the "Khlysti" by one who was initiated into their mysteries: "Among them men and women
alike take upon themselves the calling of teachers and
prophets, and in this character they lead a strict, ascetic
life, refrain from the most ordinary and innocent pleasures,
exhaust themselves by long fasting and wild, ecstatic religious exercises, and abhor marriage. Under the excitement caused by their supposed holiness and inspiration,
they call themselves not only teachers and prophets, but
also 'Saviors,' 'Redeemers,' 'Christs,' 'Mothers of God.
Generally speaking, they call themselves simply Gods,
and pray to each other as to real Gods and living Christs
or Madonnas. When several of these teachers come together at a meeting, they dispute with each other in a

vain, boasting way as to which of them possesses most grace and power. In this rivalry they sometimes give each other lusty blows on the ear, and he who bears the blows most patiently, turning the other cheek to the smiter, acquires the reputation of having most holiness."

Another sect belonging to this category is the Jumpers, among whom the erotic element is disagreeably prominent. Here is a description of their religious meetings, which are held during summer in the forest, and during winter in some outhouse or barn: "After due preparation prayers are read by the chief teacher, dressed in a white robe and standing in the midst of the congregation. At first he reads in an ordinary tone of voice, and then passes gradually into a merry chant. When he remarks that the chanting has sufficiently acted on the hearers, he begins to jump. The hearers, singing likewise, follow his example. Their ever increasing excitement finds expression in the highest possible jumps. This they continue as long as they can—men and women alike yelling like enraged savages. When all are thoroughly exhausted, the leader declares that he hears the angels singing"—and then begins a scene which cannot be here described.

It is but fair to add that we know very little of these peculiar sects, and what we do know is furnished by avowed enemies. It is very possible, therefore, that some of them are not nearly so absurd as they are commonly represented, and that many of the stories told are mere calumnies.

Until quite recently the Government showed itself very hostile to sectarianism, and occasionally endeavored to suppress it. This was natural enough as regards these fantastic sects, but it seems strange that the peaceful, industrious, honest Molokánye and Stundisti should have been put under the ban. Why is it that a Russian peasant should be punished for holding doctrines which are openly professed, with the sanction of the authorities, by his neighbors, the German colonists?

To understand this the reader must know that according to Russian conception there are two distinct kinds of heresy, distinguished from each other, not by the doctrines held, but by the nationality of the holder. It seems to a

Russian in the nature of things that Tatars should be Mahometans, that Poles should be Roman Catholics, and that Germans should be Protestants; and the mere act of becoming a Russian subject is not supposed to lay the Tatar, the Pole, or the German under any obligation to change his faith. These nationalities, therefore, have always been allowed the most perfect freedom in the exercise of their respective religions, so long as they refrained from disturbing by propagandism the divinely established order of things.

This is the received theory, and we must do the Russians the justice to say that they have habitually acted up to it. If the Government has sometimes attempted to convert alien races, the motive has always been political, and the efforts have never awakened much sympathy among the people at large, or even among the clergy. In like manner the missionary societies which have sometimes been formed in imitation of the Western nations have never received much popular support. Thus with regard to aliens this peculiar theory led to very extensive religious toleration. With regard to the Russians themselves the theory had a very different effect. If in the nature of things the Tatar is a Mahometan, the Pole a Roman Catholic, and the German a Protestant, it is equally in the nature of things that the Russian should be a member of the Orthodox Church. On this point the written law and public opinion were in perfect accord. If an Orthodox Russian became a Roman Catholic or a Protestant, he was amenable to the criminal law, and was at the same time condemned by public opinion as an apostate and renegade—almost as a traitor. Now there is a change for the better. In March, 1903, liberty of conscience was solemnly proclaimed by the Tsar as a general principle, and since that time the principle has been gradually introduced into the legislation, but we must not expect that the old conceptions on the subject will immediately disappear.

As to the future of these heretical sects it is impossible to speak with confidence. The more gross and fantastic will probably disappear as primary education spreads among the people; but the Protestant sects seem to possess much more vitality. For the present, at least, they are rapidly spreading. I have seen large villages where, according to the testimony of the inhabitants, there was not a single heretic fifteen years before, and where one-half of the population had already become Molokánye; and this change, be it remarked, had taken place without any propagandist organization and before the principle of toleration had been proclaimed. The civil and ecclesiastical authorities were well aware of the existence of the movement, but they were powerless to prevent it. The few efforts which they made were without effect, or worse than useless. Among the Stundists corporal punishment was tried as an antidote—without the concurrence, it is to be hoped, of the central authorities—and to the Molokánye of the province of Samára a learned monk was sent in the hope of converting them from their errors by reason and eloquence. What effect the birch twigs had on the religious convictions of the Stundists I have not been able to ascertain, but I assume that they were not very efficacious, because the sect remained at least as numerous as before.

Of the mission in the province of Samára I happen to know more, and can state on the evidence of many peasants—some of them Orthodox—that the only immediate effect was to stir up religious fanaticism, and to induce a certain number of Orthodox to go over to the heretical camp. In their public discussions the disputants could find no common ground on which to argue, for the simple reason that their fundamental conceptions were different. The monk spoke of the Church as the terrestrial representative of Christ and the sole possessor of truth, whilst his opponents knew nothing of a Church in this sense, and held simply that all men should live in accordance with the dictates of Scripture. Once the monk consented to argue with them on their own ground, and on that occasion he sustained a signal defeat, for he could not produce a single passage recommending the veneration of Icons— a practice which the Russian peasants consider an essential part of Orthodoxy. After this he always insisted on the authority of the early Ecumenical Councils and the Fathers of the Church—an authority which his antagonists did not recognize. Altogether the mission was a complete failure, and all parties regretted that it had been undertaken. "It was a great mistake," remarked to me confidentially an Orthodox peasant—"a very great mistake! The Molokánye are a cunning people. The monk was no match for them; they knew the Scriptures a great deal better than he did. The Church should not condescend to discuss with heretics."

It is often said that these heretical sects are politically disaffected, and the Molokánye are thought to be specially dangerous in this respect. Perhaps there is a certain foundation for this opinion, for men are naturally disposed to doubt the legitimacy of a power that systematically persecutes them; but with regard to the Molokánye, I believe the accusation to be a groundless calumny. Political ideas seemed entirely foreign to their modes of thought. During my intercourse with them I often heard them refer to the police as "wolves which have to be fed," but I never heard them speak of the Emperor otherwise than in terms of filial affection and veneration.

CHAPTER · XXI

The Dissenters

WE must be careful not to confound those heretical sects, Protestant and Fantastical, of which I have spoken in the preceding chapter, with the more numerous Dissenters or Schismatics, the descendants of those who seceded from the Russian Church—or more correctly from whom the Russian Church seceded—in the seventeenth century. So far from regarding themselves as heretics, these latter consider themselves more orthodox than the official Orthodox Church. They are conservatives, too, in the social as well as the religious sense of the term. Among them are to be found the last remnants of old Russian life, untinged by foreign influences.

The Russian Church . . . has always paid inordinate attention to ceremonial observances, and somewhat neglected the doctrinal and moral elements of the faith which it professes. This peculiarity greatly facilitated the spread of its influence among a people accustomed to pagan rites and magical incantations, but it had the pernicious effect of confirming in the new converts their superstitious belief in the virtue of mere ceremonies. Thus the Russians became zealous Christians in all matters of external observance, without knowing much about the spiritual meaning of the rites which they practiced. They looked upon the rites and sacraments as mysterious charms which preserved them from evil influences in the present life and secured them eternal felicity in the life to come, and they believed that these charms would inevitably lose their efficacy if modified in the slightest degree. Extreme importance was therefore attached to the

ritual minutiae, and the slightest modification of these
minutiae assumed the importance of an historical event.
In the year 1476, for instance, the Novgorodian Chronicler
gravely relates: "This winter some philosophers (!) began
to sing, 'Oh Lord, have mercy,' and others merely, 'Lord,
have mercy.'" And this attaching of enormous importance
to trifles was not confined to the ignorant multitude. An
Archbishop of Novgorod declared solemnly that those
who repeat the word "Alleluia" only twice at certain points
in the liturgy "sing to their own damnation," and a celebrated Ecclesiastical Council, held in 1551, put such
matters as the position of the fingers when making the
sign of the cross on the same level as heresies—formally
anathematizing those who acted in such trifles contrary
to its decisions.

This conservative spirit in religious concerns had a considerable influence on social life. As there was no clear line
of demarcation between religious observances and simple
traditional customs, the most ordinary act might receive a
religious significance, and the slightest departure from a
traditional custom might be looked upon as a deadly sin. A
Russian of the olden time would have resisted the attempt
to deprive him of his beard as strenuously as a Calvinist of
the present day would resist the attempt to make him ab-
jure the doctrine of Predestination—and both for the same
reason. As the doctrine of Predestination is for the Calvinist, so the wearing of a beard was for the old Russian—an
essential of salvation. "Where," asked one of the Patriarchs
of Moscow, "will those who shave their chins stand at the
Last Day?—among the righteous adorned with beards,
or among the beardless heretics?" The question required
no answer.

In the seventeenth century this superstitious, conservative spirit reached its climax. The civil wars and foreign
invasions, accompanied by pillage, famine, and plagues,
with which that century opened, produced a widespread
conviction that the end of all things was at hand. The
mysterious number of the Beast was found to indicate the
year 1666, and timid souls began to discover signs of
that falling away from the Faith which is spoken of in the
Apocalypse. The majority of the people did not perhaps

share this notion, but they believed that the sufferings with which they had been visited were a Divine punishment for having forsaken the ancient customs. And it could not be denied that considerable changes had taken place. Orthodox Russia was now tainted with the presence of heretics. Foreigners who shaved their chins and smoked the accursed weed had been allowed to settle in Moscow, and the Tsars not only held converse with them, but had even adopted some of their "pagan" practices. Besides this, the Government had introduced innovations and reforms, many of which were displeasing to the people. In short, the country was polluted with "heresy"—a subtle, evil influence lurking in everything foreign, and very dangerous to the spiritual and temporal welfare of the Faithful—something of the nature of an epidemic, but infinitely more dangerous; for disease kills merely the body, whereas "heresy" kills the soul, and causes both soul and body to be cast into hell fire.

Had the Government introduced the innovations slowly and cautiously, respecting as far as possible all outward forms, it might have effected much without producing a religious panic; but, instead of acting circumspectly as the occasion demanded, it ran full tilt against the ancient prejudices and superstitious fears, and drove the people into open resistance. When the art of printing was introduced, it became necessary to choose the best texts of the Liturgy, Psalter, and other religious books, and on examination it was found that, through the ignorance and carelessness of copyists, numerous errors had crept into the manuscripts in use. This discovery led to further investigation, which showed that certain irregularities had likewise crept into the ceremonial. The chief of the clerical errors lay in the orthography of the word "Jesus," and the chief irregularity in the ceremonial regarded the position of the fingers when making the sign of the cross.

To correct these errors, the celebrated Nikon, who was Patriarch in the time of Tsar Alexis, father of Peter the Great, ordered all the old liturgical books and the old Icons to be called in, and new ones to be distributed; but the clergy and the people resisted. Believing these "Nikonian novelties" to be heretical, they clung to their old Icons,

their old missals and their old religious customs, as the sole
anchors of safety which could save the Faithful from
drifting to perdition. In vain the Patriarch assured the
people that the change was a return to the ancient forms
still preserved in Greece and Constantinople. "The Greek
Church," it was replied, "is no longer free from heresy:
Orthodoxy has become many-colored from the violence
of the Turkish Mahomet; and the Greeks, under the sons
of Hagar, have fallen away from the ancient traditions."

An anathema, formally pronounced by an Ecclesiastical
Council against these Nonconformists, had no more effect
than the admonitions of the Patriarch. They persevered in
their obstinacy, and refused to believe that the blessed
saints and holy martyrs who had used the ancient forms
had not prayed and crossed themselves aright. "Not those
holy men of old, but the present Patriarch and his counsellors must be heretics." "Woe to us! Woe to us!" cried the
monks of Solovetsk—a much revered monastery on an island in the White Sea—when they received the new
Liturgies. "What have you done with the Son of God?
Give Him back to us! You have changed Isus (the old
Russian form of Jesus) into Iisus! It is fearful not only to
commit such a sin, but even to think of it!" And the sturdy
monks shut their gates, and defied Patriarch, Council, and
Tsar for seven long years, till the monastery was taken by
an armed force.

The decree of excommunication pronounced by the
Ecclesiastical Council placed the Nonconformists beyond
the pale of the Church, and the civil power undertook the
task of persecuting them. Persecution had, of course,
merely the effect of confirming the victims in their belief
that the Church and the Tsar had become heretical.
Thousands fled across the frontier and settled in the
neighboring countries—Poland, Prussia, Sweden, Austria,
Turkey, the Caucasus, and Siberia. Others concealed themselves in the northern forests, and in the densely wooded
region near the Polish frontier, where they lived by
agriculture or fishing, and prayed, crossed themselves, and
buried their dead according to the customs of their forefathers. The northern forests were their favorite place of
refuge. Hither flocked many of those who wished to keep

themselves pure and undefiled. Here the more learned
men among the Nonconformists—well acquainted with
Holy Writ, with fragmentary translations from the Greek
Fathers, and with the more important decisions of the
early Ecumenical Councils—wrote polemical and edifying
works for the confounding of heretics and the confirming of
true believers. Hence were sent out in all directions zealous missionaries, in the guise of traders, peddlers, and
laborers, to sow what they called the living seed, and
what the official Church termed "Satan's tares." When the
Government agents discovered these retreats, the inmates
generally fled from the "ravenous wolves"; but on more
than one occasion a large number of fanatical men and
women, shutting themselves up, set fire to their houses,
and voluntarily perished in the flames. In Paleostrovski
Monastery, for instance—a famous resort of pilgrims, on
a rocky islet in Lake Onega—in the year 1687, no fewer
than 2,700 fanatics gained the crown of martyrdom in
this way; and many similar instances are on record. [1] As in
all periods of religious panic, the Apocalypse was carefully
studied, and the Millennial ideas rapidly spread. The signs
of the time were plain: Satan was being let loose for a
little season. Men anxiously looked for the reappearance of
Antichrist—and Antichrist appeared! The man in whom
the people recognized the incarnate spirit of evil was no
other than Peter the Great.

From the Nonconformist point of view, Peter had very
strong claims to be considered Antichrist. He had none of
the staid, pious demeanor of the old Tsars, and showed
no respect for many things which were venerated by the
people. He ate, drank, and habitually associated with
heretics, spoke their language, wore their costume, chose
from among them his most intimate friends, and favored
them more than his own people. Imagine the horror and
commotion which would be produced among pious Catholics if the Pope should some day appear in the costume of
the Grand Turk, and should choose Pashas as his chief

---

[1] A list of well-authenticated cases is given by Nilski,
Seméinaya zhizn v russkom Raskóle, St. Petersburg, 1869, part
I, pp. 55-57. The number of these self-immolators certainly
amounted to many thousands.

counsellors! The horror which Peter's conduct produced
among a large section of his subjects was not less great.
They could not explain it otherwise than by supposing him
to be the Devil in disguise, and they saw in all his important measures convincing proofs of his Satanic origin. The
newly invented census, or "revision," was a profane "numbering of the people," and an attempt to enroll in the
service of Beëlzebub those whose names were written in
the Lamb's Book of Life. The new title of Imperator was
explained to mean something very diabolical. The passport
bearing the Imperial arms was the seal of Antichrist. The
order to shave the beard was an attempt to disfigure "the
image of God," after which man had been created, and by
which Christ would recognize His own at the Last Day.
The change in the calendar, by which New Year's Day
was transferred from September to January, was the destruction of "the years of our Lord," and the introduction
of the years of Satan in their place. Of the ingenious arguments by which these theses were supported, I may quote
one by way of illustration. The world, it was explained,
could not have been created in January, as the new
calendar seemed to indicate, because apples are not ripe
at that season, and consequently Eve could not have been
tempted in the way described! [2]

These ideas regarding Peter and his reforms were
strongly confirmed by the vigorous persecutions which
took place during the earlier years of his reign. The Nonconformists were constantly convicted of political disaf-
fection—especially of "insulting the Imperial Majesty"—
and were accordingly flogged, tortured, and beheaded
without mercy. But when Peter had succeeded in putting
down all armed opposition, and found that the movement
was no longer dangerous for the throne, he adopted a
policy more in accordance with his personal character.
Whether he himself had any religious belief whatever may
be doubted; certainly he had not a spark of religious
fanaticism in his nature. Exclusively occupied with secular
concerns, he took no interest in subtle questions of religious ceremonial, and was profoundly indifferent as to how

[2] I found this ingenious argument in one of the polemical
treatises of the Old Believers.

his subjects prayed and crossed themselves, provided they obeyed his orders in worldly matters and paid their taxes regularly. As soon, therefore, as political considerations admitted of clemency, he stopped the persecutions, and at last, in 1714, issued ukases to the effect that all Dissenters might live unmolested, provided they inscribed themselves in the official registers and paid a double poll tax. Somewhat later they were allowed to practice freely all their old rites and customs, on condition of paying certain fines.

With the accession of Catherine II, "the friend of philosophers," the *Raskól*,[3] as the schism had come to be called, entered on a new phase. Penetrated with the ideas of religious toleration then in fashion in Western Europe, Catherine abolished the disabilities to which the Raskólniks were subjected, and invited those of them who had fled across the frontier to return to their homes. Thousands accepted the invitation, and many who had hitherto sought to conceal themselves from the eyes of the authorities became rich and respected merchants. The peculiar semimonastic religious communities, which had up till that time existed only in the forests of the northern and western provinces, began to appear in Moscow, and were officially recognized by the Administration. At first they took the form of hospitals for the sick, or asylums for the aged and infirm, but soon they became regular monasteries, the superiors of which exercised an undefined spiritual authority not only over the inmates, but also over the members of the sect throughout the length and breadth of the Empire.

From that time down to the present the Government has followed a wavering policy, oscillating between complete tolerance and active persecution. It must, however, be said that the persecution has never been of a very searching kind. In persecution, as in all other manifestations, the Russian Church directs its attention chiefly to external forms. It does not seek to ferret out heresy in a

[3] The term is derived from two Russian words—*ras*, asunder; and *kolot*, to split. Those who belong to the *Raskól* are called *Raskólniks*. They call themselves *Stáro-obriádtsi* (Old Ritualists) or *Starovêri* (Old Believers).

man's opinions, but complacently accepts as Orthodox
all who annually appear at confession and communion,
and who refrain from acts of open hostility. Those who
can make these concessions to conventionalities are practically free from molestation, and those who cannot so
trifle with their conscience have an equally convenient
method of escaping persecution. The parish clergy, with
their customary indifference to things spiritual and their
traditional habit of regarding their functions from the
financial point of view, are hostile to sectarianism, chiefly
because it diminishes their revenues by diminishing the
number of parishioners requiring their ministrations. This
cause of hostility, therefore, could easily be removed by a
certain pecuniary sacrifice on the part of the sectarians,
and accordingly there used to exist between them and
their parish priest a tacit contract, by which both parties
were perfectly satisfied. The priest received his income as
if all his parishioners belonged to the State Church, and
the parishioners were left in peace to believe and practice
what they pleased. By this rude, convenient method a
very large amount of toleration was effectually secured.
Whether the practice had a beneficial moral influence on
the parish clergy is, of course, an entirely different question.

When the priest had been satisfied, there still remained
the police, who likewise levied an irregular tax on hetero-
doxy; but the negotiations were generally not difficult, for
it was in the interest of both parties that they should come
to terms and live in good fellowship. Thus, from the time
of Catherine II, until 1903, when freedom of conscience
was proclaimed, the Raskólniks lived practically under the
same conditions as in the last years of Peter the Great's
reign; they paid a tax and were not molested—only the
money paid for toleration did not find its way into the Imperial Exchequer. These external changes in the history
of the *Raskól* exercised a powerful influence on its internal
development.

When formally anathematized and excluded from the
dominant Church, the Nonconformists had neither a definite organization nor a positive creed. The only tie that
bound them together was hostility to the "Nikonian novel-

ties," and all they desired was to preserve intact the beliefs and customs of their forefathers. At first they never
thought of creating any permanent organization. The more
moderate believed that the old order of things would soon
be re-established, and the more fanatical imagined that the
end of all things was at hand.[4] In either case they had only
to suffer for a little season, keeping themselves free from
the taint of heresy and from all contact with the kingdom
of Antichrist.

But years passed, and neither of these expectations
was fulfilled. The fanatics awaited in vain the sound of the
last trump and the appearance of Christ coming with His
angels to judge the world. The sun continued to rise, and
the seasons followed each other in their accustomed
courses, but the end was not yet. Nor did the civil power
return to the old faith, though Nikon fell a victim to
Court intrigues and his own overweening pride, and was
formally deposed. Tsar Alexis in the fullness of time was
gathered unto his fathers, but there was no sign of a re-
establishment of the old Orthodoxy. Gradually the leading Raskólniks perceived that they must make preparations, not for the Day of Judgment, but for a terrestrial
future—that they must create some permanent form of
ecclesiastical organization. In this work they encountered
at the very outset not only practical but also theoretical
difficulties.

So long as they confined themselves simply to resisting
the official innovations, they seemed to be unanimous;
but when they were forced to abandon this negative policy
and to determine theoretically their new position, radical
differences of opinion became apparent. All were convinced that the official Russian Church had become heretical, and that it had now Antichrist instead of Christ as its
head; but it was not easy to determine what should be
done by those who refused to bow the knee to the Son
of Destruction. According to Protestant conceptions there
was a very simple solution of the difficulty: the Nonconformists had simply to create a new Church for themselves,

---

[4] Some had coffins made, and lay down in them at night, in
the expectation that the Sécond Advent might take place before
the morning.

and worship God in the way that seemed good to them. But to the Russians of that time such notions were still more repulsive than the innovations of Nikon. These men were Orthodox to the backbone—"plus royalistes que le roi"—and according to Orthodox conceptions the founding of a new Church is an absurdity. They believed that if the chain of historic continuity were once broken, the Church must necessarily cease to exist, in the same way as an ancient family becomes extinct when its sole representative dies without issue. If, therefore, the Church had already ceased to exist, there was no longer any means of communication between Christ and His people, the sacraments were no longer efficacious, and mankind was forever deprived of the ordinary means of grace.

Now, on this important point a difference of opinion arose among the Dissenters. Some of them believed that, though the ecclesiastical authorities had become heretical, the Church still existed in the communion of those who had refused to accept the innovations. Others declared boldly that the Orthodox Church had ceased to exist, that the ancient means of grace had been withdrawn, and that those who had remained faithful must thenceforth seek salvation, not in the sacraments, but in prayer and such other religious exercises as did not require the co-operation of duly consecrated priests. Thus took place a schism among the Schismatics. The one party retained all the sacraments and ceremonial observances in the older form; the other refrained from the sacraments and from many of the ordinary rites, on the ground that there was no longer a real priesthood, and that consequently the sacraments could not be efficacious. The former party are termed *Stáro-obriádtsi*, or Old Ritualists; the latter are called *Bezpopovtsi*—that is to say, people "without priests" (*bez popóv*).

The succeeding history of these two sections of the Nonconformists has been widely different. The Old Ritualists, being simply ecclesiastical Conservatives desirous of resisting all innovations, have remained a compact body little troubled by differences of opinion. The Priestless People, on the contrary, ever seeking to discover some new effec-

tual means of salvation, have fallen into an endless number
of independent sects.

The Old Ritualists had still, however, one important
theoretical difficulty. At first they had amongst themselves
plenty of consecrated priests for the celebration of the
ordinances, but they had no means of renewing the supply. They had no bishops, and according to Orthodox belief the lower degrees of the clergy cannot be created
without episcopal consecration. At the time of the schism
one bishop had thrown in his lot with the Schismatics,
but he had died shortly afterwards without leaving a successor, and thereafter no bishop had joined their ranks.
As time wore on, the necessity of episcopal consecration
came to be more and more felt, and it is not a little interesting to observe how these rigorists, who held to the
letter of the law and declared themselves ready to die for a
jot or a tittle, modified their theory in accordance with
the changing exigencies of their position. When the priests
who had kept themselves "pure and undefiled"—free
from all contact with Antichrist—became scarce, it was
discovered that certain priests of the dominant Church
might be accepted if they formally abjured the Nikonian
novelties. At first, however, only those who had been
consecrated previous to the supposed apostasy of the
Church were accepted, for the very good reason that
consecration by bishops who had become heretical could
not be efficacious. When these could no longer be obtained
it was discovered that those who had been *baptized* previous to the apostasy might be accepted; and when even
these could no longer be found, a still further concession
was made to necessity, and *all* consecrated priests were
received on condition of their solemnly abjuring their
errors. Of such priests there was always an abundant
supply. If a regular priest could not find a parish, or if he
was deposed by the authorities for some crime or misdemeanor, he had merely to pass over to the Old Ritualists,
and was sure to find among them a hearty welcome and
a tolerable salary.

By these concessions the indefinite prolongation of Old
Ritualism was secured, but many of the Old Ritualists

could not but feel that their position was, to say the least, extremely anomalous. They had no bishops of their own, and their priests were all consecrated by bishops whom they believed to be heretical! For many years they hoped to escape from this dilemma by discovering "Orthodox"— that is to say, Old Ritualist—bishops somewhere in the East; but when the East had been searched in vain, and all their efforts to obtain native bishops proved fruitless, they conceived the design of creating a bishopric somewhere beyond the frontier, among the Old Ritualists who had in times of persecution fled to Prussia, Austria, and Turkey. There were, however, immense difficulties in the way. In the first place it was necessary to obtain the formal permission of some foreign Government; and in the second place an Orthodox bishop must be found, willing to consecrate an Old Ritualist or to become an Old Ritualist himself. Again and again the attempt was made and failed; but at last, after years of effort and intrigue, the design was realized. In 1844 the Austrian Government gave permission to found a bishopric at Bêlaya Krinitsa, in Galicia, a few miles from the Russian frontier; and two years later the deposed Metropolitan of Bosnia consented, after much hesitation, to pass over to the Old Ritualist confession and accept the diocese.[5] From that time the Old Ritualists have had their own bishops, and have not been obliged to accept the runaway priests of the official Church.

The Old Ritualists were naturally much grieved by the schism, and were often sorely tried by persecution, but they have always enjoyed a certain spiritual tranquillity, proceeding from the conviction that they have preserved for themselves the means of salvation. The position of the more extreme section of the Schismatics was much more tragical. They believed that the sacraments had irretrievably lost their efficacy, that the ordinary means of salvation were forever withdrawn, that the powers of darkness had been let loose for a little season, that the authorities

[5] An interesting account of these negotiations, and a most curious picture of the Orthodox ecclesiastical world in Constantinople, is given by Subbótin, *Istoria Bêlokrinitskoi Ierarkhii*, Moscow, 1874.

were the agents of Satan, and that the personage who
filled the place of the old God-fearing Tsars was no other
than Antichrist. Under the influence of these horrible
ideas they fled to the woods and the caves to escape from
the rage of the Beast, and to await the Second Coming
of our Lord.

This state of things could not continue permanently.
Extreme religious fanaticism, like all other abnormal
states, cannot long exist in a mass of human beings without some constant exciting cause. The vulgar necessities of
everyday life, especially among people who have to live by
the labor of their hands, have a wonderfully sobering influence on the excited brain, and must always, sooner or
later, prove fatal to inordinate excitement. A few peculiarly
constituted individuals may show themselves capable of a
lifelong enthusiasm, but the multitude is ever spasmodic in
its fervor, and begins to slide back to its former apathy as
soon as the exciting cause ceases to act.

All this we find exemplified in the history of the "Priestless People." When it was found that the world did not
come to an end, and that the rigorous system of persecution was relaxed, the less excitable natures returned to
their homes and resumed their old mode of life; and when
Peter the Great made his politic concessions, many who
had declared him to be Antichrist came to suspect that he
was really not so black as he was painted. This idea
struck deep root in a religious community near Lake
Onega (*Vuigovski Skit*), which had received special privileges on condition of supplying laborers for the neighboring mines; and here was developed a new theory which
opened up a way of reconciliation with the Government.
By a more attentive study of Holy Writ and ancient books
it was discovered that the reign of Antichrist would con-
sist of two periods. In the former, the Son of Destruction
would reign merely in the spiritual sense, and the Faithful
would not be much molested; in the latter, he would
reign visibly in the flesh, and true believers would be subjected to the most frightful persecution. The second period,
it was held, had evidently not yet arrived, for the Faithful now enjoyed "a time of freedom, and not of compulsion or oppression." Whether this theory is strictly in

accordance with Apocalyptic prophecy and Patristic theology may be doubted, but it fully satisfied those who had already arrived at the conclusion by a different road, and who sought merely a means of justifying their position. Certain it is that very many accepted it, and determined to render unto Caesar the things that were Caesar's, or, in secular language, to pray for the Tsar and to pay their taxes.

This ingenious compromise was not accepted by all the Priestless People. On the contrary, many of them regarded it as a woeful backsliding—a new device of the Evil One; and among these irreconcilables was a certain peasant called Theodosi, a man of little education, but of remarkable intellectual power and unusual strength of character. He raised anew the old fanaticism by his preaching and writings—widely circulated in manuscript—and succeeded in founding a new sect in the forest region near the Polish frontier.

The Priestless Nonconformists thus fell into two sections; the one, called *Pomórtsi*,[6] accepted at least a partial reconciliation with the civil power; the other, called Theodosians, after their founder, held to the old opinions, and refused to regard the Tsar otherwise than as Antichrist.

These latter were at first very wild in their fanaticism, but ere long they gave way to the influences which had softened the fanaticism of the Pomórtsi. Under the liberal, conciliatory rule of Catherine they lived in contentment, and many of them enriched themselves by trade. Their fanatical zeal and exclusiveness evaporated under the influence of material well-being and constant contact with the outer world, especially after they were allowed to build a monastery in Moscow. The Superior of this monastery, a man of much shrewdness and enormous wealth, succeeded in gaining the favor not only of the lower officials, who could be easily bought but even of high-placed dignitaries, and for many years he exercised a very real, if

[6] The word *Pomórtsi* means "those who live near the seashore." It is commonly applied to the inhabitants of the northern provinces—that is, those who live near the shore of the White Sea, the only maritime frontier that Russia possessed previous to the conquests of Peter the Great.

undefined, authority over all sections of the Priestless People. "His fame," it is said, "sounded throughout Moscow, and the echoes were heard in Petropol (St. Petersburg), Riga, Astrakhan, Nizhni-Novgorod, and other lands of piety"; and when deputies came to consult him, they prostrated themselves in his presence, as before the great ones of the earth. Living thus not only in peace and plenty, but even in honor and luxury, "the proud Patriarch of the Theodosian Church" could not consistently fulminate against "the ravenous wolves," with whom he was on friendly terms, or excite the fanaticism of his followers by highly colored descriptions of "the awful sufferings and persecution of God's people in these latter days," as the founder of the sect had been wont to do. Though he could not openly abandon any fundamental doctrines, he allowed the ideas about the reign of Antichrist to fall into the background, and taught by example, if not by precept, that the Faithful might, by prudent concessions, live very comfortably in this present evil world. This seed fell upon soil already prepared for its reception. The Faithful gradually forgot their old savage fanaticism, and they have since contrived, while holding many of their old ideas in theory, to accommodate themselves in practice to the existing order of things.

The gradual softening and toning down of the original fanaticism in these two sects are strikingly exemplified in their ideas of marriage. According to Orthodox doctrine, marriage is a sacrament which can only be performed by a consecrated priest, and consequently for the Priestless People the celebration of marriage was an impossibility; but for some time this did not cause them much inconvenience. In the first ages of sectarianism a state of celibacy was quite in accordance with their surroundings. Living in constant fear of their persecutors, and wandering from one place of refuge to another, the sufferers for the Faith had little time or inclination to think of family ties, and readily listened to the monks, who exhorted them to mortify the lusts of the flesh. The result, however, proved that celibacy in the creed by no means ensures chastity in practice. Not only in the villages of the Dissenters, but even in those religious communities which professed a more ascetic mode of life, a numerous class of "orphans" began to appear, who knew not who their parents were; and this ignorance of blood relationship naturally led to incestuous connections. Besides this, the doctrine of celibacy had grave practical inconveniences, for the peasant requires a housewife to attend to domestic concerns and to help him in his agricultural occupations. Thus the necessity of reestablishing family life came to be felt, and the feeling soon found expression in a doctrinal form both among the Pomórtsi and among the Theodosians. Learned dissertations were written, and disseminated in manuscript copies, violent discussions took place, and at last a great Council was held in Moscow to discuss the question.[7] The point at issue was never unanimously decided, but many accepted the ingenious arguments in favor of matrimony, and contracted marriages which were, of course, null and void in the eye of the law and of the Church, but valid in all other respects.

This new backsliding of the unstable multitude produced a new outburst of fanaticism among the stubborn few. Some of those who had hitherto sought to conceal the origin of the "orphan" class above referred to now boldly asserted that the existence of this class was a religious necessity, because in order to be saved men must repent, and in order to repent men must sin! At the same time the old ideas about Antichrist were revived and preached with fervor by a peasant called Philip, who founded a new sect called the Philipists. This sect still exists. They hold fast to the old belief that the Tsar is Antichrist, and that the civil and ecclesiastical authorities are the servants of Satan—an idea that was kept alive by the corruption and extortion for which the Administration was notorious. They do not venture on open resistance to the authorities, but the bolder members take little pains to conceal their opinions and sentiments, and may be easily recognized by their severe aspect, their Puritanical manner, and their Pharisaical horror of everything which they

[7] I cannot here enter into the details of this remarkable controversy, but I may say that in studying it I have been frequently astonished by the dialectical power and logical subtlety displayed by the disputants, some of them simple peasants.

suppose heretical and unclean. Some of them, it is said, carry this fastidiousness to such an extent that they throw away the handle of a door if it has been touched by a heretic!

It may seem that we have here reached the extreme limits of fanaticism, but in reality there were men whom even the Pharisaical Puritanism of the Philipists did not satisfy. These new zealots, who appeared in the time of Catherine II, but first became known to the official world in the reign of Nicholas I, rebuked the lukewarmness of their brethren, and founded a new sect in order to preserve intact the asceticism practiced immediately after the schism. The sect still exists. They call themselves "Christ's People" (*Christóviye Lyúdi*), but are better known under the popular names of "Wanderers" (*Stránniki*), or "Fugitives" (*Beguny*). Of all the sects they are the most hostile to the existing political and social organization. Not content with condemning the military conscription, the payment of taxes, the acceptance of passports, and everything connected with the civil and ecclesiastical authorities, they consider it sinful to live peaceably among an Orthodox— that is, according to their belief, a heretical—population, and to have dealings with any who do not share their extreme views. Holding the Antichrist doctrine in its extreme form, they declare that Tsars are the vessels of Satan, that the Established Church is the dwelling place of the Father of Lies, and that all who submit to the authorities are children of the Devil. According to this creed, those who wish to escape from the wrath to come must have neither houses nor fixed places of abode, must sever all ties that bind them to the world, and must wander about continually from place to place. True Christians are but strangers and pilgrims in the present life, and whoso binds himself to the world will perish with the world.

Such is the theory of these Wanderers, but among them, as among the less fanatical sects, practical necessities have produced concessions and compromises. As it is impossible to lead a nomadic life in Russian forests, the Wanderers have been compelled to admit into their ranks what may be called lay brethren—men who nominally belong to the sect, but who live like ordinary mortals and have some rational way of gaining a livelihood. These latter live in the villages or towns, support themselves by agriculture or trade, accept passports from the authorities, pay their taxes regularly, and conduct themselves in all outward respects like loyal subjects. Their chief religious duty consists in giving food and shelter to their more zealous brethren, who have adopted a vagabond life in practice as well as in theory. It is only when they feel death approaching that they consider it necessary to separate themselves from the heretical world, and they effect this by having themselves carried out to some neighboring wood—or into a garden if there is no wood at hand—where they may die in the open air.

Thus, we see, there is among the Russian Nonconformist sects what may be called a gradation of fanaticism, in which is reflected the history of the Great Schism. In the Wanderers we have the representatives of those who adopted and preserved the Antichrist doctrine in its extreme form—the successors of those who fled to the forests to escape from the rage of the Beast and to await the second coming of Christ. In the Philipists we have the representatives of those who adopted these ideas in a somewhat softer form, and who came to recognize the necessity of having some regular means of subsistence until the last trump should be heard. The Theodosians represent those who were in theory at one with the preceding category, but who, having less religious fanaticism, considered it necessary to yield to force and make peace with the Government without sacrificing their convictions. In the Pomórtsi we see those who preserved only the religious ideas of the schism, and became reconciled with the civil power. Lastly, we have the Old Ritualists, who differed from all the other sects in retaining the old ordinances, and who simply rejected the spiritual authority of the dominant Church. Besides these chief sections of the Nonconformists there are a great many minor denominations (tólki), differing from each other on minor points of doctrine. In certain districts, it is said, nearly every village has one or two independent sects. This is especially the case among the Don Cossacks and the Cossacks of the Ural, who are in part descendants of the men who fled from the early persecutions.

Of all the sects the Old Ritualists stand nearest to the official Church. They hold the same dogmas, practice the same rites, and differ only in trifling ceremonial matters, which few people consider essential. In the hope of inducing them to return to the official fold the Government created at the beginning of last century special churches, in which they were allowed to retain their ceremonial peculiarities on condition of accepting regularly consecrated priests and submitting to ecclesiastical jurisdiction. As yet the design has not met with much success. The great majority of the Old Ritualists regard it as a trap, and assert that the Church in making this concession has been guilty of self-contradiction. "The Ecclesiastical Council of Moscow," they say, "anathematized our forefathers for holding to the old ritual, and declared that the whole course of nature would be changed sooner than the curse be withdrawn. The course of nature has not been changed, but the anathema has been canceled." This argument ought to have a certain weight with those who believe in the infallibility of Ecclesiastical Councils.

Towards the Priestless People the Government has always acted in a much less conciliatory spirit. Its severity has been sometimes justified on the ground that sectarianism has had a political as well as a religious significance. A State like Russia cannot overlook the existence of sects which preach the duty of systematic resistance to the civil and ecclesiastical authorities and hold doctrines which lead to the grossest immorality. This argument, it must be admitted, is not without a certain force, but it seems to me that the policy adopted tended to increase rather than diminish the evils which it sought to cure. Instead of dispelling the absurd idea that the Tsar was Antichrist by a system of strict and even-handed justice, punishing merely actual crimes and delinquencies, the Government confirmed the notion in the minds of thousands by persecuting those who had committed no crime and who desired merely to worship God according to their conscience. Above all it erred in opposing and punishing those marriages which, though legally irregular, were the best pos-

sible means of diminishing fanaticism, by leading back the
fanatics to healthy social life. Fortunately these errors have
now been abandoned. A policy of greater clemency and
conciliation has been adopted, and has proved much more
efficacious than persecution. The Dissenters have not returned to the official fold, but they have lost much of their
old fanaticism and exclusiveness.

In respect of numbers the sectarians compose a very
formidable body. Of Old Ritualists and Priestless People
there are, it is said, no less than eleven millions; and the
Protestant and Fantastical sects comprise probably about
five millions more. If these numbers be correct, the sectarians constitute about a tenth of the whole population of the
Empire. They count in their ranks none of the nobles—
none of the so-called enlightened class—but they include
in their number a respectable proportion of the peasants,
a third of the rich merchant class, the majority of the Don
Cossacks, and nearly all the Cossacks of the Ural.

Under these circumstances it is important to know how
far the sectarians are politically disaffected. Some people
imagine that in the event of an insurrection or a foreign
invasion they might rise against the Government, whilst
others believe that this supposed danger is purely imaginary. For my own part I agree with the latter opinion,
which is strongly supported by the history of many important events, such as the French invasion in 1812, the
Crimean War, the Polish insurrection of 1863, and the war
with Japan. In none of these troublous times have there
been any religious disturbances. The great majority of the
Schismatics and heretics are, I believe, loyal subjects of
the Tsar. The more violent sects, which are alone capable
of active hostility against the authorities, are weak in numbers, and regard all outsiders with such profound mistrust
that they are wholly impervious to inflammatory influences from without. Even if all the sects were capable of
active hostility, they would not be nearly so formidable as
their numbers seem to indicate, for they are hostile to each
other, and are wholly incapable of combining for a common purpose.

Though sectarianism is thus by no means a serious political danger, it has nevertheless a considerable political

significance. It proves that the Russian people is by no means so docile and pliable as is commonly supposed, and that it is capable of showing a stubborn, passive resistance to authority when it believes great interests to be at stake. The dogged energy which it has displayed in asserting for centuries its religious liberty may perhaps some day be employed in the arena of secular politics.

CHAPTER · XXII

୶ଚ୍ଚ ବ୍ଚ୶

Church and State

FROM the curious world of heretics and Dissenters let us pass now to the Russian Orthodox Church, to which the great majority of the Russian people belong. It has played an important part in the national history, and has exercised a powerful influence in the formation of the national character.

Russians are in the habit of patriotically and proudly congratulating themselves on the fact that their forefathers always resisted successfully the aggressive tendencies of the Papacy, but it may be doubted whether, from a worldly point of view, the freedom from Papal authority has been an unmixed blessing for the country. If the Popes failed to realize their grand design of creating a vast European empire based on theocratic principles, they succeeded at least in inspiring with a feeling of brotherhood and a vague consciousness of common interest all the nations which acknowledged their spiritual supremacy. These nations, whilst remaining politically independent and frequently coming into hostile contact with each other, all looked to Rome as the capital of the Christian world, and to the Pope as the highest terrestrial authority. Though the Church did not annihilate nationality, it made a wide breach in the political barriers, and formed a channel for international communication by which the social and intellectual progress of each nation became known to all the other members of the great Christian confederacy. Throughout the length and breadth of the Papal Commonwealth, educated men had a common language, a common literature, a common scientific method, and to a certain extent a common jurisprudence. Western Christendom was thus all through the Middle Ages not merely an abstract conception or a geographical expression: if not a political, it was at least a religious and intellectual unit, and all the countries of which it was composed benefited more or less by the connection.

For centuries Russia stood outside of this religious and intellectual confederation, for her Church connected her not with Rome, but with Constantinople, and Papal Europe looked upon her as belonging to the barbarous East. When the Mongol hosts swept over her plains, burned her towns and villages, and finally incorporated her into the great empire of Genghis Khan, the so-called Christian world took no interest in the struggle except in so far as its own safety was threatened. And as time wore on, the barriers which separated the two great sections of Christendom became more and more formidable. The aggressive pretensions and ambitious schemes of the Vatican produced in the Greek Orthodox world a profound antipathy to the Roman Catholic Church and to Western influence of every kind. So strong was this aversion that when the nations of the West awakened in the fifteenth and sixteenth centuries from their intellectual lethargy and began to move forward on the path of intellectual and material progress, Russia not only remained unmoved, but looked on the new civilization with suspicion and fear as a thing heretical and accursed. We have here one of the chief reasons why Russia, at the present day, is in many respects less civilized than the nations of Western Europe.

But it is not merely in this negative way that the acceptance of Christianity from Constantinople has affected the fate of Russia. The Greek Church, whilst excluding Roman Catholic civilization, exerted at the same time a powerful positive influence on the historical development of the nation.

The Church of the West inherited from old Rome something of that logical, juridical, administrative spirit which had created the Roman law, and something of that ambition and dogged, energetic perseverance that had formed nearly the whole known world into a great centralized empire. The Bishops of Rome early conceived the design of reconstructing that old empire on a new basis, and long strove to create a universal Christian theocratic State, in which kings and other civil authorities should be the subordinates of Christ's Vicar upon earth. The Eastern Church, on the contrary, has remained true to her Byzantine traditions, and has never dreamed of such lofty pretensions. Accustomed to lean on the civil power, she has always been content to play a secondary part, and has never strenuously resisted the formation of national churches.

For about two centuries after the introduction of Christianity—from 988 till 1240—Russia formed, ecclesiastically speaking, part of the Patriarchate of Constantinople. The metropolitans and the bishops were Greeks by birth and education, and the ecclesiastical administration was guided and controlled by the Byzantine Patriarchs. But from the time of the Mongol invasion, when the communications with Constantinople became more difficult and educated native priests had become more numerous, this complete dependence on the Patriarch of Constantinople ceased. The Princes gradually arrogated to themselves the right of choosing the Metropolitan of Kiev—who was at that time the chief ecclesiastical dignitary in Russia—and merely sent their nominees to Constantinople for consecration. About 1448 this formality came to be dispensed with, and the Metropolitan was commonly consecrated by a Council of Russian bishops. A further step in the direction of ecclesiastical autonomy was taken in 1589, when the Tsar succeeded in procuring the consecration of a Russian Patriarch, equal in dignity and authority to the Patriarchs of Constantinople, Jerusalem, Antioch, and Alexandria.

In all matters of external form the Patriarch of Moscow was a very important personage. He exercised a certain influence in civil as well as ecclesiastical affairs, bore the official title of "Great Lord" (*Veliki Gosudár*), which had previously been reserved for the civil head of the State and habitually received from the people scarcely less veneration than the Tsar himself. But in reality he possessed very little independent power. The Tsar was the real ruler in ecclesiastical as well as in civil affairs.[1]

[1] As this is frequently denied by Russians, it may be well to quote one authority out of many that might be cited. Bishop

The Russian Patriarchate came to an end in the time of
Peter the Great. Peter wished, among other things, to
reform the ecclesiastical administration, and to introduce
into his country many novelties which the majority of the
clergy and of the people regarded as heretical; and he
clearly perceived that a bigoted, energetic Patriarch might
throw considerable obstacles in his way, and cause him infinite annoyance. Though such a Patriarch might be deposed without any flagrant violation of the canonical formalities, the operation would necessarily be attended with
great trouble and loss of time. Peter was no friend of
roundabout, tortuous methods, and preferred to remove
the difficulty in his usual thorough, violent fashion. When
the Patriarch Adrian died, the customary short interregnum was prolonged for twenty years, and when the people
had thus become accustomed to having no Patriarch, it
was announced that no more Patriarchs would be elected.
Their place was supplied by an ecclesiastical council, or
Synod, in which, as a contemporary explained, "the main-
spring was Peter's power, and the pendulum his understanding." The great autocrat justly considered that such a
Council could be much more easily managed than a stubborn Patriarch, and the wisdom of the measure has been
duly appreciated by succeeding sovereigns. Though the
idea of re-establishing the Patriarchate has more than once
been raised, and is not yet extinct, it has never been carried into execution. The Holy Synod remains the highest
ecclesiastical authority.

But the Emperor? What is his relation to the Synod
and to the Church in general?

This is a question about which zealous Orthodox Rus-

Makarii, whose erudition and good faith are alike above suspicion, says of Dmitri of the Don: "He arrogated to himself full,
unconditional power over the Head of the Russian Church, and
through him over the whole Russian Church itself" (*Istoriya
Rússkoi Tserkvi*, V., p. 101). This is said of a Grand Prince who
had strong rivals and had to treat the Church as an ally. When
the Grand Princes became Tsars and had no longer any rivals,
their power was certainly not diminished. Any further confirmation that may be required will be found in the life of the famous
Patriarch Nikon.

sians are extremely sensitive. If a foreigner ventures to hint
in their presence that the Emperor seems to have a considerable influence in the Church, he may inadvertently
produce a little outburst of patriotic warmth and virtuous
indignation. The truth is that many Russians have a pet
theory on this subject, and have at the same time a dim
consciousness that the theory is not quite in accordance
with reality. They hold theoretically that the Orthodox
Church has no "Head" but Christ, and is in some peculiar
undefined sense entirely independent of all terrestrial authority. In this respect it is often contrasted with the Anglican Church, much to the disadvantage of the latter; and
the supposed differences between the two are made a
theme for semireligious, semipatriotic exultation. Khomiakóv, for instance, in one of his most vigorous poems, predicted that God would one day take the destiny of the
world out of the hands of England in order to give it to
Russia, and he adduced as one of the reasons for this
transfer the fact that England "has chained, with sacrile-
gious hand, the Church of God to the pedestal of the vain
earthly power." So far the theory. As to the facts, it is unquestionable that the Tsar exercises a much greater influence in ecclesiastical affairs than the King and Parliament
in England. All who know the internal history of Russia
are aware that the Government does not draw a clear line
of distinction between the temporal and the spiritual, and
that it occasionally uses the ecclesiastical organization for
political purposes.

What, then, are the relations between Church and State?

To avoid confusion, we must carefully distinguish between the Eastern Orthodox Church as a whole and that
section of it which is known as the Russian Church.

The Eastern Orthodox Church[2] is, properly speaking, a
confederation of independent churches without any central authority—a unity founded on the possession of a common dogma and on the theoretical but now unrealizable
possibility of holding Ecumenical Councils. The Russian
National Church is one of the members of this ecclesiastical confederation. In matters of faith it is bound by the

[2] Or Greek Orthodox Church, as it is sometimes called.

decisions of the ancient Ecumenical Councils, but in all other respects it enjoys complete independence and autonomy.

In relation to the Orthodox Church as a whole the Emperor of Russia is nothing more than a simple member, and can no more interfere with its dogmas or ceremonial than a King of Italy or an Emperor of the French could modify Roman Catholic theology; but in relation to the Russian National Church his position is peculiar. He is described in one of the fundamental laws as "the supreme defender and preserver of the dogmas of the dominant faith," and immediately afterwards it is said that "the Autocratic Power acts in the ecclesiastical administration by means of the most Holy Governing Synod, created by it." [3] This describes very fairly the relations between the Emperor and the Church. He is merely the defender of the dogmas, and cannot in the least modify them; but he is at the same time the chief administrator, and uses the Synod as an instrument.

Some ingenious people who wish to prove that the creation of the Synod was not an innovation represent the institution as a resuscitation of the ancient local councils; but this view is utterly untenable. The Synod is not a council of deputies from various sections of the Church, but a permanent college, or ecclesiastical senate, the members of which are appointed and dismissed by the Emperor as he thinks fit. It has no independent legislative authority, for its legislative projects do not become law till they have received the Imperial sanction; and they are always published, not in the name of the Church, but in the name of the Supreme Power. Even in matters of simple administration it is not independent, for all its resolutions require the consent of the Procureur, a layman nominated by his Majesty. In theory this functionary protests only against those resolutions which are not in accordance with the civil law of the country; but as he alone has the right to address the Emperor directly on ecclesiastical concerns, and as all communications between the Emperor and the Synod pass through his hands, he possesses in reality considerable

[3] Svod Zakonov I., §§ 42, 43.

power. Besides this, he can always influence the individual members by holding out prospects of advancement and decorations, and if this device fails, he can make the refractory members retire, and fill up their places with men of more pliant disposition. A Council constituted in this way cannot, of course, display much independence of thought or action, especially in a country like Russia, where no one ventures to oppose openly the Imperial will.

It must not, however, be supposed that the Russian ecclesiastics regard the Imperial authority with jealousy or dislike. They are all most loyal subjects, and generally warm adherents of autocracy. Those ideas of ecclesiastical independence which are so common in Western Europe, and that spirit of opposition to the civil power which animates the Roman Catholic clergy, are entirely foreign to their minds. If a bishop sometimes complains to an intimate friend that he has been brought to St. Petersburg and made a member of the Synod merely to append his signature to official papers and to give his consent to foregone conclusions, his displeasure is directed, not against the Emperor, but against the Procureur. He is full of loyalty and devotion to the Tsar, and has no desire to see his Majesty excluded from all influence in ecclesiastical affairs, but he feels saddened and humiliated when he finds that the whole government of the Church is in the hands of a lay functionary, who may be a military man, and who looks at all matters from a layman's point of view.

This close connection between Church and State and the thoroughly national character of the Russian Church is well illustrated by the history of the local ecclesiastical administration. The civil and the ecclesiastical administration have always had the same character and have always been modified by the same influences. The terrorism which was largely used by the Muscovite Tsars and brought to a climax by Peter the Great appeared equally in both. In the episcopal circulars, as in the Imperial ukases, we find frequent mention of "most cruel corporal punishment," "cruel punishment with whips, so that the delinquent and others may not acquire the habit of practicing such insolence," and much more of the same kind. And these terribly severe measures were sometimes directed against very

venial offenses. The Bishop of Vologda, for instance, in
1748 decrees "cruel corporal punishment" against priests
who wear coarse and ragged clothes,[4] and the records of
the Consistorial courts contain abundant proof that such
decrees might be rigorously executed. When Catherine II
introduced a more humane spirit into the civil administration, corporal punishment was at once abolished in the
Consistorial courts, and the procedure was modified according to the accepted maxims of civil jurisprudence. But
I must not weary the reader with tiresome historical details. Suffice it to say that, from the time of Peter the Great
downwards, the character of all the more energetic sovereigns is reflected in the history of the ecclesiastical administration.

Each province, or "government," forms a diocese, and
the bishop, like the civil governor, has a Council which
theoretically controls his power, but practically has no
controlling influence whatever. The Consistorial Council,
which has in the theory of ecclesiastical procedure a very
imposing appearance, is in reality the bishop's *chancellerie,*
and its members are little more than secretaries, whose
chief object is to make themselves agreeable to their superior. And it must be confessed that, so long as they remain what they are, the less power they possess the better
it will be for those who have the misfortune to be under
their jurisdiction. The higher dignitaries have at least
larger aims and a certain consciousness of the dignity of
their position; but the lower officials, who have no such
healthy restraints and receive ridiculously small salaries,
grossly misuse the little authority which they possess, and
habitually pilfer and extort in the most shameless manner.
The Consistories are, in fact, what the public offices were
in the time of Nicholas I.

The higher ecclesiastical administration has always been
in the hands of the monks, or "Black Clergy," as they are
commonly termed, who form a large and influential class.
The monks who first settled in Russia were, like those who
first visited northwestern Europe, men of the earnest, ascetic, missionary type. Filled with zeal for the glory of

[4] Známenski, *Prikhódskoe Dukhovénstvo v Rossíi so vrémeni
refórmy Petrá,* Kazán, 1873.

God and the salvation of souls, they took little or no thought for the morrow, and devoutly believed that their Heavenly Father, without whose knowledge no sparrow falls to the ground, would provide for their humble wants. Poor, clad in rags, eating the most simple fare, and ever ready to share what they had with anyone poorer than themselves, they performed faithfully and earnestly the work which their Master had given them to do. But this ideal of monastic life soon gave way in Russia, as in the West, to practices less simple and austere. By the liberal donations and bequests of the faithful the monasteries became rich in gold, in silver, in precious stones, and above all in land and serfs. Troitsa, for instance, possessed at one time 120,000 serfs and a proportionate amount of land, and it is said that at the beginning of the eighteenth century more than a fourth of the entire population had fallen under the jurisdiction of the Church. Many of the monasteries engaged in commerce, and the monks were, if we may credit Fletcher, who visited Russia in 1588, the most intelligent merchants of the country.

During the eighteenth century the Church lands were secularized, and the serfs of the Church became serfs of the State. This was a severe blow for the monasteries, but it did not prove fatal, as many people predicted. Some monasteries were abolished and others were reduced to extreme poverty, but many survived and prospered. These could no longer possess serfs, but they had still three sources of revenue: a limited amount of real property, Government subsidies, and the voluntary offerings of the faithful. At present there are about 500 monastic establishments, and the great majority of them, though not wealthy, have revenues more than sufficient to satisfy all the requirements of an ascetic life.

Thus in Russia, as in Western Europe, the history of monastic institutions is composed of three chapters, which may be briefly entitled: asceticism and missionary enterprise; wealth, luxury, and corruption; secularization of property and decline. But between Eastern and Western monasticism there is at least one marked difference. The monasticism of the West made at various epochs of its history a vigorous, spontaneous effort at self-regeneration, which found expression in the foundation of separate Orders, each of which proposed to itself some special aim—some special sphere of usefulness. In Russia we find no similar phenomenon. Here the monasteries never deviated from the rules of St. Basil, which restrict the members to religious ceremonies, prayer, and contemplation. From time to time a solitary individual raised his voice against the prevailing abuses, or retired from his monastery to spend the remainder of his days in ascetic solitude; but neither in the monastic population as a whole, nor in any particular monastery, do we find at any time a spontaneous, vigorous movement towards reform. During the last two hundred years reforms have certainly been effected, but they have all been the work of the civil power, and in the realization of them the monks have shown little more than the virtue of resignation. Here, as elsewhere, we have evidence of that inertness, apathy, and want of spontaneous vigor which form one of the most characteristic traits of Russian national life. In this, as in other departments of national activity, the spring of action has lain not in the people, but in the Government.

It is only fair to the monks to state that in their dislike of progress and change of every kind they merely reflect the traditional spirit of the Church to which they belong. The Russian Church, like the Eastern Orthodox Church generally, is essentially conservative. Anything in the nature of a religious revival is foreign to her traditions and character. *Quieta non movere* is her fundamental principle of conduct. She prides herself on being above terrestrial influences.

The modifications that have been made in her administrative organization have not affected her inner nature. In spirit and character she is now what she was under the Patriarchs in the time of the Muscovite Tsars, holding fast to the promise that no jot or tittle shall pass from the law till all be fulfilled. To those who talk about the requirements of modern life and modern science she turns a deaf ear. Partly from the predominance which she gives to the ceremonial element, partly from the fact that her chief aim is to preserve unmodified the doctrine and ceremonial as determined by the early Ecumenical Councils, and

partly from the low state of general culture among the
clergy, she has ever remained outside of the intellectual
movements. The attempts of the Roman Catholic Church
to develop the traditional dogmas by definition and de-
duction, and the efforts of Protestants to reconcile their
creeds with progressive science and the ever varying intellectual currents of the time, are alike foreign to her nature. Hence she has produced no profound theological
treatises conceived in a philosophical spirit, and has made
no attempt to combat the spirit of infidelity in its modern
forms. Profoundly convinced that her position is impregnable, she has "let the nations rave," and scarcely deigned
to cast a glance at their intellectual and religious struggles.
In a word, she is "in the world, but not of it."

If we wish to see represented in a visible form the peculiar characteristics of the Russian Church, we have only
to glance at Russian religious art, and compare it with that
of Western Europe. In the West, from the time of the
Renaissance downwards, religious art has kept pace with
artistic progress. Gradually it emancipated itself from archaic forms and childish symbolism, converted the lifeless typical figures into living individuals, lit up their dull
eyes and expressionless faces with human intelligence and
human feeling, and finally aimed at archeological accuracy in costume and other details. Thus in the West the
Icon grew slowly into the naturalistic portrait, and the rude
symbolical groups developed gradually into highly finished historical pictures. In Russia the history of religious
art has been entirely different. Instead of distinctive
schools of painting and great religious artists, there has
been merely an anonymous traditional craft, destitute of
any artistic individuality. In all the productions of this
craft the old Byzantine forms have been faithfully and
rigorously preserved, and we can see reflected in the modern Icons—stiff, archaic, expressionless—the immobility
of the Eastern Church in general, and of the Russian
Church in particular.

To the Roman Catholic, who struggles against science
as soon as it contradicts traditional conceptions, and to the
Protestant, who strives to bring his religious beliefs into
accordance with his scientific knowledge, the Russian

Church may seem to resemble an antediluvian petri-
faction, or a cumbrous line-of-battle ship that has been
long stranded. It must be confessed, however, that the
serene inactivity for which she is distinguished has had
very valuable practical consequences. The Russian clergy
have neither that haughty, aggressive intolerance which
characterizes their Roman Catholic brethren, nor that bitter, uncharitable, sectarian spirit which is too often to be
found among Protestants. They allow not only to heretics,
but also to members of their own communion, the most
complete intellectual freedom, and never think of anathematizing anyone for his scientific or unscientific opinions. All that they demand is that those who have been
born within the pale of Orthodoxy should show the
Church a certain nominal allegiance; and in this matter of
allegiance they are by no means very exacting. So long as
a member refrains from openly attacking the Church and
from going over to another confession, he may entirely
neglect all religious ordinances and publicly profess scientific theories logically inconsistent with any kind of dogmatic religious belief, without the slightest danger of incurring ecclesiastical censure.

This apathetic tolerance may be partly explained by the
national character, but it is also to some extent due to the
peculiar relations between Church and State. The Government vigilantly protects the Church from attack, and at
the same time prevents her from attacking her enemies.
Hence religious questions are never discussed in the press,
and the ecclesiastical literature is all historical, homiletic,
or devotional. The authorities allow public oral discussions
to be held during Lent in the Kremlin of Moscow between
members of the State Church and Old Ritualists; but these
debates are not theological in our sense of the term. They
turn exclusively on details of Church History, and on the
minutiae of ceremonial observance.

From time to time there has been a good deal of vague
talk about a possible union of the Russian and Anglican
Churches. If by "union" is meant simply union in the
bonds of brotherly love, there can be, of course, no objection to any amount of such *pia desideria;* but if anything
more real and practical is intended, the project is an

absurdity. A real union of the Russian and Anglican
Churches would be as difficult of realization, and is as un-
desirable, as a union of the Russian Duma and the British
House of Commons.[4]

[4] I suppose that the more serious partisans of the union
scheme mean union with the Eastern Orthodox, and not with
the Russian, Church. To them the above remarks are not addressed. Their scheme is, in my opinion, unrealizable and undesirable, but it contains nothing absurd.

6 : *Industrialization and Revolution*

CHAPTER XXIII

இந்த இ

Revolutionary Nihilism
and the Reaction

THE rapidly increasing enthusiasm for reform after the Crimean War did not confine itself to practical measures such as the emancipation of the serfs, the creation of local self-government, and the thorough reorganization of the law courts and legal procedure. In the younger section of the educated classes, and especially among the students of the universities and technical colleges, it produced a feverish intellectual excitement and wild aspirations which culminated in what is commonly known as Nihilism.

In a preceding chapter I pointed out that during the last two centuries all the important intellectual movements in Western Europe have been reflected in Russia, and that these reflections have generally been what may fairly be termed exaggerated and distorted reproductions of the originals.[1] Roughly speaking, the Nihilist movement in Russia may be described as the exaggerated, distorted reflection of the earlier Socialist movements of the West; but it has local peculiarities and local coloring which deserve attention.

The Russian educated classes had been well prepared by their past history for the reception and rapid development of the Socialist virus. For a century and a half the country had been subjected to a series of drastic changes, administrative and social, by the energetic action of the

[1] *See* Chapter XII.

autocratic power, with little spontaneous co-operation on the part of the people. In a nation with such a history, Socialistic ideas naturally found favor, because all Socialist systems, until quite recent times, were founded on the assumption that political and social progress must be the result not of slow natural development, but rather of philosophic speculation, legislative wisdom, and administrative energy.

This assumption lay at the bottom of the reform enthusiasm in St. Petersburg at the commencement of Alexander II's reign. Russia might be radically transformed, it was thought, politically and socially, according to abstract scientific principles, in the space of a few years, and be thereby raised to the level of West European civilization, or even higher. The older nations had for centuries groped in darkness, or stumbled along in the faint light of practical experience, and consequently their progress had been slow and uncertain. For Russia there was no necessity to follow such devious, unexplored paths. She ought to profit by the experience of her elder sisters, and avoid the errors into which they had fallen. Nor was it difficult to ascertain what these errors were, because they had been discovered, examined and explained by the most eminent thinkers of France, Germany and England, and efficient remedies had been prescribed. Russian reformers had merely to study and apply the conclusions at which these eminent authorities had arrived, and their task would be greatly facilitated by the fact that they could operate on virgin soil, untrammeled by the feudal traditions, religious superstitions, metaphysical conceptions, romantic illusions, aristocratic prejudices, and similar obstacles to social and political progress which existed in Western Europe.

Such was the extraordinary intellectual atmosphere in which the Russian educated classes lived during the early years of the sixties. On "the men with aspirations" who had longed in vain for more light and more public activity under the obscurantist, repressive regime of the preceding reign, it had an intoxicating effect. The more excitable and sanguine amongst them now believed seriously that they had discovered a convenient short cut to national prosperity, and that for Russia a grandiose social and political milennium was at hand.[2]

In these circumstances it is not surprising that one of the most prominent characteristics of the time was a boundless, childlike faith in the so-called "latest results of science." Infallible science was supposed to have found the solution of all political and social problems. What a reformer had to do—and who was not a would-be reformer in those days?—was merely to study the best authorities. Their works had been long rigidly excluded by the press censure, and now that it was possible to obtain them, they were read with avidity.

Chief among the new, infallible prophets whose works were profoundly venerated was Auguste Comte, the inventor of Positivism. In his classification of the sciences, the crowning of the edifice was sociology, which taught how to organize human society on scientific principles. Russia had merely to adopt the principles laid down and expounded at great length in the *Cours de Philosophie Positive*. There Comte explained that humanity had to pass through three stages of intellectual development—the religious, the metaphysical, and the positive—and that the most advanced nations, after spending centuries in the first two, were entering on the third. Russia must endeavor, therefore, to get into the positive stage as quickly as possible, and there was reason to believe that, in consequence of certain ethnographical and historical peculiarities, she could make the transition more quickly than other nations. After Comte's works, the book which found, for a time, most favor was Buckle's *History of Civilisation*, which seemed to reduce history and progress to a matter of statistics, and which laid down the principle that progress is always in the inverse ratio of the influence of theological conceptions. This principle was regarded as of great practical importance, and the conclusion drawn from it was that rapid national progress was certain if only the influ-

---

[2] I was not myself in St. Petersburg at that period, but on arriving a few years afterwards I became intimately acquainted with men and women who had lived through it, and who still retained much of their early enthusiasm.

ence of religion and theology could be destroyed. Very popular, too, was John Stuart Mill, because he was "imbued with enthusiasm for humanity and female emancipation"; and in his tract on Utilitarianism he showed that morality was simply the crystallized experience of many generations as to what was most conducive to the greatest good of the greatest number. The minor prophets of the time, among whom Büchner occupied a prominent place, are too numerous to mention.

Strange to say, the newest and most advanced doctrines appeared regularly, under a very thin and transparent veil, in the St. Petersburg daily press, and especially in the thick monthly magazines, which were as big as, or bigger than, our venerable quarterlies. The art of writing and reading "between the lines," not altogether unknown under the Draconian regime of Nicholas I, was now developed to such a marvelous extent that almost anything could be written clearly enough to be understood by the initiated without calling forth the thunderbolts of the press censure, which was now only intermittently severe. Indeed, the press censors themselves were sometimes carried away by the reform enthusiasm. One of them long afterwards related to me that during "the mad time," as he called it, in the course of a single year he had received from his superiors no less than seventeen reprimands for passing objectionable articles without remark.

The movement found its warmest partisans among the students and young literary men, but not a few graybeards were to be found among the youthful apostles. All who read the periodical literature became more or less imbued with the new spirit; but it must be presumed that many of those who discoursed most eloquently had no clear idea of what they were talking about; for even at a later date, when the novices had had time to acquaint themselves with the doctrines they professed, I often encountered the most astounding ignorance. Let me give one instance by way of illustration: A young gentleman who was in the habit of talking glibly about the necessity for scientifically reorganizing human society, declared to me one day that not only sociology, but also biology, should be taken into consideration. Confessing my com-

plete ignorance of the latter science, I requested him to enlighten me by giving me an instance of a biological principle which could be applied to social regeneration. He
looked confused, and tried to ride out of the difficulty on
vague general phrases; but I persistently kept him to the
point, and maliciously suggested that as an alternative he
might cite to me a biological principle which could *not*
be used for such a purpose. Again he failed, and it became
evident to all present that of biology, about which he
talked so often, he knew absolutely nothing but the name!
After this, I frequently employed the same pseudo-Socratic
method of discussion, and very often with a similar result.
Not one in fifty, perhaps, ever attempted to reduce the
current hazy conceptions to a concrete form. The enthusiasm was not the less intense, however, on that account.

At first the partisans of the movement seemed desirous
of assisting, rather than of opposing or undermining, the
Government, and so long as they merely talked academi-
cally about scientific principles and similar vague entities,
the Government felt no necessity for energetic interference; but as early as 1861 symptoms of a change in the
character of the movement became apparent. A secret
society of officers organized a small printing press in
the building of the Headquarters Staff and issued
clandestinely three numbers of a periodical called the
Velikoruss (*Great Russian*), which advocated administrative reform, the convocation of a constituent assembly,
and the emancipation of Poland from Russian rule. A few
months later (April, 1862) a seditious proclamation appeared, professing to emanate from a central revolutionary
committee, and declaring that the Románovs must expiate
with their blood the misery of the people.

These symptoms of an underground revolutionary agitation caused alarm in the official world, and repressive measures were at once adopted. Sunday schools for the working
classes, reading rooms, students' clubs, and similar institutions which might be used for purposes of revolutionary
propaganda were closed; several trials for political offenses
took place; the most popular of the monthly periodicals,
the *Contemporary*, was suspended for a time, and its
editor, Chernyshevski, arrested. There was nothing to show

that Chernyshevski was implicated in any treasonable designs, but he was undoubtedly the leader of a group of youthful writers whose aspirations went far beyond the intentions of the Government, and it was thought desirable to counteract his influence by shutting him up in prison. Here he wrote and published, with the permission of the authorities and the *imprimatur* of the press censure, a novel called *Chto delat'?* (What is to be done?), which was regarded at first as a most harmless production, but which is now considered one of the most influential and baneful works in the whole range of Nihilist literature. As a novel it had no pretensions to artistic merit, and in ordinary times it would have attracted little or no attention, but it put into concrete shape many of the vague Socialist and Communist notions that were at the moment floating about in the intellectual atmosphere, and it came to be looked upon by the young enthusiasts as a sort of informal manifesto of their new-born faith. It was divided into two parts; in the first was described a group of students living according to the new ideas in open defiance of traditional conventionalities, and in the second was depicted a village organized on the communistic principles recommended by Fourier. The first was supposed to represent the dawn of the new era; the second, the goal to be ultimately attained. When the authorities discovered the mistake they had committed in allowing the book to be published, it was at once confiscated and withdrawn from circulation, whilst the author, after being tried by the Senate, was exiled to northeastern Siberia and kept there for nearly twenty years.[3]

[3] Chernyshevski was a man of encyclopedic knowledge, and specially conversant with political economy. According to the testimony of those who knew him intimately, he was one of the ablest and most sympathetic men of his generation. During his exile a bold attempt was made to rescue him, and very nearly succeeded. A daring youth, disguised as an officer of gendarmes and provided with forged official papers, reached the place where he was confined and procured his release, but the officer in charge had vague suspicions, and insisted on the two travelers being escorted to the next post station by a couple of Cossacks. The rescuer tried to get rid of the escort by means of his revolver, but he failed in the attempt, and the fugitives were

With the arrest and exile of Chernyshevski the young would-be reformers were constrained to recognize that they had no chance of carrying the Government with them in their endeavors to realize their patriotic aspirations. Police supervision over the young generation was increased and all kinds of associations, whether for mutual instruction, mutual aid, or any other purpose, were discouraged or positively forbidden. And it was not merely in the mind of the police that suspicion was aroused. In the opinion of the great majority of moderate, respectable people the young enthusiasts were becoming discredited. The violently seditious proclamations with which they were supposed to sympathize, and a series of destructive fires in St. Petersburg, erroneously attributed to them, frightened timid Liberals and gave the Reactionaries, who had hitherto remained silent, an opportunity of preaching their doctrines with telling effect. The celebrated novelist, Turgenev, long the idol of the young generation, had inadvertently, in *Fathers and Sons,* invented the term Nihilist, and it at once came to be applied as an opprobrious epithet, notwithstanding the efforts of Pisarev, a popular writer of remarkable talent, to prove to the public that it ought to be regarded as a term of honor.

Pisarev's defense of Nihilism made no impression outside of his own small circle. According to popular opinion the Nihilists were a band of fanatical young men and women, mostly medical students, who had determined to turn the world upside down and to introduce a new kind of social order, founded on the most advanced principles of social equality and Communism. As a first step towards the great transformation they had reversed the traditional order of things in the matter of *coiffure:* the males allowed their hair to grow long, and the female adepts cut their hair short, adding occasionally the additional badge of blue spectacles. Their unkempt appearance naturally shocked the aesthetic feelings of ordinary people, but to this they were indifferent. They had raised themselves above the

---

arrested. In 1883 Chernyshevski was transferred to the milder climate of Astrakhan, and in 1889 he was allowed to return to his native town, Sarátov, where he died a few months afterwards.

level of popular notions, took no account of so-called public opinion, gloried in Bohemianism, despised Philistine respectability, and rather liked to scandalize old-fashioned people imbued with antiquated prejudices.

This was the ridiculous side of the movement, but underneath the absurdities there was something serious. These young men and women, who were themselves terribly in earnest, were systematically hostile, not only to accepted conventionalities in the matter of dress, but to all manner of shams, hypocrisy, and cant in the broad Carlylean sense of those terms. To the "beautiful souls" of the older generation, who had habitually, in conversation and literature, shed pathetic tears over the defects of Russian social and political organization without ever moving a finger to correct them—especially the landed proprietors who talked and wrote about civilization, culture, and justice while living comfortably on the revenues provided for them by their unfortunate serfs—they had the strongest aversion; and this naturally led them to condemn in strong language the worship of aesthetic culture. But here again they fell into exaggeration. Professing extreme utilitarianism, they explained that the humble shoemaker who practices his craft diligently is, in the true sense, a greater man than a Shakespeare or a Goethe, because humanity has more need of shoes than of dramas and poetry.

Such silly paradoxes provoked, of course, merely a smile of compassion; what alarmed the sensible, respectable "Philistine" was the method of cleansing the Augean stable recommended by these enthusiasts. Having discovered in the course of their desultory reading that most of the ills that flesh is heir to proceed directly or indirectly from uncontrolled sexual passion and the lust of gain, they proposed to seal hermetically these two great sources of crime and misery by abolishing the old-fashioned institutions of marriage and private property. When society, they argued, would be so organized that all the healthy instincts of human nature could find complete and untrammeled satisfaction, there would be no motive or inducement for committing crimes or misdemeanors. For thousands of years humanity had been sailing on a wrong tack. The great lawgivers of the world, religious and civil, in their ignorance of physical science and positivist methods, had created institutions, commonly known as law and morality, which were utterly unfitted to human nature, and then the magistrate and the moralist had endeavored to compel or persuade men and women to conform to them, but their efforts had failed most signally. In vain the police had threatened and punished, and the priests had preached and admonished. Human nature had systematically and obstinately rebelled, and was still rebelling, against the unnatural constraint. It was time, therefore, to try a new system. Instead of continuing, as had been done for thousands of years, to force men and women, as it were, into badly fitting, unelastic clothes which cause intense discomfort and prevent all healthy muscular action, why not adapt the costume to the anatomy and physiology of the human frame? Then the clothes would no longer be rent, and those who wore them would be contented and happy.

Unfortunately for the progress of humanity, there were serious obstacles in the way of this radical change of system. The absurd, antiquated and pernicious institutions and customs were supported by abstruse metaphysical reasons and enshrined in mystical, romantic sentiment, and in this way they might still be preserved for generations unless the axe were laid to the root of the tree. Now, it was said, is the critical moment. Russia must be made to rise at once from the metaphysical to the positivist stage of intellectual development; metaphysical reasoning and romantic sentiment must be rigorously discarded; and everything must be brought to the touchstone of naked practical utility.

One might naturally suppose that men holding such opinions must be materialists of the grossest type—and, indeed, many of them gloried in the name of materialist and atheist—but such an inference would be erroneous. While denouncing metaphysics, they were themselves metaphysicians in so far as they were constantly juggling with abstract conceptions, and letting themselves be guided in their walk and conversation by *à priori* deductions; while ridiculing romanticism, they had romantic sentiment enough to make them sacrifice their time, their property, and sometimes even their life, to the attainment

of an unrealizable ideal; and while congratulating themselves on having passed from the religious to the positivist
stage of intellectual development, they frequently showed
themselves animated with the spirit of the early martyrs!

Rarely have the strange inconsistencies of human nature
been so strikingly exemplified as in these unpractical, anti-
religious fanatics. In dealing with them I might easily,
without very great exaggeration, produce a most amusing
caricature, but I prefer describing them as they really were.
A few years after the period here referred to I knew some
of them intimately, and I must say that, without at all
sharing or sympathizing with their opinions, I could not
help respecting them as honorable, upright, quixotic men
and women who had made great sacrifices for their convictions. One of them whom I have specially in view at
this moment, suffered patiently for years from the utter
shipwreck of his generous illusions, and when he could no
longer hope to see the dawn of a brighter day, he ended
by committing suicide. Yet that man believed himself to
be a realist, a materialist, and a utilitarian of the purest
water, and habitually professed a scathing contempt for
every form of romantic sentiment! In reality he was personally one of the best and most sympathetic men I have ever
known.

To return from this digression. So long as the subversive opinions were veiled in abstract language, they raised
misgivings in only a comparatively small circle; but when
schoolteachers put them into a form suited to the juvenile
mind, they were apt to produce startling effects. In a satirical novel of the time a little girl is represented as coming
to her mother and saying, "Little mamma! Maria Ivan'na,
our new schoolmistress, says there is no God and no Tsar,
and that it is wrong to marry!" Whether such incidents
actually occurred in real life, as several friends assured me,
I am not prepared to say, but certainly people believed
that they might occur in their own families, and that was
quite sufficient to produce alarm even in the ranks of the
Liberals, to say nothing of the rapidly increasing army of
the Reactionaries.

To illustrate the general uneasiness produced in St.
Petersburg, I may quote here a letter written in October,

1861, by a man who occupied one of the highest positions in the Administration. As he had the reputation of being an ultra-Radical who sympathized overmuch with Young Russia, we may assume that he did not take an exceptionally alarmist view of the situation:

"You have not been long absent—merely a few months; but if you returned now, you would be astonished by the progress which the Opposition, one might say the Revolutionary Party, has already made. The disorders in the University do not concern merely the students. I see in the affair the beginning of serious dangers for public tranquillity and the existing order of things. Young people, without distinction of costume, uniform and origin, take part in the street demonstrations. Besides the students of the University there are the students of other institutions, and a mass of people who are students only in name. Among these last are certain gentlemen in long beards and a number of *révolutionnaires* in crinoline, who are of all the most fanatical. Blue collars—the distinguishing mark of the students' uniform—have become the *signe de ralliement*. Almost all the professors and many officers take the part of the students. The newspaper critics openly defend their colleagues. Mikhailov has been convicted of writing, printing and circulating one of the most violent proclamations that ever existed, under the heading, 'To the young generation!' Among the students and the men of letters there is unquestionably an organized conspiracy, which has perhaps leaders outside the literary circle. . . . The police are powerless. They arrest anyone they can lay hands on. About eighty people have been already sent to the fortress and examined, but all this leads to no practical result, because the revolutionary ideas have taken possession of all classes, all ages, all professions, and are publicly expressed in the streets, in the barracks, and in the Ministries. I believe the police itself is carried away by them! What this will lead to, it is difficult to predict. I am very much afraid of some bloody catastrophe. Even if it should not go to such a length im-

mediately, the position of the Government will be
extremely difficult. Its authority is shaken, and all are
convinced that it is powerless, stupid and incapable.
On that point there is the most perfect unanimity
among all parties of all colors, even the most opposite.
The most desperate 'planter' [4] agrees in that respect
with the most desperate Socialist. Meanwhile, those
who have the direction of affairs do almost nothing,
and have no definite aim in view. At present the Emperor is not in the capital, and now, more than at any
other time, there is complete anarchy in the absence
of the master of the house. There is a great deal of
bustle and talk, and all blame they know not whom." [5]

The expected revolution did not take place, but timid
people had no difficulty in perceiving signs of its approach.
The press continued to disseminate, under a more or less
disguised form, ideas which were considered dangerous.
The *Kólokol*, a Russian revolutionary paper published in
London by Herzen and strictly prohibited by the press
censure, found its way in large quantities into the country,
and . . . was read by thousands, including the higher
officials and the Emperor himself, who found it regularly
on his writing table, laid there by some unknown hand. In
St. Petersburg, the arrest of Chernyshevski and the suspen-
sion of his magazine, the *Contemporary*, made the writers a
little more cautious in their mode of expression, but the
spirit of their articles remained unchanged. These energetic, intolerant leaders of public opinion were *novi ho-
mines* not personally connected with the social strata in
which moderate views and retrograde tendencies had begun to prevail. Mostly sons of priests or of petty officials,
they belonged to a recently created literary proletariat,
composed of young men with boundless aspirations and
meager material resources, who earned a precarious sub-

[4] An epithet commonly applied, at the time of the Emancipation, to the partisans of serfage and the defenders of the proprietors' rights.

[5] I found this interesting letter thirty-five years ago among
the private papers of Nicholas Milútin, who played a leading
part as an official in the reforms of the time.

sistence by journalism or by giving lessons in private families. Living habitually in a world of theories and unrestrained by practical acquaintance with public life, they were ready, from the purest and most disinterested motives, to destroy ruthlessly the existing order of things in order to realize their crude notions of social regeneration. Their heated imagination showed them in the near future a New Russia, composed of independent federated Communes, without any bureaucracy or any central power—a happy land in which everybody virtuously and automatically fulfilled his public and private duties, and in which the policemen and all other embodiments of material constraint were wholly superfluous.

Governments are not easily converted to Utopian schemes of that idyllic type, and it is not surprising that even a Government with liberal humanitarian aspirations like that of Alexander II should have become alarmed and should have attempted to stem the current. What is to be regretted is that the repressive measures adopted were a little too Oriental in their character. Scores of young students of both sexes—for the Nihilist army included a strong female contingent—were secretly arrested and confined for months in unwholesome prisons, and many of them were finally exiled, without any regular trial, to distant provinces in European Russia or to Siberia. Their exile, it is true, was not at all so terrible as is commonly supposed, because political exiles are not usually confined in prisons or compelled to labor in the mines, but are obliged merely to reside at a given place under police supervision. Still, such punishment was severe enough for educated young men and women, especially when their lot was cast among a population composed exclusively of peasants and small shopkeepers or of Siberian aborigines, and where there were no means of satisfying the most elementary intellectual wants. For those who had no private resources the punishment was particularly severe, because the Government granted merely a miserable monthly pittance, hardly sufficient to purchase food of the coarsest kind, and there was rarely an opportunity of adding to the meager official allowance by intellectual or manual labor. In all cases the treatment accorded to the exiles wounded their sense of justice and increased the existing discontent among their friends and acquaintances. Instead of acting as a deterrent, the system produced a feeling of profound indignation against the authorities, and ultimately transformed not a few sentimental dreamers into active conspirators.

At first there was no conspiracy or regularly organized secret society, and nothing of which the criminal law in Western Europe could have taken cognizance. Students met in each other's rooms to discuss prohibited books on political and social science, and occasionally short essays on the subjects discussed were written in a revolutionary spirit by members of the coterie. This was called mutual instruction. Between the various coteries or groups there were private personal relations, not only in the capital, but also in the provinces, so that manuscripts and printed papers could be transmitted from one group to another. From time to time the police captured these academic disquisitions, and made raids on the meetings of students who had come together merely for conversation and discussion; and the fresh arrests caused by these incidents increased the hostility to the Government.

In the letter above quoted it is said that the revolutionary ideas had taken possession of all classes, all ages, and all professions. This may have been true with regard to St. Petersburg, but it could not have been said of the provinces. There the landed proprietors were in a very different frame of mind. They had to struggle with a multitude of urgent practical affairs which left them little time for idyllic dreaming about an imaginary millennium. Their serfs had been emancipated, and what remained to them of their estates had to be reorganized on the basis of free labor. Into the semichaotic state of things created by such far-reaching changes, legal and economic, they did not wish to see any more confusion introduced, and they did not at all feel that they could dispense with the Central Government and the policeman. On the contrary, the Central Government was urgently needed in order to obtain a little ready money wherewith to reorganize the estates in the new conditions, and the police organization required to be strengthened in order to compel the emancipated serfs to fulfill their legal obligations. These men and their families were, therefore, much more conservative than the class commonly designated "the young generation," and they naturally sympathized with the "Philistines" in St. Petersburg who had been alarmed by the exaggerations of the Nihilists.

Even the landed proprietors, however, were not so entirely free from discontent and troublesome political aspirations as the Government would have desired. They had not forgotten the autocratic and bureaucratic way in which the Emancipation had been prepared, and their indignation had been only partially appeased by their being allowed to carry out the provisions of the law without much bureaucratic interference. So much for their discontent. As for their reform aspirations, they thought that, as a compensation for having consented to the liberation of their serfs and for having been expropriated from about a half of their land, they ought to receive extensive political rights, and be admitted, like the upper classes in Western Europe, to a fair share in the government of the country. Unlike the fiery young Nihilists of St. Petersburg, they did not want to abolish or paralyze the central power; what they wanted was to co-operate with it loyally, and to give their advice on important questions by means of representative institutions. They formed a constitutional group so moderate in its aims that it might have been used as a convenient safety valve for the explosive forces which were steadily accumulating under the surface of society, but it never found favor in the official world. When some of its leading members ventured to hint in the press and in loyal addresses to the Emperor that the Government would do well to consult the country on important questions, their respectful suggestions were coldly received or bluntly rejected by the bureaucracy and the autocratic power.

The more the revolutionary and constitutional groups sought to strengthen their position, the more pronounced became the reactionary tendencies in the official world, and these received in 1863 an immense impetus from the Polish insurrection, with which the Nihilists and even some of the Liberals sympathized. The students of the St. Petersburg University, for example, scandalized their more patriotic fellow countrymen by making a pro-Polish demonstration.

That ill-advised attempt on the part of the Poles to recover their independence had a curious effect on Russian public opinion. Alexander II, with the warm approval of the more Liberal section of the educated classes, was in the course of creating for Poland almost complete administrative autonomy under the viceroyalty of a Russian Grand Duke; and the Emperor's brother Constantine was preparing to carry out the scheme in a generous spirit. Soon it became evident that what the Poles wanted was not administrative autonomy, but political independence, with the frontiers which existed before the first partition! Trusting to the expected assistance of the Western Powers and the secret connivance of Austria, they raised the standard of insurrection, and some trifling successes were magnified by the pro-Polish press into important victories. As the news of the rising spread over Russia, there was a moment of hesitation. Those who had been for some years habitually extolling liberty and self-government as the normal conditions of progress, who had been sympathizing warmly with every Liberal movement, whether at home or abroad, and who had put forward a voluntary federation of independent Communes as the ideal state organism, could not well frown on the political aspirations of the Polish patriots. The Liberal sentiment of that time was so extremely philosophical and cosmopolitan that it hardly distinguished between Poles and Russians, and liberty was supposed to be the birthright of every man and woman, to whatever nationality they might happen to belong. But underneath these beautiful artificial clouds of cosmopolitan Liberal sentiment lay the volcano of national patriotism, dormant for the moment, but by no means extinct. Though the Russians are in some respects the most cosmopolitan of European nations, they are at the same time capable of indulging in violent outbursts of patriotic fanaticism; and events in Warsaw brought into hostile contact these two contradictory elements in the national character.

The struggle was only momentary. Ere long the patriotic feelings gained the upper hand and crushed all cosmopolitan sympathy with political freedom. The *Moscow Gazette*, the first of the papers to recover its mental equilibrium, thundered against the pseudo-Liberal sentimentalism which would, if unchecked, necessarily lead to the dismemberment of the Empire; and its editor, Katkov, became for a time the most influential private individual in the country. A few, indeed, remained true to their convictions. Herzen, for instance, wrote in the *Kólokol* a glowing panegyric on two Russian officers who had refused to fire on the insurgents; and here and there a good Orthodox Russian might be found who confessed that he was ashamed of Muraviev's extreme severity in Lithuania. But such men were few, and they were commonly regarded as traitors, especially after the ill-advised diplomatic intervention of the Western Powers. Even Herzen, by his publicly expressed sympathy with the insurgents, lost entirely his popularity and influence among his fellow countrymen. The great majority of the public thoroughly approved of the severe, energetic measures adopted by the Government, and when the insurrection was suppressed, men who had a few months previously spoken and written in magniloquent terms about humanitarian Liberalism joined in the ovations offered to Muraviev! At a great dinner given in his honor, that ruthless administrator of the old Muscovite type, who had systematically opposed the emancipation of the serfs and had never concealed his contempt for the Liberal ideas in fashion, could ironically express his satisfaction at seeing around him so many "new friends"! [6]

This revulsion of public feeling gave the Moscow Slavophils an opportunity of again preaching their doctrine that the safety and prosperity of Russia were to be found, not in the Liberalism and Constitutionalism of Western Europe, but in patriarchal autocracy, Eastern Orthodoxy,

[6] In fairness to Count Muraviev I must say that he was not so black as he was painted in the Polish and West European press. He left an interesting autobiographical fragment relating to the history of this time, but it is not likely to be printed for some years. As an historical document it is valuable, but must be used with caution by the future historian. A copy of it was for some time in my possession, but I was bound by a promise not to make extracts.

and the peculiarities of Russian nationality. Thus the reactionary tendencies gained ground; but Alexander II,
while causing all political agitation to be repressed, did not
at once abandon his policy of introducing radical reforms
by means of the autocratic power. On the contrary, he
gave orders that the preparatory work for creating local
self-government and reorganizing the law courts should
be pushed on energetically. The important laws for the establishment of the Zemstvo and for the great judicial reforms, which I have described in previous chapters, both
date from the year 1864.

These and other reforms of a less important kind made
no impression on the young irreconcilables. A small group
of them, under the leadership of a certain Ishútin, formed
in Moscow a small secret society, and conceived the design
of assassinating the Emperor, in the hope that his son and
successor, who was erroneously supposed to be imbued
with ultra-Liberal ideas, might continue the work which
his father had begun and had not the courage to complete.
In April, 1866, the attempt on the life of the Emperor was
made by a youth called Karakózov as his Majesty was
leaving a public garden in St. Petersburg, but the bullet
happily missed its mark, and the culprit was executed.

This incident formed a turning point in the policy of the
Government. Alexander II began to fear that he had gone
too far, or, at least, too quickly, in his policy of radical
reform. An Imperial rescript announced that law, property,
and religion were in danger, and that the Government
would lean on the Noblesse and other conservative elements of society. The two periodicals which advocated the
most advanced views (*Sovreménnik* and *Rússkoye Slóvo*)
were suppressed permanently, and precautions were taken
to prevent the annual assemblies of the Zemstvo from giving public expression to the aspirations of the moderate
Liberals.

A secret official inquiry showed that the revolutionary
agitation proceeded in all cases from young men who were
studying, or had recently studied, in the universities, the
seminaries, or the technical schools, such as the Medical
Academy and the Agricultural Institute. Plainly, therefore,
the system of education was at fault. The semimilitary

system of the time of Nicholas had been supplanted by one in which discipline was reduced to a minimum and the study of natural science formed a prominent element. Here, it was thought, lay the chief root of the evil.

Englishmen may have some difficulty in imagining a possible connection between natural science and revolutionary agitation. To them the two things must seem wide as the poles asunder. Surely mathematics, chemistry, physiology, and similar subjects have nothing to do with politics. When a young Englishman takes to studying any branch of natural science, he gets up his subject by means of lectures, textbooks, and museums or laboratories, and when he has mastered it, he probably puts his knowledge to some practical use. In Russia it is otherwise. Few students confine themselves to their speciality. The majority of them dislike the laborious work of mastering dry details, and with the presumption which is often found in conjunction with youth and a smattering of knowledge, they aspire to become social reformers, and imagine themselves specially qualified for such activity.

But what, it may be asked, has social reform to do with natural science? I have already indicated the connection in the Russian mind. Though very few of the students of that time had ever read the voluminous works of Auguste Comte, they were all more or less imbued with the spirit of the Positivist Philosophy, in which all the sciences are subsidiary to sociology, and social reorganization is the ultimate object of scientific research. The imaginative Positivist can see with prophetic eye Humanity reorganized on strictly scientific principles. Cool-headed people who have had a little experience of the world, if they ever indulge in such delightful dreams, recognize clearly that this ultimate goal of human intellectual activity, if it is ever to be reached, is still a long way off in the misty distance of the future; but the would-be social reformers among the Russian students of the sixties were too young, too inexperienced, and too presumptuously self-confident to recognize this plain, simple truth. They felt that too much valuable time had been already lost, and they were madly impatient to begin the great work without further delay. As soon as they had acquired a smattering of chemistry, physiology, and biology, they imagined themselves capable of reorganizing human society from top to bottom, and when they had acquired this conviction they were of course unfitted for the patient, plodding study of details.

To remedy these evils, Count Dimitri Tolstoy, who was regarded as a pillar of Conservatism, was appointed Minister of Public Instruction, with the mission of protecting the young generation against pernicious ideas, and eradicating from the schools, colleges, and universities all revolutionary tendencies. He determined to introduce more discipline into all the educational establishments, and to supplant to a certain extent the superficial study of natural science by the thorough study of the classics—that is to say, Latin and Greek. This scheme, which became known before it was actually put into execution, produced a storm of discontent in the young generation. Discipline at that time was regarded as an antiquated and useless remnant of patriarchal tyranny, and young men who were impatient to take part in social reorganization resented being treated as naughty schoolboys. To them it seemed that the Latin grammar was an ingenious instrument for stultifying youthful intelligence, destroying intellectual development, and checking political progress. Ingenious speculations about the possible organization of the working classes and grandiose views of the future of humanity are so much more interesting and agreeable than the rules of Latin syntax and the Greek irregular verbs!

Count Tolstoy could congratulate himself on the efficacy of his administration, for from the time of his appointment there was a lull in the political excitement. During three or four years there was only one political trial, and that an insignificant one; whereas there had been twenty between 1861 and 1864, and all more or less important. I am not at all sure, however, that the educational reform, which created much momentary irritation and discontent, had anything to do with the improvement in the situation. In any case, there were other and more potent causes at work. The excitement was too intense to be long-lived, and the fashionable theories too fanciful to stand the wear and tear of everyday life. They evaporated, therefore, with amazing rapidity when the leaders of the movement had disappeared—Chernyshevski and others by exile, and Dobrolubov and Pisarev by death—and when among the less prominent representatives of the young generation many succumbed to the sobering influences of time and experience or drifted into lucrative professions. Besides this, the reactionary currents were making themselves felt, especially since the attempt on the life of the Emperor. So long as these had been confined to the official world they had not much affected the literature, except externally through the press censure, but when they permeated the reading public their influence was much stronger. Whatever the cause, there is no doubt that, in the last years of the sixties, there was a subsidence of excitement and enthusiasm, and the peculiar intellectual phenomenon which had been nicknamed Nihilism was supposed to be a thing of the past. In reality, the movement of which Nihilism was a prominent manifestation had merely lost something of its academic character, and was entering on a new stage of development.

CHAPTER XXIV

Socialist Propaganda, Revolutionary Agitation, and Terrorism

COUNT TOLSTOY's educational reform had one effect which was not anticipated: it brought the revolutionists into closer contact with Western Socialism. Many students, finding their position in Russia uncomfortable, determined to go abroad and continue their studies in foreign universities, where they would be free from the inconveniences of police supervision and press censure. Those of the female sex had an additional motive to emigrate because they could not complete their studies in Russia, but they had more difficulty in carrying out their intention, because parents naturally disliked the idea of their daughters going abroad to lead a Bohemian life, and they very often obstinately refused to give their consent. In such cases the persistent daughter found herself in a dilemma. Though she might run away from her family and possibly earn her own living, she could not easily cross the frontier without a passport; and without the parental sanction a passport could not be obtained. Of course she might marry and get the consent of her husband, but most of these young ladies objected to the trammels of matrimony. Occasionally the problem was solved by means of a fictitious marriage, and when a young man could not be found to co-operate voluntarily in the arrangement, the terrorist methods which the revolutionists adopted a few years later for other purposes might be employed. I have heard of at least one case in which an ardent female devotee of medical science threatened to shoot a student who was going abroad if he did not submit to the matrimonial ceremony and allow her to accompany him to the frontier as his official wife!

Strange as this story may seem, it contains nothing inherently improbable. At that time the energetic young ladies of the Nihilist school were not to be diverted from their purposes by trifling obstacles. We shall meet some of them hereafter, displaying great courage and tenacity in revolutionary activity. One of them, as I have already mentioned, attempted to murder the Prefect of St. Petersburg, and another, a young person of considerable refinement and great personal charm, gave the signal for the assassination of Alexander II, and expiated her crime on the scaffold without the least sign of repentance.

Most of the studious *émigrés* of both sexes went to Zürich, where female students were admitted to the medical classes. Here they made the acquaintance of noted Socialists from various countries who had settled in Switzerland, and being in search of panaceas for social regeneration, they naturally fell under their influence. At the same time they read with avidity the works of Proudhon, Lassalle, Büchner, Marx, Flerovski, Pfeiffer and other writers of "advanced" opinions.

Among the apostles of Socialism living at that time in Switzerland, they found a sympathetic fellow countryman in the famous Anarchist Bakúnin, who had succeeded in escaping from Siberia. His ideal was the immediate overthrow of all existing Governments, the destruction of all administrative organization, the abolition of all *bourgeois* institutions, and the establishment of an entirely new order of things on the basis of a free federation of productive Communes, in which all the land should be distributed among those capable of tilling it and the instruments of production confided to co-operative associations. Efforts to obtain mere political reforms, even of the most radical type, were regarded by him with contempt as miserable palliatives, which could be of no real, permanent benefit to the masses, and might be positively injurious by prolonging the present era of *bourgeois* domination.

For the dissemination of these principles a special organ called *The Cause of the People* (*Narodnoye Dyelo*) was founded in Geneva in 1868 and was smuggled across the Russian frontier in considerable quantities. It aimed at drawing away the young generation from Academic Nihilism to more practical revolutionary activity, but it evidently remained to some extent under the old influences, for it indulged occasionally in very abstract philosophical disquisitions. In its first number, for example, it published a program in which the editors thought it necessary to declare that they were materialists and atheists, because the belief in God and a future life, as well as every other kind of idealism, demoralizes the people, inspiring it with mutually contradictory aspirations, and thereby depriving it of the energy necessary for the conquest of its natural rights in this world, and the complete organization of a free and happy life. At the end of two years this organ for moralizing the people collapsed from want of funds, but other periodicals and pamphlets were printed, and the clandestine relations between the exiles in Switzerland and their friends in St. Petersburg were maintained without difficulty, notwithstanding the efforts of the police to cut the connection. In this way Young Russia became more and more saturated with the extreme Socialist theories current in Western Europe.

Thanks partly to this foreign influence and partly to their own practical experience, the would-be reformers who remained at home came to understand that academic talking and discussing could bring about no serious results. Students alone, however numerous and however devoted to the cause, could not hope to overthrow or coerce the Government. It was childish to suppose that the walls of the autocratic Jericho could be overthrown by the blasts of academic trumpets. Attempts at revolution could not be successful without the active support of the people, and consequently the revolutionary agitation must be extended to the masses.

So far there was complete agreement among the revolutionists, but with regard to the *modus operandi* emphatic differences of opinion appeared. Those who were carried away by the stirring accents of Bakúnin imagined that if the masses could only be made to feel themselves the victims of administrative and economic oppression, they would rise and free themselves by a united effort. According to this view all that was required was that popular discontent should be excited and that precautions should be taken to ensure that the explosions of discontent should take place simultaneously all over the country. The rest might safely be left, it was thought, to the operation of natural forces and the inspiration of the moment. Against this dangerous illusion warning voices were raised. Lavróv, for example, while agreeing with Bakúnin that mere political reforms were of little or no value, and that any genuine improvement in the condition of the working classes could proceed only from economic and social reorganization, maintained stoutly that the revolution, to be permanent and beneficial, must be accomplished, not by demagogues directing the ignorant masses, but by the people as a whole, *after it had been enlightened and instructed as to its true interests.* The preparatory work would necessarily require a whole generation of educated propagandists, living among the laboring population, rural and urban.

For some time there was a conflict between these two currents of opinion, but the views of Lavróv, which were simply a practical development of academic Nihilism, gained far more adherents than the violent anarchical proposals of Bakúnin, and finally the grandiose scheme of realizing gradually the Socialist ideal by indoctrinating the masses was adopted with enthusiasm. In St. Petersburg, Moscow, and other large towns, the student associations for mutual instruction, to which I have referred in the foregoing chapter, became centers of popular propaganda, and the academic Nihilists were transformed into active missionaries. Scores of male and female students, impatient to convert the masses to the gospel of freedom and terrestrial felicity, sought to get into touch with the common people by settling in the villages as schoolteachers, medical practitioners, midwives, etc., or by working as common factory hands in the industrial centers. In order to obtain employment in the factories and conceal their real purpose, they procured false passports, in which they were described as belonging to the lower classes; and even those who settled in the villages lived generally under assumed names. Thus was formed a class of professional revolutionists, sometimes called the Illegals, who were liable to be arrested at any moment by the police. As compensation for the privations and hardships which they had to endure, they had the consolation of believing that they were advancing the good cause. The means they usually employed for making converts were informal conversations and pamphlets expressly written for the purpose. The more enthusiastic and persevering of these missionaries continued their efforts for months and years, remaining in communication with the headquarters in the capital or some provincial town in order to report progress, obtain a fresh supply of pamphlets, and get their forged passports renewed.

This extraordinary movement was called "going in among the people," and it spread among the young generation like an epidemic. In 1873 it was suddenly reinforced by a detachment of fresh recruits. Over a hundred Russian students were recalled by the Government from Switzerland, in order to save them from the baneful influence of Bakúnin, Lavróv, and other noted Socialists, and a large proportion of them joined the ranks of the propagandists.[1]

With regard to the aims and methods of the propagandists, a good deal of information was obtained in the course of a judicial inquiry instituted in 1875. A peasant, who was at the same time a factory worker, informed the police that certain persons were distributing revolutionary pamphlets among the factory hands, and as a proof of what he said he produced some pamphlets which he had himself received. This led to an investigation, which showed that a number of young men and women, evidently belonging to the educated classes, were disseminating revolutionary ideas by means of pamphlets and conversation. Arrests followed, and it was soon discovered

[1] Instances of "going in among the people" had happened as early as 1864, but they did not become frequent till after 1870.

that these agitators belonged to a large secret association,
which had its center in Moscow, and local branches in
Ivanovo, Tula, and Kiev. In Ivanovo, for instance—a manufacturing town about a hundred miles to the northeast
of Moscow—the police found a small apartment inhabited
by three young men and four young women, all of whom,
though belonging by birth to the educated classes, had
the appearance of ordinary factory workers, prepared their
own food, did with their own hands all the domestic work,
and sought to avoid everything which could distinguish
them from the laboring population. In the apartment were
found 240 copies of revolutionary pamphlets, a considerable sum of money, a large amount of correspondence in
cipher, and several forged passports.

How many persons the society contained it is impossible
to say, because a large proportion of them eluded the
vigilance of the police; but many were arrested, and ultimately forty-seven were condemned. Of these, eleven
were nobles, seven were sons of parish priests, and the remainder belonged to the lower classes—that is to say, the
small officials, burghers, and peasants. The average age of
the prisoners was twenty-four, the oldest being thirty-six
and the youngest under seventeen! Only five or six were
over twenty-five, and none of these were ringleaders. The
female element was represented by no less than fifteen
young persons, whose ages were on an average under
twenty-two. Two of these, to judge by their photographs,
were of refined, prepossessing appearance, and seemingly
little fitted for taking part in wholesale massacres such as
the society talked of organizing.

The character and aims of the society were clearly depicted in the documentary and oral evidence produced at
the trial. According to the fundamental principles, there
should exist among the members absolute equality, complete mutual responsibility and full frankness and confidence with regard to the affairs of the association. Among
the conditions of admission we find that the candidate
should devote himself entirely to revolutionary activity;
that he should be ready to sever all ties, whether of
friendship or of love, for the good cause; that he should
possess great powers of self-sacrifice and the capacity

for keeping secrets; and that he should consent to become, when necessary, a common laborer in a factory. The desire to maintain absolute equality is well illustrated by the article of the statutes regarding the administration: the officebearers are not to be chosen by election, but all members are to be officebearers in turn, and the term of office must not exceed one month!

The avowed aim of the society was to destroy the existing social order, and to replace it by one in which there should be no private property and no distinctions of class or wealth; or, as it is expressed in one document, "to found on the ruins of the present social organization the Empire of the working classes." The means to be employed were indicated in a general way, but each member was to adapt himself to circumstances, and was to devote all his energies to forwarding the cause of the revolution. For the guidance of the inexperienced, the following means were recommended: simple conversations, dissemination of pamphlets, the exciting of discontent, the formation of organized groups, the creation of funds and libraries. These, taken together, constitute, in the terminology of revolutionary science, "propaganda," and thereafter comes "agitation." The technical distinction between these two processes is that propaganda has a purely preparatory character, and aims merely at enlightening the masses regarding the true nature of the revolutionary cause, whereas agitation aims at exciting an individual or a group to acts which are considered, in the existing regime, as illegal. In time of peace "pure agitation" was to be carried on by means of organized bands which should frighten the Government and the privileged classes, draw away the attention of the authorities from less overt kinds of revolutionary action, raise the spirit of the people, and thereby render it more accessible to revolutionary ideas, obtain pecuniary means for further activity, and liberate political prisoners. In time of insurrection the members should give to popular movements every assistance in their power, and impress on them a Socialistic character. The central administration and the local branches should establish relations with publishers, and take steps to secure a regular supply of prohibited books from abroad. Such are a few

characteristic extracts from a document which might fairly
be called a treatise on revolutionology.

As a specimen of the revolutionary pamphlets circulated
by the propagandists and agitators I may give here a
brief account of one which is well known to the political
police. It is entitled *Khítraya Mekhánika* (Cunning Machinery), and gives a graphic picture of the ideas and
methods employed. The *mise en scène* is extremely simple.
Two peasants, Stepán and Andréi, are represented as
meeting in a gin shop and drinking together. Stepán is
described as good and kindly when he has to do with men
of his own class, but very sharp-tongued when speaking
with a foreman or manager. Always ready with an answer,
he can on occasion silence even an official! He has traveled
all over the Empire, has associated with all sorts and conditions of men, sees everything most clearly, and is, in
short, a very remarkable man. One of his excellent
qualities is that, being "enlightened" himself, he is always
ready to enlighten others, and he now finds an opportunity of displaying his powers.

When Andréi, who is still unenlightened, proposes that
they should drink another glass of vodka, he replies that
the Tsar, together with the nobles and traders, bars the
way to his throat. As his companion does not understand
this metaphorical language, he explains that if there were
no Tsars, nobles, or traders, he could get five glasses of
vodka for the sum that he now pays for one glass. This
naturally suggests wider topics, and Stepán gives something like a lecture. The common people, he explains, pay
by far the greater part of the taxation, and at the same
time do all the work; they plough the fields, build the
houses and churches, work in the mills and factories, and
in return they are systematically robbed and beaten. And
what is done with all the money that is taken from them?
First of all, the Tsar gets nine million of rubles—enough
to feed half a province—and with that sum he amuses
himself, has hunting parties, feasts, eats, drinks, makes
merry, and lives in stone houses. He gave liberty, it is
true, to the peasants; but we know what the Emancipation really was. The best land was taken away and the
taxes were increased, lest the muzhik should get fat and

lazy. The Tsar is himself the richest landed proprietor and manufacturer in the country. He not only robs us as much as he pleases, but he has sold into slavery (by forming a national debt) our children and grandchildren. He takes our sons as soldiers, shuts them up in barracks so that they should not see their brother peasants, and hardens their hearts so that they become wild beasts, ready to rend their parents. The nobles and traders likewise rob the poor peasants. In short, all the upper classes have invented a bit of cunning machinery by which the muzhik is made to pay for their pleasures and luxuries.

The people, however, will one day rise and break this machinery to pieces. When that day comes they must break every part of it, for if one bit escapes destruction, all the other parts of it will immediately grow up again. All the force is on the side of the peasants, if they only knew how to use it. Knowledge will come in time. They will then destroy this machine, and perceive that the only real remedy for all social evils is brotherhood. People should live like brothers, having no *mine* and *thine*, but all things in common. When we have created brotherhood, there will be no riches and no thieves, but right and righteousness without end. In conclusion, Stepán addresses a word to "the torturers": "When the people rise, the Tsar will send troops against us, and the nobles and capitalists will stake their last ruble on the result. If they do not succeed, they must not expect any quarter from us. They may conquer us once or twice, but we shall at last get our own, for there is no power that can withstand the whole people. Then we shall cleanse the country of our persecutors, and establish a brotherhood in which there will be no *mine* and *thine,* but all will work for the common weal. We shall construct no cunning machinery, but shall pluck up evil by the roots, and establish eternal justice!"

The above-mentioned distinction between Propaganda and Agitation, which plays a considerable part in revolutionary literature, had at that time more theoretical than practical importance. The great majority of those who took an active part in the movement confined their efforts to indoctrinating the masses with Socialistic and subversive ideas, and sometimes their methods were rather child-

ish. As an illustration I may cite an amusing incident related by one of the boldest and most tenacious of the revolutionists, who subsequently acquired a certain sense of
humor. He and a friend were walking one day on a country road, when they were overtaken by a peasant in his
cart. Ever anxious to sow the good seed, they at once entered into conversation with the rustic, telling him that he
ought not to pay his taxes, because the *chinóvniks* robbed
the people, and trying to convince him by quotations from
Scripture that he ought to resist the authorities. The prudent muzhik whipped up his horse and tried to get out of
hearing, but the two zealots ran after him and continued the sermon till they were completely out of breath.
Other propagandists were more practical, and preached a
species of agrarian Socialism which the rural population
could understand. At the time of the Emancipation, the
peasants were convinced, as I have mentioned in a previous chapter, that the Tsar meant to give them all the land,
and to compensate the landed proprietors by salaries.
Even when the law was read and explained to them, they
clung obstinately to their old convictions, and confidently
expected that the *real* emancipation would be proclaimed
shortly. Taking advantage of this state of things, the propagandists to whom I refer confirmed the peasants in their
error, and sought in this way to sow discontent against the
proprietors and the Government. Their watchword was
"Land and Liberty," and they formed for a good many
years a distinct group, under that title (*Zemlya i Volya,*
or more briefly *Zemlevoltsi*).

In the St. Petersburg group, which aspired to direct
and control this movement, there were one or two men
who held different views as to the real object of propaganda and agitation. One of these, Prince Kropotkin, has
told the world what his object was at that time. He hoped
that the Government would be frightened and that the autocratic power, as in France on the eve of the Revolution,
would seek support in the landed proprietors, and call together a National Assembly. Thus a constitution would be
granted, and though the first Assembly might be conservative in spirit, autocracy would be compelled in the long
run to yield to parliamentary pressure.

No such elaborate projects were entertained, I believe, by the majority of the propagandists. Their reasoning was much simpler: "The Government, having become reactionary, tries to prevent us from enlightening the people; we will do it in spite of the Government!" The dangers to which they exposed themselves only confirmed them in their resolution. Though they honestly believed themselves to be realists and materialists, they were at heart romantic idealists, panting to do something heroic. They had been taught by the apostles whom they venerated, from Belinski downwards, that the man who simply talks about the good of the people, and does nothing to promote it, is among the most contemptible of human beings. No such reproach must be addressed to them. If the Government opposed and threatened, that was no excuse for inactivity. They must be up and doing. "Forward! forward! Let us plunge into the people, identify ourselves with them, and work for their benefit! Suffering is in store for us, but we must endure it with fortitude!" The type which Chernyshevski had depicted in his famous novel, under the name of Rakhmétov—the youth who led an ascetic life and subjected himself to privation and suffering as a preparation for future revolutionary activity— now appeared in the flesh. If we may credit Bakúnin, these Rakhmétovs had not even the consolation of believing in the possibility of a revolution, but as they could not and would not remain passive spectators of the misfortunes of the people, they resolved to go in among the masses, in order to share with them fraternally their sufferings, and at the same time to teach and prepare, not theoretically, but practically, by their living example.[2] This is, I believe, an exaggeration. The propagandists were, for the most part, of incredibly sanguine temperament.

The success of the propaganda and agitation was not at all in proportion to the numbers and enthusiasm of those who took part in it. Most of these displayed more zeal than mother-wit and discretion. Their Socialism was too abstract and scientific to be understood by rustics, and when they succeeded in making themselves intelligible

[2] Bakúnin: *Gosudarstvennost' i Anarkhiya* (State-organization and Anarchy). Zürich, 1873.

they awakened in their hearers more suspicion than sympathy. The muzhik is a very matter-of-fact practical person, totally incapable of understanding what Americans call "highfaluting" tendencies in speech and conduct, and as he listened to the preaching of the new gospel, doubts and questionings spontaneously rose in his mind: "What do those young people, who betray their gentlefolk origin by their delicate white hands, their foreign phrases, their ignorance of the common things of everyday peasant life, really want? Why are they bearing hardships and taking so much trouble? They tell us it is for our good, but we are not such fools and simpletons as they take us for. They are not doing it all for nothing. What do they expect from us in return? Whatever it is, they are evidently evildoers, and perhaps *moshenniki* (swindlers). Devil take them!" And thereupon the cautious muzhik turns his back upon his disinterested, self-sacrificing teachers, or goes quietly and denounces them to the police! It is not only in the pages of Cervantes that we encounter Don Quixotes and Sancho Panzas!

Occasionally a worse fate befell the missionaries. If they allowed themselves, as they sometimes did, to "blaspheme" against religion or the Tsar, they ran the risk of being maltreated on the spot. I have heard of one case in which the punishment for blasphemy was applied by sturdy peasant matrons. Even when the propagandists escaped such mishaps they had not much reason to congratulate themselves on their success. After three years of arduous labor the hundreds of apostles could not boast of more than a score or two of converts among the genuine working classes, and even these few did not all remain faithful unto death. Some of them, however, it must be admitted, labored and suffered to the end with the courage and endurance of true martyrs.

It was not merely the indifference or hostility of the masses that the propagandists had to complain of. The police soon got on their track, and did not confine themselves to persuasion and logical arguments. Towards the end of 1873 they arrested some members of the central directing group in St. Petersburg, and in the following May they discovered in the province of Sarátov an affiliated organization with which nearly 800 persons were connected, about one-fifth of them belonging to the female sex. A few came of well-to-do families—sons and daughters of minor officials or small landed proprietors—but the great majority were poor students of humbler origin, a large contingent being supplied by the sons of the poor parish clergy. In other provinces the authorities made similar discoveries. Before the end of the year a large proportion of the propagandists were in prison, and the centralized organization, so far as such a thing existed, was destroyed. Gradually it dawned on the minds even of the Don Quixotes that pacific propaganda was no longer possible, and that attempts to continue it could lead only to useless sacrifices.

For a time there was universal discouragement in the revolutionary ranks; and among those who had escaped arrest there were mutual recriminations and endless discussions about the causes of failure and the changes to be made in modes of action. The practical result of these recriminations and discussions was that the partisans of a slow, pacific propaganda retired to the background, and the more impatient revolutionary agitators took possession of the movement. These maintained stoutly that, as pacific propaganda had become impossible, stronger methods must be adopted. The masses must be organized so as to offer successful resistance to the Government. Conspiracies must, therefore, be formed, local disorders provoked, and blood made to flow. The part of the country which seemed best adapted for experiments of this kind was the southern and southeastern region, inhabited by the descendants of the turbulent Cossack population which had raised formidable insurrections under Stenka Razin and Pugachév in the seventeenth and eighteenth centuries. Here, then, the more impatient agitators began their work. A Kiev group called the *Buntari* (rioters), composed of about twenty-five individuals, settled in various localities as small shopkeepers or horse dealers, or wandered about as workmen or pedlars.

One member of the group has given us in his Reminiscences an amusing account of the experiment. Everywhere the agitators found the peasants suspicious and inhospitable, and consequently they had to suffer a great deal of discomfort. Some of them at once gave up the task as hopeless. The others settled in a village and began operations. Having made a topographical survey of the locality, they worked out an ingenious plan of campaign; but they had no recruits for the future army of insurrection, and if they had been able to get recruits, they had no arms for them, and no money wherewith to purchase arms or anything else. In these circumstances they gravely appointed a committee to collect funds, knowing very well that no money would be forthcoming. It was as if a shipwrecked crew in an open boat, having reached the brink of starvation, appointed a committee to obtain a supply of fresh water and provisions! In the hope of obtaining assistance from headquarters a delegate was sent to St. Petersburg and Moscow to explain that for the arming of the population about a quarter of a million of rubles was required. The delegate brought back thirty second-hand revolvers! The Revolutionist who confesses all this[3] recognizes that the whole scheme was childishly impractical: "We chose the path of popular insurrection because we had faith in the revolutionary spirit of the masses, in its power and its invincibility. That was the weak side of our position; and the most curious part of it was that we drew proofs in support of our theory from history—from the *abortive* insurrections of Razin and Pugachév, which took place in an age when the Government had only a small regular army and no railways or telegraphs! We did not even think of attempting a propaganda among the military!"

In the district of Chigirin the agitators had a little momentary success, but the result was the same. There a student called Stefánovich pretended that the Tsar was struggling with the officials to benefit the peasantry, and he showed the simple rustics a forged imperial manifesto in which they were ordered to form a society for the purpose of raising an insurrection against the officials, the nobles, and the priests. At one moment (April, 1877)

[3] Debogorio-Mokriévich: *Vospominaniya* (Reminiscences). Paris, 1894-99.

the society had about 600 members, but a few months later it was discovered by the police, and the leaders and peasants were arrested.

When it had thus become evident that propaganda and agitation were alike useless, and when numerous arrests were being made daily, it became necessary for the Revolutionists to reconsider their position, and some of the more moderate proposed to rally to the Liberals, as a temporary measure. Hitherto there had been very little sympathy and a good deal of openly avowed hostility between Liberals and Revolutionists. The latter, convinced that they could overthrow the autocratic power by their own unaided efforts, had looked askance at Liberalism because they believed that parliamentary discussions and party struggles would impede rather than facilitate the advent of the Socialist millennium, and strengthen the domination of the *bourgeoisie* without really improving the condition of the masses. Now, however, when the need of allies was felt, it seemed that constitutional government might be used as a steppingstone for reaching the Socialist ideal, because it must grant a certain liberty of the press and of association, and it would necessarily abolish the existing autocratic system of arresting, imprisoning and exiling, on mere suspicion, without any regular form of legal procedure. As usual, an appeal was made to history, and arguments were easily found in favor of this course of action. The past of other nations had shown that in the march of progress there are no sudden leaps and bounds, and it was therefore absurd to imagine, as the Revolutionists had hitherto done, that Russian Autocracy could be swallowed by Socialism at a gulp. There must always be periods of transition, and it seemed that such a transition period might now be initiated. Liberalism might be allowed to destroy, or at least weaken, Autocracy, and then it might be destroyed in its turn by Socialism of the most advanced type.

Having adopted this theory of gradual historic development, some of the more practical Revolutionists approached the more advanced Liberals and urged them to more energetic action; but before anything could be arranged, the more impatient Revolutionists—notably the group called the *Narodovoltsi* (National-will-ists)—intervened, denounced what they considered an unholy alliance, and proposed a policy of terrorism by which the Government might be frightened into a more conciliatory attitude. Their idea was that the officials who displayed most zeal against the revolutionary movement should be assassinated, and that every act of severity on the part of the Administration should be answered by an act of "revolutionary justice."

As it was evident that the choice between these two courses of action must determine in great measure the future character and ultimate fate of the movement, there was much discussion between the two groups; but the question did not long remain in suspense. Soon the extreme party gained the upper hand, and the Terrorist policy was adopted. I shall let the Revolutionists themselves explain this momentous decision. In a long proclamation published some years later it is explained thus:

"The revolutionary movement in Russia began with the so-called 'going in among the people.' The first Russian Revolutionists thought that the freedom of the people could be obtained only by the people itself, and they imagined that the only thing necessary was that the people should absorb Socialistic ideas. To this it was supposed that the peasantry were naturally inclined, because they already possessed, in the Rural Commune, institutions which contained the seeds of Socialism, and which might serve as a basis for the reconstruction of society according to Socialist principles. The propagandists hoped, therefore, that in the teachings of West European Socialism the people would recognize its own instinctive creations in riper and more clearly defined forms, and that it would joyfully accept the new teaching.

"But the people did not understand its friends, and showed itself hostile to them. It turned out that institutions born in slavery could not serve as a foundation for the new construction, and that the man who was yesterday a serf, though capable of taking part in disturbances, was not fitted for conscious revolutionary

work. With pain in their hearts the Revolutionsts had
to confess that they were deceived in their hopes of
the people. Around them were no social revolutionary
forces on which they could lean for support, and yet
they could not reconcile themselves with the existing
state of violence and slavery. Thereupon awakened a
last hope—the hope of a drowning man who clutches
at a straw: a little group of heroic and self-sacrificing
individuals might accomplish with their own strength
the difficult task of freeing Russia from the yoke of
autocracy. They had to do it themselves, because there
was no other means. But would they be able to accomplish it? For them that question did not exist. The
struggle of that little group against autocracy was
like the heroic means on which a doctor decides when
there is no longer any hope of the patient's recovery.
Terrorism was the only means that remained, and it
had the advantage of giving a natural vent to pent-up
feelings, and of seeming a reaction against the cruel
persecutions of the Government. The party called the
Narodnaya Volya (National Will) was accordingly
formed, and during several years the world witnessed
a spectacle that had never been seen before in history.
The *Narodnaya Volya*, insignificant in numbers but
strong in spirit, engaged in single combat the powerful
Russian Government. Neither executions, nor imprisonment with hard labor, nor ordinary imprisonment
and exile, could destroy the energy of these Revolutionists. Under their shots fell, one after the other, the
most zealous and typical representatives of arbitrary
action and violence. . . ."

It was at this time, in 1877, when propaganda and agitation among the masses were being abandoned for the
system of terrorism, but before any assassinations had
taken place, that I accidentally came into personal relations with some prominent adherents of the revolutionary
movement. One day a young man of sympathetic appearance, whom I did not know and who brought no credentials, called on me in St. Petersburg and suggested to me
that I might make public through the English press what

he described as a revolting act of tyranny and cruelty committed by General Trepov, the Prefect of the city. That official, he said, in visiting recently one of the prisons, had noticed that a young political prisoner called Bogolúbov did not salute him as he passed, and he had ordered him to be flogged in consequence. To this I replied that I had no reason to disbelieve the story, but that I had equally no reason to accept it as accurate, as it rested solely on the evidence of a person with whom I was totally unacquainted. My informant took the objection in good part, and offered me the names and addresses of a number of persons who could supply me with any proofs that I might desire.

At his next visit I told him I had seen several of the persons he had named, and that I could not help perceiving that they were closely connected with the revolutionary movement. I then went on to suggest that as the sympathizers with that movement constantly complained that they were systematically misrepresented, calumniated and caricatured, the leaders ought to give to the world an accurate account of their real doctrines, and in this respect I should be glad to assist them. Already I knew something of the subject, because I had many friends and acquaintances among the sympathizers, and had often had with them interminable discussions. With their ideas, so far as I knew them, I felt bound to confess that I had no manner of sympathy, but I flattered myself, and he himself had admitted, that I was capable of describing accurately and criticizing impartially doctrines with which I did not agree. My new acquaintance, whom I may call Dimitri Ivan'ich, was pleased with the proposal, and after he had consulted with some of his friends, we came to an agreement by which I should receive all the materials necessary for writing an accurate account of the doctrinal side of the movement. With regard to any conspiracies that might be in progress, I warned him that he must be strictly reticent, because if I came accidentally to know of any terrorist designs I should consider it my duty to warn the authorities. For this reason I declined to attend any secret conclaves, and it was agreed that I should be instructed without being initiated.

The first step in my instruction was not very satisfactory or encouraging. One day Dimitri Ivan'ich brought me a large manuscript, which contained, he said, the real doctrines of the Revolutionists and the explanation of their methods. I was surprised to find that it was written in English, and I perceived at a glance that it was not at all what I wanted. As soon as I had read the first sentence I turned to my friend and said:

"I am very sorry to find, Dimitri Ivan'ich, that you have not kept your part of the bargain. We agreed, you may remember, that we were to act towards each other in absolutely good faith, and here I find a flagrant bit of bad faith in the very first sentence of the manuscript which you have brought me. The document opens with the statement that a large number of students have been arrested and imprisoned for distributing books among the people. That statement may be true according to the letter, but it is evidently intended to mislead. These youths have been arrested, as you must know, not for distributing ordinary books, as the memorandum suggests, but for distributing books *of a certain kind*. I have read some of them, and I cannot feel at all surprised that the Government should object to their being put into the hands of the ignorant masses. Take, for example, the one entitled *Khítraya Mekhánika*, and others of the same type. The practical teaching they contain is that the peasants should be ready to rise and cut the throats of the landed proprietors and officials. Now, a wholesale massacre of the kind may or may not be desirable in the interests of society, and justifiable according to some new code of higher morality. That is a question into which I do not enter. All I maintain is that the writer of this memorandum, in speaking of 'books,' meant to mislead me."

Dimitri Ivan'ich looked puzzled and ashamed. "Forgive me," he said; "I am to blame—not for having attempted to deceive you, but for not having taken precautions. I have not read the manuscript, and I could not if I wished, for it is written in English, and I know no language but my mother tongue. My friends ought not to have done this. Give me back the paper, and I shall take care that nothing of the sort occurs in future."

This promise was faithfully kept, and I had no further reason to complain. Dimitri Ivan'ich gave me a considerable amount of information, and lent me a valuable collection of revolutionary pamphlets. Unfortunately the course of tuition was suddenly interrupted by unforeseen circumstances, which I may mention as characteristic of life in St. Petersburg at the time. My servant, an excellent young Russian, more honest than intelligent, came to me one morning with a mysterious air, and warned me to be on my guard, because there were "bad people" going about. On being pressed a little, he explained to me what he meant. Two strangers had come to him, and after offering him a few rubles had asked him a number of questions about my habits—at what hour I went out and came home, what persons called on me, and much more of the same sort. "They even tried, sir, to get into your sitting room; but of course I did not allow them. I believe they want to rob you!"

It was not difficult to guess who these "bad people" were, who took such a keen interest in my doings, and who wanted to examine my apartment in my absence. Any doubts I had on the subject were soon removed. On the morrow and following days I noticed that whenever I went out, and wherever I might walk or drive, I was closely followed by two unsympathetic-looking individuals —so closely that when I turned round sharp they ran into me. The first and second times this little incident occurred they received a strong volley of unceremonious vernacular; but when we became better acquainted we simply smiled at each other knowingly, as the old Roman augurs are supposed to have done when they met in public unobserved. There was no longer any attempt at concealment or mystification. I knew I was being shadowed, and the shadowers could not help perceiving that I knew it. Yet, strange to say, they were never changed!

The reader probably assumes that the secret police had somehow got wind of my relations with the Revolutionists. Such an assumption presupposes on the part of the police an amount of intelligence and perspicacity which they do not usually possess. On this occasion they were on an entirely wrong scent, and the very day when

I first noticed my shadowers a high official, who seemed to regard the whole thing as a good joke, told me confidentially what the wrong scent was. At the instigation of an ex-ambassador, from whom I had the misfortune to differ in matters of foreign policy, the *Moscow Gazette* had denounced me publicly by name as a person who was in the habit of visiting daily the Ministry of Foreign Affairs —doubtless with the nefarious purpose of obtaining by illegal means secret political information—and the police had concluded that I was a fit and proper person to be closely watched. In reality, my relations with the Russian Foreign Office, though inconvenient to the ex-ambassador, were perfectly regular and aboveboard—sanctioned, in fact, by Prince Gorchakov—but the indelicate attentions of the secret police were none the less extremely unwelcome, because some intelligent police agent might get on to the real scent, and cause me serious inconvenience. I determined, therefore, to break off all relations with Dimitri Ivan'ich and his friends, and postpone my studies to a more convenient season; but that decision did not entirely extricate me from my difficulties. The collection of revolutionary pamphlets was still in my possession, and I had promised to return it. For some little time I did not see how I could keep my promise without compromising myself or others, but at last—after having had my shadowers carefully shadowed in order to learn accurately their habits, and having taken certain elaborate precautions, with which I need not trouble the reader, as he is not likely ever to require them—I paid a visit secretly to Dimitri Ivan'ich in his small room, almost destitute of furniture, handed him the big parcel of pamphlets, warned him not to visit me again, and bade him farewell.

Thereupon we went our separate ways, and I saw him no more. Whether he subsequently played a leading part in the movement I never could ascertain, because I did not know his real name; but if the conception which I formed of his character was at all accurate, he probably ended his career in Siberia, for he was not a man to look back after having put his hand to the plough. That is a peculiar trait of the Russian Revolutionists of the period in question. Their passion for realizing an impossible ideal was incurable. Many of them were again and again arrested; and as soon as they escaped, or were liberated, they almost invariably went back to their revolutionary activity, and worked energetically until they again fell into the clutches of the police.

From this digression into the sphere of personal reminiscences I return now, and take up again the thread of the narrative.

We have seen how the propaganda and the agitation had failed, partly because the masses showed themselves indifferent or hostile, and partly because the Government adopted vigorous repressive measures. We have seen, too, how the leaders found themselves in face of a formidable dilemma; either they must abandon their schemes or they must attack their persecutors. The more energetic among them, as I have already stated, chose the latter alternative, and they proceeded at once to carry out their policy. In the course of a single year (February, 1878, to February, 1879) a whole series of terrorist crimes were committed; in Kiev, an attempt was made on the life of the Public Prosecutor, and an officer of gendarmerie was stabbed; in St. Petersburg the Chief of the Political Police of the Empire (General Mezentsev) was assassinated in broad daylight in one of the central streets, and a similar attempt was made on his successor (General Drenteln); at Kharkov the Governor (Prince Kropotkin) was shot dead when entering his residence. During the same period two members of the revolutionary organization, accused of treachery, were "executed" by order of local Committees. In most cases the perpetrators of the crimes contrived to escape. One of them became well known in Western Europe as an author under the pseudonym of Stepniak.

Terrorism had not the desired effect. On the contrary, it stimulated the zeal and activity of the authorities, and in the course of the winter of 1878-9 hundreds of arrests— some say as many as 2,000—were made in St. Petersburg alone. Driven to desperation, the Revolutionists still at large decided that it was useless to assassinate mere officials; the *fons et origo mali* must be reached; a blow must be struck at the Tsar himself! The first attempt was made by a young man called Solovyév, who fired several shots at

Alexander II as he was walking near the Winter Palace, but none of them took effect.

This policy of aggressive terrorism did not meet with universal approval among the Revolutionists, and it was determined to discuss the matter at a Congress of delegates from various local circles. The meetings were held in June, 1879, two months after Solovyév's unsuccessful attempt, at two provincial towns, Lipetsk and Vorónezh. It was there agreed in principle to confirm the decision of the terrorist *Narodovoltsi*. As the Liberals were not in a position to create liberal institutions or to give guarantees for political rights, which were the essential condition of any Socialist agitation, there remained for the revolutionary party no other course than to destroy the despotic autocracy. Thereupon a program of action was prepared, and an Executive Committee elected. From that moment, though there were still many who preferred milder methods, the Terrorists had the upper hand, and they at once proceeded to centralize the organization and to introduce stricter discipline, with greater precautions to ensure secrecy.

The Executive Committee imagined that autocracy might be destroyed by assassinating the Tsar, and several carefully planned attempts were made. The first plan was to wreck the Emperor's special train when the Imperial family were returning to St. Petersburg from the Crimea. Mines were accordingly laid at three separate points, but they all failed. At the last of the three points (near Moscow) a train was blown up, but it was not the one in which the Imperial family was traveling.

Not at all discouraged by this failure, nor by the discovery of its secret printing press by the police, the Executive Committee next tried to attain its object by an explosion of dynamite in the Winter Palace at the hour when the Imperial family usually assembled at dinner. The execution was entrusted to a certain Halturin, one of the few Revolutionists of peasant origin. As an exceptionally clever carpenter and polisher he easily found regular employment in the palace, and he contrived to make a rough plan of the building. This plan, on which the dining hall was marked with an ominous red cross, fell into the hands of the police, and they made what they considered a careful investigation, but they failed to unravel the plot and did not discover the dynamite, concealed in the carpenter's sleeping quarters. Halturin showed wonderful coolness while the search was going on, and continued to sleep every night on the explosive, though it caused him excruciating headaches. When he was assured by the chemist of the Executive Committee that the quantity collected was sufficient, he exploded the mine at the usual dinner hour, and contrived to escape uninjured.[4] In the guard room immediately above the spot where the dynamite was exploded ten soldiers were killed and fifty-three wounded, and in the dining hall the floor was wrecked, but the Imperial family escaped in consequence of not sitting down to dinner at the usual hour.

For this barbarous act the Executive Committee publicly accepted full responsibility. In a proclamation placarded in the streets of St. Petersburg it declared that, while regretting the death of the soldiers, it was resolved to carry on the struggle with the autocratic power until the social reforms should be entrusted to a Constituent Assembly, composed of members freely elected and furnished with instructions from their constituents.

Finding police repression so ineffectual, Alexander II determined to try the effect of conciliation, and for this purpose he placed General Loris Mélikov at the head of the Government, with semidictatorial powers (February, 1880). The experiment did not succeed. By the Terrorists it was regarded as "a hypocritical Liberalism outwardly and a veiled brutality within," while in the official world it was condemned as an act of culpable weakness on the part of the autocracy. One consequence of it was that the Executive Committee was encouraged to continue its efforts, and, as the authorities became less vigilant, it was enabled to improve the revolutionary organization. In a circular sent to the affiliated provincial associations it explained that the only source of legislation must be the

---

[4] After living some time in Rumania he returned to Russia under the name of Stepánov, and in 1882 he was tried and executed for complicity in the assassination of General Strelnikov.

national will,[5] and as the Government would never accept such a principle, its hand must be forced by a great popular insurrection, for which all available forces should be organized. The peasantry, as experience had shown, could not yet be relied on, but efforts should be made to enrol the workmen of the towns. Great importance was now attached to propaganda in the army; but as few conversions had been made among the rank and file, attention was to be directed chiefly to the officers, who would be able to carry their subordinates with them at the critical moment.

While thus recommending the scheme of destroying autocracy by means of a popular insurrection in the distant future, the Committee had not abandoned more expeditious methods, and it was at that moment hatching a plot for the assassination of the Tsar. During the winter months his Majesty was in the habit of holding on Sundays a small parade in the riding school near the Michael Square in St. Petersburg. On Sunday, March 3rd, 1881, the streets by which he usually returned to the Palace had been undermined at two places, and on an alternative route several conspirators were posted with hand grenades concealed under their greatcoats. The Emperor chose the alternative route. Here, at a signal given by Sophia Perovski, the first grenade was thrown by a student called Ryssakóv, but it merely wounded some members of the escort. The Emperor stopped and got out of his sledge, and as he was making inquiries about the wounded soldiers, a second grenade was thrown by a youth called Grinevitski, with fatal effect. Alexander II was conveyed hurriedly to the Winter Palace, and died almost immediately.

By this act the members of the Executive Committee proved their energy and their talent as conspirators, but they at the same time showed their short-sightedness and their political incapacity; for they had made no preparations for immediately seizing the power which they so ardently coveted—with the intention of using it, of course,

[5] Hence the designation *Narodovoltsi* (which, as we have seen, means literally National-will-ists), adopted by this section of the revolutionaries.

entirely for the public good. If the facts were not so well authenticated, we might dismiss the whole story as incredible. A group of young people, certainly not more than thirty or forty in number, without any organized material force behind them, without any influential accomplices in the army or the official world, without any prospect of support from the masses, and with no plan for immediate action after the assassination, deliberately provoked the crisis for which they were so hopelessly unprepared. It has been suggested that they expected the Liberals to seize the supreme power, but this explanation is evidently an afterthought, because they knew that the Liberals were as unprepared as themselves, and they regarded them at that time as dangerous rivals. Besides this, the explanation is quite irreconcilable with the proclamation issued by the Executive Committee immediately afterwards. The most charitable way of explaining the conduct of the conspirators is to suppose that they were actuated more by blind hatred of the autocracy and its agents than by political calculations of a practical kind—that they acted simply like a wounded bull in the arena, which shuts its eyes and recklessly charges its tormentors.

The murder of the Emperor had not at all the effect which the *Narodovoltsi* anticipated. On the contrary, it destroyed their hopes of success. Many people of liberal convictions who sympathized vaguely with the revolutionary movement without taking part in it, and who did not condemn very severely the attacks on police officials, were horrified when they found that the would-be reformers did not spare even the sacred person of the Tsar! At the same time, the police officials, who had become lax and inefficient under the conciliatory regime of Loris Mélikov, recovered their old zeal, and displayed such inordinate activity that the revolutionary organization was paralyzed and in great measure destroyed. Six of the regicides were condemned to death, and five of them publicly executed, amongst the latter Sophia Perovski, one of the most active and personally sympathetic personages among the Revolutionists. Scores of those who had taken an active part in the movement were in prison or in exile. For a short time the propaganda was continued among military and naval

officers, and various attempts at reorganization, especially
in the southern provinces, were made, but they all failed.
A certain Degaiev, who had taken part in the formation
of military circles, turned informer, and aided the police.
By his defection a considerable number of officers, and also
Vera Filipov, a young person of remarkable ability and
courage, who was the leading spirit in the attempts at reorganization, were arrested. From time to time the leaders
living abroad sent emissaries to revive the propaganda,
but these efforts were all fruitless.

One of the active members of the revolutionary party,
Leo Deutsch, who has since published his Memoirs, relates
how the tide of revolution ebbed rapidly at this time.
"Both in Russia and abroad," he says, "I had seen how the
earlier enthusiasm had given way to skepticism; men had
lost faith, though many of them would not allow that it
was so. It was clear to me that a reaction had set in for
many years." Of the attempts to resuscitate the movement he says: "The untried and unskillfully managed societies were run to earth before they could undertake anything definite, and the unity and interdependence which
characterized the original band of members had disappeared." With regard to the want of unity, another prominent revolutionist (Máslov) wrote to a friend (Dragomá-
nov) at Geneva in 1882 in terms of bitter complaint. He
accused the Executive Committee of trying to play the
part of chief of the whole revolutionary party, and declared that its centralizing tendencies were more despotic
than those of the Government. Distributing orders among
its adherents without initiating them into its plans, it insisted on unquestioning obedience. The Socialist youth,
ardent adherents of Federalism, were indignant at this
treatment, and began to understand that the Committee
used them simply as *chair à canon*. The writer described
in vivid colors the mutual hostility which reigned among
various fractions of the party, and which manifested itself
in accusations and even in denunciations; and he predicted
that the *Narodnaya Volya*, which had organized the various acts of terrorism, culminating in the assassination of
the Emperor, would never develop into a powerful revolutionary party. It had sunk into the slough of untruth,

and it could only continue to deceive the Government and
the public.

In the mutual recriminations several interesting admis-
sions were made. It was recognized that neither the educated classes nor the common people were capable of
bringing about a revolution: the former were not numerous enough, and the latter were devoted to the Tsar and
did not sympathize with the revolutionary movement,
though they might perhaps be induced to rise at a moment
of crisis. It was considered doubtful whether such a rising
was desirable, because the masses, being insufficiently prepared, might turn against the educated minority. In no
case could a popular insurrection attain the object which
the Socialists had in view, because the power would either
remain in the hands of the Tsar—thanks to the devotion of
the common people—or it would fall into the hands of the
Liberals, who would oppress the masses worse than the
autocratic Government had done. Further, it was recognized that acts of terrorism were worse than useless, because they were misunderstood by the ignorant, and
tended to inflame the masses against the leaders. It
seemed necessary, therefore, to return to the pacific propaganda. Tikhomirov, who was nominally directing the
movement from abroad, became utterly discouraged, and
wrote in 1884 to one of his emissaries in Russia (Lopá-
tin): "You now see Russia, and can convince yourself that
it does not possess the material for a vast work of reorganization. . . . I advise you seriously not to make superhu-
man efforts, and not to make a scandal in attempting the
impossible. . . . If you do not want to satisfy yourself
with trifles, come away and await better times."

In examining the material relating to this period one sees
clearly that the revolutionary movement had got into a
vicious circle. As pacific propaganda had become impossible, in consequence of the opposition of the authorities
and the vigilance of the police, the Government could be
overturned only by a general insurrection; but the general insurrection could not be prepared without pacific
propaganda. As for terrorism, it had become discredited.
Tikhomirov himself came to the conclusion that the terrorist idea was altogether a mistake, not only morally, but

also from the point of view of political expediency. A party, he explained, has either the force to overthrow the Government, or it has not; in the former case it has no need of political assassination, and in the latter the assassinations have no effect, because Governments are not so stupid as to let themselves be frightened by those who cannot overthrow them. Plainly there was nothing to be done but to wait for better times, as he had suggested, and the better times did not seem to be within measurable distance. He himself, after publishing a brochure entitled "Why I Ceased to be a Revolutionist," made his peace with the Government, and others followed his example. In one prison nine made formal recantations, among them Emiliánov, who held a reserve bomb ready when Alexander II was assassinated.

Occasional acts of terrorism showed that there was still fire under the smoldering embers, but such acts were few and far between. The last serious incident of the kind during this period was the regicide conspiracy of Sheviryév in March, 1887. The conspirators, carrying the bombs, were arrested in the principal street of St. Petersburg, and five of them were hanged. The railway accident of Borki, which happened in the following year, and in which the Imperial family had a very narrow escape, ought perhaps to be added to the list, because there is reason to believe that it was the work of Revolutionists.

By this time all the cooler heads among the Revolutionists, especially those who were living abroad in personal safety, had come to understand that the Socialist ideal could not be attained by popular insurrection, terrorism, or conspiracies, and consequently that further activity on the old lines was absurd. Those of them who did not abandon the enterprise in despair reverted to the idea that the autocratic power, impregnable against frontal attacks, might be destroyed by prolonged siege operations. This change of tactics is reflected in the revolutionary literature. In 1889, for example, the editor of the Svobódnaya Rossía declared that the aim of the movement now was political freedom—not only as a steppingstone to social reorganization, but as a good in itself. This is, he explains, the only revolution possible at present in Russia.

"For the moment there can be no other immediate practical aim. Ulterior aims are not abandoned, but they are not at present within reach. . . . The Revolutionists of the seventies and the eighties did not succeed in creating among the peasantry or the town workmen anything which had even the appearance of a force capable of struggling with the Government; and the Revolutionists of the future will have no greater success until they have obtained such political rights as personal inviolability. Our immediate aim, therefore, is a National Assembly controlled by local self-government, and this can be brought about only by a union of all the revolutionary forces."

There were still indications, it is true, that the old spirit of terrorism was not yet quite extinct: Captain Zolotýkhin, for example, an officer of the Moscow secret police, was assassinated by a female revolutionist in 1890. But such incidents were merely the last fitful sputterings of a lamp that was going out for want of oil. In 1892 Stepniak declared it evident to all that the professional Revolutionists could not alone overthrow autocracy, however great their energy and heroism; and he arrived at the same conclusion as the writer just quoted. After reviewing the situation as a whole, he says: "It is only from the evolutionist's point of view that the struggle with autocracy has a meaning. From any other standpoint it must seem a sanguinary farce—a mere exercise in the art of self-sacrifice!" Such are the conclusions arrived at in 1892 by a man who had been in 1878 one of the leading Terrorists, and who had with his own hand assassinated General Mezentsev, Chief of the Political Police.

Thus the revolutionary movement, after passing through four stages, which I may call the academic, the propagandist, the insurrectionary, and the terrorist, had failed to accomplish its object. One of those who had taken an active part in it, and who, after spending two years in Siberia as a political exile, escaped and settled in Western Europe, could write thus: "Our revolutionary movement is dead, and we who are still alive stand by the bier of our beautiful departed, and discuss what is wanting in her. One of us thinks that her nose might be improved; another suggests a change in her chin or her hair. We do not notice the essential, that what our beautiful departed wants is life; that it is not a matter of hair or eyebrows, but of a living soul, which formerly concealed all defects and made her beautiful, and which now has flown away. Any changes and improvements which we may imagine are utterly insignificant in comparison with what is really wanting, and what we cannot give; for who can breathe a living soul into a corpse?"

In truth, the movement which I have endeavored to describe was at an end; but another movement, having the same ultimate object, was coming into existence, and it constitutes one of the essential factors of the present situation. Some of the exiles in Switzerland and Paris had become acquainted with the Social Democratic and Labor movements in Western Europe, and they believed that the strategy and tactics employed in these movements might be adopted in Russia. How far they have succeeded in carrying out this policy, I shall relate presently; but before entering on this subject I must explain how the application of such a policy had been rendered possible by changes in the economic conditions. Russia had begun to create rapidly a great manufacturing industry and an industrial proletariat. This will form the subject of the next chapter.

CHAPTER XXV

Industrial Progress
and the Proletariat

FIFTY years ago Russia was still essentially a peasant Empire, living by agriculture of a primitive type, and supplying her other wants chiefly by home industries, as was the custom in Western Europe during the Middle Ages.

For many generations her rulers had been trying to transplant into their wide dominions the arts and crafts of the West, but they had formidable difficulties to contend with, and their success was not nearly so great as they desired. We know that as far back as the fourteenth century there were cloth workers in Moscow, for we read in the chronicles that the workshops of these artisans were sacked when the town was stormed by the Tatars. Workers in metal also had appeared in some of the larger towns by that time, but they do not seem to have risen much above the level of ordinary blacksmiths. They were destined, however, to make more rapid progress than other classes of artisans, because the old Tsars of Muscovy, like other semibarbarous potentates, admired and envied the industries of more civilized countries mainly from the military point of view. What they wanted most was a plentiful supply of good arms wherewith to defend themselves and attack their neighbors, and it was to this object that their most strenuous efforts were directed.

As early as 1475 Ivan III, the grandfather of Ivan the Terrible, sent a delegate to Venice to seek out for him an architect who, in addition to his own craft, knew how to make guns; and in due course appeared in the Kremlin a certain Muroli, called Aristotle by his contemporaries on account of his profound learning. He undertook "to build churches and palaces, to cast big bells and cannons, to fire off the said cannons, and to make every sort of castings very cunningly"; and for the exercise of these various arts it was solemnly stipulated in a formal document that he should receive the modest salary of ten rubles monthly. With regard to the military products, at least, the Venetian faithfully fulfilled his contract, and in a short time the Tsar had the satisfaction of possessing a "cannon house," subsequently dignified with the name of "arsenal." Some of the natives learned the foreign art, and just over a century later (1586) a Russian, or at least a Slav, called Chekhov, produced a famous "Tsar cannon," weighing as much as 96,000 pounds.

The connection thus established with the mechanical arts of the West was always afterwards maintained, and we find frequent notices of the fact in contemporary writers. In the reign of the grandfather of Peter the Great, for example, two paper works were established by an Italian; and velvet for the Tsar and his *Boyárs*, gold brocades for ecclesiastical vestments, and rude kinds of glass for ordinary purposes were manufactured under the august patronage of the enlightened ruler. His son Alexis went a good many steps farther, and scandalized his God-fearing Orthodox subjects by his love of foreign heretical inventions. It was in his German suburb of Moscow that young Peter, who was to become "the Great," made his first acquaintance with the useful arts of the West.

When the great reformer came to the throne he found in his Tsardom, besides many workshops, some ten foundries, all of which were under orders "to cast cannons, bombs, and bullets, and to make arms for the service of the State." This seemed to him only a beginning, especially for the mining and iron industry, in which he was particularly interested. By importing foreign artificers and placing at their disposal big estates, with numerous serfs, in the districts where minerals were plentiful, and by carefully stipulating that these foreigners should teach his subjects well, and conceal from them none of the secrets of the

craft, he created in the Ural a great iron industry, which
still exists at the present day. Finding by experience that
State mines and State ironworks were a heavy drain on
his insufficiently filled treasury, he transferred some of
them to private persons, and this policy was followed occasionally by his successors. Hence the gigantic fortunes
of the Demidovs and other families. The Shuválovs, for
example, in 1760 possessed, for the purpose of working
their mines and ironworks, no less than 33,000 serfs and a
corresponding amount of land. Unfortunately, the concessions were generally given, not to enterprising business-
men, but to influential Court dignitaries, who confined
their attention to squandering the revenues, and not a few
of the mines and works reverted to the Government.

The army required not only arms and ammunition, but
also uniforms and blankets. Great attention, therefore, was
paid to the woolen industry from the reign of Peter downwards. In the time of Catherine there were already 120
cloth factories, but they were on a very small scale, according to modern conceptions. Ten factories in Moscow, for
example, had amongst them only 104 looms, 130 workers,
and a yearly output valued at 200,000 rubles.

While thus largely influenced in its economic policy by
military considerations, the Government did not entirely
neglect other branches of manufacturing industry. Ever
since Russia had pretensions to being a civilized power its
rulers have always been inclined to pay more attention to
the ornamental than the useful—to the varnish rather than
the framework of civilization—and we need not therefore
be surprised to find that, long before the native industry
could supply the materials required for the ordinary wants
of humble life, attempts were made to produce such
things as Gobelin tapestries. I mention this merely as an
illustration of a characteristic trait of the national character, the influence of which may be found in many other
spheres of official activity.

If Russia did not attain the industrial level of Western
Europe, it was not from want of ambition and effort on the
part of the rulers. They worked hard, if not always wisely,
for this end. Manufacturers were exempted from rates and
taxes, and even from military service, and some of them,

as I have said, received large estates from the Crown on the understanding that the serfs should be employed as workmen. At the same time they were protected from foreign competition by prohibitive tariffs. In a word, the manufacturing industry was nursed and fostered in a way to satisfy the most thoroughgoing Protectionist, especially those branches which worked up native raw material such as ores, flax, hemp, wool, and tallow. Occasionally the official interference and anxiety to protect public interests went farther than the manufacturers desired. On more than one occasion the authorities fixed the price of certain kinds of manufactured goods, and in 1754 the Senate, being anxious to protect the population against fires, ordered all glass and iron works within a radius of 200 versts around Moscow to be destroyed! In spite of such obstacles, the manufacturing industry as a whole made considerable progress. Between 1729 and 1762 the number of establishments officially recognized as factories rose from 26 to 335.

These results did not satisfy Catherine II, who ascended the throne in 1762. Under the influence of her friends the French Encyclopédistes, she imagined for a time that the official control might be relaxed, and that the system of employing serfs in the factories and foundries might be replaced by free labor, as in Western Europe; monopolies might be abolished, and all liege subjects, including the peasants, might be allowed to embark in industrial undertakings as they pleased, "for the benefit of the State and the nation." All this looked very well on paper, but Catherine never allowed her sentimental Liberalism to injure seriously the interests of her Empire, and she accordingly refrained from putting the *laissez-faire* principle largely into practice. Though a good deal has been written about her economic policy, it is hardly distinguishable from that of her predecessors. Like them, she maintained high tariffs, accorded large subsidies, and even prevented the export of raw material, in the hope that it might be worked up at home; and when the prices in the woolen market rose very high she compelled the manufacturers to supply the army with cloth at a price fixed by the authorities. In short, the old system remained practically unimpaired, and notwithstanding the steady progress made during the reign of Nicholas I (1825-55), when the number of factory hands rose from 210,000 to 380,000, the manufacturing industry as a whole continued to be, until the serfs were emancipated in 1861, a hothouse plant which could flourish only in an officially heated atmosphere.

There was one branch of it, however, to which this remark does not apply. The art of cotton spinning and cotton weaving struck deep root in Russian soil. After remaining for generations in the condition of a cottage industry—the yarn being distributed among the peasants, and worked up by them in their own homes—it began, about 1825, to be modernized. Though it still required to be protected against foreign competition, it rapidly outgrew the necessity for direct official support. Big factories driven by steam power were constructed, the number of hands employed rose to 110,000, and the foundations of great fortunes were laid. Strange to say, many of the future millionaires were uneducated serfs. Sava Morózov, for example, who was to become one of the industrial magnates of Moscow, was a serf belonging to a proprietor called Ryumin; most of the others were serfs of Count Sheremetyev—the owner of a large estate on which the industrial town of Ivanovo had sprung up—who was proud of having millionaires among his serfs, and who never abused his authority over them. The great movement, however, was not effected without the assistance of foreigners. Foreign foremen were largely employed, and in the work of organization a leading part was played by a German called Ludwig Knoop. Beginning life as a commercial traveler for an English firm, he soon became a large cotton importer, and when in 1840 a feverish activity was produced in the Russian manufacturing world by the Government's permission to import English machines, his firm supplied these machines to the factories on condition of obtaining a share in the business. It has been calculated that it obtained in this way a share in no less than 122 factories, and hence arose among the peasantry a popular saying:

> "Where there is a church, there you find a pope,
> And where there is a factory, there you find a Knoop." [1]

[1] Gdye tserkov—tam pop;
A gdye fabrika—tam Knop.

The biggest creation of the firm was a factory built at Narva in 1856, with nearly half a million spindles driven by water power.

In the second half of last century a revolution was brought about in the manufacturing industry generally by the emancipation of the serfs, the rapid extension of railways, the facilities for creating limited liability companies, and by certain innovations in the financial policy of the Government. The emancipation put on the market an unlimited supply of cheap labor; the construction of railways in all directions increased a hundredfold the means of communication; and the new banks and other credit institutions, aided by an overwhelming influx of foreign capital, encouraged the foundation and extension of industrial and commercial enterprises of every description. For a time there was great excitement. It was commonly supposed that in all matters relating to trade and industry Russia had suddenly jumped up to the level of Western Europe, and many people in St. Petersburg, carried away by the prevailing enthusiasm for Liberalism in general and the doctrines of Free Trade in particular, were in favor of abolishing Protection as an antiquated restriction on liberty and an obstacle to economic progress.

At one moment the Government was disposed to yield to the current, but it was restrained by an influential group of conservative political economists, who appealed to patriotic sentiment, and by the Moscow manufacturers, who declared that Free Trade would ruin the country. After a little hesitation it proceeded to raise, instead of lower, the Protectionist tariff. In 1869-76 the *ad valorem* duties were, on an average, under thirteen per cent, but from that time onwards they rose steadily until the last five years of the century, when they averaged thirty-three per cent, and were for some articles very much higher. In this way the Moscow industrial magnates were protected against the influx of cheap foreign goods, but they were not saved from foreign competition, for many foreign manufacturers, in order to enjoy the benefit of the high duties, founded factories in Russia. Even the firmly established cotton industry suffered from these intruders. Industrial suburbs containing not a few cotton factories owned by foreign capitalists sprang up around St. Petersburg; and a small Polish village called Lodz, near the German frontier, grew rapidly into a prosperous town of 400,000 inhabitants, and became a serious rival to the ancient Muscovite capital. So severely was the competition of this young upstart felt that the Moscow merchants petitioned the Emperor to protect them by drawing a customs frontier round the Polish provinces, but their petition was not granted.

Under the shelter of the high tariffs the manufacturing industry as a whole has made rapid progress, and the cotton trade has kept well to the front. At the beginning of 1909, according to the official reports, the number of industrial establishments of all kinds under Government inspection amounted to 32,601, employing 2,042,115 hands.

The progress of the mineral industries has been not less remarkable than that of the cotton manufacturers. Originally confined to the northern parts of the country, they received about half a century ago a powerful impulse from the discovery that some of the southern provinces, especially the Don basin, contained in close proximity to each other enormous quantities of iron ore and large beds of good coal. Thanks to this discovery, and to other facts of which I shall have occasion to speak presently, this district, which had previously been purely agricultural and pastoral, has outstripped the famous Ural region, and has become the Black Country of Russia. The vast lonely Steppe, where formerly one saw merely peasant farmers, shepherds, and the *Chumák*,[2] driving along somnolently with his big, long-horned white bullocks, is now dotted over with busy industrial settlements of mushroom growth and great ironworks; while at night the landscape is lit up with the lurid flames of gigantic blast furnaces. In this wonderful transformation, as in the history of Russian industrial progress generally, a great part was played by foreigners. The pioneer who did most in this district was a Welshman, John Hughes, who began life as the son and

---

[2] The *Chumák*, a familiar figure in the songs and legends of Little Russia, was the carrier who, before the construction of railways, transported the grain to the great markets, and brought back merchandise to the interior.

pupil of a blacksmith, and whose sons are now directors of the biggest of the South Russian ironworks.

Much as the South has progressed industrially in recent years, it still remains far behind those industrial portions of the country which were thickly settled at an earlier date. From this point of view the most important region is the group of provinces clustering round Moscow; next comes the St. Petersburg region, including Livonia; and thirdly Poland. As for the various kinds of industry, the most important category is that of textile fabrics, the second that of articles of nutrition, and the third that of ores and metals. The total production, if we may believe certain statistical authorities, places Russia now among the industrial nations of the world in the fifth place, immediately after the United States, England, Germany, and France, and a little before Austria.

The man who has in recent times carried out most energetically the policy of protecting and fostering native industries is M. Witte, a name now familiar to Western Europe. An avowed disciple of the great German economist, Friedrich List, about whose works he published a brochure in 1888, he held firmly, from his youth upwards, the doctrine that "each nation should above all things develop harmoniously its natural resources to the highest possible degree of independence, protecting its own industries and preferring the national aim to the pecuniary advantage of individuals." As a corollary to this principle he declared that purely agricultural countries are economically backward and intellectually stagnant, being condemned to pay tribute to the nations who have learned to work up their raw products into more valuable commodities. The good old English doctrine that certain countries were intended by Providence to be eternally agricultural, and that their function in the economy of the universe is to supply raw material for the industrial nations, was always in his eyes an abomination—an ingenious, nefarious invention of the Manchester school, astutely invented for the purpose of keeping the younger nations permanently in a state of economic bondage for the benefit of English manufacturers. To emancipate Russia from this thralldom by enabling her to create a great native industry, sufficient to supply all her own wants, was the aim of his policy and the constant object of his untiring efforts. Those who have had the good fortune to know him personally must have often heard him discourse eloquently on this theme, supporting his views by quotations from the economists of his own school, and by illustrations drawn from the history of his own and other countries.

A necessary condition of realizing this aim was that there should be high tariffs. These already existed, and they might be raised still higher, but in themselves they were not enough. For the rapid development of native industry an enormous capital was required, and the first problem to be solved was how this capital could be obtained. At one moment the energetic Minister conceived the project of creating a fictitious capital by inflating the paper currency; but this idea proved unpopular, and when broached in the Council of State it encountered determined opposition. Being a practical man without inveterate prejudices, M. Witte gave up the scheme which he could not carry through, and adopted the views of his opponents. He would introduce a gold currency as recommended; but how was the requisite capital to be obtained? It must be procured from abroad, somehow, and the simplest way seemed to be to stimulate the export of native products. For this purpose the railways were extended,[3] the traffic rates manipulated, and the means of transport improved generally.

A certain influx of gold was thus secured, but not nearly enough for the object in view. Some more potent means, therefore, had to be employed, and the inventive Minister evolved a new scheme. If he could only induce foreign capitalists to undertake manufacturing industries in Russia, they would, at one and the same time, bring into the country an enormous amount of capital, and also co-operate powerfully in that development of the national industry which he so ardently desired. No sooner had he roughly sketched out his plan—for he was not a man to let the grass grow under his feet—than he set himself to

[3] During the ten years of his financial administration (1893-1903) the railway system was extended from 20,287 to 37,128 miles.

put it into execution by letting it be known in the financial world that the Government was ready to open a great field for lucrative investments, in the form of profitable enterprises under the control of those who subscribed the capital.

Foreign capitalists responded warmly to the call. Crowds of concession hunters, projectors, company promoters, *et hoc genus omne,* collected in St. Petersburg, offering their services on the most tempting terms; and all of them who could make out a plausible case were well received at the Ministry of Finance. It was there explained to them that in many branches of industry, such as the manufacture of textile fabrics, there was little or no room for newcomers, but that in others the prospects were most brilliant. Take, for example, the iron industries of Southern Russia. The boundless mineral wealth of that region was still almost intact, and the few works which had been there established were paying very large dividends. The works founded by John Hughes, for example, had repeatedly divided considerably over twenty per cent, and there was little fear for the future, because the Government had embarked on a great scheme of railway extension, requiring an unlimited amount of rails and rolling stock. What better opening could be desired? Certainly the opening seemed most attractive, and into it rushed the crowd of company promoters, followed by stock jobbers and brokers, playing lively pieces of what the Germans call *Zukunftsmusik.* An unwary and confiding public, especially in Belgium and France, listened to the enchanting strain of the financial sirens, and invested largely. Quickly the number of completed ironworks in that region rose from nine to seventeen, and in the short space of three years the output of pig iron was nearly doubled. In 1900 there were 44 blast furnaces in working order, and ten more were in course of construction. And all this time the Imperial revenue increased by leaps and bounds, so that the introduction of the gold currency was effected without difficulty. M. Witte was declared to be the greatest Minister of his time—a Russian Colbert or Turgot, or perhaps the two rolled into one.

Then came a change. Competition and overproduction

led naturally to a fall in prices, and at the same time the demand decreased, because the railway-building activity of the Government slackened. Alarmed at this state of things, the banks which had helped to start and foster the huge and costly enterprises contracted their credits. By the end of 1899 the disenchantment was general and widespread. Some of the companies were so weighted by the preliminary financial obligations, and had conducted their affairs in such careless, reckless fashion, that they had to shut down their mines and close their works. Even solid undertakings suffered. The shares of the Briansk works, for example, which had given dividends as high as 30 per cent, fell from 500 to 230. The Mamontov companies—supposed to be one of the strongest financial groups in the country—had to suspend payment, and numerous other failures occurred. Nearly all the commercial banks, having directly participated in the industrial concerns, were rudely shaken. M. Witte, who had been for a time the idol of a certain section of the financial world, became very unpopular, and was accused of having misled the investing public. Among the accusations brought against him some at least could easily be refuted. He may have made mistakes in his policy, and may have been himself oversanguine, but surely, as he subsequently replied to his accusers, it was no part of his duty to warn company promoters and directors that they should refrain from overproduction, and that their enterprises might not be as remunerative as they expected. As to whether there is any truth in the assertion that he held out prospects of larger Government orders than he actually gave, I cannot say. That he cut down prices, and showed himself a hard man to deal with, there seems no doubt.

The reader may naturally be inclined to jump to the conclusion that the commercial crisis just referred to was the direct cause of M. Witte's fall. Such a conclusion would not be quite accurate. The crisis happened in the winter of 1899-1900, and M. Witte remained Finance Minister until the autumn of 1903. His fall was the result of more complicated causes, and these I propose now to explain, because the explanation will throw light on certain very curious and characteristic conceptions which were then current among the Russian educated classes and have not yet entirely disappeared.

Of course there were certain causes of a purely personal kind, but I shall dismiss them in a very few words. I remember once asking a well-informed friend of M. Witte's what he thought of him as an administrator and a statesman. The friend replied: "Imagine a Negro of the Gold Coast let loose in modern European civilization!" This reply, like most epigrammatic remarks, is a piece of gross exaggeration, but it has a modicum of truth in it. In the eyes of well-trained Russian officials M. Witte was a titanic, reckless character, capable at any moment of playing the part of the bull in the china-shop. As a masterful person, brusque in manner and incapable of brooking contradiction, he had made for himself many enemies; and his restless, irrepressible energy had led him to encroach on the provinces of all his colleagues. Possessing as he did the control of the purse, his interference could not easily be resisted. The Ministers of the Interior, War, Agriculture, Public Works, Public Instruction, and Foreign Affairs had all occasion to complain of his incursions into their departments.

Altogether M. Witte was an inconvenient personage in an Administration in which strong personality is regarded as entirely out of place, and in which personal initiative is supposed to reside exclusively in the Tsar. In addition to all this he was a man who felt keenly, and when he was irritated he did not always keep the unruly member under strict control. If I am correctly informed, it was some imprudent and not very respectful remarks, repeated by a subordinate and transmitted by a Grand Duke to the Tsar, which were the immediate cause of his transfer from the influential post of Minister of Finance to the ornamental position of President of the Council of Ministers; but that was merely the proverbial last straw that breaks the camel's back. His position was already undermined, and it is the undermining process which I wish to describe.

The first to work for his overthrow were the Agrarian Conservatives. They could not deny that, from the purely fiscal point of view, his administration was a marvelous success; for he was rapidly doubling the revenue, and he had succeeded in replacing the fluctuating depreciated paper currency by a gold coinage; but they maintained that he was killing the goose that laid the golden eggs. Evidently the taxpaying power of the rural classes was being overstrained, for they were falling more and more into arrears in the payment of their taxes, and their impoverishment was yearly increasing. All their reserves had been exhausted, as was shown by the famines of 1891-2, when the Government had to spend hundreds of millions to feed them. Whilst the land was losing its fertility, those who had to live by it were increasing in numbers at an alarming rate. Already in some districts one-fifth of the peasant households had no longer any land of their own, and of those who still possessed land a large proportion had no longer the cattle and horses necessary to till and manure their allotments. No doubt M. Witte was beginning to perceive his mistake, and had done something to palliate the evils by improving the system of collecting the taxes and abolishing the passport dues, but such merely palliative remedies could have little effect. While a few capitalists were amassing gigantic fortunes, the masses were slowly and surely advancing to the brink of starvation. The welfare of the agriculturists, who constitute nine-tenths of the whole population, was being ruthlessly sacrificed, and for what? For the creation of a manufacturing industry which rested on an artificial, precarious basis, and which had already begun to decline.

So far the Agrarians, who championed the interests of the agricultural classes. Their views were confirmed and their arguments strengthened by an influential group of men whom I may call, for want of a better name, the philosophers or doctrinaire interpreters of history, who have, strange to say, more influence in Russia than in any other country.

The Russian educated classes desire that the nation should be wealthy and self-supporting, and they recognize that for this purpose a large manufacturing industry is required; but they are reluctant to make the sacrifices necessary to attain the object in view, and they imagine that, somehow or other, these sacrifices may be avoided. Sympathizing with this frame of mind, the doctrinaires explain that the rich and prosperous countries of Europe and America obtained their wealth and prosperity by so-called "Capitalism"—that is to say, by a peculiar social organization, in which the two main factors are a small body of rich capitalists and manufacturers, and an enormous pauper proletariat living from hand to mouth, at the mercy of the heartless employers of labor. Russia had lately followed in the footsteps of those wealthy countries, and if she continued to do so she would inevitably be saddled with the same disastrous results—plutocracy, pauperism, unrestrained competition in all spheres of activity, and a greatly intensified struggle for life, in which the weaker would necessarily go to the wall.[4]

Happily there was, according to these theorists, a more excellent way, and Russia might adopt it if she only remained true to certain mysterious principles of her past historic development. Without attempting to expound those mysterious principles, to which I have repeatedly referred in previous chapters, I may mention briefly that the traditional patriarchal institutions on which the theorists founded their hopes of a happy social future for their country were the rural Commune, the native home industries, and the peculiar co-operative institutions called *Artéls*. How these remnants of a semipatriarchal state of society were to be practically developed in such a way as to withstand the competition of manufacturing industry organized on modern "Capitalist" lines, no one could explain satisfactorily, but many people indulged in ingenious speculations on the subject, like children planning the means of diverting with their little toy spades a formidable inundation. In my humble opinion, the whole theory was a delusion; but it was held firmly—I might almost say fanatically—by those who, in opposition to the indiscriminate admirers of West European and American civilization, considered themselves genuine Russians and exceptionally good patriots. M. Witte never belonged to that

[4] Free competition in all spheres of activity, leading to social inequality, plutocracy, and pauperism, is the favorite bugbear of Russian theorists; and who is not a theorist in Russia? The fact indicates the prevalence of Socialist ideas among the educated classes.

class. He believed that there was only one road to national prosperity—the road by which Western Europe had traveled—and along this road he tried to drive his country as rapidly as possible. He threw himself, therefore, heart and soul into what his opponents called "Capitalism," by raising State loans, organizing banks and other credit institutions, encouraging the creation and extension of big factories, which must inevitably destroy the home industries, and even—*horribile dictu!*—undermining the rural Commune, and thereby adding to the ranks of the landless proletariat, in order to increase the amount of cheap labor for the benefit of the capitalists.

With the arguments thus supplied by Agrarians and doctrinaires, quite honest and well meaning according to their lights, it was easy to sap M. Witte's position. Among his opponents, the most formidable was the late M. Plehve, Minister of the Interior—a man of a totally different stamp. A few months before his tragic end, I had a long and interesting conversation with him, and I came away deeply impressed. Having repeatedly had conversations of a similar kind with M. Witte, I could compare, or rather contrast, the two men. Both of them evidently possessed an exceptional amount of mental power and energy, but in the one it was volcanic, and in the other it was concentrated and thoroughly under control. In discussion, the one reminded me of the self-taught, slashing swordsman; the other of the dexterous fencer, carefully trained in the use of the foils, who never launches out beyond the point at which he can quickly recover himself. As to whether M. Plehve was anything more than a bold, energetic, clever official, there may be differences of opinion, but he certainly could assume the airs of a profound and polished statesman, capable of looking at things from a much higher point of view than the ordinary *chinóvnik*, and he had the talent of tacitly suggesting that a great deal of genuine, enlightened statesmanship lay hidden under the smooth surface of his cautious reserve. When speaking of his colleague, M. Witte, his language was most correct, but it was not difficult to infer that he was decidedly hostile to the policy of the Ministry of Finance.

From other sources I learned the chief cause of this

hostility. Being Minister of the Interior, and having served long in the Police Department, M. Plehve considered that his first duty was the maintenance of public order and the protection of the person and autocracy of his august master. He was therefore the determined enemy of revolutionary tendencies, in whatever garb or disguise they might appear; and as a statesman he had to direct his attention to everything likely to increase those tendencies in the future. Now it seemed to him that in the financial policy which had been followed for some years there were germs of future revolutionary fermentation. The peasantry were becoming impoverished, and were therefore more likely to listen to the insidious suggestions of Socialist agitators; and already agrarian disturbances had occurred in the provinces of Kharkov and Poltava. The industrial proletariat which was being rapidly created was being secretly organized by the revolutionary Social Democrats, and already there had been serious labor troubles in some of the large towns. For any future revolutionary movement the proletariat would naturally supply recruits. Then, at the other end of the social scale, a class of rich capitalists was being created, and everybody who has read a little history knows that a rich and powerful *tiers-état* cannot be permanently conciliated with autocracy. Though himself neither an Agrarian nor a Slavophil doctrinaire, M. Plehve could not but have a certain sympathy with those who were forging thunderbolts for the official annihilation of M. Witte. He was too practical a man to imagine that the hands on the dial of economic progress could be set back and a return made to moribund patriarchal institutions; but he thought that at least the pace might be moderated. The Minister of Finance need not be in such a desperate, reckless hurry, and it was desirable to create conservative forces which might counteract the revolutionary forces which his impulsive colleague was inadvertently calling into existence.

Some of the forgers of thunderbolts went a great deal farther, and asserted or insinuated that M. Witte was himself consciously a revolutionist, with secret, malevolent intentions. In support of their insinuations they cited certain cases in which well-known Socialists had been appointed professors in academies under the control of the Ministry of Finance, and they pointed to the Peasant Bank, which enjoyed M. Witte's special protection. At first it had been supposed that the bank would have an antirevolutionary influence by preventing the formation of a landless proletariat and increasing the number of small landowners, who are always and everywhere conservative so far as the rights of private property are concerned. Unfortunately its success roused the fears of the more conservative section of the landed proprietors. These gentlemen, as I have already mentioned, pointed out that the estates of the nobles were rapidly passing into the hands of the peasantry, and that, if this process were allowed to continue, the hereditary noblesse, which had always been the surest support of the throne, would drift into the towns and there sink into poverty or amalgamate with the commercial plutocracy. Thus they would help to form a *tiers-état*, which would be hostile to the autocratic power.

In these circumstances it was evident that the headstrong Minister of Finance could maintain his position only so long as he enjoyed the energetic support of the Emperor, and this support, for reasons which I have indicated above, failed him at the critical moment. While his work was still unfinished he was suddenly compelled to relinquish his post and accept a position in which, it was supposed, he would cease to have any great influence on the Administration.

Thus fell the Russian Colbert-Turgot, or whatever else he may be called. Whether financial difficulties in the future will lead to his reinstatement as Minister of Finance remains to be seen; but in any case his work cannot be undone. He has increased manufacturing industry to an unprecedented extent, and, as M. Plehve perceived, the industrial proletariat, which manufacturing industry on capitalist lines always creates, has provided a new field of activity for the revolutionists. I return, therefore, to the development of the revolutionary movement in order to describe its more recent phases.

CHAPTER · XXVI

❦

A New Phase of the Revolutionary Movement

THE development of manufacturing industry on capitalist lines, and the consequent formation of a large industrial proletariat, naturally produced great disappointment among the numerous theorists who had believed that in some way or other Russia would escape "the festering sores of Western civilization." Experience had proved that the belief was an illusion, and those who had tried to check the natural course of industrial progress were constrained to confess that their efforts had been futile. Big factories were increasing in size and numbers, while cottage industries were disappearing or falling under the power of middlemen, and the *Artéls* had not advanced a step in their expected development. The factory workers, all of peasant origin, were losing their connection with their native villages, and abandoning their allotments of the Communal land. They were becoming, in short, an hereditary caste in the town population, and the Slavophil dream of every factory worker having a house in the country could no longer be indulged in. Nor was there any prospect of a change for the better in the future. With the increase of competition among the manufacturers, the uprooting of the muzhik from the soil must go on more and more rapidly, because employers must insist more and more on having thoroughly trained operatives ready to work steadily all the year round.

This state of things had a curious effect on the course of the revolutionary movement.

Let me recall very briefly the successive stages through which the movement had already passed. It had been inaugurated, as we have seen, by the Nihilists, the ardent young representatives of a "storm-and-stress" period, in which the venerable traditions and respected principles of the past were rejected and ridiculed, and the newest ideas of Western Europe were eagerly adopted and distorted. Like the majority of their educated countrymen, they believed that, in the race of progress, Russia was about to overtake and surpass the nations of the West, and that this desirable result was to be attained by making a *tabula rasa* of existing institutions, and reconstructing society according to the plans of Proudhon, Fourier, and the other writers of the early Socialist school.

When the Nihilists had expended their energies and exhausted the patience of the public in theorizing, talking, and writing, a party of action came upon the scene. Like the Nihilists, they desired political, social, and economic reforms of the most thoroughgoing kind, but they believed that such things could not be effected by the educated classes alone, and they determined to call in the co-operation of the people. For this purpose they tried to convert the masses to the gospel of Socialism. Hundreds of them became missionaries and "went in among the people." But the gospel of Socialism proved unintelligible to the uneducated, and the more ardent, incautious missionaries fell into the hands of the police. Those of them who escaped, perceiving the error of their ways, but still clinging to the hope of bringing about a political, social, and economic revolution, determined to change their tactics. The emancipated serf had shown himself incapable of "prolonged revolutionary activity," but there was reason to believe that he was, like his forefathers in the time of Stenka Razin and Pugachev, capable of rising and murdering his oppressors. He must be used, therefore, for the destruction of the autocratic power and the bureaucracy, and then it would be easy to reorganize society on a basis of universal equality, and to take permanent precautions against capitalism and the creation of a Proletariat. This was the second phase of the movement.

The hopes of the agitators proved as delusive as those of the propagandists. The muzhik turned a deaf ear to their instigations, and the police soon prevented their further activity. Thus the would-be root-and-branch reformers found themselves in a dilemma. Either they must abandon their schemes for the moment or they must strike immediately at their persecutors. They chose, as we have seen, the latter alternative, and after vain attempts to frighten the Government by acts of terrorism against zealous officials, they assassinated the Tsar himself; but before they had time to think of the constructive part of their task, their organization was destroyed by the autocratic power and the bureaucracy, and those of them who escaped arrest had to seek safety in emigration to Switzerland and Paris. Thus ended the third phase.

Then arose, all along the line of the defeated, decimated Revolutionists, the cry, "What is to be done?" Some replied that the shattered organization should be reconstructed, and a number of secret agents were sent successively from Switzerland for this purpose. But their efforts, as they themselves confessed, were fruitless, and despondency seemed to be settling down permanently on all, except a few fanatics, when a voice was heard calling on the fugitives to rally round a new banner and carry on the struggle by entirely new methods. The voice came from a revolutionologist (if I may use such a term) of remarkable talent, called M. Plekhánov, who had settled in Geneva with a little circle of friends, calling themselves the "Labor-Emancipation Group." His views were expounded in a series of interesting publications, the first of which was a brochure entitled "Socialism and the Political Struggle," published in 1883.

According to M. Plekhánov and his disciples the revolutionary movement had been conducted up to that moment on altogether wrong lines. All previous revolutionary groups had acted on the assumption that the political revolution and the economic reorganization of society must be effected simultaneously, and consequently they had rejected contemptuously all proposals for reforms, however radical, of a merely political kind. These had been considered, as I have mentioned in a previous chapter, not only as worthless, but as positively prejudicial to the interests of the working classes, because so-called political liberties and parliamentary government would be sure to consolidate the domination of the *bourgeoisie*. That such had generally been the immediate effect of parliamentary institutions was admitted, but it did not follow that the creation of such institutions should be opposed. On the contrary, they ought to be welcomed, not merely because, as some revolutionists had already pointed out, propaganda and agitation could be more easily carried on under a constitutional regime, but because constitutionalism is certainly the most convenient, and perhaps the only, road by which the socialistic ideal can ultimately be attained. This is a dark saying, but it will become clearer when I have explained, according to the new apostles, a second error into which their predecessors had fallen.

That second error was the assumption that all true friends of the people, whether Conservatives, Liberals, or Revolutionaries, ought to oppose to the utmost the development of capitalism. In the light of Karl Marx's discoveries in economic science everyone must recognize this to be an egregious mistake. That great authority, it was said, had proved that the development of capitalism was irresistible, and his conclusions had been confirmed by the recent history of Russia, for all the economic progress made during the last half-century had been on capitalist lines.

Even if it were possible to arrest the capitalist movement it is not desirable from the revolutionary point of view. In support of this thesis Karl Marx is again cited. He has shown that capitalism, though an evil in itself, is a necessary stage of economic and social progress. At first it is prejudicial to the interests of the working classes, but in the long run it benefits them, because the ever growing Proletariat must, whether it desires it or not, become a political party, and as a political party it must one day break the domination of the *bourgeoisie*. As soon as it has obtained the predominant political power, it will confiscate, for the public good, the instruments of production—factories, foundries, machines, etc.—by expropriating the capitalists. In this way all the profits which accrue from production on a large scale, and which at present go into the pockets of the capitalists, will be distributed equally among the workmen.

Thus began the fourth phase of the revolutionary

movement, and, like all previous phases, it remained for some years in the academic stage, during which there were endless discussions on theoretical and practical questions. Lavróv, the prophet of the old propaganda, treated the new ideas "with grandfatherly severity," and Tikhomirov, the leading representative of the moribund *Narodnaya Volya*, which had prepared the acts of terrorism, maintained stoutly that the West European methods recommended by Plekhánov were inapplicable to Russia. The Plekhánov group replied in a long series of publications, partly original, and partly translations from Marx and Engels, explaining the doctrines and aims of the Social Democrats.

Seven years were spent in this academic literary activity —a period of comparative repose for the Russian secret police—and then, about 1890, the propagandists of the new school began to work cautiously in St. Petersburg. At first they confined themselves to forming little secret circles for making converts, and they found that the ground had been to some extent prepared for the seed which they had to sow. The workmen were discontented, and some of the more intelligent amongst them, who had formerly been in touch with the propagandists of the older generation, had learned that there was an ingenious and effective means of getting their grievances redressed. How was that possible? By combinations and strikes. For the uneducated workers this was an important discovery, and they soon began to put the suggested remedy to a practical test. In the autumn of 1894 labor troubles broke out in the Nevski engineering works and the arsenal, and in the following year in the Thornton factory and the cigarette manufactories. In all these strikes the Social Democratic agents took part behind the scenes. Avoiding the main errors of the old propagandists, who had offered the workmen merely abstract Socialist theories which no uneducated person could reasonably be expected to understand, they adopted a more rational method. Though impervious to abstract theories, the Russian workman is not at all insensible to the prospect of bettering his material condition, and getting his everyday grievances redressed. Of these grievances the ones he felt most keenly were the long hours, the low wages, the fines arbitrarily imposed by the managers, and the brutal severity of the foremen. By helping him to have these grievances removed, the Social Democratic agents might gain his confidence, and when they had come to be regarded by him as his real friends they might widen his sympathies, and teach him to feel that his personal interests were identical with the interests of the working classes as a whole. In this way it would be possible to awaken in the industrial proletariat generally a sort of *esprit de corps,* which is the first condition of political organization.

On these lines the agents set to work. Having formed themselves into a secret association called the "Union for the Emancipation of the Working Classes," they gradually abandoned the narrow limits of coterie-propaganda and prepared the way for agitation on a larger scale. Among the discontented workmen they distributed a large number of carefully written tracts, in which the material grievances were formulated, and the whole political system, with its police, gendarmes, Cossacks, and tax gatherers, was criticized in no friendly spirit, but without violent language. In introducing into the program this political element, great caution had to be exercised, because the workmen did not yet perceive clearly any close connection between their grievances and the existing political institutions, and those of them who belonged to the older generation regarded the Tsar as the incarnation of disinterested benevolence. Bearing this in mind, the Union circulated a pamphlet for the enlightenment of the laboring population, in which the writer refrained from all reference to the autocratic power, and described simply the condition of the laboring classes, the heavy burdens they had to bear, the abuses of which they were the victims, and the inconsiderate way in which they were treated by their employers. This pamphlet was eagerly read, and from that moment, whenever labor troubles arose, the men applied to the Social Democratic agents to assist them in formulating their grievances.

Of course, the assistance had to be given secretly, because there were always police spies in the factories, and all persons suspected of aiding the labor movement were liable to be arrested and exiled. On January 4th, 1896, for example, when the Social Democrats were holding a secret meeting, 115 of them were arrested by the police. Notwithstanding this incident and others of a similar kind, the work was carried on with great energy, and in the summer of 1896 the field of operations was extended. During the coronation ceremonies of that year the factories and workshops in St. Petersburg were closed, and the men considered that for these days they ought to receive wages as usual. When their demand was refused, 30,000 of them went out on strike. The Social Democratic Union seized the opportunity and distributed tracts in large quantities. For the first time such tracts were read aloud at workmen's meetings and applauded by the audience. The Union encouraged the workmen in their resistance, but advised them to refrain from violence, so as not to provoke the intervention of the police and the military, as they had imprudently done on some previous occasions. When the police did intervene and expelled some of the strike leaders from St. Petersburg, the agitators had an excellent opportunity of explaining that the authorities were the protectors of the employers and the enemies of the working classes. These explanations counteracted the effect of an official proclamation to the workmen, in which M. Witte tried to convince them that the Tsar was constantly striving to improve their condition. The struggle was decided, not by arguments and exhortations, but by a more potent force: having no funds for continuing the strike, the men were compelled by starvation to resume work.

This is the point at which the labor movement began to be conducted on a large scale and by more systematic methods. In the earlier labor troubles, the strikers had not understood that the best means of bringing pressure on employers was simply to refuse to work, and they had often proceeded to show their dissatisfaction by ruthlessly destroying their employers' property. This had brought the police, and sometimes the military, on the scene, and numerous arrests had followed. Another mistake made by the inexperienced strikers was that they had neglected to create a reserve fund from which they could draw the means of subsistence when they no longer received wages and could no longer obtain credit at the factory provision store. Efforts were now made to correct these two mistakes, and with regard to the former they were fairly successful, for wanton destruction of property ceased to be a prominent feature of labor troubles; but strong reserve funds have not yet been created, so that the strikes have never been of long duration.

Though the strikes had led, so far, to no great practical, tangible results, the new ideas and aspirations were spreading rapidly in the factories and workshops, and they had already struck such deep root that some of the genuine workmen wished to have a voice in the managing committee of the Union, which was composed exclusively of educated men. When a request to that effect was rejected by the committee a lengthy discussion took place, and it soon became evident that underneath the question of organization lay a most important question of principle. The workmen wished to concentrate their efforts on the improvement of their material condition, and to proceed on what we should call trade-unionist lines, whereas the committee wished them to aim at the acquisition of political rights. Great determination was shown on both sides. An attempt of the workmen to found and disseminate a secret periodical of their own with the view of emancipating themselves from the "Politicals" ended in failure; but they received sympathy and support from some of the educated members of the party, and in this way a schism took place in the Social Democrat camp. After repeated ineffectual attempts to find a satisfactory compromise the question was submitted to a Congress, which was held in Switzerland in 1900; but the discussions merely accentuated the differences of opinion, and the two parties constituted themselves into separate independent groups. The one following Plekhánov, and calling itself the Revolutionary Social Democrats, held to the Marx doctrines in all their extent and purity, and maintained the necessity of constant agitation in the political sense. The other, calling itself the Union of Foreign Social Democrats, inclined to the trade-unionism program, and proclaimed the necessity of being guided by political expediency rather than inflexible dogmas. Between the two groups a wordy warfare was carried on for some time in pedantic, technical language; but, though habitually brandishing their weapons and denouncing their antagonists in true Homeric style, they were really allies, struggling towards a common end—two sections of the Social Democratic party differing from each other merely on questions of tactics.

The two divergent tendencies have often reappeared in the subsequent history of the movement. During ordinary peaceful times the economic or trade-unionist tendency can generally hold its own, but as soon as disturbances occur and the authorities have to intervene, the political current quickly gains the upper hand. This was exemplified in the labor troubles which took place at Rostov-on-the-Don in 1902. During the first two days of the strike the economic demands alone were put forward, and in the speeches which were delivered at the meetings of workmen no reference was made to political grievances. On the third day one orator ventured to speak disrespectfully of the autocratic power, but he thereby provoked signs of dissatisfaction in the audience. On the fifth and following days, however, several political speeches were made, ending with the cry of "Down with Tsarism!" and a crowd of 30,000 workmen agreed with the speakers. Thereafter occurred similar strikes in Odessa, the Caucasus, Kiev, and Central Russia, and they all had a political rather than a purely economic character.

I must now endeavor to explain clearly the point of view and plan of campaign of this new movement, which I may call the revolutionary Renaissance.

The ultimate aim of the new reformers was the same as that of all their predecessors—the thorough reorganization of Society on Socialistic principles. According to their doctrines, Society as at present constituted consists of two great classes, called variously the exploiters and the exploited, the shearers and the shorn, the capitalists and the workers, the employers and the employed, the tyrants and the oppressed; and this unsatisfactory state of things must go on so long as the so-called *bourgeois* or capitalist regime continues to exist. In the new heaven

and the new earth of which the Socialist dreams, this unjust distinction is to disappear; all human beings are to be
equally free and independent, all are to co-operate spontaneously with brains and hands to the common good, and
all are to enjoy in equal shares the natural and artificial
good things of this life.

So far there has never been any difference of opinion
among the various groups of Russian thoroughgoing revolutionists. All of them, from the antiquated Nihilist down
to the Social Democrat of the latest type, have held these
views. What has differentiated them from each other is the
greater or less degree of impatience to realize the ideal.

The most impatient were the Anarchists, who grouped
themselves around Bakúnin. They wished to overthrow
immediately by a frontal attack all existing forms of
government and social organization, in the hope that
chance, or evolution, or natural instinct, or sudden inspiration, or some other mysterious force, would create something better. They themselves declined to aid this mysterious force even by suggestions, on the ground that, as
one of them has said, "to construct is not the business of
the generation whose duty is to destroy." Notwithstanding the strong impulsive element in the national character,
these reckless, ultraimpatient doctrinaires never became
numerous, and never succeeded in forming an organized
group, probably because the young generation in Russia
were too much occupied with the actual and future condition of their own country to embark on schemes of cosmopolitan anarchism such as Bakúnin recommended.

Next in the scale of impatience came the group of believers in Socialist agitation among the masses, with a
view to overturning the existing Government and putting
themselves in its place as soon as the masses were sufficiently organized to play the part destined for them. Between them and the Anarchists the essential points of difference were that they admitted the necessity of some
years of preparation, and they intended, when the existing regime was overturned, not to preserve indefinitely
the state of anarchy, but to put in the place of autocracy,
limited monarchy, or the republic, a strong, despotic,
provisional Government thoroughly imbued with Socialis-

tic principles. As soon as this temporary despotism had
laid firmly the foundations of the new order of things it
was to call together a National Assembly, from which
it was to receive, I presume, a bill of indemnity for the
benevolent tyranny which it had temporarily exercised
during the period of transition.

Impatience a few degrees less intense produced the
next group, the partisans of pacific Socialist propaganda.
They maintained that there was no necessity for over-
throwing the old order of things till the masses had been
intellectually prepared for the new, and they objected to
the foundation of the new regime being laid by despots,
however well intentioned in the Socialist sense. The people
must be made happy and preserved in a state of happiness
by the people themselves.

In the last place came the least impatient of all, the
Social Democrats, who differ widely from all the preceding
categories.

All previous revolutionary groups had systematically rejected the idea of a gradual transition from the *bourgeois*
to the Socialist regime. They would not listen to any suggestion about a constitutional monarchy or a democratic
republic even as a mere intermediate stage of social development. All such things, as part and parcel of the
bourgeois system, were anathematized. There must be no
halfway houses between present misery and future happiness; for many weary travelers might be tempted to settle
there in the desert, and fail to reach the promised land.
"Ever onward" should be the watchword, and no time
should be wasted on the foolish struggles of political parties and the empty vanities of political life.

Not thus thought the Social Democrat. He was much
wiser in his generation. Having seen how the attempts of
the impatient groups had ended in disaster, and knowing
that, if they had succeeded, the old effete bureaucracy
would probably have been replaced by a young, vigorous despotism more objectionable than its predecessor, he
determined to try a more circuitous but surer road to the
goal which the impatient revolutionaries had in view. In
his opinion the distance from the present Russian regime
protected by autocracy to the future Socialist paradise

was far too great to be traversed in a single stage, and he knew of one or two comfortable rest houses on the way. First there was the rest house of Constitutionalism, with parliamentary institutions. For some years the *bourgeoisie* would doubtless have a parliamentary majority, but gradually, by persistent effort, the Fourth Estate would gain the upper hand, and then the Socialist millennium might be proclaimed. Meanwhile, what had to be done was to gain the confidence of the masses, especially of the factory workers, who were more intelligent and less conservative than the peasantry, and to create powerful labor organizations as material for a future political party.

This program implied, of course, a certain unity of action with the constitutionalists, from whom, as I have said, the revolutionists of the old school had stood sternly aloof. There was now no question of a formal union, and certainly no idea of "a union of hearts," because the Socialists knew that their ultimate aim would be strenuously opposed by the Liberals, and the Liberals knew that an attempt was being made to use them as a cat's-paw; but there seemed to be no reason why the two groups should not observe towards each other a benevolent neutrality, and march side by side as far as the half-way house, where they could consider the conditions of the further advance.

When I first became acquainted with the Russian Social Democrats, I imagined that their plan of campaign was of a purely pacific character; and that they were, unlike their predecessors, an evolutionary, as distinguished from a revolutionary, party. Subsequently I discovered that this conception was not quite accurate. In ordinary quiet times they used merely pacific methods, and they felt that the Proletariat was not yet sufficiently prepared, intellectually and politically, to assume the great responsibilities reserved for it in the future. Moreover, when the moment should come for getting rid of the autocratic power, they preferred a gradual process of liquidation to a sudden cataclysm. So far they might be said to be evolutionaries rather than revolutionaries, but their plan of campaign did not entirely exclude violence. They did not consider it their duty to oppose the use of violence on the part of the more impatient sections of the revolutionists, and they had no scruples about utilizing disturbances for the attainment of their own ends. Public agitation, which is always likely in Russia to provoke violent repression by the authorities, they regarded as necessary for keeping alive and strengthening the spirit of opposition; and when force was used by the police they approved of the agitators using force in return. To acts of terrorism, however, they were opposed on principle.

Who, then, were the Terrorists who assassinated so many great personages? In reply to this question I must introduce the reader to another group of the revolutionists who have usually been in hostile, rather than friendly, relations with the Social Democrats, and who call themselves the Socialist-Revolutionaries (*Sotsialísty-Revolutsionéry*).

Like other revolutionary groups, the Socialist-Revolutionaries declared their ultimate aim to be the transfer of political authority from the autocratic power to the people, and the complete reorganization of the national life on the most advanced principles of Socialism. On certain points they were at one with the Social Democrats. They recognized, for example, that the social reorganization must be preceded by a political revolution, that much preparatory work was necessary, and that attention should be directed first to the industrial proletariat as the most intelligent section of the masses. On the other hand they maintained, in opposition to the Social Democrats, that it was a mistake to confine the revolutionary activity to the working classes of the towns, who were not strong enough to overturn the autocratic power. The agitation ought, therefore, to be extended to the peasantry, who were quite "developed" enough to understand at least the idea of land-nationalization; and for the carrying out of this part of the program a special organization was created.

With so many opinions in common it seemed at one moment as if the Social Democrats and the Socialist-Revolutionaries might unite their forces for a combined attack on the Government; but, apart from the mutual jealousy and hatred which so often characterize revolutionary as well as religious sects, they were prevented from coalescing, or even cordially co-operating, by profound differences both in doctrine and in method.

The Social Democrats were essentially doctrinaires. Thoroughgoing disciples of Karl Marx, they believed in the so-called immutable laws of social progress, according to which the Socialistic ideal can be reached only through capitalism, while the intermediate political revolution, which is to substitute the will of the people for the autocratic power, must be effected by the conversion and organization of the industrial proletariat. With the spiritual pride of men who feel themselves to be the incarnations or avatars of immutable law, they were inclined to look down with something very like contempt on mere empirics who were ignorant of scientific principles and were guided by considerations of practical expediency. The Socialist-Revolutionaries seemed to them to be empirics of this kind because they rejected the tenets, or at least denied the infallibility, of the Marx school, clung to the idea of partially resisting the overwhelming influence of capitalism in Russia, hoped that the peasantry would play an important part in bringing about the political revolution, and were profoundly convinced that the advent of political liberty might be greatly accelerated by the use of terrorism. On this last point they stated their views very frankly in a pamphlet which they published in 1902 under the title of "Our Task" (*Nasha Zadacha*). It is here said:

> "One of the powerful means of struggle, dictated by our revolutionary past and present, is political Terrorism, consisting of the annihilation of the most injurious and influential personages of Russian autocracy. . . . Systematic Terrorism, in conjunction with other forms of open mass struggle (industrial riots and agrarian risings, demonstrations, etc.) which receive from Terrorism an enormous, decisive significance, will lead to the disorganization of the enemy. Terrorist activity will cease only with the victory over autocracy and the complete attainment of political liberty. Besides its chief significance as a means of disorganizing, Terrorist activity will serve at the same time as a

means of propaganda and agitation, a form of open struggle taking place before the eyes of the whole people, undermining the prestige of Government authority, and calling into life new revolutionary forces, while the oral and literary propaganda is being continued without interruption. Lastly, the Terrorist activity serves for the whole secret revolutionary party as a means of self-defense and of protecting the organization against the injurious elements of spies and treachery."

In accordance with this theory a "militant organization" (*Boevaya Organizatsia*) was formed, and it soon set to work with revolvers and bombs. First an attempt was made on the life of Pobêdonostsev; then the Minister of the Interior, Sipiágin, was assassinated; next, attempts were made on the lives of the Governors of Vilna and Kharkov; thereafter the Governor of Ufa, the Vice-Governor of Elizabetpol, M. Plehve, the Grand Duke Serge, and many others fell victims to the Terrorist policy.

Though the Social Democrats had no sentimental squeamishness about bloodshed, they objected to this policy on the ground that acts of Terrorism were unnecessary and were apt to prove injurious rather than beneficial to the Revolutionist cause. One of the main objects of every intelligent revolutionary party should be to awaken all classes from their habitual apathy and induce them to take an active part in the political movement; but Terrorism must have a contrary effect by suggesting that political freedom is to be attained, not by the steady pressure and persevering co-operation of the people, but by startling, sensational acts of individual heroism.

The efforts of these two Revolutionary parties, as well as of minor groups, to get hold of the industrial proletariat did not escape the notice of the authorities; and during the labor troubles of 1896, on the suggestion of M. Witte, the Government had considered the question as to what should be done to counteract the influence of the agitators. On that question it had no difficulty in coming to a decision: the condition of the working classes must be improved. An expert official was accordingly instructed to write a report on what had already been done in that direction. In this report it was shown that the Government had long been thinking about the subject. Not to speak of a still-born law about a ten hours' day for artisans, dating from the time of Catherine II, an Imperial commission had been appointed as early as 1859, but nothing practical came of its deliberations until 1882, when legislative measures were taken for the protection of women and children in factories. A little later (1886) other grievances were dealt with and partly removed by regulating contracts of hire, providing that the money derived from deductions and fines should not be appropriated by the employers, and creating a staff of factory inspectors who should take care that the benevolent intentions of the Government were duly carried out. Having reviewed all these official efforts in 1896, the Government passed in the following year a law prohibiting night work and limiting the working day to eleven and a half hours.

This did not satisfy the workmen. Their wages were still low, and it was difficult to get them increased becauses strikes and all forms of association were still, as they had always been, criminal offenses. On this point the Government remained firm so far as the law was concerned, but it gradually made practical concessions by allowing the workmen to combine for certain purposes. In 1898, for example, in Kharkov, the Engineers' Mutual Aid Society was sanctioned, and thereafter it became customary to allow the workmen to elect delegates for the discussion of their grievances with the employers and inspectors.

Finding that these concessions did not check the growing influence of the Social Democratic agitators among the operatives, the Government resolved to go a step farther; it would organize the workers on purely trade-unionist lines, and would thereby combat the Social Democrats, who always advised the strikers to mix up political demands with their material grievances. The project seemed to have a good prospect of success, because there were many workmen, especially of the older generation, who did not at all like the mixing up of politics, which so often led to arrest, imprisonment and exile, with the practical concerns of everyday life.

The first attempt of the kind was made in Moscow, under the direction of a certain Zubátov, chief of the secret police, who had been himself a revolutionary in his youth, and afterwards an *agent provocateur*. He organized a large workmen's association, with reading rooms, lectures, discussions and other attractions, and sought to convince the members that they should turn a deaf ear to the Social Democratic agents, and look only to the Government for the improvement of their condition. In order to gain their sympathy and confidence, he instructed his subordinates to take the side of the workmen in all labor disputes, while he himself brought official pressure to bear on the employers. By this means he made a considerable number of converts, and for a time the association seemed to prosper, but he did not possess the extraordinary ability and tact required to play the complicated game successfully, and he committed the fatal mistake of using the office-bearers of the association as detectives for the discovery of the "ill-intentioned." This tactical error had its natural consequences. As soon as the workmen perceived that their professed benefactors were police spies, who did not obtain for them any real improvement of their condition, the popularity of the association rapidly declined. At the same time, the factory owners complained to the Minister of Finance that the police, who ought to be guardians of public order, and who had accused the factory inspectors of stirring up discontent in the laboring population, were themselves creating troubles by inciting the workmen to make inordinate demands. The Minister of Finance at the moment was M. Witte, and the Minister of Interior, responsible for the acts of the police, was M. Plehve, and between these two official dignitaries, who were already in very strained relations, Zubátov's activity formed a new bone of contention. In these circumstances, it is not surprising that the very risky experiment came to an untimely end.

SIR DONALD MACKENZIE WALLACE, newspaper correspondent, editor, and author, was born in Scotland in 1841. He attended the universities at Glasgow and Edinburgh, the Ecole de Droit in Paris, and the universities of Berlin and Heidelberg, where he received the degree of Doctor of Laws in 1867. While studying Comparative Law in Germany, Wallace accepted a private invitation to visit Russia. He remained there for five years (1870-5), returning to England in 1876. His outstanding two-volume work on Russia, originally published in 1877, was revised in 1905 and again in 1912. After the outbreak of the Russo-Turkish War he began an active career as foreign correspondent for *The Times* (London), which he represented at St. Petersburg in 1877-8; at the Berlin Congress in June and July 1878; and afterward for six years at Constantinople, where he was an eyewitness to many of the dramatic events of the 1880's. During Lord Dufferin's five years as Viceroy of India, 1884-9, Wallace served as his secretary. He then returned to *The Times* as Director of the Foreign Department. In 1889, when *The Times* took over the *Encyclopaedia Britannica*, Wallace, along with Hugh Chisholm, edited the extra volumes needed to bring the Tenth Edition up to date. In 1905 he returned for the last time to *The Times* as a correspondent, attending the Conference at Portsmouth, New Hampshire, which produced the peace between Russia and Japan. He then retired to travel and study. He died at the age of seventy-seven in 1919. His works include *Egypt and the Egyptian Question* (1883), *The Web of Empire* (1902), and *Our Russian Ally* (1914).

CYRIL E. BLACK became a full Professor of History at Princeton University in 1954. A native of Bryson City, North Carolina, Dr. Black spent his boyhood in Turkey and Bulgaria, and returned to take his A.B. degree at Duke University in 1936. He has also studied at Vienna, Berlin, and Besançon; he obtained his Master's Degree and Doctorate at Harvard University. Since 1938 Dr. Black has been teaching at Princeton. He is the author of *The Establishment of Constitutional Government in Bulgaria*, editor of *Rewriting Russian History* (1956), co-author of *Twentieth Century Europe* (1950), and contributor to numerous scholarly journals. For the year 1960-1 he is a Fellow of the Center for Advanced Study in the Behavioral Sciences, Stanford, California.

THE TEXT of this book is set on the Linotype in CALEDONIA, a typeface designed by *W. A. Dwiggins*, who was responsible for so much that is good in contemporary book design.

f